LEARNING THAT LASTS

LEARNING THAT LASTS

Challenging, Engaging, and Empowering Students with Deeper Instruction

Ron Berger
Libby Woodfin
Anne Vilen

Foreword by Jal Mehta

Director of Video Production: David Grant

A Wiley Brand

Published by Jossey-Bass
A Wiley Brand

One Montgomery Street, Suite 1000, San Francisco, CA 94104-4594—www.josseybass.com

Jossey-Bass books and products are available through most bookstores. To contact Jossey-Bass directly call
our Customer Care Department within the U.S. at 800-956-7739, outside the U.S. at 317-572-3986, or
fax 317-572-4002.

Wiley publishes in a variety of print and electronic formats and by print-on-demand. Some material
included with standard print versions of this book may not be included in e-books or in print-on-demand.
If this book refers to media such as a CD or DVD that is not included in the version you purchased, you may
download this material at http://booksupport.wiley.com. For more information about Wiley products, visit
www.wiley.com.

Library of Congress Cataloging-in-Publication Data
Library of Congress Cataloging-in-Publication Data has been applied for and is on file with the Library
of Congress.

9781119253457 (Paperback)
9781119253549 (ePub)
9781119253525 (ePDF)

Cover Design: Wiley
Cover Image: © EL Education

Printed in the United States of America
FIRST EDITION
PB Printing   10 9 8 7 6 5 4 3 2 1

Contents

DVD Contents

On the DVD in the back of this book you'll find our *Core Practices in Action* video series. These videos—which we direct you to at various points throughout the book—show key practices in action with students and teachers in schools throughout the United States.

Chapter 1

1. Grappling with New Concepts during a Common Core Math Workshop
2. Thinking and Speaking Like Scientists through a Science Talk
3. Debrief Circles
4. Students Own Their Progress
5. Redirecting a Lesson with Exemplars

Chapter 2

6. Curriculum Design: The Four Ts
7. Reading and Thinking Like Scientists—Day 1: Strategies for Making Meaning from Complex Scientific Text
8. Reading and Thinking Like Scientists—Day 2: Deepening Conceptual Understanding through Text-Based Tasks
9. Prioritizing Evidence to Address a Document-Based Question
10. Policing in America: Using Powerful Topics and Texts to Challenge, Engage, and Empower Students
11. Preparing for an Academic Conversation, Day 1: Analyzing a Scientific Document
12. Preparing for An Academic Conversation, Day 2: Constructing Arguments Using Science Notebooks

You can also view the video clips at: www.wiley.com/go/eleducation

Foreword

I recently attended a Global Cities Education Network meeting in Shanghai. Present were representatives from East and West—five cities from North America, plus Shanghai, Singapore, Seoul, Hiroshima, and Melbourne. Despite their varied histories and cultures, all were part of a "twenty-first century learning" working group, which was seeking ways to help their students develop the knowledge and skills—critical thinking, collaboration, communication, problem solving—that have always been valuable but are now increasingly central to educational agendas worldwide.

EL Education (formerly known as Expeditionary Learning) started working on these issues twenty-five years ago. Founded on a conviction that students need to master core academic knowledge and skills, become producers of high-quality work, and develop into ethical, caring, and responsible human beings, EL Education is one of the few networks of schools that was tackling a "twenty-first century agenda" before the term was coined. There are now more than 150 EL Education schools. They include both charter and regular public schools, and they are located in urban centers, rural outposts, and everywhere in between. They have some hard evidence of success in core skills: for example, a recent Mathematica evaluation found that a sample of EL Education middle schools produced statistically significant gains in both math and reading compared to otherwise similar middle schools.[1] But what is distinctive about EL Education is that when it achieves success it does so through a model that does not prize test scores as the ultimate goal. Rather, its approach is rooted in a vision of both what it wants its learners to become and what sort of pedagogy might get them there.

To step back for a moment, part of the reason that creating good education is so difficult is that it requires integrating different kinds of virtues. On the one hand, powerful education is exciting: it connects to students' identities and their sense of life's purpose, and, in so doing, creates the energy and momentum that we see and feel in classrooms at their best. At the same time, if learning is going to be worth much, it requires discipline and persistence on the students' part—a willingness to acknowledge that subjects are complex, that learning is hard, and that it is only by doing and re-doing that real quality is produced. On the teachers' part, it similarly requires the creativity to craft challenges that will capture the students' imagination—often by taking what is on the surface and setting it slightly askew—and it requires the exceptionally careful planning and attention to detail that, together, organize how that learning will be carried out.

Many places have one or the other halves of this equation in place, but it is rare to find both. This is what my colleague, Sarah Fine, and I found over five years of researching a wide variety of American schools. There are a number of schools, particularly those of the No Excuses variety, that have embraced the more conservative virtues of discipline and practice, and, in so doing, have enabled their students to acquire more core disciplinary knowledge than had previously been the case. Many of these schools are now discovering that some of their students are struggling in the more open-ended environment of college, and are trying to revisit how to keep their core virtues and practices while also making learning more engaging and self-directed. Conversely, many of the more progressive, project-based schools that we have researched have been relatively successful in creating projects that tap into students' identities and motivation, but they worry that their students are often not adequately developing core content knowledge in disciplinary subjects. The challenge of integrating these contrasting virtues is what makes deeper learning, and the deeper instruction that would produce it, so difficult to achieve.

EL Education puts this integration front and center. Take the issue of standards and its relationship to project-based instruction. The typical approach makes traditional instruction the meat and potatoes of the diet—follow the textbook, do the problems—and intersperses occasional forays into projects which are largely disconnected from the core content but are intended to be the more engaging part of the curriculum. In the EL Education approach, teachers get together during the summer, examine the core standards that students are expected to master over the coming year, and then develop units which are anchored by meaningful projects but which simultaneously incorporate the content that targets the standards. Such an approach makes the learning purposeful and integrated for the students, while easing teachers' anxiety that projects are stealing time from the core content that will be measured on state tests.

A related idea that EL Education has championed is that the same standard can give rise to very different lessons. Say that the standard asks students to understand data scatterplots. A typical lesson might give students some fictional data—for example, thirty students' height and weight—and ask them to graph it, draw a best fit line, and reach a conclusion about the relationship between height and weight. An EL Education lesson might ask students to take repeated samples of the local water supply and see whether there is a relationship between the cleanliness of the water and the rate of toxic dumping. This investigation might then spark an effort to fight pollution in their cities. Both lessons would teach students how to plot data and think about the relationships between X and Y, but the EL Education lesson invites students into a real world context and shows them why statistics is worth learning. Perhaps for these reasons, EL Education's open-source curriculum has become an increasingly popular resource for traditional public schools: its grades 3 through 8 ELA curriculum is now being used in more than 500 districts in 39 states, including half of New York state's 700 districts.

In the pages that follow, Ron Berger, Libby Woodfin, and Anne Vilen show you how to create such lessons. Much of the existing literature is either at the level of theory, with little practical guidance, or it offers oversimplified prescriptions that tend not to survive contact with real students. This book is different. It treats its reader with respect—it firmly acknowledges that the discretion and wisdom of the teacher are central in bringing any lesson to life. But, at the same time, it offers many concrete examples, in different disciplines for different ages, of how to create lessons that both connect to standards and connect to students. And it organizes these examples into categories, so that as teachers are trying to develop their practice within a particular type of lesson (say, a workshop approach to math), they can see what such a practice might look like at its best. All of these lessons come from EL Education schools—they draw on the work of practicing EL Education teachers, and you hear the voices of real EL Education students. Many of the lessons are illustrated with videos or photos of student work, consistent with EL Education's longtime emphasis on examining models as a central vehicle for learning.

To be sure, these lessons represent EL Education at its best; not every school or every classroom in its network meets this formidable standard. As you will see in a few pages, a critique that Sarah and I wrote about one of its schools became a catalyst for some of EL Education's recent efforts to help its schools to live up to the network's considerable aspirations. The challenge for EL Education schools, like the challenge for the nation, is to discover how to embed the deeper instruction described in this book in many more classrooms.

To achieve that goal, each and every teacher will need to grapple with what it means to do deep or powerful instruction. And this book can help with that. Its lessons are not the kind you read once and then just "apply" to practice; rather, the book is a resource that is meant to be used *in conversation* with practice. Try some of these ideas with your students; see what catches and what falls flat; and then return to these pages and see whether there is a refinement, a wrinkle, or a different lesson that might better suit your needs. And do this in a community of like-minded teachers with whom you can share your discoveries and vent your frustrations as you seek to move from your current teaching self to its next iteration.

* * *

Each year, Ron Berger has come to visit my class at the Harvard Graduate School of Education. Ron's approach is always the same: he radiates optimism about the potential of what students can do, and then he shows a series of slides and videos depicting how work unfolds in the best EL Education classrooms. Frequently these videos feature students developing multiple drafts of a single piece of work—a first sketch of a butterfly or snake done by a first or second grader, looking like the typical drawing of a young child, and then, after student critiques and revisions and several subsequent drafts, a final version, looking like something you might want to hang on your living room wall. Each year, this visit is described by many students as their most consequential moment of learning—not only in my class, not only during their time at Harvard, but over their professional careers—because the students and their first drafts are so recognizable and their final results are so exceptional.

Austin's Butterfly Drafts

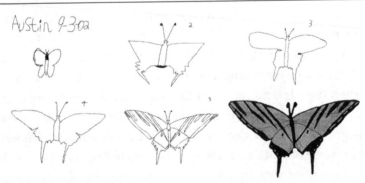

I recently read the book *Resonate*, which argues that the most powerful presentations are ones in which the audience is the hero and the presenter is the guide.[2] The idea is that giving a presentation is like inviting the audience to go on a quest with you, inspiring them towards the limits of the possible, acknowledging that getting there will be difficult, and offering an idea, tool, or concept that will help them on this journey, a journey that will long outlast the short occasion of the talk. Ron's work is like that—people come into contact with him only for a little while, but they leave inspired to try to incorporate his ideas into their practice for a lifetime. I hope this book will help you on your own journey; the ideas contained within it and the people who developed them have certainly been consequential for mine.

Jal Mehta
Cambridge, MA

NOTES

1. Ira Nichols-Barrer and Joshua Haimson, "Impacts of Five Expeditionary Learning Middle Schools on Student Achievement," July 2013, *Mathematica Policy Research*. This was a quasi-experimental study in which students at EL Education schools were matched with comparable students from surrounding public schools. It cannot reach as definitive causal conclusions as a lottery study, but it does employ a variety of techniques to try to ensure that the EL Education students and the students to whom they were being compared were matched on as many characteristics as possible.

2. Nancy Duarte, *Resonate: Present Visual Stories That Transform Audiences* (Hoboken, NJ: John Wiley and Sons, 2010).

Preface

Learning That Lasts addresses the most important challenge in education today: teaching quality. The research on this topic is unequivocal; there is no factor more closely correlated with student success. We often frame the problem as a "teacher quality" problem, rather than a "teaching quality" problem. Unfortunately, this small distinction has held us back from taking meaningful steps toward improvement. In this country we tend to believe that great teachers are born great, and therefore a student's experience in school is tied to the immutable personality traits or innate skills of his or her teachers. In other professions, such beliefs would seem ridiculous. We would never assume that doctors or firefighters are born good at what they do. Instead, we would assume that they have had extensive training and that they are continually learning new skills and staying motivated to do their best.

This is a book about *teaching* quality. It is about the capacity of teachers—all teachers—to get better at what they do. It honors their creativity and independence, but also provides them with the tools and inspiration they need to grow as professionals. This is also a book about the capacity of students. When they are challenged, engaged, and empowered through deeper instruction, they can fulfill their highest aspirations as students and people.

At EL Education we take a multidimensional view of student achievement, one that encompasses mastery of knowledge and skills, character, and high-quality work. The prevailing narrow view of student achievement, based primarily on tests of basic skills, does not reflect what families want for their children. Basic skills are vital, but families also want their children to develop higher-order skills and critical thinking, and they want them to be respectful, thoughtful, and happy. Businesses want students who are ready to be productive, independent, and collaborative workers, and creative problem solvers. Communities want students who are informed, contributing citizens and good people.

When students complete their formal education, their achievement will no longer be measured by high stakes tests. Instead, it is the quality of their work and character that will determine their success. The deeper instructional practices described in *Learning That Lasts* are designed to build students' skills across all three dimension of achievement and prepare them for success in and beyond school.

Like all of EL Education's books, this is not a theoretical text but rather a collection of practices and models from remarkably successful schools and classrooms. *Learning That Lasts* mines decades of wisdom from our most effective teachers, school leaders, and instructional coaches about how to plan and deliver instruction that is challenging, engaging and empowering for students. We hope this book and the accompanying videos of powerful practice can be both an inspiration and a practical guide for teachers and leaders, helping us all to get better at unleashing the power of students to do more than they ever thought possible.

Scott Hartl
President and CEO, EL Education
New York, NY

Acknowledgments

This is the fourth book we've written in collaboration with dozens of EL Education staff members, teachers, school leaders, and students. It is never easy to write in collaboration with so many; however, it is always well worth it. The result is a book filled with deeper instructional practices from some of the most inspiring classrooms in the country, classrooms where students and teachers alike are challenged, engaged, and empowered.

Nearly thirty EL Education staff members made significant contributions to *Learning That Lasts* by developing outlines, interviewing teachers, reviewing drafts, or simply guiding our thinking. There are only three names on the cover, but this book would not be possible without the contributions of the following staff members:

Tony Altucher	Enid Dodson
Dale Bergerhofer	Molly Dykman-Wilson
Sarah Boddy	Cyndi Gueswel
Stephanie Burke Bishop	Gwyneth Hagan
Mia Chmiel	Lucia Kaempffe
Linda D'Acquisto	Eugenie Kang
Marcia DeJesús-Rueff	Aurora Kushner
Rayna Dineen	Steven Levy
Cheryl Becker Dobbertin	Jon Mann

Dave Manzella

Martha Martin

Kerry Meehan-Richardson

Jill Mirman

Kate Palumbo

Jaime Passchier

Deborah Pinto

Suzanne Nathan Plaut

Meg Riordan

Kippy Smith

Colleen Stanevich

Dina Strasser

Rebecca Tatistcheff

Jen Wood

A heartfelt thanks goes to the teachers, leaders, and students who told us their stories, shared their practice with us, reviewed our drafts, and allowed our video cameras to capture them at work. It is one thing to hypothesize about what will work in the classroom and quite another to *show* what works. Thank you for allowing us to show and not just tell:

Meg Alexander

Blaire Baron

Lynn Bass

Eric Beck

Rhonda Berkower

Ali Bernstein

Jovanne Buckmire

Liz Butler

Louise Cadwell

Sydney Chaffee

Jill Clark

Valencia Clay

Monet Cooper

Perli Cunanan

Ben Daley

Kelly DiGiacinto

Arin Dineen

Stephanie Doane

Chris Dolgos

Karen Dresden

Maria Ekmalian

Jes Ellis

Jenna Gampel

Corey Goodrich

Megan Hall

Lane Harlow

Linda Henke

Jeff Heyck-Williams

Peter Hill

Teresa Hill

Shannon Hillman

Mona Iehl

Giselle Isbell

Toni Jackson

Steve Jenkins

Heather Kabot

Kavitha Kasargod

Caitlin LeClair

Marin Leroy

Eric Levine

Joanna Lewton

Maureen Lockner

Anna Loring

Steve Mahoney

Brianna Markoff

Joy Marts

Susan McCray

Val McKern

Reenie McMains

Stuart Miles

Hillary Mills

Michele Morenz

Matt Newsum

Marielle Palombo

Jessica Proffitt

Jeff Robin

Thomas Rochowicz

Elyse Rosenberg

Lubía Sánchez

Bill Simmons

Bobby Shaddox

Jianan Shi

Anne Simpson

Elizabeth Smallwood

Emily Stainer

Matt Strand

Justin Sybenga

Carri Thomason

Fran Taffer

Brooke Teller

Erin Wheeler

Roger White

Kathy White

Chris Widmaier

Aubrey Wilk

Lisa Wing

Claire Wolff

Rob Yongue

Jill Znaczko

Mark Zucker

Special thanks to Leah Rugen, our coauthor on other projects who helped us craft the chapter on differentiated instruction; Jal Mehta, who catalyzed our renewed focus on deeper instruction, wrote our Foreword, and has been a mentor for this work in many ways; the students—Edward, Lukas, and Elena—who shared their wisdom with us; and Marjorie McAneny, our editor and champion.

And last, but not least, our deepest gratitude to our filmmaker David Grant, a former EL Education teacher who can tell the story of strong classroom practice better than anyone in the business.

About the Authors

Ron Berger is chief academic officer for EL Education, overseeing resources and professional learning for schools nationally. Berger works closely with the Harvard Graduate School of Education, where he did his graduate work, and currently teaches a course that uses exemplary student work to illuminate academic standards. Prior to his work with EL Education and Harvard, Berger was a public school teacher and master carpenter in rural Massachusetts for more than twenty-five years. Berger is an Annenberg Foundation Teacher Scholar and received the Autodesk Foundation National Teacher of the Year award. His previous books include *An Ethic of Excellence, A Culture of Quality, Leaders of Their Own Learning: Transforming Schools through Student-Engaged Assessment, Transformational Literacy: Making the Common Core Shift with Work That Matters*, and *Management in the Active Classroom*. Berger's writing and speaking center on inspiring quality and character in students, specifically through project-based learning, original scientific and historical research, service learning, and the infusion of arts. He works with the national character education movement to embed character values into the core of academic work.

Libby Woodfin is the director of publications for EL Education. Woodfin started her career as a fifth- and sixth-grade teacher at the original lab school for the Responsive Classroom in Greenfield, Massachusetts, and went on to become a counselor at a large comprehensive high school. Woodfin started with EL Education in 2007 while completing graduate work at the Harvard Graduate School of Education. Throughout her career, Woodfin has written articles, chapters, and books about important issues in education. Her previous books include *Leaders of*

Their Own Learning: Transforming Schools through Student-Engaged Assessment, Transformational Literacy: Making the Common Core Shift with Work That Matters, Management in the Active Classroom, and *Familiar Ground: Traditions That Build School Community.*

Anne Vilen is a staff writer and school coach for EL Education. She began her career in academic publishing and freelance writing, then earned a master's degree in teaching and taught language arts at levels ranging from sixth grade to college. Vilen served as director of program and professional development for seven years at an EL Education mentor school before joining EL Education in 2011. In her twenty years as an editor, writer, and teacher, she has published dozens of poems, essays, and articles. Her previous books include *Transformational Literacy: Making the Common Core Shift with Work That Matters* and *Sisters and Workers in the Middle Ages.*

About EL Education

ᴱᴸ Education

EL Education (formerly Expeditionary Learning) is a leading K–12 nonprofit that is meeting the national challenge to raise student achievement across diverse schools and communities. Combining challenging work with the joy of discovery and pride in mastery, EL Education prepares students to become contributing citizens with both the skills and character necessary for success throughout college, work, and life.

EL Education's portfolio of instructional materials and coaching services draws on 20-plus years of success in more than 150 schools in the EL Education network, serving 4,000 teachers and 45,000 students in 30 states. Based on founding principles of meaningful work, character, and respect for teachers, EL Education's offerings transform teaching and learning to promote habits of scholarship and character that lead to high student achievement, regardless of student background. In addition to success on standardized tests, EL Education students demonstrate critical thinking, intellectual courage, and emotional resilience; they possess the passion and the capacity to contribute to a better world. For more information, visit www.ELeducation.org.

The Change Our Students Need

* Agree
♥ Aspire
? Argue

In a high school English classroom in Portland, Maine, students sit transfixed as they listen to the passionate instructions of their teacher, Susan McCray. They have just returned from a week in New York City, where they interviewed victims of Hurricane Sandy and worked with them to restore damaged homes, all in preparation for telling their stories with documentary films. They feel tremendous pressure: they are now the keepers of the personal narratives of the families they interviewed—stories of tragedy and courage—and they need to tell those stories with integrity and power. "This is an incredible responsibility," McCray tells her students before they embark on this academic and personal adventure. Their writing and filmmaking must be brilliant: these families deserve no less.

McCray has planned the sequence of her instruction so that students are reaching a personal epiphany: we all have life stories, and our stories matter. The families that her students interviewed have stories that matter, and the students themselves, many of them refugees, also have stories that matter. This is now becoming clear to them. Her students can create beautiful narratives of the families they met, and they can also create beautiful narratives for their own lives. They have the power to do great things, and as they sit together processing their experience with McCray they see this.

Nationally, success statistics for low-income students in public high schools are bleak. But something different and important is going on at Casco Bay High School. The quality of instruction is unusually strong, and the results are transformational. Every year, nearly every student makes it to graduation on time and is accepted to college. Ninety-eight percent of Casco Bay students, many of whom are low income and/or English language learners, have been accepted to college in the past decade. These students go to college with a mission: to succeed academically so that they can contribute to a better world.

As a nation, we strive continually to improve America's schools and do a better of job of preparing students for success in college, career, and life. We mandate new policies, new structures, and new standards. But none of this will matter if we fail to make changes in the classroom, where learning actually takes place. Educational research has made it clear: the quality of teaching is the single most important factor in student success. But we cannot mandate great instruction. We need to inspire it and shepherd it.

This book presents a new vision for classroom instruction that sharpens and deepens what is asked of teachers and students. It is the opposite of a "teacher-proof"

Photo: Rhonda Farnham

solution. Instead, it is predicated on a model of instruction through which teachers become expert planners of learning experiences for students and continuously grow in the acuity and depth of their craft knowledge and content knowledge. It is not a theoretical vision. It is a model of instruction that was derived and improved in some of the nation's most successful public schools—schools that are beating the odds to create remarkable achievement—sited primarily in urban and rural low-income communities.

Our vision of instruction is also predicated on an expanded notion of what constitutes high achievement for students. More than 150 years ago, public schools were founded in America with a world-shaking aspiration: to provide free education that would prepare students to be scholars, skilled workers, and contributing citizens of our new democratic nation. America's definition of student achievement has narrowed over the years. Today, when we refer to a school as "high-achieving," those words refer solely to one thing: good test scores on basic skills in two subjects. There is no mention of whether students are work-ready and life-ready or have the skills and dispositions to be respectful and active citizens.

Our vision of instruction reclaims the original mission of public schools. And, because we have continually evolved as a nation in our embodiment of justice for all, our vision affirms our new national charge to apply that educational mission equally to all students from all backgrounds.

We define student achievement as having three dimensions:

1. Mastery of knowledge and skills

2. Character

3. High-quality student work

This is a book for teachers, school leaders, and those who help to prepare and coach teachers who wish to help students achieve in each of these dimensions. It is not a theoretical book—it is a practical guide filled with structures, strategies, and resources, grounded in examples and stories from successful schools. It presents a detailed picture of how more ambitious and effective instruction—instruction that is challenging, engaging, and empowering for students—can look across grade levels and disciplines, and across a range of school settings. It focuses on *deeper instruction* and paints a portrait of *learning that lasts*, which is something that all students need and all students deserve.

What Are the Outcomes We Want?

When a student is finished with school and moves into adult life, she will be judged not by her ability to perform on a test of basic skills, but by the quality of her work and character. This holds true regardless of what career or life role she chooses. *Deeper instruction* is an effort to improve students' readiness for college, careers, and life by prioritizing what matters most in our global economy and helping students achieve lives of integrity, joy in learning, and contribution.

The model of instruction in this book disrupts the classic paradigm of teacher-centered instruction, described by educator Paolo Freire as the "banking model" of education, in which teachers make "deposits" of knowledge into the empty containers of students' heads. Instead, deeper instruction allows students for much of their time in school to be the thinkers and doers, collaborating, creating knowledge, and engaging in work that matters. Although mastering core academic content is critical, deeper instruction supports students to acquire that knowledge through challenging real-world work, deep engagement, and meaningful application.

Deeper instruction promotes *deeper learning* in students, which is defined by six outcomes:

1. Mastery of core academic content

2. Critical thinking and problem solving

3. Collaboration

4. Effective communication

5. Self-directed learning and

6. Academic mindsets

Deeper instruction honors the multidimensional nature of student achievement. Student achievement on standardized tests, which has dominated educational policy for decades and has therefore greatly influenced life in schools, has resulted in a reductionist view of what it means for students to succeed. Assessments are important, but so too is the work that students create, and the dispositions and skills students acquire to become capable and honorable scholars, citizens, and human beings.

Our focus on deeper instruction not only prioritizes positive character and quality work as essential components of student achievement, but also supports students to build mastery of knowledge and skills with more understanding and ownership. It equips teachers with strategies and skills to create rich learning experiences that empower students to be leaders of their own learning.

For teachers and leaders this may seem impossible given the pressures of high-stakes testing. The beauty is that there is no tradeoff here. The schools in our network that are most successful in deeper instruction, whose students shine in the depth and quality of their thinking, their work, and their citizenship, are also schools that excel on high-stakes state assessments. Their test scores significantly exceed comparable schools, in all subjects and with all subgroups of students.

Many of the secondary schools described in this book, working primarily with low-income students, are getting 100 percent of graduates into college. We don't have to choose between deeper learning and success on high-stakes assessments and college attainment—deeper instruction serves both goals.

How Do We Define Deeper Instruction?

We all want our students to learn deeply. We want them to feel energized and empowered by what their minds can do and to flexibly apply their knowledge to new situations. We want them to move beyond rote memorization of facts up the Bloom's Taxonomy pyramid—understanding, applying, analyzing, evaluating, and creating knowledge. This is what makes learning last.

Despite what is a fairly universal goal, teachers are often challenged by the dilemma of how to help students learn deeply. There are many pressures that impinge on life in the classroom—among them are inadequate curricular materials, classroom management challenges, lack of training or experience working with diverse learning styles, pressure to succeed on standardized tests, and a lack of time. Time may in fact be the greatest hurdle a teacher faces—time to plan strong lessons, time to nurture students' creativity, time to push students beyond the facts in a textbook. These hurdles often result in instructional choices that may result in short-term or narrowly defined achievements but not necessarily long-term, meaningful learning.

Our goal with this book then is to provide teachers and school leaders with practical tools for deeper instruction. But what exactly is deeper instruction? We propose a three-pronged framework to help teachers plan and deliver deeper instruction:

1. Deeper Instruction *Challenges* Students

Challenge is at the heart of deeper instruction. Grappling with new ideas and problems will productively challenge students when they have enough background knowledge to feel anchored, enough scaffolding to feel supported, and enough time and intellectual freedom to wrestle with complex ideas that stimulate their thinking. A productive challenge stretches students to go beyond what they may think is possible. This stretch leads to new learning.

Our approach to challenge is twofold. First, students must be challenged with rigorous, sophisticated material that engages them in higher-order reading, writing, thinking, and discussion. Second, students must be challenged to gain conceptual understanding and to apply (or transfer) it to new situations.

The following questions can guide teachers when planning for challenge:

- How challenging are the tasks I'm asking students to complete? How complex is the required thinking?

- Am I giving students an opportunity to grapple? Am I making space for uncertainty or creative puzzling?

- What questions should I ask? What is the purpose of each?

2. Deeper Instruction *Engages* Students

Engagement is fueled by curiosity and connection. When students feel that their learning has purpose and is connected to the real world, they become more engaged—their curiosity about and connection to their academic content is heightened. Often purpose is connected to the choices teachers make when they create compelling long-term curricula for students. Purpose in *daily* lessons connects to curricula, but it is also fostered through the collaboration among students as they think and do together every day. Students drive themselves forward toward deeper layers of learning because they have a "need to know" and they are buoyed by the collaborative efforts of their peers. Prioritizing this collaboration—which is built on a foundation of relationship, trust, and effective communication—is a key to deeper instruction. Collaborative grappling with compelling problems and ideas strengthens students' connections to each other, the classroom, and school and greatly increases their engagement with learning.

Curricular and instructional choices that lead to deeper engagement are intimately tied to the first part of this framework: appropriate levels of challenge. It is difficult for students to feel that "need-to-know" excitement when they spend too much time doing tasks with a low level of cognitive demand, if they already know what's being taught, or if they are lost in what they don't know and can't figure out how to move forward.

The following questions can guide teachers when planning for engagement:

- Do I know what students already know? What texts, tasks, or experiences will help them learn about the topic more deeply?

- Will my questions encourage discussion? What protocols, prompts, or lesson formats will push students to ask questions of each other?

- Is there a framing question or task that connects to an authentic personal, disciplinary, or social issue? If so, is this connection being used to engage students *and* deepen their thinking?

3. Deeper Instruction *Empowers* Students with Tools for Learning

The third part of the framework for deeper instruction focuses on helping students become self-directed learners with strong habits of scholarship. Designing lessons that challenge and engage students goes hand in hand with designing lessons that support this metacognition. Deeper instruction allows students to understand where their learning is headed and to track their progress along the way. And, most important, it gives students the opportunity to debrief learning experiences in order to synthesize their learning, connect it to larger disciplinary concepts, and reflect on their own process as learners.

Key to our approach to empowering students as learners is fostering their growth mindset, instilling in them the belief that they can "get smart" through effort. Intelligence is not something that they're born with, but something that they develop through perseverance and strong habits of scholarship. When students adopt this mindset they can produce extraordinary high-quality work and achieve at levels they may not have thought possible. Learning is within their control.

The following questions can guide teachers when planning for empowerment:

- How will I structure the lesson so that students take responsibility for their learning? How will they assess and track their progress? How will we debrief learning experiences?

- What scaffolding can I provide to help students do high-quality work?

- Are there parts of the lesson that I can turn over to students to lead?

- Does the lesson give students an opportunity to articulate why the learning matters?

See Table I.1 for the indicators of deeper instruction, aligned to each part of this framework.

Table I.1 Indicators of Deeper Instruction

CHALLENGING	**Learning is courageous; it embraces a process of risk taking, growth, and revision.** • Students may struggle individually and collectively; they expect to make mistakes along the way. • Students understand that uncertainty, grappling, and/or playful exploration are a part of learning. • Teachers explicitly and implicitly communicate a growth mindset to students.	**Learning is planned to meet and exceed standards.** • Students are working at tasks and toward targets that are clearly aligned with standards and, when possible, go beyond standards. • Students demonstrate understanding of disciplinary big ideas, ways of thinking, and skills. • Students apply their understanding to produce work that demonstrates complexity, craftsmanship, and authenticity.	**Learning is cognitively rigorous.** • Students are applying, analyzing, evaluating, and/or creating during a significant portion of the lesson or arc of lessons (not simply remembering). • Students think critically. They synthesize complex ideas and consider multiple perspectives.
ENGAGING	**Learning is active.** • Students are engaged in productive work throughout the class. • Students create ideas and work that have value and are worthy of peer and class discussion and critique. • Teachers regularly use protocols and strategies that encourage all students to participate and be accountable for learning.	**Learning results from pursuing worthy questions.** • Teachers and students ask questions that promote critical thinking and inquiry. • Students are given sustained opportunities to ask questions and engage in scholarly dialogue with other students. • Students ask and answer questions that require reading, writing, and using evidence from sources, or require mathematical and scientific exploration.	**Learning is purposeful.** • Students understand how their new learning connects to past learning (i.e., not a series of disconnected lessons). • Students understand how the work they are doing connects to real-world issues, needs, careers, and lives. • When appropriate, students do work that simulates professional work that happens in the discipline or field.
EMPOWERING	**Learning fosters responsibility.** • Students become ethical people and effective learners who develop the mindsets, skills, and character they need for success in college, career, and life. • Students have specific roles and responsibilities for working in groups and learn to collaborate and communicate effectively. • Students put their learning to use to improve their communities. • Teachers elevate student voice and leadership in classrooms and across the school.	**Learning is self-assessed and peer-assessed.** • Teachers involve students in discussing and creating goals for learning and criteria for success. • Teachers provide frequent feedback to students along the way and teach students how to self-assess, revise, and critique and support peers. • Students reflect on and track their own progress toward learning targets based on meaningful data. • Students have regular opportunities to debrief learning experiences.	**Learning inspires students to create work of high quality.** • Teachers have high expectations and provide thoughtful scaffolding to support high-quality work. • Students use models, critique, and descriptive feedback to improve their work through multiple drafts. • Students create work that is of higher quality than they thought was possible and take pride in their own craftsmanship and growth. • Students can articulate why their learning matters and transfer knowledge and skills to novel, meaningful tasks and situations.

Deeper instruction can be a powerful difference-maker in students' lives. A teacher's thoughtful intention to challenge, engage, and empower her students drives deeper learning and, in many cases, students' investment in school. If we're lucky, we've experienced it ourselves. And if so, we have likely been struck by the difference between walking into a classroom where deeper instruction was a focus for our teacher and a classroom where we sat passively listening to the teacher, taking notes, and watching the clock. A learning environment like this can transform how we feel about school and our futures as students, learners, and citizens. The academic mindset we develop as a result paves the way for deeper learning.

Academic Mindsets: A Foundation For Deeper Learning

Academic mindsets are the motivational components that influence a student's engagement with his or her learning. These mindsets determine why and under what conditions students will dig in to master knowledge and skills, problem solve, collaborate with their peers, and persevere with their learning, even when it is difficult. Nothing we do as teachers is as important as our influence on these mindsets. Even with access to all of the information in the world, which is literally at their fingertips, without positive academic mindsets, students may not be motivated to access it. Camille Farrington (2013), a researcher from the University of Chicago and a co-developer of the concept of academic mindsets, describes them as "the energy source that fuels students' engagement in deeper learning activities" (p. 3). She states, "Students with positive academic mindsets work harder, engage in more productive academic behaviors [(e.g., class participation, homework)], and persevere to overcome obstacles to success" (p. 4).

Students enter classrooms with existing academic mindsets that affect their engagement but their mindsets can also be shaped positively by deeper learning experiences. When instruction challenges, engages, and empowers students, teachers can and do influence their attitudes and beliefs about themselves as learners.

The four academic mindsets draw from research on human motivation and basic psychological needs:

1. *I belong in this learning community.* Students have a connection with their peers and teachers and feel that they are part of a learning community. As a result, they see setbacks as a normal part of learning rather than a sign that they are "out of place."

2. *I can succeed at this.* Students more willingly engage in tasks when they believe they can succeed. If they anticipate failure, they will likely refrain from investing effort or devalue the importance of the task to maintain a sense of their own competence. This sense of self-efficacy is malleable and can be nurtured through feedback, goal setting, and thoughtfully scaffolded instruction.

3. *My ability and competence will grow with my effort.* Based on the work of Carol Dweck (2006), students with a growth mindset believe that the "brain is a muscle" that gets stronger with use. Students with fixed mindsets believe that intelligence is something they are either born with or not. A growth mindset helps students see challenges or mistakes as an opportunity to learn—they are motivated toward mastery rather than performance.

4. *This work has value for me.* Students are able to focus on their academic work when it connects to their lives, their futures, or their interests. When it is not valued, they have to expend considerably more effort to focus on it and are less likely to remember it.

Teachers who intentionally foster students' academic mindsets create an environment that encourages students to take on meaningful challenges within a supportive learning community. Teachers see every student as capable of meeting the target with the right scaffolding and practice. They approach learning as a process that involves making mistakes and learning from those mistakes to find success. They design many opportunities for critique and revision of student work. They name and reinforce character traits that lead to growth. They recognize and celebrate effort and innovation in their classrooms. And, finally, they approach lesson planning with a growth mindset of their own—as a process of carefully choreographing interactions between students and ideas or skills, reflecting afterward on the results of the dynamics, and planning again to achieve a better result.

The deeper instructional strategies and practices described in this book are designed to build these mindsets in all students. From compelling case studies, to problem-based math, to differentiated instruction, our approach is designed to help students feel a sense of belonging and self-efficacy in their schools and classrooms, where they see that their work has value and they believe that their effort will help them grow and get smarter.

About This Book: A Multimedia Toolkit for Teachers and Leaders

Chapter 1: Planning and Delivering Lessons That Challenge, Engage, and Empower

The lesson is the basic unit of instruction. It is the package in which we wrap curriculum and the vehicle we use to deliver content and skills. Lessons that challenge, engage, and empower students must be carefully crafted and skillfully delivered to maximize deeper learning. This chapter describes such lessons, including three specific lesson formats—the workshop model, protocol-based lessons, and discovery-based lessons—as well as the essential elements of any lesson, no matter its name or format, and shows what they look like and sound like in action in classrooms representing all types of students and schools.

Chapter 2: Laying the Foundation for Deeper Learning with Literacy

Literacy—reading, writing, speaking, and listening—is the foundation of deeper learning. Even in the digital age, perhaps *especially* in the digital age, reading closely for detail, nuance, and context is the key to academic and career success. Deeper instruction depends on all teachers building their capacity to teach students how to learn from texts. This chapter builds on our previous book, *Transformational Literacy: Making the Common Core Shift with Work That Matters* (2014), with examples and illustrations from social studies and science teachers in elementary, middle, and high schools who have transformed literacy challenges into learning successes.

Chapter 3: Creating Scientists and Historians

The big ideas of human history reside in science and social studies curricula (including history and, in high schools, other social science electives like psychology or anthropology). Nevertheless, these content areas are infamously a mile wide and an inch deep, cluttered with too many standards and high-stakes testing that measures success in esoteric facts and forgettable minutiae. This chapter shows teachers how to reframe that instructional dilemma so that students meet standards and succeed on tests while still doing the real work of scientists and historians: asking authentic questions, researching multiple answers, and presenting the evidence behind their claims publicly.

Chapter 4: Reimagining Mathematics Instruction

Of all subjects, mathematics raises a fundamental question about the teacher's role. Is it to deliver content (e.g., facts, algorithms, formulas, definitions) or to create opportunities for students to build understanding? Because of this question, we often seek quick answers—the magic curriculum that will deliver the right content in the right way—rather than learning how to build and customize lessons that will create independent, facile problem solvers. This chapter presents a fresh lesson structure for mathematics—Math Workshop 2.0—that prioritizes individual and collaborative problem solving and conceptual understanding. Drawing from a case study of a public school that has achieved incredible success in mathematics, we offer strategies for building a culture of mathematical inquiry and success across a school.

Chapter 5: Teaching in and through the Arts

The arts—visual arts, music, theater, dance, and design—are at the heart of deeper instruction. Art inspires students to see beauty, engages them in the complexity of the world, and empowers them to communicate their deepest feelings and their most innovative ideas. Art is both a motivating force in other academic areas and a core subject area in its own right, with deep inherent value for building creative and conceptual skills. In this chapter, we describe instructional practices for teaching art and for integrating art with other subject areas for deeper interdisciplinary understanding. This chapter is punctuated with multiple examples of student art work—supported by lesson plans, rubrics, and other documents—from Models of Excellence: The Center for High-Quality Student Work, a repository of writing, artwork, and other projects curated by EL Education in partnership with the Harvard Graduate School of Education (http://modelsofexcellence.eleducation.org/).

Chapter 6: Differentiating Instruction

Differentiation is an expectation in every school, but there's a wide gap between expecting it and doing it. Meeting the needs of all students through differentiation often requires shifts in schoolwide structures like staffing and collaborative planning as well as changes in how teachers deliver lessons. This chapter addresses how to create a culture that values diversity and inclusion and how to teach in ways that let every student lead his or her own learning.

Chapter 1

Planning and Delivering Lessons That Challenge, Engage, and Empower

OVERVIEW

A Call to Action

In December 2011, Jal Mehta and Sarah Fine, researchers from the Harvard Graduate School of Education, visited the Springfield Renaissance School, a 6–12 public district school in Springfield, Massachusetts, the state's second-largest school district. They were in the midst of a large-scale tour of high schools across the United States looking for evidence of deeper learning.

At Renaissance they observed classes and interviewed students, teachers, and the school's founding principal, Steve Mahoney. In a follow-up e-mail to Mahoney after their visit, Mehta noted the palpably strong and positive culture at the school and its amazing results. Since opening in 2006, nearly all of Renaissance's students have graduated on time and 100 percent of those graduates have been accepted to college. For many years the students have beaten the odds in their city with dedication and perseverance, and they have set a new bar for their school district and the city. And as a result, students, families, and faculty feel deeply connected to and proud to be part of the community at their mission-driven school.

Mehta also, however, noted areas that were less strong, particularly in the depth of instructional rigor observed during lessons. He cited a few bright spots but found many examples of low-level tasks and students who could recall information (the lowest level of Bloom's Taxonomy: See Figure 1.1) but seemed to lack true understanding of concepts. Overall, both researchers found that classroom instruction across the school didn't move students often enough up the taxonomy

Figure 1.1   Bloom's Revised Taxonomy

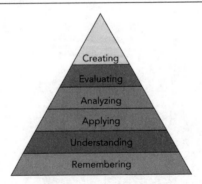

of complexity. Despite strong structures for supporting instruction, including frequent observations by administrators, Renaissance as a school had not yet created the rigorous instruction across classrooms to which they aspired.

Mahoney likes to joke about Mehta's comprehensive and candid e-mail: "He tore us apart!" he'll say with a grin. Instead of feeling defensive about the critical parts of the analysis, Mahoney took the e-mail as a welcome provocation to improve. At Renaissance, Mahoney shared the e-mail with his staff, and it sparked their development of an instructional checklist to be used for data collection and as a catalyst for conversation about instructional practice following administrator observations. The checklist reflected a renewed focus on checking for understanding strategies and what Mahoney refers to as his "obsession" with good debriefs at the conclusion of every lesson. Mahoney also shared the e-mail with EL Education's national staff and mentor principals, who used it as a common reading during their summer meeting and subsequently began a multiyear effort to increase instructional rigor in their schools.

Though Mahoney takes no comfort in this fact, Mehta and Fine found evidence of deeper learning only very rarely on their national tour of "good" high schools. Almost every school they visited was struggling with rigorous daily instruction. Schools everywhere, even high-achieving and highly regarded schools, struggle in ways similar to Renaissance. It is often easier to consider the ways that curricular choices (e.g., challenging projects or texts) can lead to deeper learning. But daily instruction that compels students to build conceptual understanding is difficult to define and difficult to find in action. This chapter begins our exploration of deeper instruction by lifting up effective instructional strategies that help students learn deeply during daily lessons in any discipline.

Why This Practice Matters

Our focus on the lesson acknowledges repeated studies that show that teacher quality and instructional practices are the greatest predictor of student achievement (Goe & Stickler, 2008). The lesson is the heart of the instructional core (City et al., 2009) where teachers, students, and the content interact every day. Creating classrooms where deeper learning flourishes requires teachers' and leaders' persistent effort to create high-quality lessons where the interactions that occur within this core are planned and delivered purposefully. This focus is important for the following key reasons.

Students Need *Challenge*

A college- and career-ready education must prepare students for jobs that don't yet exist and global problems that haven't yet been defined. Preparing students to thrive intellectually and emotionally in the twenty-first century means they have to be facile and resilient problem solvers. As students in one of our schools often say, "The harder the problems, the more our brains grow." Unless we have lesson structures that compel students to take on complex work and do the thinking themselves, they will leave their K–12 education unprepared for what awaits them.

Students Need *Engagement*

Students of every demographic are distracted by technology. Cell phones, the Internet, media, music, and the "noise" of the marketplace bombard our daily lives with information, opinions, sales pitches, and data. One goal of any lesson, then, must be to captivate students and motivate them to dig in. This does not mean to *entertain* them. It means rather to *intrigue* them, to *engage* them in discovering connections, making meaning, and grappling with challenge. Lessons that engage students impel them to become self-directed and independent in pursuing knowledge and honing skills.

Students Need *Empowerment*

Purposeful lesson design and delivery is critical to empowering students with tools for leading their own learning. Creating time and structures for students to understand their learning goals, own their progress, and synthesize and reflect helps them develop responsibility and independence as learners. As teachers, we often admire those students who are self-directed in their learning and wish our other students were just as motivated and confident. We need to embrace the fact that the lessons we plan and deliver can serve to cultivate empowered, self-directed learners or, just the opposite, discourage those dispositions in our students.

Getting started with lessons that engage, challenge, and empower students begins with reflection, planning, and centering lessons within the big picture of teaching and learning. In the Getting Started section that follows we explore the key decision points for teachers by mapping the lesson planning process onto the deeper instruction framework. By unpacking what it means to plan lessons that challenge, engage, and empower students, we move one step closer to answering the call for deeper learning.

GETTING STARTED

Planning Lessons That Challenge, Engage, and Empower Students

Planning the 45, 60, or 90 minutes of each lesson is some of the most challenging and important work a teacher can do. Whether designing a lesson from scratch or customizing a lesson provided with a published curriculum, getting the details right really matters. There are timeless questions that every teacher wrestles with:

- What do I most want my students to learn?

- How will I know if they understand?

- How will I challenge them?

- How will I help make the learning last?

- How will I meet the needs of my diverse learners?

But wrestle we must, because the lesson plans that result from our answers are the best tools we have to promote deeper learning.

A good lesson is the heart of deeper instruction, bringing to life the body of knowledge and skills students need. Indeed, the lesson is how a teacher brings any curriculum to life. Thus, when planning a lesson it is critical to first consider the curriculum for the unit, semester, or year and the knowledge, skills, and concepts required by grade-level standards. Nesting the lesson intentionally within the content, and sequencing lessons in a way that makes the content compelling, challenging, and authentic is work that goes hand in hand with creating and delivering any one individual lesson.

We understand that some teachers build lessons themselves, some regularly customize lessons provided in a curriculum, and still others are expected to follow a lesson plan provided to them almost exactly as it is written. We encourage teachers in all of these circumstances to make use of the deeper instruction structures and strategies we present here as much as is feasible. The structures and strategies can be a foundation for creating an original lesson sequence or can be used to modify and enhance lesson plans that are already created. Because teachers are professionals who need to respond to the needs of their students, there is no teacher-proof curriculum that can effectively script lessons for every group of students.

Planning in the context of curriculum (whether district provided or teacher created) and keeping the destination of students' learning in mind are critical to planning for deeper instruction. "When I am lesson planning," says Thomas Rochowicz, a former high school history teacher at the Washington Heights Expeditionary Learning School (WHEELS) in New York City, "I have the unit plan open. I first think,

> how does this lesson fit within the context of the unit and the week? I think about the final projects that students will do and the knowledge and skills they will need in order to be successful on the learning targets for the project. The hardest work for me comes in the planning, writing the targets, choosing the texts, identifying the protocol, and deciding how much time each element will take. After that, I am playing the role of facilitator as students dig in to develop their understanding. I coach, but the students are taking ownership for their learning."

By keeping the end in mind and sequencing his lessons to get students to the target in a productive and timely fashion, Rochowicz can devote the rest of his attention to keeping his students challenged and engaged during the lesson itself.

Planning for Challenge

The 1980s documentary, *A Private Universe,*[1] is a cautionary tale and a good opportunity to reflect on the importance of keeping the end in mind when designing lessons, particularly the tasks we ask students to complete in order to demonstrate their learning. In the documentary, Harvard University graduates, still wearing their caps and gowns, are asked to describe why the Earth has seasons. Nearly all of them, despite years of science education and degrees from one of the most prestigious universities in the world, promote the same misconception. They state, often with earnest gesticulations, that the Earth moves around the sun in a highly exaggerated elliptical pattern. When the earth is at the end nearest the sun it is summer and when it is at the far end it is winter. They repeat a misconception common even among adults: that the seasons are caused by the changing distance between the Earth and the sun.

The solar system is something that we begin studying in elementary school and often come back to in classes throughout our education. Why do our misconceptions persist? It is likely that the concepts were never fully understood and etched deeply in our brains in the first place. When we learn things for tests, but never have to apply that knowledge to new settings or use it to teach others or create something of value, the learning often does not last. Facts, like times tables or the order of the eight planets (or nine, depending on one's age), can be memorized. Understanding of concepts, like why we have seasons on Earth, is not built by sheer memorization. If our goal in a lesson sequence is to build conceptual understanding, we have to plan a lesson that requires students to demonstrate conceptual understanding, such as explaining the concepts to others.

Describing tricky concepts is challenging, even for adults. It often takes multiple attempts, and we may discover new and better ways to do it each time we try. We may start with gestures, move on to drawings, and finally arrive at models to help us. The open-ended nature of such tasks is what makes them challenging and important for our students. Asking students to describe or replicate the concept, like the producers of *A Private Universe* did, is the best way for teachers to ensure that students are moving beyond recall to true understanding. Rather than increasing challenge for our students by assigning more difficult reading (e.g., one grade level up) or a larger problem set, focusing on tasks that require them to uncover and explain simple concepts may provide more bang for the buck.

Second-grade teacher Rob Yongue and his colleagues at Glenwood Elementary in Decatur, Georgia, gave their students just such a task. Reflecting two Georgia science standards, they asked students to explain not only what causes the seasons, but also what a year represents on Earth and on other planets.

Students had to explain cosmic phenomena related to the sun, moon, and stars through scientific illustrations and written explanations based on research, reading, and observation. This task assessed both students' understanding of the concepts *and* their skill in communicating them. It measured students' mastery of knowledge and skills through a performance assessment that gave credit to high-quality work. Toward this product, students revised their work multiple times, not for neatness or beauty (though the results are neat and beautiful), but for scientific accuracy and detail—the criteria used to evaluate real-world scientific communication. Notice how one of the students' pages, shown in Figure 1.2, correctly renders the Earth's orbit as nearly circular.

Figure 1.2   Second-Grade Solar System Project

A Year in the Making
By Ava and Tiara

The sun is big and very important. Our year is 365 days long. It takes Earth 365 days or one year to orbit the sun. If we were farther from the sun, our year would be longer. If we were closer, our year would be shorter. Other planets have longer or shorter years because they are farther or closer to the sun. Without the sun we wouldn't have a year.

This shows Earth traveling around the sun.

One year on Uranus is the same as almost 84 years on Earth.

This example shows that even young students, when held to a rigorous standard, can demonstrate an understanding of complex concepts. The key, says Yongue, is "dialogue, continued questioning, and lots of revision. It took many drafts for kids to get it right and to understand why the changes were important to communicating a scientific picture of what we see in the sky."

At High Tech High, a public charter school in San Diego, tenth-grade economics students were given a task that similarly challenged them with new skills and complex concepts. They each chose an economic term and were required to explain that term in writing for a lay audience, so that anyone could understand it, even someone who had never studied economics. They also created a wood cut–style illustration that illuminated the term. Finally, they had to write an essay about a contemporary issue that is an example of how that term, and the concept it represents, exists in a real-life situation. The final product, a book titled *Economics Illustrated,* which contains all of the terms explored by the entire class, is a joy to read—the descriptions and artistic representations make the concepts highly accessible (Figure 1.3). The students succeed in bringing economics to life in a way that no textbook can.

Figure 1.3 Economics Illustrated

Take, for example, Nathan's description of the economic concept of "signaling." He uses a Harvard degree (ironically) as an example of a signal to future employers that an applicant has the right amount of education for the job. Nathan then goes on to write an essay titled "The Rise of Education Inflation," which describes how the value of college degrees has gone down as more and more people obtain them. A college degree no longer signals the same thing that it once did, when fewer people had them—today's master's degree is yesterday's bachelor's degree. He closes by arguing that a Harvard degree is still a stronger signal than a degree from his local school, San Diego State (even if graduates can't explain why we have seasons).

Use Learning Targets to Increase the Level of Rigor in Daily Lessons

Zooming in from the big picture of where the lesson fits in the arc of the curriculum, the teacher's next step is to consider the specific objectives for a particular lesson. Beyond content objectives, this includes the *kind of thinking* (e.g., knowing, reasoning, doing) and *depth of thinking* (e.g., remembering, analyzing, creating) expected of students.

Our approach to instruction and assessment promotes the use of learning targets as a way to reframe traditional teacher-centered objectives into more student-centered targets that students themselves own. Learning targets, written in student-friendly language and reflected on throughout a lesson, transfer ownership for meeting objectives from the teacher to the student. They are written in concrete, student-friendly language—beginning with the stem "I can"—shared with students, posted in the classroom, and tracked carefully by students and teachers during the process of learning.[2]

Learning targets involve much more than tacking the words "I can" in front of a teacher's objective for a lesson or in front a sentence copied from state standards. The statements must help students describe the goals for their learning and give them an anchor for tracking their progress. For example, in one first-grade classroom in Massachusetts, a state standard called for all students to "understand the monetary value of standard US coinage." This is a reasonable and useful standard, but putting the words "I can" in front of that sentence would not make it understandable or motivating to any first grader. The teacher in this classroom used the learning target: "I can make change for a quarter in many different ways." This was exciting for the students. They all got good at it and could demonstrate it to their friends and families. When they were done they had met the intent of the state standard beautifully.

In the sample learning targets in Table 1.1, notice how important the verb is for identifying the intended learning. Approaching a lesson with the student-centered outcome, "I can communicate my understanding of these patterns through an accurate and detailed scientific diagram" is much different than approaching it with the teacher-centered objective: "Cover lab 3.1 from the text." A learning target can help teachers shift their mindsets from covering content to motivating students to uncover concepts and ideas.

Table 1.1 Examples of Daily Learning Targets

Second-Grade *Skylights* Project	Tenth-Grade *Economics Illustrated* Project
I can demonstrate curiosity and critical thinking by asking questions about the sun, moon, and stars.	I can cite strong and thorough evidence to support an analysis of informational text.
I can explain what causes the seasons based on evidence of change and patterns in space.	I can generate and evaluate analogies that will best illustrate an economic concept for someone unfamiliar with economics.
I can communicate my understanding of these patterns through an accurate and detailed scientific diagram.	I can explain an economic term artistically.

In our 2014 book, *Leaders of Their Own Learning: Transforming Schools through Student-Engaged Assessment*, we explore how teachers can attend to learning target "types"—knowledge, reasoning, and skill—as a helpful starting place for analyzing what students should understand and be able to do in any given lesson (see Table 1.2). Labeling learning targets is helpful, but it may not be enough when considering the overall rigor of a lesson. Teachers also need to consider the complexity of student tasks and assessments linked to the learning targets. Hess's Cognitive Rigor Matrix (Table 1.3) is a useful tool to analyze this component of a lesson. If, for example, your exit ticket, or a "pop quiz" given at the end of a lesson, asks student to recall facts from their text, you can map that onto the matrix and see that it is the lowest level of Bloom's Taxonomy (Remember) and of Webb's Depth-of-Knowledge Levels (Level 1: Recall and Reproduction). This isn't a bad thing necessarily—often

Table 1.2 Knowledge, Reasoning, and Skills Learning Targets

	Knowledge	Skill	Reasoning
Explanation	Knowledge, facts, concepts to be learned outright or retrieved using reference materials	Use of knowledge to perform an action; demonstration is emphasized	Thinking proficiencies—using knowledge to solve a problem, make a decision, plan, and so on
Sample verbs	Explain, describe, identify, tell, name, list, define, label, match, choose, recall, recognize, select	Observe, listen, perform, conduct, read, speak, write, assemble, operate, use, demonstrate, measure, model, collect, dramatize	Analyze, compare and contrast, synthesize, classify, infer, evaluate

Source: ETS (Educational Testing Service); Stiggins, Rick J.; Arter, Judith J.; Chappuis, Jan; Chappuis, Steve, Classroom Assessment for Student Learning: Doing It Right - Using It Well, 1st Edition, (c) 2008. Reprinted by permission of Pearson Education, Inc., Upper Saddle River, NJ.

Table 1.3 Cognitive Rigor Matrix

Revised Bloom's Taxonomy	Webb's DOK Level 1 Recall & Preproduction	Webb's DOK Level 2 Skills & Concepts	Webb's DOK Level 3 Strategic Thinking/ Reasoning	Webb's DOK Level 4 Extended Thinking
Remember Retrieve knowledge from long-term memory, recognize, recall, locate, identify	Recall, recognize, or locate basic facts, details, events, or ideas explicit in texts Read words orally in connected text with fluency & accuracy			
Understand Construct meaning, clarify, paraphrase, represent, translate, illustrate, give examples, classify, categorize, summarize, generalize, infer a logical conclusion, predict, compare/ contrast, match like ideas, explain, construct models	Identify or describe literary elements (characters, setting, sequence etc.) Select appropriate words when intended meaning/definition is clearly evident Describe/explain who, what, where, when, or how Define/describe facts, details, terms, principles Write simple sentences	Specify, explain, show relationships; explain why, cause-effect Give non-examples/examples Summarize results, concepts, ideas Make basic inferences or logical predictions from data or texts Identify main ideas or accurate generalizations of texts Locate information to support explicit/implicit central ideas	Explain, generalize, or connect ideas using supporting evidence (quote, example, text reference) Identify/make inferences about explicit or implicit themes Describe how word choice, point of view, or bias may affect the readers' interpretation of a text Write multiparagraph composition for specific purpose, focus, voice, tone, and audience	Explain how concepts or ideas specifically relate to other content domains or concepts Develop generalizations of the results obtained or strategies used and apply them to new problem situations
Apply Carry out or use a procedure in a given situation; carry out (apply) to a familiar task), or use (apply) to an unfamiliar task	Use language structure (prefix/ suffix) or word relationships (synonym/antonym) to determine meaning of words Apply rules or resources to edit spelling, grammar, punctuation, conventions, word use Apply basic formats for documenting sources	Use context to identify the meaning of words/phrases Obtain and interpret information using text features Develop a text that may be limited to one paragraph Apply simple organizational structures (paragraph, sentence types) in writing	Apply a concept in a new context Revise final draft for meaning or progress ion of ideas Apply internal consistency of text organization and structure to composing a full composition Apply word choice, point of view, style to impact readers'/ viewers' interpretation of a text	Illustrate how multiple themes (historical, geographic, social) may be interrelated Select or devise an approach among many alternatives to research a novel problem

Analyze Break into constituent parts, determine how parts relate, differentiate between relevant/irrelevant, distinguish, focus, select, organize, outline, find coherence, deconstruct (e.g., for bias or point of view)	Identify whether specific information is contained in graphic representations (e.g., map, chart, table, graph, T-chart, diagram) or text features (e.g., headings, subheadings, captions) Decide which text structure is appropriate to audience and purpose	Categorize/compare literary elements, terms, facts/details, events Identify use of literary devices Analyze format, organization, and internal text structure (signal words, transitions, semantic cues) of different texts Distinguish relevant/irrelevant information; fact/opinion Identify characteristic text features; distinguish between texts, genres	Analyze information within data sets or texts Analyze interrelationships among concepts, issues, problems Analyze or interpret author's craft (literary devices, viewpoint, or potential bias) to create or critique a text Use reasoning, planning, and evidence to support inferences	Analyze multiple sources of evidence, or multiple works by the same author, or across genres, time periods, themes Analyze complex/abstract themes, perspectives, concepts Gather, analyze, and organize multiple information sources Analyze discourse styles
Evaluate Make judgments based on criteria, check, detect inconsistencies or fallacies, judge, critique			Cite evidence and develop a logical argument for conjectures Describe, compare, and contrast solution methods Verify reasonableness of results Justify or critique conclusions drawn	Evaluate relevancy, accuracy, and completeness of information from multiple sources Apply understanding in a novel way, provide argument or justification for the application
Create Reorganize elements Into new patterns/ structures, generate, hypothesize, design, plan, produce	Brainstorm ideas, concepts, problems, or perspectives related to a topic or concept	Generate conjectures or hypotheses based on observations or prior knowledge and experience	Synthesize information within one source or text Develop a complex model for a given situation Develop an alternative solution	Synthesize information across multiple sources or texts Articulate a new voice, alternate theme, new knowledge or perspective

Source: © 2009 Karin K. Hess's Cognitive Rigor Matrix. For full article, go to www.nciea.org.

students do need to memorize basic facts—but you should take care to not stay stuck at this level day after day. View it as one part of a sequence of lessons.

Knowing where a task falls on the matrix can inform backward planning, helping teachers ensure that the learning targets will scaffold students' learning appropriately through an arc of lessons. Perhaps on Monday recall is important, but by Friday you want students to be able to analyze the interrelationships among concepts, issues, or problems (Analyze on Bloom's and Level 3: Strategic Thinking and Reasoning on Webb's). Using the matrix can be especially helpful for considering tasks that fall in the Extended Thinking column, emphasizing real-world application, cross-disciplinary connections, problem solving, and creative thinking—all important aspects of deeper learning.

Planning for Engagement

Too often engagement is confused with attention. If students are paying attention or not acting out, we assume they're engaged with the lesson. Often we see students *complying* with the teacher's directions, but to assure that they are engaging with the content and skills in a lesson we need to delve deeper. When lessons are designed to feed students' curiosity and connection—compelling all students to work collaboratively and to grapple with real problems—we see students engaged in active and intentional learning. We see it in how they interact with the lesson and also in the work they produce during the lesson.

Feeding curiosity fuels students' motivation to learn

Worthy curriculum is a necessary ingredient for engaging lessons, and one we address more in the discipline-specific chapters to come. Here we focus on how the design of daily lessons can impel students to engage with their learning. What follows are descriptions of three lesson structures—workshop lessons, protocol-based lessons, and discovery-based lessons—that foster engagement because they get students reading, thinking, talking, writing, and investigating. Regardless of structure, key to any lesson, no matter its name, length, or intended learning, are the following components: an opening that hooks students into the worthiness of the work with which they are about to engage; time for students to grapple with concepts, ideas, texts, or problems; frequent checks for understanding; and a debrief or synthesis. These components are unpacked a bit more in the In Practice section of this chapter.

The Workshop Model

The workshop model has long been a structured yet versatile "container" for introducing or elaborating concepts, skills, and thinking strategies in any subject area. It can be flexed for different time frames or modified to accommodate the needs of a particular group of students or a variety of instructional activities. Although it is flexible, the workshop model has distinct components that limit the amount of teacher talk and make time for students to *think* and *do*, apply their learning, and reflect on what they've learned. The workshop model also staunchly fosters collaboration, communication, and responsibility by structuring roles and time for students to work together, independently, and on tasks that hold them accountable for their learning.

When the Common Core standards were introduced, one of the first things we did was revise the workshop model to address the demand for new capacities for students. We call it Workshop 2.0. Workshop 2.0 for reading and math features a small but important shift in the basic workshop instructional sequence, putting individual grappling with complex text (or, in mathematics, complex problems) before a mini-lesson, peer discussion, or group work. Updating the classic "I do, we do, you do" sequence of Workshop 1.0, Workshop 2.0 prioritizes time for independent, productive struggle with complex text or problems. Figure 1.4 is a comparison of Readers' Workshop 1.0 and 2.0. (Math Workshop 2.0 is discussed at length in Chapter 4).

Figure 1.4 Comparison between Readers' Workshops 1.0 and 2.0

Workshop 1.0	Workshop 2.0
Introduction/Mini-lesson The teacher engages students, links the topic to previous learning, and provides direct instruction and modeling on one aspect of the learning target.	Three steps now launch a workshop: **Engage:** Students engage with a question, quote, object, picture, or activity that spurs thinking and engages them in the lesson's purpose/topic. **Grapple:** Students grapple independently with a complex text (this may mean reading silently in their heads while the teacher reads aloud). **Discuss:** Students follow a structured protocol to discuss the reading with a peer or group, re-reading and referring to the text to support their comments.
Guided Practice All students try the modeled task as the teacher observes and assesses understanding. Teacher provides support and targeted instruction as needed.	**Focus:** Guided practice and mini-lessons are used as needed to "mop up" whatever students can't figure out on their own during the engage, grapple, and discuss phases.
Practice/Application All students have the opportunity to apply the task independently. The teacher may differentiate tasks as needed.	**Apply:** During this phase, differentiation of task is acceptable, but not differentiation of the text or learning targets. Shorter sections of the same text may be used when appropriate.
Share The teacher creates structure for all students to share their work and progress towards the learning target.	
Debrief The teacher supports all students in making connections between the specific learning target and the larger context, assessing proficiency, and identifying next steps and goals.	**Synthesis:** The share and debrief phases are now part of the synthesis phase wherein students share their thinking, reflect on progress toward the learning target(s), make generalizations regarding strategies and content, and discuss transfer to other contexts.

When would you choose workshop 2.0?

Workshop 2.0 does not *replace* Workshop 1.0. There are times when Workshop 1.0 is still the most appropriate choice. But we believe Workshop 2.0 is an important additional lesson structure that builds different skills in students and should be included in the quiver of lesson structures that a teacher uses. Because the standard workshop model is well known and described effectively and elegantly in a number of books, most notably *That Workshop Book* by Samantha Bennett (2007), we focus on illuminating what makes Workshop 2.0 different and how and when it may be useful.

The major difference between Workshop 1.0 and 2.0 is that Workshop 2.0 begins with students grappling individually and then constructing meaning through peer discussion rather than with the teacher modeling the thinking. When learning certain skills, Workshop 1.0 is a better choice. Students often benefit from modeling with a mini-lesson before attempting a new skill. Consider a highly technical skill like learning to drive: having a lesson first, before being thrown into the driver's seat, is crucial. Similarly, there are academic skills that would be frustrating and discouraging for students—and ultimately unsuccessful—to take on without teacher modeling and guidance to begin.

However, if we always model for students how to approach challenges, they are not being prepared to confidently address problems without teacher previews and scaffolding. Because teacher modeling is typically intended to give students as many supports as possible, teachers may end up doing some of the struggling and thinking for students ahead of time. Though it is not the intent of Workshop 1.0, in practice this modeling may allow students to avoid dealing with complex text and problems on their own. It explicitly prevents for students the shock of confronting complex text or problems "cold"—on their own and without careful preview. This is a positive thing in many instances, but if this were always the case, students may not be prepared to individually tackle difficult challenges on high stakes tests, in school, or in real life.

Choosing between Workshop 2.0 and the traditional Workshop 1.0 for a lesson should be based on the professional judgment of teachers. The questions that teachers can ask themselves are

- Do students have sufficient strategies and background knowledge so that grappling with the text or problems in the lesson *before they have teacher modeling* can be successful (i.e., not easy or immediately successful, but offering entry points toward success)?

- Is there important information for students to know ahead of diving into materials or content that should be covered in a mini-lesson to ensure that materials, class norms, student confidence, and the momentum of learning are not harmed?

What does workshop 2.0 look like in action?

The workshop model has earned its reputation as the go-to lesson format for many teachers. Because it can be used for any subject matter at any grade level and prioritizes engagement, it is eminently useful for teachers. With practice, Workshop 2.0 is another powerful tool for digging deep and amplifying students' thinking and doing. In the Snapshot that follows, and in the accompanying video, notice the level of engagement in Giselle Isbell's fifth graders at Anser Charter School in Boise, Idaho. Each stage of the Workshop 2.0 lesson is highlighted.

SNAPSHOT: Workshop 2.0 Lesson: Fifth-Grade Mathematics

Giselle Isbell's fifth graders at Anser Charter School in Boise, Idaho, have gotten accustomed to grappling with challenging problems on their own before she teaches them new strategies for solving them. A typical mathematics class begins with a student reading a word problem aloud and all students taking a few minutes to **GRAPPLE** with the problem independently before Isbell does any instruction. On a day when students are wrestling with decimal operations—dividing 2.58 acres into six evenly sized garden plots—students come up with more than one way to determine how big the plots need to be. Up until now students have only practiced division with whole numbers. A few students, working on their own, get completely stuck or reach the wrong answer. Isbell circulates while students are working and asks probing questions to nudge their thinking into new territory.

Before any students shut down in frustration, she gives them a chance at their tables to **DISCUSS** their strategies and solutions with each other. During this time, students must critique each other's reasoning and defend their own while following the class discussion norms. Isbell reminds them of those norms—listen closely, respect air time, share ideas—before they begin. "I think it's important to work as a group [after you try to solve it yourself], because even if the person got it wrong, they might give you a hint, and then you're, like, 'Oh, I know how to do this now,' and then you can help them," one of her students explains.

Isbell carefully observes how students are working on the problem and talking about it during the discussion time. What she sees informs how she explains the strategies in the brief, explicit **FOCUS** lesson that follows the table discussions. Here, she introduces and unpacks the lesson's learning target so that students know exactly what they need to be able to do and are positioned to own their own learning. Then Isbell both demonstrates multiple strategies for dividing decimals and invites students to explain which strategy is most efficient and why.

Most of the class period is dedicated to **APPLICATION** time, during which most students practice their mathematical thinking on similar problems, using multiple strategies. Some students, identified during the grapple and discuss time, begin their application by practicing together under Isbell's guidance. This illustrates a key difference between the Workshop 1.0 lesson structure, in which all students participated in guided practice, and Workshop 2.0, where the application time is fully differentiated to challenge students who are ready to move on and to support students who are not.

The lesson ends with a time for **SYNTHESIS**, in which Isbell invites the class to reflect on whether they have met the learning target, addressing both content and the process by which they learned it. "It's a time for us to think about where we are going next," she says. "Now that they have some experience with the strategies, it's wonderful to see them think about how they would transfer that understanding to a new problem. They feel empowered to move forward. They want to know what's going to come next."

 WATCH Video 1: Grappling with New Concepts during a Common Core Math Workshop

Protocol-Based Lessons

Familiar protocols for reading, writing, discussion, and sharing liberate students to focus their attention on *what* they're learning, rather than *how*. A protocol-based lesson gives students a structure that levels the playing field for engagement so that all students can embrace the challenge of the content or skill being taught. Protocols don't rely on the teacher being center stage; instead, once students have mastered the protocol, they are empowered to manage their own reading, thinking, talking, writing, and doing about the topic.

Protocols are not typically full lessons; most often they represent one part of a lesson, however, certain protocols are comprehensive enough that they can serve as an entire lesson. Protocols can range in length from very simple (and short) discussion protocols like "think, pair, share"—students consider a question, compare ideas with a neighbor, and share out to the full group—which can occur in the midst of any lesson type, to multistep protocol-based lessons. Building Background Knowledge workshops and Socratic Seminars are common examples of protocol-based lessons (see Appendix A: Sample Protocol-Based Lessons). The value of a protocol-based lesson is in its "rules." Students work productively and can fairly share roles because protocols follow predictable and clear guidelines.[3]

When would you choose a protocol-based lesson?

Protocols articulate the process and procedures for learning with exactitude—and the exactitude matters. It's appropriate to choose a protocol-based lesson when *how* students do something will affect *what* they get out of it, and you want them to use the same procedure on multiple occasions throughout the year. For example, taking the time to teach, model, and practice listening to a peer's work, identifying specific strengths and weakness, giving constructive feedback, and making a plan for revision will pay off in much better writing over the course of a year.

What does a protocol-based lesson look like in action?

A full lesson based on a multistep protocol takes students deeper into a process or a topic and, once the guidelines have been explicitly taught and rehearsed, holds students accountable for making their way through the procedure to the learning target. In the Snapshot that follows, students in Eric Levine's tenth-grade biology class at the Springfield Renaissance School are using a Science Talk protocol to practice thinking and speaking like scientists, using evidence from complex texts, original research, and authentic data. The steps of the Science Talk protocol can be found in Appendix A.

SNAPSHOT: Science Talk Protocol: Tenth Grade

Eric Levine's students are in the midst of a learning expedition (see box) called "Resistance," which is focused on the global crisis of antibiotic-resistant bacteria. Prior to today's Science Talk, students had conducted original research at their school, collecting samples from locker rooms, bathrooms, the cafeteria, and other key locations around the school. In addition to their own original research, students read articles and other research about the topic. By the time they engage in the Science Talk protocol they are well equipped with data and background knowledge.

> **Learning expeditions** are the signature curricular structure in EL Education schools that make content standards come alive for students. They are interdisciplinary studies, usually lasting six to twelve weeks, led by a teacher or teaching team. Learning expeditions are based on standards, aligned with local curriculum maps, and focused on essential content and skills. Each learning expedition includes guiding questions, kickoff experiences, case studies, projects, lessons, fieldwork, experts, service learning, and a culminating event that features high-quality student work.

Levine begins today's Science Talk by focusing students on the class anchor chart for what it means to think, talk, and write like a scientist. This list, which students built together after watching videos of scientists talking about their work, includes such reminders as *provide evidence, cite your sources, build off each other's ideas,* and *ask questions.* Students then share their personal goals for the Science Talk. "My goal is to build off of others' ideas," says one student. Another states that she wants to "focus on providing evidence." This step, combined with the debrief at the end of the Science Talk, in which students reflect on their process as learners, is key to deeper instruction—it empowers students with tools for learning.

The next step in the protocol is introducing the questions that will guide students through their Science Talk. The questions are strategically pre-planned by Levine so that students start with the big picture and then hone in on their data. Finally, students have the opportunity to dig into the *So What:* Why is this an important global issue?

- Is antibiotic resistance a global threat? Why?
- What do our own data tell us about the problem?
- What can scientists, politicians, and the public do about it? What do the experts say? What do our own data say about the solution?

Students move quickly from discussing the evidence presented in their reading—addressing the first question—to their own research. They begin to make connections between what they noticed in their research and what they have been reading. One student states, "I noticed that where we clean the most and where we care for the most, like the gym and the bathroom and the nurse's office, have more antibiotic resistance." He surmises that this is "due to the fact that all the cleaning materials that we use have ingredients that we put into antibiotics." Another student follows up by referencing the class data stating that 34 percent of the bacteria in the school are resistant to amoxicillin (this is the same student who set a goal for himself to "build off of others' ideas").

When students have sufficiently addressed the second question, they move on to the final question, getting to the *So What?* Students cite data from their research about successful state-level policy efforts in the United States. One student suggests that Massachusetts should "follow the lead" of states that have lower levels of antibiotic resistance. Another suggests tighter regulations and follow-up with doctors who prescribe antibiotics.

Reflecting on the protocol, one student states, "I *am* thinking more like a scientist during the Science Talk. I use relevant information that scientists use, I use data, and I use what I researched." You can view Levine and his students engaged in this Science Talk in the accompanying video.

 WATCH Video 2: Thinking and Speaking Like Scientists through a Science Talk

Discovery-Based Lessons

The label "discovery-based" covers a range of lesson formats that have in common an inductive approach to teaching. Essentially, the teacher provides neither the answer nor direct instruction in how to find the answer. Instead, students are given only the materials they will need to solve a problem, conduct an experiment, or meet a challenge. Students, often working in teams, marshal their prior knowledge and critical thinking skills to discover their own methodology and answers to the problem. The discovery-based lesson concludes with students explaining their process and product and generalizing from this specific task to draw conclusions about "how things work" in other similar domains or tasks (see Figure 1.5). Proponents of this approach (e.g., Jerome Bruner, Jean Piaget) note that this process replicates scientific inquiry, in which scientists "discover" general patterns and principles of nature by hypothesizing about and then investigating specific cases that yield significantly similar results.

Figure 1.5 The Discovery Cycle

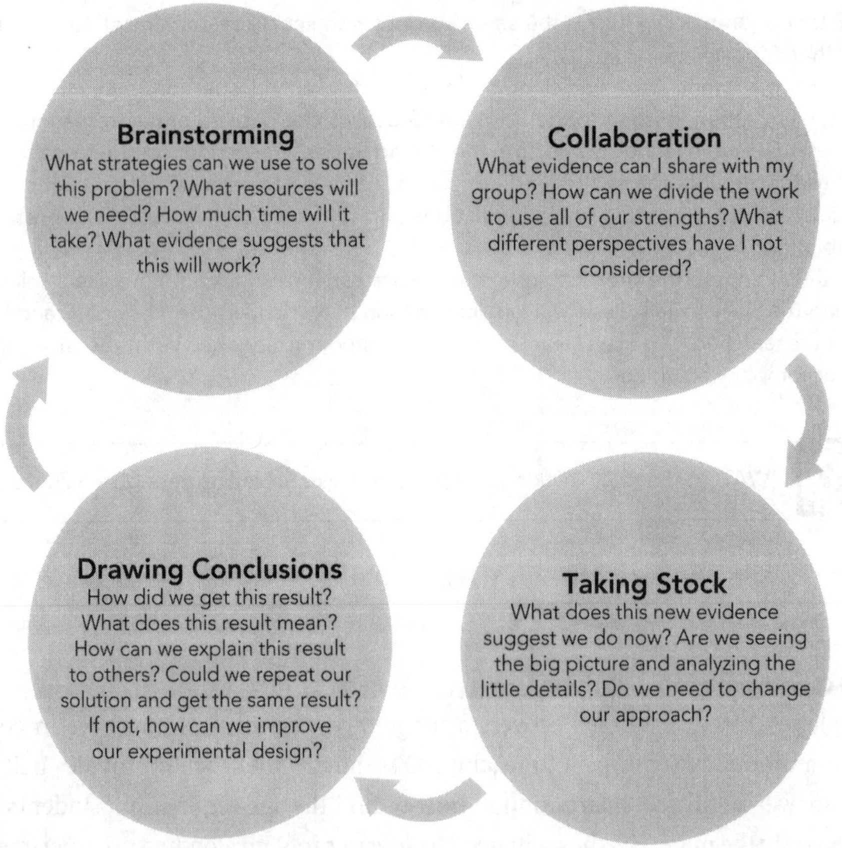

Brainstorming
What strategies can we use to solve this problem? What resources will we need? How much time will it take? What evidence suggests that this will work?

Collaboration
What evidence can I share with my group? How can we divide the work to use all of our strengths? What different perspectives have I not considered?

Drawing Conclusions
How did we get this result? What does this result mean? How can we explain this result to others? Could we repeat our solution and get the same result? If not, how can we improve our experimental design?

Taking Stock
What does this new evidence suggest we do now? Are we seeing the big picture and analyzing the little details? Do we need to change our approach?

When would you choose a discovery-based lesson?

Discovery-based lesson structures, such as the Five Es,[4] in which students Engage, Explore, Explain, Extend, and Evaluate a problem, are often effective structures for science, mathematics and even social studies lessons when the class has met two conditions:

1. Students have been supported in developing sufficient prior knowledge and skills so that they have ideas of where to begin with the problem.

2. Students have been engaged with sufficient desire and motivation so that they are eager to tackle the problem without instruction.

Absent these conditions, discovery-based lessons may result in only a few students feeling successful or, worse, devolve into chaos and generalized frustration when students flounder with the realization that they have no idea how to approach the task.

The Five Es lesson design can also disrupt instructional patterns in the classroom that unintentionally favor the participation of some students and disengage the disengaged even further. The staff at Delaware Ridge Elementary School in Kansas City, Kansas, decided to focus on Five Es lessons as a way to cut down on the amount of teacher talk and engage more students. Former principal Cindy Kapeller notes, "Our experience has been that students who are less motivated are sometimes most intrigued by the Five Es. Our more advanced students tend to like precise answers, they like knowing. In the Five Es, there's a lot of not knowing. Some of our students who have to work really hard on a daily basis, even students with learning disabilities, become leaders in these Five Es experiences because they have more experience with having to work hard to get to the answer over time."

What does a discovery-based lesson look like in action?

In the Snapshot that follows, primary teacher Bill Simmons from Gill Elementary School in Gill, Massachusetts, engages a diverse class of students in rich learning without having to do much at all during the actual lesson other than observe students. The hard work for him was all done ahead of time: building a class culture with clear norms and routines for work, training students to be self-directed in setting and cleaning up, and getting the materials just right.

SNAPSHOT: Discovery-Based Lesson: First, Second, and Third Grades

Bill Simmons has more than the usual range of student needs in his classroom. He is teaching a multi-age primary class of first, second, and third graders that includes a few students with highly challenging special needs. For many lessons, he needs to differentiate by grades or skill levels. For this lesson, however, all students are together. Students enter the classroom in the morning to find that a section of the room is set up with a large glass aquarium filled with dirt, moss, and plants. Next to it are stacks of small plastic aquaria and bins of dirt, sticks, moss, and plants, along with science supplies—hand lenses, rulers, and science notebooks.

Simmons explains to students that each of them will be adopting a land snail to take care of and study. Each student is assigned a partner (most pairs are an older and younger student working together). The pairs will share responsibility for a plastic aquarium home for two snails. The large glass aquarium is home to all of the snails for the time being. Simmons gives a few quick instructions about how to handle snails carefully, modeling with a live snail, and then students are sent off to join their partners. Their instructions:

- Look carefully at the model environment in the glass aquarium.
- Take a plastic aquarium and supplies and build an environment similar to the model environment.
- Choose two snails from the model environment to adopt and place them in their new home. Be sure you can tell them apart.
- Observe them closely, adding notes and drawings in your science journals, focusing on:
  - What do you notice about the snails' bodies and behavior?
  - What questions do you have about your snails?

For the next 25 minutes, there is almost no need for an adult to be in the classroom. The students are captivated by the task, building elaborate miniature environments and then peering intently and discovering all kinds of things about their snails. They are brimming with questions. Simmons circulates around the room making sure students are calm and focused, but saying very little. He takes notes on the questions he hears from students.

The lesson ends with three steps. First, Simmons gathers all the students on the carpet and they chart their questions. They are excited to share all the things they learned, but he keeps the focus only on their questions. Second, Simmons hands out index cards and students are asked to name their snails and create a sign with the snails' names and their names and tape it onto the front of their snail homes. Last, they are asked to clean up.

When the cleaning is done and his student-inspectors give him the thumbs-up that everything looks good, Simmons dismisses them for recess. He has to compel many students to go out to the playground because so many of them want to stay inside and watch their snails.

Other Lesson Formats

Occasionally teachers may choose other formats for lessons, including delivering a traditional lecture, showing a video, or providing an entire class period of independent project time. These lessons are mostly used at the beginning of a unit when a specific resource (an expert's lecture, a compelling video segment) provides rich content and essential information that in subsequent lessons students will manipulate and apply, or toward the end of a unit when students are strictly applying their learning through the creation of products (e.g., research papers, essays).

Lectures and videos deserve particular attention because they have traditionally been the default lesson structure in so many classrooms. These formats are not inherently "wrong"; lectures and educational videos can be compelling and informative. However, when we focus on student learning, not on what is covered in the lesson, we need to consider what students actually take away. Teachers who use these formats regularly must be careful to maximize active ways to engage students in reflection, checking for understanding, or strategic questioning during these lessons. Simply pausing a video at strategic moments so that students can record their thinking on a well-designed graphic organizer goes a long way to making sure that students not only watch but also respond to a video. New technology, such as Zaption, can equip teachers to customize a video by building reflections, assessments, and class discussion right into the flow of the video itself. Punctuating a lecture, even with an "audience" of 100 students, with turn-and-talk questions gives every student a chance to participate. Checking for understanding using answer clickers, a cold-call technique, or exit tickets livens the dialogue between teacher and students, and provides useful data for that lesson or the next lesson.

Regardless of the lesson format, teachers would do well to do more listening than talking, asking strategic questions and giving students time and encouragement to answer them with evidence from their reading, discussion, and experience. Dylan Wiliam, writing in *Educational Leadership*, even suggests that teachers pose a question and give students *an* answer, then challenge students to argue why the answer is correct or not correct by supporting their answer with points from their notes (Wiliam, 2014). Additional questioning techniques are described in the In Practice section of this chapter.

It is fair to say that lesson planning is both a necessary craft for the novice teacher and an elegant art for the master teacher. Mastering the basics of the lesson formats described here gives teachers room to explore new and more challenging texts, devise real-world inquiry-based investigations, and fine-tune strategies for differentiation. Although predetermined lesson structures like those discussed here don't guarantee engagement or deeper learning, they do help teachers focus on the challenge, engagement, and empowerment that are crucial to deeper instruction.

Planning for Empowerment

As referenced in the opening of this chapter, Steve Mahoney from the Springfield Renaissance School has an obsession with debriefs. "We want teachers to circle kids up at the end of every class," he says. "'What did we learn today? What was the process? How did we do as a team? How does this connect to what we did yesterday? How does it connect to what we're doing as we move forward? How does it connect to the big picture of the whole course?'" Mahoney's obsession has become part of the instructional checklist that guides lesson planning at Renaissance. Quality debriefs, even when time is tight, are something that every teacher is expected to prioritize in the 5 to 10 minutes at the end of every lesson. Debriefs like these are a key strategy for Renaissance teachers to help their students track their progress toward learning targets, synthesize and solidify their understanding of concepts, reflect on their process as learners, and prepare to transfer their learning to new situations.

Sixth-grade teacher Maria Ekmalian, featured in the accompanying video, often uses a debrief protocol in which her students form an inner circle and an outer circle so that they rotate to new partners and answer questions that help them reflect on the day's learning. "Students are able to speak to each other and hold each other accountable for what they were learning and how they were learning it," she says. Often they will answer simple reflective questions such as "What did you notice? What did you wonder?" In today's lesson about ratios, in which students apply the concept by making waffles, one student reflects, "I wondered if it would fully rise and I wondered if it would be thin." At the end of the debrief, Ekmalian refocuses students on their learning target: "I can describe the relationship between two quantities." She asks the inside circle to tell the outside circle what it meant to describe that relationship today. The same girl who wondered whether her waffle would rise or be thin commented to her partner: "It meant you had to have enough batter to balance out the water."

 WATCH Video 3: Debrief Circles

"Debrief is where kids get the deeper learning and the deeper understanding," says Ekmalian. Her comment reveals the essence of why deeper instruction matters. A lesson that challenges, engages, and empowers goes beyond following a set curriculum or textbook chapter or meeting required standards. It challenges students with higher-order thinking, develops student ownership and intrinsic engagement in learning, and cultivates students' awareness of and responsibility for their own learning process.

Ekmalian's lesson was designed to allow students to grapple with the concept of ratios with a real-world problem and to work together to come up with a solution. The debrief was the key to empowering them as learners—they reflected on why their waffles turned out well (or not) and how this related to the mathematical concept of describing the relationship between two quantities. This ability to transfer knowledge and skills empowers students. It is what they need to succeed in work and in life—and it's the deeper objective of every great lesson.

Debrief circles, which can be used in the synthesis portion of a Workshop 2.0 lesson, are one strategy for empowering students with tools for learning, but they aren't the only one. Other lesson designs have reflection baked in as well. For example, a Socratic Seminar protocol can be set up like a Fishbowl in which the outer circle observes and makes "metacognitive insights" about the inner circle's process or progress toward learning targets (e.g., "I noticed Raj using evidence directly from the text"). The Evaluate portion of a Five Es lesson is a chance for students to reflect on the success (or failure) of their approach to a problem.

Just understanding the purpose and their responsibilities during all the parts of a lesson can also be empowering for students. This "self-knowledge" becomes a lever for engagement and empowerment. Lane Harlow, a former third-grade teacher at Tollgate Elementary in Aurora, Colorado, spends a lesson at the beginning of the year teaching students the purpose and expectation for each part of the workshop model lesson component. "Students thrive when they understand the structure of their day," she says. "Furthermore, they like the predictability of the daily routines. Once students understand the *why* and *how* of the lesson format, everything just flows together and less time is wasted setting up, settling down, and repeatedly explaining new or different structures. I know the routines also help me be a better-prepared teacher because they offer me a framework in which to think through the learning."

The familiarity with protocols and routines fosters confidence. Carri Thomason, an elementary school teacher at Pocatello Community Charter School in Idaho, begins each day's mathematics lesson with a protocol she calls "My favorite mistake." As students get started on the *grapple* portion of the workshop, she floats and looks for common errors.

> "Then I post them, dramatically, as my favorite mistake (it's important that my favorite mistake is one made by lots of students, that way no one feels picked on and it is never revealed by me who made the mistakes). I make a huge deal about how the mistake is so clever that kids would have to be mathematical geniuses to find and correct the mistake I've shared. Of course, the kids find and fix the mistake. We have a discussion about why that mistake is made and how we can avoid it in the future. Then we begin the lesson. My point is this: We all make mistakes. The only bad mistake is one we don't try to learn from."

Build Structures That Help Students Track and Own Their Progress toward Learning Goals

To design a lesson that empowers students with a deep understanding of how they learn as well as what they've learned, punctuate the lesson with opportunities for students to track their progress. "Tracking progress charts," used by students as a group to reflect on class progress or by individual students to track progress on specific learning targets, are one such tool. For an example of students tracking their data, see the accompanying video.

 WATCH Video 4: Students Own Their Progress

Portfolios that include drafts of student work and feedback from peers and teachers, anchored in explicit rubric criteria, are a more holistic long-term way of tracking progress toward quality work. Teachers can plan for students to use a portfolio for a single project or for an entire year's course. Lessons can be planned to allow students to dig into their work and assess their progress toward long-term learning targets or standards. Finally, daily or weekly reflections (e.g., exit tickets), in which students describe the progress they've made toward targets and provide evidence for their claims are a narrative way for students to track their own progress.

Whatever structures you choose to support students in owning their own learning need to be identified as part of the lesson planning, and time must be dedicated to teaching students how to use the structure. Thereafter, time must occasionally be set aside for students to reflect, track their progress, and report that progress in a systematic way.

Plan for Differentiation

Planning instructional moves—including protocols and assessments—to meet the needs of diverse learners is key to deeper learning. Done well, differentiated instruction challenges, engages, and empowers students. Students who are less ready for the reading, writing, or speaking required by a lesson or students who have already mastered the content of a lesson require special attention. They may need different materials, more or less scaffolding, or a modified setting. A detailed description of the many ways that teachers can effectively differentiate for all kinds of learners is offered in Chapter 6: Differentiating Instruction.

As we see in the In Practice section that follows, students themselves are full partners in the teaching and learning enterprise. Challenge, engagement, and empowerment begin with an effective plan for deeper instruction. But they come to fruition only when the plan is executed.

IN PRACTICE

From Planning to *Delivering* Lessons That Challenge, Engage, and Empower

Throughout a series of lessons, Anne Simpson's kindergarten students at Two Rivers Public Charter School in Washington, D.C., have been learning how to make text-to-self connections. Today, in order to push their thinking even further, she has planned a new lesson that will introduce them to the concept of text-to-text connections. Using the fictional story "Trouper," about a rescued dog, and the nonfiction text "Everything Dogs," Simpson asks her students to make connections between the two texts.

Simpson reads passages aloud to students and asks them to write their text-to-text connections on sticky notes. As they are working independently, she moves among them and asks them about the connections they are identifying. Up until this point, Simpson thought the lesson was going pretty well, but listening to her students as they work tells her a different story—students are reverting back to text-to-self connections. "I had really high expectations," she says, "but about halfway through my lesson I realized they really weren't getting to the point where I wanted them to be and I had to switch gears." She quickly transitions the students into independent learning centers and revisits her plan for the lesson.

At this point, one student, Ozzy, approaches Simpson and asks a simple but critical question: "What's a text-to-text connection?" Simpson sits with him and by asking him questions and looking together at the texts she is able to steer him toward a solid understanding of the concept. He is finally able to make text-to-text connections, and his work becomes the exemplar she needs to help the rest of the class. "Kids learn so much more from their peers," Simpson says. "He will share his thoughts with other kids and be able to word it in a way that the other kids will understand probably much better than I'll be able to word it."

Upon reflection, Simpson notes, "Today I asked them to do too much too fast." Despite this false start, Simpson is able, in the end, to lead her students (with Ozzy's help) to the learning she hoped they would gain from the lesson. Key to her ultimate success was her ability to listen closely to what her students were telling her and her willingness to change her plan to accommodate their needs. View this lesson in the accompanying video.

 WATCH Video 5: Redirecting a Lesson with Exemplars

Plan Great Lessons, but Be Prepared for Anything

Planning lessons is essential. Planning is the rehearsal time when teachers can identify and refine opportunities for deeper instruction. But delivering a great lesson is less like following a script and more like live interactive theater, in which actors and audience members tell a collaborative story. Each performance is different, depending on the energy, skills, and interests of the audience. The actors, under the leadership of a director, have prepared and rehearsed their opening lines, the structure of the play, and a repertoire of strategic moves that draw the audience in and engage them—not as passive observers, but as central characters—in the story that unfolds. The magic of interactive theater is not on the page of the script, but in the spark of connection as the story, the professional actors, and the untrained audience members interact.

This interactive magic is very much like what happens in classrooms everywhere as teachers develop their own repertoire of strategic moves and students interact with the content, each other, and their teachers within the instructional core. Teachers, like directors, must know their students, organize their material, and determine both the how and the when of delivering it. In the theater of the classroom, however, the content, not the teacher, is the main actor on the stage. The teacher is the director behind the scenes, and her goal is to engage students with the content—to bring students into the story, where they become center stage, interacting with words, numbers, ideas, and each other.

As we saw in Anne Simpson's kindergarten classroom, sometimes students don't progress as you intend them to. And, just like she did, it's important to recognize when it's time to turn the page of your script or toss it out and write a new one. Abandoning your plan should not be seen as a failure. In fact, knowing when to "flip the script" usually indicates that you are clear about what you want students to learn, and you have checked for understanding along the way—this is good practice. After all, the most ambitious and well-written lesson is not worth much if students leave the room more confused than they were when they walked in. Changing course is part of being a teacher. In the theater of the classroom, there is no one right way to do things, and there's certainly no way to predict how twenty or thirty diverse learners will interact with the content, each other, and you.

In this section we shift from the planning of challenging, engaging, and empowering lessons to what it takes to deliver them. There is no doubt that there is an art to delivering lessons well, but this art can be learned. It is not something bestowed on great teachers from birth. It is something that comes from practice, willingness to learn from others, and a belief that improvement is within our control. Primarily we focus on a few key lesson components—no matter the design—that are essential for the success of any lesson: an opening that hooks students into the worthiness of the work with which they are about to engage; time for students to grapple with concepts, ideas, texts, or problems; frequent checks for understanding; and a debrief or synthesis.

Setting a Course for Learning with a Strong Opening

How many times have we heard our students ask, "Why do we have to do this?" How many times have we said this ourselves throughout our own educational journey? Answering this question by helping students understand why their hard work matters is a critical ingredient when designing curricula and lessons, but too often it is left out of the plan. The worth of a lesson does not need to be *justified* to students as in "You'll need to know this for next week's test." Those are just words. Instead, lessons should begin with a "hook" that will naturally build students' curiosity and fuel their motivation to do their best work. This hook may come from a table full of mysterious materials at the start of a discovery-based lesson. It may come from a challenging grapple problem during a Workshop 2.0 lesson. Or, it may come from a beautiful model of high-quality work that students aspire to replicate. These thoughtfully planned lesson openings invite students into a learning space where they can answer the question "Why?" for themselves.

A strong opening engages students with their questions and makes them want to seek answers

Reenie McMains, a sixth-grade teacher at Sierra Expeditionary Learning School in Truckee, California, recalls starting a lesson with a mathematics problem in which she intentionally withheld the units of measurement from students. "Pretty soon," she says, "students started asking, 'What measurement are we talking about here? Are these triangles even comparable?' Next, a student conjectured that he could use the Pythagorean theorem to solve for the missing variables in the measurements, if only he knew how to calculate square roots. "So then the math we were learning became purposeful. They were hooked," she reflects. She then shared the daily learning target with students, who were by then primed and ready: *I can develop a complex mathematical question based on observations.*

Don't Just Write Learning Targets; Use Them to Leverage Growth

As discussed in the Getting Started section, we recommend learning targets as a tool to plan purposeful lessons and sequences of lessons that move students up Bloom's Taxonomy. McMain's example is a good one for demonstrating their value in engaging students in the lesson, hooking them in to the learning that is before them. Learning targets can be used strategically and wisely. They can also be used poorly. Simply writing them on the board or reading them aloud at the start of the lesson is not enough. This does little to engage students in their learning. The target must be introduced at the right time, unpacked in discussion with students so that they understand it and can own it, and referred to throughout a lesson so that students can articulate the connection between what they are doing and what they aim to know and be able to do at the end of the lesson. Thomas Rochow-icz, from WHEELS in NYC, almost always shares the learning target(s) with students at the beginning of class, and, often, he shares what the student's exit ticket (i.e., assessment) will be at the end of the class at the same time. When students are consciously aiming for the target, they work harder to develop the skills and knowledge they will need to "hit it" on the assessment.

In the hands of teachers, learning targets are a powerful tool for planning for challenge and engagement. In the hands of students they are equally powerful as a tool for empowerment. As one eighth-grade student at the Odyssey School of Denver states, "I know I understand the learning target when I feel the confidence to say 'I can.'" Knowing where they're headed gives students ownership over their progress. If they can't say "I can," they know they haven't met the target. A former Odyssey student, Elena Fulton, subsequently attended a large comprehensive high school in Denver where teachers don't use learning targets. She reflects on how she handled the transition: "Learning targets guided and supported my learning for all of my nine years, and by the time I graduated, I could not bear to part with them. In fact, it had not even occurred to me that traditional schools don't use learning targets regularly, if at all. Walking into my first class freshman year . . . almost without thinking, I created a target for myself based on the writing prompt and reading assignment on the board."

Connect the Intended Learning to Students' Prior Knowledge

Connecting students to what they already know about a topic is a productive way to ground them in the learning. Prior knowledge or skills become a firm surface from which to launch new learning. Connecting with "what I know" facilitates their "need to know" and thus engages them in deeper learning. Incorporating this step in the opening of any lesson is also a way of situating students within the broad landscape of their learning; it's a way of saying "This is where we've been, this is where we are, and this is where we're going next." The daily learning target then becomes just one step on the staircase to meeting a standard (or, over a student's K–12 education, on the staircase to college- and career-readiness).

Share Models of High-Quality Work

Another engaging way to open a lesson and motivate through inspiration is with compelling and beautiful student work or professional work. No amount of teacher talk or written guidelines can achieve what a model can. A model creates a vision of what quality looks like and allows students to create specific criteria, in their own words, of what quality looks like. When a teacher in one of our schools in Maine put out a gallery of models—professional-looking local field guides created by students of different ages in schools across the country—his students were captivated. They immediately wanted to create something equally impressive and useful. They argued about their favorite guides and favorite features. They argued about what features they could borrow for their own project. They wanted to come to consensus about what quality work would look like so that they could begin the work right away.

Particularly when introducing a challenging assignment or product as the outcome of a lesson, seeing a model of how other students or professionals have done something similar can kick start students' understanding of where they are headed and motivate them to persevere with their own work, to do more than they may have thought possible. How to critique a model of high-quality work *with students* so that students identify and articulate the criteria for quality is explored at length in Chapter 2.

Grappling with Problems, Ideas, and Concepts

A well-designed opportunity for students to grapple with problems, texts, ideas, or concepts is where the rich brew of deeper instruction is most powerful. This is where asking the right questions—as opposed to giving the right answers—can give students a challenge that they can sink their teeth into. Allowing them to grapple with that question collaboratively engages them in co-constructing knowledge and empowers them as they learn that they can discover the "answers" with their own ingenuity.

Grappling is baked into the lesson structures described in the Getting Started section. No matter what the lesson structure, however, using complex texts or tasks that are initially confounding to students is a strategy that should be approached thoughtfully so that it is productive and empowering for students. The following list provides an overview of strategies teachers can use to create a class culture in which challenge or struggle is viewed as a way to learn, not as a barrier to learning:

- Build common language in your classroom for "grappling"—you don't have to call it grappling, but label it for students. Make it a class routine with specific strategies (e.g., re-reading, annotating, collaborating).

- Give students tangible successes early in the year by designing tasks you know they can be successful with and supporting them to do them with quality. Give students lots of individual feedback to help them grow and regularly point out their growth.

- Talk explicitly about the importance of taking on challenges in order to learn. When appropriate, read and discuss with students short pieces of research about having a growth mindset and its impact on learning.

- Use group initiatives to practice grappling with a challenge, tenacity, and problem solving—discuss application to classroom lessons when debriefing the initiative.

- Engage students in discussions that make the link between character traits and the grapple phase of your lessons: What does perseverance look like? What are tips for helping yourself keep going when the going is hard?

- Create meaningful metaphors for instilling a growth mindset (e.g., the mind is a muscle that can get stronger).

- Do a "zones of comfort" activity: draw concentric circles for the comfort, risk, and danger zones. Students identify the types of experiences they have that fall into the different zones. Point out that the risk zone is our learning zone—we learn best when we are a little uncomfortable.

Harness the Power of Questions

The first and easiest shift teachers can make when incorporating more productive struggle into lessons is moving from asking questions with "right" answers to asking open-ended questions. In Workshop 2.0 and discovery-based lessons, curiosity and engagement stem from an opening problem or question that students encounter right out of the gate. Reenie McMains, from Sierra Expeditionary

Learning School, often puts an intriguing question, like "Do round things fly?," on the board to start her Inquiry Friday lessons. "When they come to me from fifth grade, this sometimes stumps them," she says. "They are used to being told how to do things. Then I try to be less helpful."

Open-ended questions invite students to generate their own ideas, defend them with reasoning and evidence, elaborate on them, and build on them with new questions (Alber, 2013). These are also questions that can't be answered by the teacher himself. They are questions that beg for real-time, original answers rather than the scripted solutions from the answer key. They are questions that allow the teacher to see and hear student thinking, questions that push students to engage fully in the lesson content and to make connections between concepts and back to the text, and to take responsibility for articulating their learning in their own words.

"If the questions are not causing students to struggle and think, they are probably not worth asking," says Dylan Wiliam (2014, p. 16). Formulating challenging and meaningful questions takes time and forethought and should be part of the lesson-planning process. Preparing questions in advance allows teachers to differentiate and contextualize the questions in the sequence of the lesson so that all students have access and opportunity to dig deep for the answers. Pre-planned strategic questions advance the discussion of a text, the understanding of a topic, or the synthesis of the lesson's activities. They demand that students think deeply and critically (not just that they remember or relate to their own experience).

Teachers will not always have the answers to good questions. Students will not always find the answers. A classroom dialogue based on inquiry makes failure a real possibility. But through perseverance, collaboration, and multiple attempts—perhaps guided by redirection after assessment—students can, and do, succeed over time. Just as important, they learn that asking hard questions, looking for answers, and evaluating the evidence to support their answers is what educated people do.

Questions are powerful tools for teachers. They are also powerful tools for students. The Common Core literacy standards ask students to ask and answer questions about key details (reading anchor standard R.1) and to conduct

> The purpose of strategic questions is to enhance comprehension, not to assess it.
>
> *–Suzanne Plaut, director of Curriculum Design, EL Education*

research based on self-generated questions (writing anchor standard W.7). But how do we teach students to ask the right questions? In *The Language of Learning: Teaching Students Core Thinking, Listening, and Speaking Skills*, Margaret Berry Wilson (2014) emphasizes the importance of teaching students to identify the purpose of different types of questions. "By understanding the purpose behind every question, students can better clarify their own thinking and make strategic decisions about what to ask in a given situation." She describes a lesson in which students generate questions about a text and then sort them according to their purpose:

- *Clarifying questions*: To understand what you read, heard, or saw
- *Background questions*: To understand more about the history behind what you read, heard, or saw
- *Opinion-seeking questions*: To find out what others think about what you read, heard, or saw
- *Challenging questions*: To find out whether you believe or trust what you read, heard, or saw

Finally, Wilson recommends that instead of giving students the pat response "Good question," teachers should point out what kind of question students are asking and how it will help them reach their learning target. For example, when a student asks, "How does being a vegetarian qualify this writer to evaluate the health impacts of genetically modified foods?" the teacher might answer, "Your question challenges us to determine whether or not this source is biased and valid. It will help you identify strong evidence for your argument." When students understand the different types of questions, and how they flesh out a concept, they are more likely to generate multiple questions and different types of questions (Wilson, 2014).

In the Strategy Close Up that follows, Dan Rothstein and Luz Santana of the Right Question Institute offer a protocol for teaching students to ask their own questions.

STRATEGY CLOSE UP: The Question Formulation Technique

The Question Formulation Technique[5] prescribes these specific instructional moves to help students prioritize a list of brainstormed questions, select one, and improve it before beginning an investigation.

1. Ask a small group of students to write as many questions as they can about the topic in a short amount of time.

2. Students then talk about each question on the list: What is its purpose? Is it open ended or closed? Is it a testable question? What sources would provide answers?
3. Students categorize questions according to Bloom's Taxonomy, then "choose three questions that move you up the ladder."
4. Select the one that can be researched accurately and reliably. This also might be a starting point for further research.

As is true with all protocols, the Question Formulation Technique must be explicitly taught and practiced. Initially it may require a full 50-minute period for students to do it successfully. Once students know how and why to generate critical questions, the teacher can and should step back into the role of facilitator and coach.

Checking for Understanding: Knowing What They Know Empowers Students

As Anne Simpson discovered, a well-planned lesson can still fall short if students don't reach the target of the lesson. Consequently, an essential part of deeper instruction is checking for understanding. Our approach to checking for understanding involves both the quick checks that happen during the course of daily lessons, like what we saw Simpson doing in her kindergarten classroom, and the deeper kind of check that occurs when we design tasks that require students to describe their conceptual understanding, like we saw in the *Economics Illustrated* example in the Getting Started section.

Quick checks encompass a wide range of techniques—formal and informal, oral and written, verbal and nonverbal—used by teachers and students to track what students understand and can do throughout a lesson. As a result of this ongoing assessment, teachers and students make adjustments to what they are doing to ensure that gaps in understanding are addressed and that students who have mastered concepts may comfortably move on to another learning task.

It is important that these kinds of quick checks are meant to get a true read on *every* student's progress, not just on the progress of some students. Too often you will hear teachers asking questions—"What year did the Civil War start?" "How much is 7 + 5?" "What does an adverb do?" Often, if no student answers the question immediately, you will hear the teacher himself give the answer. Or, if two or three students raise their hands to answer the question, the teacher may listen to the answer, clarify if necessary, and then move on, assuming that most students understand the material. Dylan Wiliam notes that these off-the-cuff, lower-level questions don't provide accurate assessment data for the teacher, and they give opportunity and affirmation only to those students who already know the answer; those who don't raise their hands still don't know, and, worse, don't know how to find out (Wiliam, 2014).

Strategies that ask all students to reflect, assess themselves, and communicate their own sense of their progress toward the learning target are much more valuable, both for the teacher and for the students. What follows are some examples of quick checks that involve all students in self-assessment:

- *Heads together.* Students stand up and literally put their heads together (huddle) to respond to a question. After a minute or so, "heads apart" and debrief answers with the class.

- *Think-pair-share.* Given a prompt or a question, students think first independently and then turn to share their thinking with partners. Partners may be assigned strategically to match students with different or similar strengths. Partners may also be asked to share out with the whole class.

- *Electronic response systems.* "Clickers," or apps like "Poll Everywhere," enable teachers to ask a question and get instant data about students' understanding.

- *Exit tickets.* This involves short writing in response to a prompt or question that all students complete at the end of the lesson. Well-crafted exit tickets can also serve as a pre-assessment for the next lesson.

Quick checks give teachers important information about students' collective and sometimes individual progress toward targets so that they can adjust instruction if necessary. They often don't, however, provide a granular picture of whether individual students have met long-term objectives or demonstrated deep understanding of concepts and skills. Checking for this kind of understanding requires locating high-quality summative assessments at strategic points in a series of lessons. The design of the assessment is critical; it must match the thinking task (knowledge, skill, or reasoning) identified in the learning targets (Table 1.2). A multiple-choice test may allow you to check for a student's ability to analyze or evaluate, say, the best of three options. However, an essay might be a better way to see a student's logical reasoning abilities in support of a claim. Often, a truly complex task—an artifact, piece of writing, demonstration, or presentation— is needed to assess higher-order thinking skills on the upper levels of Bloom's Taxonomy. Such tasks may be on-demand, such as an essay or dialogue in a world language class. Or, they can be tasks student work on and revise over time in class as they apply the learning of daily lessons.

Synthesizing and Reflecting on Learning

One of the hallmarks of a lesson that empowers students is that it helps them learn how to learn. At the end of a lesson, synthesizing and reflecting on learning with students enables them to "file" the learning away for transfer to a new lesson or learning opportunity. As we saw in Maria Ekmalian's class earlier in this chapter, an opportunity to debrief learning invites students to reflect on the big ideas they are taking away from the lesson. During this important part of any lesson, students reflect not only on what they learned, but also on how they learned it.

The debrief may also ask students to weigh the value of a strategy or behavior that helped them be successful that day, for example, "What strategies did you use to annotate your article that helped you discover the bias of its author?" Often, questions that get at this metacognition will arise from teachers observing students at work, seeing them have *aha*'s or overcome obstacles. Helping them process these experiences will support the development of positive work habits and a growth mindset Finally, synthesis and reflection invites students to connect their learning to bigger disciplinary concepts: "How is today's news story similar or different to what you've learned about economics in the 1920s?"

When time is short, as it often is at the end of a lesson, inviting students to answer synthesis or reflection questions in pairs, trios, or quads rather than speaking them out to the whole group will create more opportunities for participation. In any case, a debrief is a time for student voices to have the last word, for them to name and store for later the skills, understanding, and reasoning that have made them successful in the day's lesson.

The Critical Moves for Planning and Delivering Lessons That Challenge, Engage, and Empower

Planning and delivering challenging, engaging, and empowering lessons takes intention and practice. So that students can become leaders of their own learning, teachers must make thoughtful choices about lesson structure and content and attend to the nuanced choreography of the teaching and learning steps that students and teachers take during a lesson. Table 1.4 illustrates the who, what, and why of lessons that challenge, engage, and empower.

Table 1.4 The Who, What, and Why of Lessons That Challenge, Engage, and Empower

What Do Teachers Do?	What Do Students Do?	What's the Result?
Consider the curriculum. Plan daily lessons in the context of where you've been and where you're headed.	N/A	Lessons and sequences of lessons build the long-term skills, knowledge, and understandings students need to meet standards and learn deeply.
Plan for challenge. Focus on skills and tasks that demand cognitive rigor and demonstrate mastery of required standards.	N/A	Lessons intentionally move students up Bloom's Taxonomy and lead to deeper learning.
Plan for engagement. Choose a lesson structure in which students are doing the thinking, reading, writing, talking, and investigating.	N/A	Students do the cognitive work in the classroom and have a need-to-know orientation to their learning.
Plan for empowerment. Identify protocols, assessments, structures, and differentiation strategies that give all students tools for leading their own learning	N/A	Students develop the habits and skills of efficacious learners.
Launch the lesson with purpose. Name learning targets, connect to real-world issues, and set expectation for (or share models of) what students will do at the end.	Name the purpose of the lesson and take aim to meet the target. They identify strategies for meeting expectations and feel confident they can succeed.	Students create high-quality work and work toward mastery of knowledge and skills.
Insist that students grapple. Ask strategic questions and support students with graphic organizers, anchor charts, and other ways of representing their thinking.	Persevere through challenges because of structures that allow for grappling. They learn to debate and disagree and use evidence to support their ideas. They ask and answer deep questions.	Students know how to formulate focused questions and how to seek their own answers. They value evidence and develop routines and note-taking strategies for organizing, remembering, and archiving their ideas.
Actively use the learning target with students throughout the lesson to promote ownership of learning. Use well-designed formative and summative assessments to check for understanding and adjust instruction.	Assess their progress and articulate where they are going and how they'll get there. They understand the data and how it reflects their learning.	Students take responsibility for the results of their learning. They analyze their own data, reflect on academic choices, and revise their habits and actions to get different results.

What Do Teachers Do?	What Do Students Do?	What's the Result?
Provide opportunities for students to synthesize and reflect on what and how they learn.	Articulate both what they learned and how they learned it. They reflect on the process and the product.	Students can adapt to different and more complex learning situations. They are resourceful and resilient.

SCHOOLWIDE IMPLEMENTATION

Making Teaching Practice Transparent

In the introduction to this book we explored the concept of *academic mindsets*, including the importance of students' growth mindsets—their belief in their own capacity to "get smart" through hard work and persistence. But teachers need a growth mindset too. Believing that we can improve our craft as teachers builds our confidence and skill, and this is ultimately the path to better outcomes for our students. But how do we improve our craft as teachers? It is not as simple as reading a book or keeping up our professional development credits. It takes deep commitment from school communities to set up systems and structures to make teaching practice transparent and that allow others to plan with us, observe us, give us feedback, and learn from us.

At Two Rivers Public Charter School in Washington, D.C., the entire school community made such a commitment to improving their craft, particularly with planning and delivering great lessons. They agreed on common language and common structures, and to continually analyze when and why their lessons were working. Though the staff didn't decide to all follow one particular kind of lesson design, they did decide to bring common structures to lessons in all classrooms. They spent six months' worth of faculty meetings, in fact, studying one common component of all of their lessons: the debrief at the end of every lesson. They focused on such strategies as having one to three students or groups share rather than the whole class, identifying the key concepts in a lesson that they wanted students to synthesize, and creating some form of exit ticket to collect data on what every student took away from the lesson. Together they sharpened their practice for concluding lessons.

Teaching can be a lonely profession. Unless we consciously decide to do otherwise, or work in a school like Two Rivers that has committed to the practice, we may rarely, if ever, find ourselves looking at other teachers' lesson plans or observing them teach. This has always been true in American schools, even though research shows that peer observation and collaborative analysis of lesson plans and student work leads to sharp improvement in teacher practice (Darling-Hammond & Richardson, 2009).

In other parts of the world—most notably Japan—teaching is viewed as a collaborative endeavor in which continuous improvement over the long term is an integral part of the profession. The Japanese lesson study is one of the best examples of focused, collaborative work that can affect the planning and implementation of lessons and, most important, the results for students. The steps of the Japanese lesson study include:[6]

1. *Defining the problem.* A group of teachers (often grade-level or disciplinary groups) collaboratively define a problem that can be addressed in the course of lesson. Usually this comes from a problem of practice in their classrooms (e.g., using proper punctuation when writing dialogue), though sometimes it comes from policymakers seeking teacher input on national priorities.

2. *Planning the lesson.* Teachers collaboratively plan a lesson to address the problem. The lesson plan is presented to schoolwide faculty for critique and then revised to prepare it for implementation. This initial planning may take several months.

3. *Teaching the lesson.* Teachers collaboratively prepare materials and conduct dress rehearsals. The actual lesson is then conducted by one teacher while the rest of the group observes.

4. *Evaluating the lesson and reflecting on its effect.* The teacher who taught the lesson reflects first on how the lesson went, including its problems. Other members of the group then offer critique of the lesson. Because the lesson is a group product and everyone in the group feels ownership, the focus is on the flaws of the lesson itself, not the teacher.

5. *Revising the lesson.* Based on specific misunderstandings of the students, the group might change the materials, activities, questions asked, and so on.

6. *Teaching the revised lesson.* Once the lesson is revised, it is taught to a different class, sometimes by the same teacher but often by a different teacher. All members of the school faculty attend.

7. *Evaluating and reflecting again.* As before, the teacher who taught the lesson reflects first. Then the entire faculty reflects on the success of the lesson, focusing on how well it addressed the defined problem and student learning.

8. *Sharing the results.* Most lesson study groups produce a report that details their work. This report is used in the school and sometimes is forwarded to educational authorities for wider dissemination.

The term "lesson study" is used rather loosely in the United States. Rarely does it refer to a process as comprehensive as the Japanese model, instead focusing on less robust classroom observation structures. School leaders may never find a way to engage teachers in a highly regimented lesson study like the Japanese, but making time and space in the school calendar for observation and critique, and, ideally, some kind of collaborative planning process, can make a difference.

Achieving consistent teaching practices throughout a school requires intentional and strategic leadership. To start with, leaders must make the time for teachers to engage with each other around the questions that drive their lesson planning. "How can I increase the level of challenge here?" "What's a better hook for this lesson?" "How will I help my students show that they can transfer their knowledge and skills to novel situations?" There is no reason to struggle with these questions alone. Collaboration in planning and structures that engage teachers in respectfully giving and receiving feedback on lesson plans and implementation improve learning. They can also go a long way in diminishing the isolation that so many teachers feel when they shut the doors to their classrooms.

Key Leadership Actions

Lay the Groundwork

- Be explicit and relentless in creating a professional culture that is safe for teachers to share their questions and struggles in order to grow together. Celebrate a growth mindset across the school so that faculty feel empowered to take risks, to open their classrooms to peer and coach observation, and do not feel they have to close their doors and bury their lesson plans to hide weaknesses in their instruction.

- Create structures for planning. Time is the most elusive commodity for most teachers, especially for those in the first few years of their careers; they often need school leaders to help them find planning time.

- Develop norms for effective collaboration and common systems for facilitating and documenting grade-level or subject-area planning meetings.

- Consider developing a common lesson-planning template that prompts teachers, especially novice teachers, to incorporate common lesson design elements (e.g., an engaging hook" time to grapple, a debrief).

Build Teachers' Capacity

- Be the lead learner. Attend professional development on lesson design and engagement strategies alongside teachers. Model lessons for teachers so that teachers see that leaders too have a growth mindset about improving school-wide practice.

- Develop a multipronged strategy for professional learning around planning and delivering lessons that includes whole-staff professional learning, intensive and collaborative coaching for individual teachers, and planning and revision of plans within teaching teams.

- With individuals and teams, develop a theory of action (i.e., If we do X, then we expect to see Y). Collect data on these actions and analyze the results.

Support Teachers to Deepen Their Practice

- Schedule regular learning walks to analyze patterns of practice across the grade level, department, or building—and the impact these practices have on students' learning. If possible, invite teachers or teams to also conduct learning walks. Table 1.5 is an example of a learning walk note-catcher focused on the quality of questioning in the classroom. You can also use the Indicators of Deeper Instruction (Table I.1) to focus observations on deeper learning.

- Conduct a formal lesson study in which teachers plan a common lesson, observe each other teaching it, then analyze and revise their practices collaboratively. Share the Japanese model with them and decide together on an adaptation that will work in your setting.

Table 1.5 Observation Note-Catcher for Questioning in the Classroom

Category	Accomplished indicators . . . *The lesson includes*	Observations
Questions are planned	Questions aligned to the learning targets Strategies to make questions visible to students (charts, visual aids) Thinking extenders and challenge questions with an emphasis on probing Protocols or strategies to encourage students to ask their own questions	
Questions focus on specific content, concepts, skill and character targets	Warm-up questions to clarify learning targets and illuminate schema Questions that build on schema and increase in complexity Questions that clarify criteria for success and help students determine next steps	
Questions emphasize critical thinking and metacognition	Questions focused on critical thinking: top four levels of Bloom's Revised Taxonomy Questions that promote metacognition (thinking about thinking)	
Questions are structured to promote engagement and deep thinking of all learners in varied patterns of dialogue	Structures for think-time to promote deep thinking by all students Note-taking, illustration, written conversations or quick-check strategies to help all students engage during think time Cold call, no opt out, whiteboards and/or other whole-class engagement strategies Strategies to support students to ask their own questions Student-centered protocols that create varied patterns of dialogue	

COMMON CHALLENGES

Planning Lessons without a Long-Term Curriculum Map

Know how the lesson fits into the big picture. Lessons that are compelling in and of themselves, but not anchored in the larger purpose and arc of a long-term curriculum, may succeed in the moment but fail to move students toward the overarching goals for the work. These lessons sometimes fall into the category of "activities." When teachers sit down to plan and begin the conversation with an excited gasp and the phrase, "We could do . . ." beware! Beginning with the big picture and the long-term targets in mind will help teachers plan backward to individual lessons that follow a road map to lasting success.

Aiming Low

Design complex and challenging tasks. In order for students to strengthen their intellectual muscles, the tasks we ask them to complete must stretch them cognitively. Teachers can ask themselves a series of questions:

- What did students learn that they didn't know before?

- Did the task—reading, writing, questioning, discussing, writing, problem solving—involve higher-order thinking skills like analyzing, evaluating, or creating?

- Did they read complex text, conduct research, or use evidence to support their thinking?

- Did I ask them to synthesize ideas and apply what they learned in new work?

- How did this learning advance them toward the long-term targets of this unit?

Writing Vague Lesson Plans

Plan how you will challenge, engage, and empower students by writing down the lesson steps. Many lessons fail because they are too loosely constructed or teachers write them to comply with school policy but don't actually use them. Identify the teacher moves and directions for student moves throughout the lesson, including time for such things as grappling, annotating a text, discussing collaboratively using a protocol, or applying learning to solve a problem. Do the task yourself to troubleshoot problems that may arise for your students. Lesson plans should also identify when and how students and the teacher will assess progress and debrief the lesson. It is important that the written lesson plan is a living document that guides instruction and that teachers reflect on afterward, annotate for revision, and save with plans to improve the next time around.

Too Much Teacher Talk

Structure ample time for student work and student voices. With so much going on in the classroom, it's easy to be unaware of who is doing the talking during a lesson. Observation feedback focused simply on the types of questions a teacher asks, the amount of wait-time he or she gives students, the use of cold calling or another method to reinforce accountability, and the depth of students' answers is a great way to push more and deeper student talk in the classroom. Attending to tight time frames for the various components of the workshop model or the other lesson structures introduced in this chapter will also help teachers shift from teacher-centered to student-centered teaching, where what students are doing and saying is at the heart of the classroom conversation. Leaders Lynn Bass and Elizabeth Smallwood at Tapestry Charter High School in Buffalo, New York, confronted this problem by collecting data about the ratio of teacher talk to student talk. They visited each classroom for 10 minutes and recorded who was doing the most talking during each minute. This data dramatically shifted teachers' practice. They became much more mindful and intentional about making room for students' voices. See Figure 1.6 for a sample data collection form used at Tapestry.

Forgetting to Assess What's Being Learned

Students and teachers must track students' progress. In the sincere effort to cover all the content, teachers sometimes rush through without pausing for an assessment of whether individual students are "getting it" along the way. The bell rings and that sound, mid-sentence, is the end of the lesson, rather than any strategic debrief or assessment of the skills and knowledge taught. Although the teacher may have taught a great deal, it's very possible the students have learned little. Assessment—both formative and summative—is the lynchpin of learning. It keeps the wheel of learning turning because students and teachers both know intimately the topography of where they've been and where the trail is headed next.

Figure 1.6   Teacher Talk versus Student Talk Recording Form

Week _____   93 | 32%
290 | 68%
goal 75%

Department		Goal: To spend 10 minutes in the class, not the 2nd 5 minutes or the last 5 minutes											
		T-Teacher talking to whole class/traditional questioning/ giving directions/lecturing or other presentation of information (TEACHER CENTERED INSTRUCTION)											
		S- Students engaged in independent, partners or group work/discussion protocol/workshop/ teacher talking to small group or individual (STUDENT CENTERED INSTRUCTION)											
English		Sara	7	S	S	S	S	S	S	S	S	S	S	cold call Pack Quiz
		Anthony	② ②	T	T	T	T	T	T	T	T	T	T	student
		Jesse	①	S	S	S	S	S	S	S	S	S	S	Productive
	25/50	Simon	⑦	T	T	T	T	T	T	T	T	T	T	Video
		Terra	⑫ 7	T	S	T	T	T	T	S	S	S	S	evidence Gallery wage
Social Studies	9 40	Fred	①	T	T	T	T	S	S	S	S	S	S	Push discussion
		Tricia	⑦	T	T	S	S	S	S	T	T	S	S	Jigsaw
		Jessica	②	S	S	S	S	S	S	S	S	S	S	PKT
		Nate	①	S	S	S	S	S	S	S	S	S	S	White Boards
Math	20/4	Marlena	②	S	S	S	S	S	T	S	S	S	S	Board
		Milton	②	T	T	T	T	T	T	T	T	T	T	Think Pair
		Mitch	⑥	S	S	S	S	S	T	S	S	T	T	Traditional
		Karrie	②	T	T	T	S	S	T	T	S	S	T	Lab
	?	Eric	①	S	S	S	S	S	S	S	S	S	S	Lab
Science	10/20	Taryn	①	S	S	S	S	S	S	S	S	S	S	Lab
		Mike	⑥	S	S	S	S	S	S	S	S	S	S	video Notes
		Hillary	①	T	T	T	T	T	T	T	S	S	S	Lab
		Grant	②	S	S	S	S	S	S	S	S	S	S	Lab
	?	Martin	①	T	T	T	S	S	S	S	S	S	S	Test review
Spanish	13/20	Lauren	①	T	T	S	T	T	T	T	T	T	T	resume
		Jenine	①	T	S	S	S	S	S	T	S	S	S	Essay
		Adriana	③	T	S	S	S	S	T	S	S	S	S	Stations
Physical Education		Matt K.	⑬	S	S	S	S	S	S	S	S	S	S	Matt Picts
		Dan	⑧	S	S	S	S	S	S	S	S	S	S	graphon
Honors		Geoff	①	T	T	T	T	T	T	T	T	T	S	Project
Arts		Dan	①	T	T	S	S	S	S	S	S	S	S	
290		Edreys	135	T	T	S	S	S	S	S	S	S	S	
		Joe	①23	S	S	S	S	T	S	S	S	S	S	
		Chris	234	T	S	S	T	S	S	T	S	S	S	Reflection

Overlooking the Needs of Some Students

Support all learners. It can be tempting to simply teach to the middle, but careful assessment will often reveal that although most students have met the learning targets, some fall far short and a few met them before or moments after the lesson began. A lesson designed to meet the needs only of most students, allows the "some" and the "few" to fall through the cracks. Successful differentiation is a tremendous challenge for teachers; however, careful planning prior to the lesson can help teachers identify places to provide additional scaffolds for some or fewer scaffolds for others so that by the time the lesson is delivered all students experience just right challenges. Chapter 6 covers differentiation comprehensively.

Avoiding Change

Cultivate a growth mindset. Learn from colleagues and commit to changing your practice. Teams that consistently and collaboratively implement high-quality lessons continually critique and improve what they've done before. With lesson planning, technology is your friend. Composing lessons digitally and saving them to a shared electronic space on which others can critique, add to, or revise a lesson for their own class streamlines and elevates this process. Teachers rarely have enough time to sit down together and finish planning. An electronic sharing system, and a commitment to continual improvements that address shifting standards, student needs, and other parameters (class size, classroom technology, staffing support, schedule changes), allow teachers to work smarter, not harder, to develop lessons that challenge, engage, and empower students.

Notes

1. The original documentary can be viewed on YouTube.

2. Our work with learning targets is founded on the assessment for learning practices of Rick Stiggins, Judith Arter, Jan Chappuis, and Steve Chappuis and the Assessment Training Institute.

3. Appendix B: The What, Why, and How of Protocols, outlines the important ingredients in any protocol and provides a recipe for introducing protocols to students.

4. The Biological Science Curriculum Study (BSCS), a team led by Principal Investigator Roger Bybee, developed the instructional model for constructivism, called the "Five Es." Other models have been adapted from this model, including the 6E and 7E models.

5. The Question Formulation Technique (adapted from the Right Question Institute: http://rightquestion.org/educators/resources/).

6. Stigler, J. W., & Hiebert, J. (1999). *The teaching gap: Best ideas from the world's teachers for improving education in the classroom.* New York, NY: Free Press.

Chapter 2

Laying the Foundation for Deeper Learning with Literacy

OVERVIEW

A Foundation for Deeper Learning

Literacy is the bedrock of learning. Strong literacy skills determine academic success and, often, success beyond school. When students can manipulate information and ideas both accurately and fluently, and when they read not only for knowledge, but also for joy and wonder, their capacity to learn and express themselves rests on a stable foundation unlikely to crumble even in a seismic educational or life event.

For many students, no matter their background or first language, learning to read complex text and write in academic formats can create new choices and pathways for the future. When a person can tease apart the vocabulary, esoteric references, and data of a scientific journal article, for example, she is better prepared to judge the validity of its content and to understand how it supports or fails to support her own choices as a citizen, patient, or policy leader. Furthermore, when a student seeks camaraderie, inspiration, or solace in poems or literature, she has a friend for life—and a doorway into the universal cultural expression of humankind: storytelling.

Nevertheless, enabling students to become confident speakers, readers, and writers in the language of professionals, scholars, wordsmiths, and the marketplace is a challenge for teachers everywhere. Teaching literacy raises enduring questions:

- How do we motivate "shallow" or nonreaders?

- How do we get students to read for detail rather than general ideas?

- How do we teach students to incorporate what they read into what they write?

- How do we fortify the reading students choose with texts that have a higher vocabulary "vitamin and mineral" count?

- How do we address the needs of readers and writers with a variety of interests, readiness, and styles?

And beyond the challenges of teaching literacy, the goal of deeper learning for all students is a next-level challenge for even the most seasoned of teachers. This demands that students know not just *what* they are reading or writing about, but also *why* they are reading and writing. Deeper instruction shows students that communication—reading, writing, and speaking—is a purposeful and powerful tool.

The examples and illustrations in this chapter show teachers in schools across the country at work making the bedrock of literacy through deeper instruction. These teachers provide students with both pick axe and shovel—the strategies to read and write precisely, with variety, and in volume. They also show that through studious apprenticeship, all teachers—not just English language arts (ELA) teachers—can learn to plan and teach lessons that invite and encourage students to become dexterous and determined wordsmiths. Braced with the skills to analyze difficult text, apply their understanding to new contexts, and effectively create their own texts, students have what they need to adapt to any challenge. They are resilient learners. They are innovative learners. They are fearless learners. And like deeper learners everywhere, they want to know more about the intricate connections between what's "out there" and the inner workings of their own experience.

Deeper instructional practices in literacy begin with purposeful lesson planning and curriculum choices that sift standards-based topics of study through relevant, compelling literature and informational text so that students are challenged with work that goes beyond standards. Leading with worthy texts, teachers help students connect what they're reading to real-world ideas and problems. They give students the tools to do the hard work of close reading and authentic, high-quality writing. They develop lessons that address ascending levels of Bloom's Taxonomy (see Figure 1.1) and boost students up the ladder of complexity into a difficult text. They model and critique real-world writing formats, while steering students toward audiences of informed and eager readers.

The deeper instructional practices in this chapter teach students that reading, writing, listening, and speaking are powerful levers. The point of literacy is communication—understanding and being understood—and it is the work of all teachers, not just ELA teachers. Every teacher has a role in helping students believe "What I know matters, and what I say—out loud and in writing—counts in the marketplace of ideas."

Why These Practices Matter

Because reading, writing, and speaking are the gateway to learning, instruction that challenges, engages, and empowers students to walk confidently into the arena of language matters from the earliest years right up through adulthood. Deeper instruction in literacy prepares students for college and beyond. This matters for a number of reasons.

The Right Kind of Challenge Builds Students' Literacy Muscles

As the foundation for deeper learning, literacy instruction that is appropriately challenging for students, and that is coherent and connected across multiple lessons and multiple disciplines, is especially critical. Teachers must take care to select complex and compelling texts that build students' reading muscles and academic vocabulary banks and help them see reading as a way to learn about the world. They must help students use evidence from their reading in their writing and see the value in writing for an authentic audience that wants to hear what they have to say. Moreover, to produce work of high quality, and to do so with integrity, students need to sort ideas that hold up to scrutiny from ones that don't. They need to engage in decision making and problem solving by comparing notes, questioning sources, and referring back to specific examples, facts, and research.

Deeper instructional practices in literacy entice students out of their comfort zone and into deeper levels of challenge, where grappling with words, texts, and ideas is worthy and exciting work. Helping students establish a growth mindset about these challenges will ensure that their literacy foundation is strong and sturdy and something they can keep building on throughout their lives.

Purposeful Reading, Writing, Thinking, and Speaking Fuels Engagement

Deeper literacy instruction cultivates the fruitful exchange of ideas in response to worthy questions raised in classes across the curriculum. Reading for and writing with evidence are essential ways to discover and articulate answers to questions. In conversation with each other and their teachers, students explore new perspectives, discuss fresh research, and develop a more nuanced understanding of a topic. Deeper learners understand how their reading, writing, and speaking in class connects to what they have learned before and to what they are learning across the curriculum. Further, worthy questions take students beyond the classroom, where they apply their literacy skills and understanding in real work for the benefit of their communities. For this reason, literacy feels purposeful and that purpose fuels engagement and quality work.

Deeper Literacy Instruction Empowers Students to Be Self-Directed Learners

Instructional strategies that boost all students into challenging texts that engage them in active, collaborative, and interesting ways of digging for meaning are not a quick fix. However, they are surely part of empowering students as learners, capable of defining their own destiny. For Edward Brown, a graduate of the Springfield Renaissance School, who went on to Brown University to study literary arts, the experience of dissecting literature paragraph by paragraph and of having his own arguments critiqued over and over again made it possible for him to "level up" to a great volume of reading in college.

"At college, I may have to read thirty or forty pages a night for a class, but I always know what I'm looking for in my reading. At Renaissance we read things that were just as hard, even though they weren't as long. We read the Constitution, the Declaration of Independence, *The Great Gatsby*, and a lot of informational articles. They were dense, and they gave me a grasp of how much harder it would be in college, but I also learned strategies for taking a text apart and analyzing it and understanding it." When Brown went to college, he says, he knew two things that assured him that he could meet the demands of Brown University. "I knew how to manage my time. And I knew how to pinpoint what I wasn't so good at and design a plan for improving on it. That's what I'm still doing here at Brown."

Challenging, engaging, and empowering students as readers, writers, speakers, and thinkers so that they carry their skills up to the next grade level or the next stage in life is the focus of this chapter. In the Getting Started section that follows, we see how two second-grade teachers deliver a rich and rigorous science unit that coherently connects reading, writing, speaking, and listening.

GETTING STARTED

Learning That Makes a Difference

At Centennial School for Expeditionary Learning in Denver, Colorado, the playground wood chips were recently replaced with a poured rubber surface. The new surface allows students in the school's multi-intensive severe needs program, including many who use wheelchairs, to join their friends from the regular education program at recess. Second-grade writers made that happen.

Inspired by their study of simple machines, the students put their learning into action. After reading about friction and wheels and experimenting with how wheels rolled on their existing playground surface, they discussed how unfair it seemed that none of the playground equipment was accessible to some of their friends who used wheelchairs. So they wrote and presented their opinions, loaded with evidence from their studies, to district officials. "Never in my thirty years of working in education have I seen students advocate for other students the way you have done today," John Liberatore, director of Denver Public Schools' Student Services Department, told the students.

Six months later, as the playground is getting an upgrade, second-grade teachers Ali Bernstein and Fran Taffer see how the experience of making a difference through writing changed their students. "Our students got an intrinsic desire to do fabulous work and push themselves further than they thought they could go because they discovered that school is a place where there is purpose. When we read and write, there should be a reason for it that leads to action. Students just got a $90,000 playground. That's powerful." Taffer's and Bernstein's commitment to deeper instruction invited students to apply their learning about persuasive writing to a real-world problem and a real audience. It was just the beginning. "Now we are wondering what these students will do next. They've got the writing bug now, and they are unstoppable!," says Taffer.

Using the Four Ts—Topic, Text, Target, Task—to Challenge, Engage, and Empower Students

Getting started with deeper literacy instruction begins as professional preparation—excavating the terrain of what students want and need to learn, driven by standards, curricular requirements, and student interests and abilities. In this chapter and elsewhere we propose that the Four Ts (see Figure 2.1)—topic, text, target, task—can help teachers craft learning experiences for students that are challenging, engaging, and empowering, no matter if they are creating curriculum from scratch or seeking merely to amend or enhance existing curriculum.

For example, in preparing the unit that would lead their second graders to write the persuasive letters that would get district leaders' attention, Bernstein and Taffer "crossed their 'Ts'" in the following way. They chose the **topic** of simple machines because it matched second graders' eagerness to get into the gears and

Figure 2.1 The Four Ts: Topic, Text, Target, Task

Topic: The topic "ties together" a unit of study.

The topic brings coherence to the unit of study. It is the "what" students are learning about, often connected to specific content knowledge. While students may be able to meet the standards without it, a compelling, relevant topic helps students to develop their skills more deeply as readers and writers. The best topics teach the standards through real world issues, original research, primary source documents, and the opportunity to engage with the community. They lend themselves to the creation of authentic tasks and products.

Text: The complex texts (books/articles) that students will read closely, and additional texts that ensure students experience a "volume of reading" at their independent reading level.

The text is the primary vehicle through which the topic is taught. Carefully selected texts at the text complexity band for a given grade level give students access to the topic and content targets through close and careful reading. Choose text judiciously to ensure it is "worthy" in terms of the knowledge it will help students build about the world and the opportunities it presents for students to master specific literacy standards.

Target: The learning targets derived from literacy and content standards.

The learning targets name what students need to know and be able to do. They are derived from the standards and informed by analysis of the assessment of the standard. Learning targets are contextualized to the topic, prepare students for and guide the task, and ensure proper, deep analysis of the text. Texts can be chosen for their ability to master particular standards/targets.

Task: The culminating assignment—a product or performance task.

The culminating task gives students the opportunity to read for and write with specific textual evidence and to meaningfully apply the standards (targets). This is different from just writing "about" what one has read. The best tasks give students the opportunity to address authentic need and an authentic audience related to the topic.

figure out how things work. This topic also addressed Colorado's standards for physical science, so they knew it would help them address the learning **targets** their students were expected to meet. Weaving the science content standards together with their literacy standards helped them determine the right **task** for their students. Writing persuasive letters in response to a real-world problem involving simple machines would give students an authentic purpose for reading for and writing with evidence. Therefore, the **texts** they would need would be ones that helped students solve that problem. In other words, they needed texts that would inspire and empower students to be informed readers and speakers in their own community. View the accompanying video to see how this same framework can be used to create curriculum.

Thinking intentionally through the lens of the Four Ts as part of the planning process helps teachers assess whether their instruction will be deep and effective for all learners. By asking "Is my topic relevant and compelling?" "Are my texts challenging and engaging?" "Do these targets unpack required standards?" "Are my tasks purposeful and complex?" teachers can identify the blind alleys and wild goose chases that often derail the best instructional intentions.

Bringing Text to Life through Compelling TOPICS

Every teacher has the student who protests as soon as the book is brought out, "Why do we have to read this? How will I ever use this in my life?" Whether working with second graders or high school students, we should be able to answer that question, not only by explaining how the skills of analyzing and arguing are the skill set of successful professionals and citizens, but also by connecting challenging, canonical, or esoteric texts to students' real lives. This means first of all taking our students seriously as people with interests, viewpoints, and a stake in their own communities. When teaching a literacy unit, it means asking the questions "What matters to my students? What texts will bring this topic to life for them and give them the opportunity to build their reading muscles?"

The Strategy Close Up that follows demonstrates the strategy of partnering fiction from another time and place with contemporary informational texts about a compelling topic. The literature introduces students to authors and themes that build their understanding of the genre and craft of fiction. The informational text enables them to apply the same themes—and vocabulary—to a broader context and to see relevance to their own lives. This strategy is especially useful when seeking opportunities to deepen instruction within an existing curriculum.

STRATEGY CLOSE UP: Connecting Classic Literature to Contemporary Issues

Valencia Clay, a middle school literacy teacher at Southwest Baltimore Charter School, regularly uses African American literary classics—the poetry of Langston Hughes, Lorraine Hansbury's *A Raisin in the Sun*, Ralph Ellison's *Invisible Man*—to capture the attention of her students, many of whom are African American. But in eighth grade, her standards dictate that her students study literature from the Holocaust. Her students are participating in book clubs on *The Diary of Anne Frank*, *The Book Thief*, and Elie Weisel's *Night*. To help students relate to issues that might seem like ancient history from another continent and culture, she partnered the literary reading with a nonfiction study of articles on police profiling of black men.

Students were soon immersed in discussions of how the Nazis used propaganda and policy to manipulate the perceptions of mainstream Germans and in a parallel discussion of media bias and stereotyping in the contemporary American context. Looking at these issues side by side gave students a better understanding of how stereotyping—anywhere, anytime—works to undercut an accurate and complex picture of a diverse society. Many of Clay's students have themselves been the victims of racial stereotyping, and this connection made reading and writing purposeful in her classroom. "Students began to ask deep questions about media bias and whether the media is fair," she says. "They wanted to know more about the points of view of everyone involved, including the police." Students read news accounts, tweets from the protest line, and photos that one student had brought back from Ferguson, Missouri.

Then, based on the multiple perspectives gained from their nonfiction and fiction reading, students wrote point-of-view stories of their own: from the perspective of the bullet that killed Michael Brown, the perspective of a police siren during a riot, and the perspectives of perpetrators, victims, resisters, and bystanders in response to racial conflict. Discussing and writing from multiple perspectives about current events helped students understand the complexity of relationships in Nazi Germany too, says Clay. And getting the perspective right mattered to them because it connected to their real lives.

Deepening Literacy Instruction in the Content Areas

Some of the most compelling topics for students are embedded in current scientific controversies and contemporary social issues. This means that content-area classes are a ripe opportunity for deeper literacy instruction. Indeed, because gaining knowledge, vocabulary, and critical reading strategies are interdependent, and because evidence from multiple studies (EL Education, Liben, & Liben, 2015) vigorously points out that deeper learning results from infusing literacy acquisition into knowledge building, content-area reading is often the best place to teach literacy. Yet teachers of social studies and science often feel it is not their job to teach literacy skills in their classes. They feel that this is not what they were hired or trained to do; they are *history teachers* or *chemistry teachers*, not *reading and writing teachers*. At the same time, when asked how satisfied they are with their students' ability to read and write about historical or scientific content, almost all are frustrated. This lack of content-specific literacy diminishes clarity and quality in almost all assignments but is rarely addressed proactively.

This is not just stubbornness on the part of content-area teachers. They are aware that the specific vocabulary and conventions of their fields are unlikely to be examined in English classes, and that students need help in this area. But they don't feel prepared to teach literacy, and they have so much content to cover that they can't imagine where they could find the time to do so.

The strategies and stories from content-area teachers who have overcome the same challenges in this chapter and Chapter 3: Creating Scientists and Historians, provide tools for science and history teachers to also become literacy teachers. We believe that when all teachers focus with their students on making sense of the texts they are reading and analyze what good writing looks like in their discipline, everyone wins. The students become more self-reliant and skilled, and the teachers are more gratified and successful.

Perhaps most important, the students become more capable and confident as young scientists and historians. Science teacher Peter Hill, getting ready to dive into reading a scientific article with his students, explains: "I was talking with a scientist and he said that 'My job is 10 percent experimenting, 40 percent writing, and 50 percent reading.' So I wanted my students to have a middle school experience of that in the classroom."

Specifically, new, more rigorous standards for literacy in the content areas and the demands of science and social science professions require that students not only read for literal understanding but also read for implications, biases, and context. In order to achieve deep understanding of disciplinary concepts, students need to act like historical or scientific detectives, examining and evaluating the evidence with accuracy and precision. Historians, for example, must be aware of changes in the meaning of vocabulary over time, and must read for how words are contextualized in the period or culture represented by a given text. Scientists read scientific diagrams, symbols, and data as closely as they do words, and at multiple levels of meaning. A chemist who has never actually seen a molecule nevertheless can visualize the three dimensional dynamics of one from its two dimensional representation on paper (Shanahan & Shanahan, 2008). The case study that follows, from a ninth-grade biology classroom, demonstrates the power of teaching students to read in the content areas.

CASE STUDY

Close Reading Scientific Journal Articles in Ninth-Grade Biology

The structure and function of DNA is a foundational concept in the discipline of biology, one many teachers replicate with a toothpick and marshmallows lab. Boston's Codman Academy biology teacher Jianan Shi wanted his students to understand the structure of DNA more deeply—by building the molecule guided only by the paradigm-shifting scientific journal article, "Molecular Structure of Nucleic Acids: A Structure for Deoxyribose Nucleic Acid," published by James Watson and Francis Crick in 1953 in the journal *Nature*. His students were mostly below grade level in reading, and the article was loaded with challenging vocabulary, so enabling students to do the reading, thinking, and learning required analyzing the article in pieces, and then reconstructing it—much as the original scientists did with DNA. See Figure 2.2 for an excerpt of this very challenging text.

"I framed it as a challenge and kept reiterating how much I believed in them," says Shi, emphasizing the importance of a growth mindset for building literacy skills. Students spent two weeks on ten paragraphs, close reading one paragraph each day, with a graphic organizer for each paragraph that guided them to identify, talk about, and write about new vocabulary, explain the process described by Watson and Crick, and build models of DNA. See the graphic organizer in Figure 2.3.

"Biology has so much vocabulary," says Shi. "It's a language unto itself and that can be a gatekeeper for many students." Shi used to assign textbook reading as homework, but for this complex text he realized "students needed the mental workout in the classroom. They needed my support and the support of talking to their peers in order to answer challenging text-dependent questions."

For further guidance on close reading primary sources, see Appendix C: Primary Source Close Reading Guide.

Providing Tools to Support Students

For some students—English language learners and students with individualized education programs (IEPs), primarily—Shi differentiated his instruction by providing them with a pre-annotated text, with the "gist" written in the margin or some words defined. This helped students who otherwise may have given up get a handle on a word or sentence that could turn the key to discovering the meaning of the whole paragraph.

For all students, Shi provided colored paper, markers, and K'NEX building blocks so that they could literally manipulate the ideas with their hands—building DNA as they read about it. Students really had to grapple with each word in the text and reproduce it through models one chunk at a time. "I kept telling them that engineers don't just follow their supervisor's directions. They have to read and figure out a working structure from mechanical manuals. They have to see the whole picture from its parts."

Figure 2.2 Excerpt of Watson and Crick Article

No. 4356 **April 25, 1953** NATURE 737

equipment, and to Dr. G. E. R. Deacon and the captain and officers of R.R.S. *Discovery II* for their part in making the observations.

[1] Young, F. B., Gerrard, H., and Jevons, W., *Phil. Mag.*, **40**, 149 (1920).
[2] Longuet-Higgins, M. S., *Mon. Not. Roy. Astro. Soc., Geophys. Supp.*, **5**, 285 (1949).
[3] Von Arx, W. S., Woods Hole Papers in Phys. Ocearog. Meteor., **11** (3) (1950).
[4] Ekman, V. W., *Arkiv. Mat. Astron. Fysik.* (Stockholm), **2** (11) (1905).

MOLECULAR STRUCTURE OF NUCLEIC ACIDS

A Structure for Deoxyribose Nucleic Acid

WE wish to suggest a structure for the salt of deoxyribose nucleic acid (D.N.A.). This structure has novel features which are of considerable biological interest.

A structure for nucleic acid has already been proposed by Pauling and Corey[1]. They kindly made their manuscript available to us in advance of publication. Their model consists of three intertwined chains, with the phosphates near the fibre axis, and the bases on the outside. In our opinion, this structure is unsatisfactory for two reasons : (1) We believe that the material which gives the X-ray diagrams is the salt, not the free acid. Without the acidic hydrogen atoms it is not clear what forces would hold the structure together, especially as the negatively charged phosphates near the axis will repel each other. (2) Some of the van der Waals distances appear to be too small.

Another three-chain structure has also been suggested by Fraser (in the press). In his model the phosphates are on the outside and the bases on the inside, linked together by hydrogen bonds. This structure as described is rather ill-defined, and for this reason we shall not comment on it.

We wish to put forward a radically different structure for the salt of deoxyribose nucleic acid. This structure has two helical chains each coiled round the same axis (see diagram). We have made the usual chemical assumptions, namely, that each chain consists of phosphate diester groups joining β-D-deoxyribofuranose residues with 3′,5′ linkages. The two chains (but not their bases) are related by a dyad perpendicular to the fibre axis. Both chains follow right-handed helices, but owing to the dyad the sequences of the atoms in the two chains run in opposite directions. Each chain loosely resembles Furberg's[2] model No. 1; that is, the bases are on the inside of the helix and the phosphates on the outside. The configuration of the sugar and the atoms near it is close to Furberg's 'standard configuration', the sugar being roughly perpendicular to the attached base. There

This figure is purely diagrammatic. The two ribbons symbolize the two phosphate—sugar chains, and the horizontal rods the pairs of bases holding the chains together. The vertical line marks the fibre axis

is a residue on each chain every 3·4 A. in the z-direction. We have assumed an angle of 36° between adjacent residues in the same chain, so that the structure repeats after 10 residues on each chain, that is, after 34 A. The distance of a phosphorus atom from the fibre axis is 10 A. As the phosphates are on the outside, cations have easy access to them.

The structure is an open one, and its water content is rather high. At lower water contents we would expect the bases to tilt so that the structure could become more compact.

The novel feature of the structure is the manner in which the two chains are held together by the purine and pyrimidine bases. The planes of the bases are perpendicular to the fibre axis. They are joined together in pairs, a single base from one chain being hydrogen-bonded to a single base from the other chain, so that the two lie side by side with identical z-co-ordinates. One of the pair must be a purine and the other a pyrimidine for bonding to occur. The hydrogen bonds are made as follows : purine position 1 to pyrimidine position 1 ; purine position 6 to pyrimidine position 6.

If it is assumed that the bases only occur in the structure in the most plausible tautomeric forms (that is, with the keto rather than the enol configurations) it is found that only specific pairs of bases can bond together. These pairs are : adenine (purine) with thymine (pyrimidine), and guanine (purine) with cytosine (pyrimidine).

In other words, if an adenine forms one member of a pair, on either chain, then on these assumptions the other member must be thymine ; similarly for guanine and cytosine. The sequence of bases on a single chain does not appear to be restricted in any way. However, if only specific pairs of bases can be formed, it follows that if the sequence of bases on one chain is given, then the sequence on the other chain is automatically determined.

It has been found experimentally[3,4] that the ratio of the amounts of adenine to thymine, and the ratio of guanine to cytosine, are always very close to unity for deoxyribose nucleic acid.

It is probably impossible to build this structure with a ribose sugar in place of the deoxyribose, as the extra oxygen atom would make too close a van der Waals contact.

The previously published X-ray data[5,6] on deoxyribose nucleic acid are insufficient for a rigorous test of our structure. So far as we can tell, it is roughly compatible with the experimental data, but it must be regarded as unproved until it has been checked against more exact results. Some of these are given in the following communications. We were not aware of the details of the results presented there when we devised our structure, which rests mainly though not entirely on published experimental data and stereochemical arguments.

It has not escaped our notice that the specific pairing we have postulated immediately suggests a possible copying mechanism for the genetic material.

Full details of the structure, including the conditions assumed in building it, together with a set of co-ordinates for the atoms, will be published elsewhere.

We are much indebted to Dr. Jerry Donohue for constant advice and criticism, especially on interatomic distances. We have also been stimulated by a knowledge of the general nature of the unpublished experimental results and ideas of Dr. M. H. F. Wilkins, Dr. R. E. Franklin and their co-workers at

Source: Watson, J. D., & Crick, F.H.C. (1953). Molecular Structure of Nucleic Acids: A Structure for Deoxyribose Nucleic Acid. *Nature, 171 ,* 737–738.

Figure 2.3 Graphic Organizer: Paragraph 3 and 4 Recording Form

Do Now (Questions 1–3): Use the reading and diagram to answer the following questions:

A nitrogenous base is a nitrogen-containing molecule. They are particularly important since they make up the building blocks of DNA and RNA.

1) **What is a nitrogenous base?**

2) **What are the five different nitrogenous bases?**

3) **What are two main types of nitrogenous bases?**

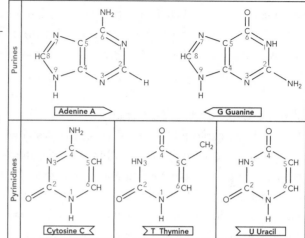

Types of nitrogen bases

At the end of the DNA reading unit, Shi's students were tired but proud. "I realized," said Shi, "that just covering my standards is an excuse not to teach things well. My students can break down any text using this method and get a lot more out of it because they did the thinking themselves. They mastered it, and then we celebrated big time."

To see a similar lesson sequence involving close reading in a middle school science classroom, view the accompanying two-part video.

WATCH
Video 7: Reading and Thinking Like Scientists—Day 1: Strategies for Making Meaning from Complex Scientific Text
Video 8: Reading and Thinking Like Scientists—Day 2: Deepening Conceptual Understanding through Text-Based Tasks

Choosing Engaging TEXTS

Texts that lead students to deeper learning serve as a second teacher in the literacy classroom. They are not just any texts. They are ones that push students to understand more and differently than the teacher's voice alone can do. Indeed, the 2006 ACT report "Reading between the Lines" showed that students who succeed in college must do more than be able to apply reading strategies like inferring and questioning. They must be able to apply those strategies to dig meaning out of *complex* text. "What students could read, in terms of its complexity, was at least as important as what they could do with what they read" (National Governors Association Center for Best Practices, Council of Chief State School Officers, Appendix A, 2010, p. 2).

Choose Outside-the-Box Texts

Previously we explored how English teacher Valencia Clay paired literature with informational text about a compelling topic. Content-area teachers, similarly, can make reading more compelling and challenging for students by supplementing or replacing textbooks with trade books and primary sources. Letters, historical photographs, documents, data sets, and artifacts are compelling and often challenging reads for students. Primary sources push students to inquire about the context of language: who's speaking, when, and for what purpose—that mediates the meaning of any text. As such, primary sources demand that students shift from a shallow regurgitation of textbook facts and platitudes, to a deep investigation of the vocabulary, structure, and style of a text written by and for someone engaged in an original transaction of meaning. See Table 2.1 for a variety of types of informational texts that can be used in the classroom. Also see the accompanying video of tenth-grade humanities students in New York City evaluating and curating sets of primary source documents to best tell the story of the holocaust.

 WATCH Video 9: Prioritizing Evidence to Address a Document-Based Question

Balance Rigor and Relevance

What if you have a compelling topic, but no textbook? A quick Google search may yield a long list of Web pages, but no clue about the rigor, relevance, or appropriateness for your students. Furthermore, if the text is not compelling for you as a teacher and adult reader—if it is not fascinating in content and ideas or beautiful or intriguing in structure and style—students will likely not find it compelling either. Whatever the content match and complexity level of the text, if it is not a

Table 2.1 Types of Informational Text

Expository	Argumentative	Instructional	Literary Nonfiction
Text books	Opinion/Editorial pieces	Training manuals	(Auto)Biographies
Reports	Speeches	Contracts	Histories
Tourism guides	Advertisement	User guides/manuals	Correspondence
Product specifications	Political propaganda	Legal documents	Curriculum vitae
Product/Service descriptions	Journal articles	Recipes	Memoirs
Magazine articles	Government documents	Product/Service descriptions	News articles
Company profiles	Legal documents		Essays
Legal documents	Tourism guides		Interviews
Agendas	Correspondence		
Correspondence	Essays		
Essays	Reviews		
Interviews	Memoirs		
Government documents			
News articles			

Source: New York State Education Department (EngageNY) (n.d.). Passage selection guidelines for assessing CCSS ELA. Retrieved from https://www.engageny.org/resource/new-york-state-passage-selection-resources-for-grade-3-8-assessments

worthy text—one that is provocative to read once and rewarding to read again—it will not motivate students to read.

So what are the factors to consider in the search to find a worthy text that is compelling, complex, and relevant to students?

Analyze complexity

A text that will give students a leg up the ladder of complexity is both rigorous and engaging for students. It is a text that enables students to discover both new information and needed information. And it is a text that engages students in thinking deeply about text structure, vocabulary, and style. In short, it is a text that is meaty enough for students to come back to multiple times and to leave each reading feeling full and satisfied. Analyze possible text candidates for quantitative complexity, qualitative complexity, and for a match with the needs of individual readers and tasks.

Quantitative complexity, based on word and sentence length, as well as syntax, is easily determined by computers that yield Lexile text measures or Flesch-Kincaid grade levels. Consider whether the complexity of the text based on these measures matches readers' ability to comprehend complex words and sentences.

Qualitative complexity is best measured by teachers employing their professional judgment, experience, and knowledge of their students and subject. It refers to more subjective criteria, including:

- *Background knowledge.* The experience that readers must bring to the text helps them understand its content and language. Sometimes, teachers can provide this background knowledge through initial lessons prior to introducing the text.
- *Language.* Is the vocabulary academic or discipline specific? Does the text rely extensively on figurative language or unconventional syntax? Shakespearean plays, poetry, and scientific journals are good examples of text with language complexity.
- *Meaning.* Are there multiple levels of meaning or purpose in the text? Ironic or satirical literature and children's books with multiple allusions that only adults will "get" (the Pixar film *Shrek* is a great example) are texts with multiple levels of meaning.
- *Structure.* Are the organization, genre, and text features conventional, compelling, or innovative? Scientific diagrams, creative nonfiction, and magical realism are just a few examples of texts with complex structures.

The needs and motivations of readers may dictate that teachers begin with a less complex text that meets students where they are, and then build on that success with something more complex. It is critical that teachers identify sections of the text that students can access independently by "having a go" on their own and sections of the text that, if not understood, will steer students in the wrong direction. These excerpts will guide lesson scaffolding, from lessons that invite students to grapple on their own to lessons that are launched with a teacher directed mini-lesson.

For further guidance on factors to consider when selecting text, see Appendix D.

Engage with relevance

A worthy text must be one that students have a purpose for reading. They want to read it because it answers questions they have. They want to read it because it is visually exciting or written in words and phrases that humor or inspire them. Or, they want to read it because it helps them understand how to write in the genre or format of an upcoming assignment. Choosing text that not only informs or engages students about a topic but also models for them how to structure their own writing is generally a wise choice. In the accompanying video see how a teacher's wise choice of a timely and highly relevant text—the Investigation of the Ferguson Police Department by the Department of Justice—deepens her students' understanding of the successes, challenges, and possibilities of policing in America.

 WATCH Video 10: Policing in America: Using Powerful Topics and Texts to Challenge, Engage, and Empower Students

If you can't find the right text, consider writing it yourself

In developing their simple machines unit for second graders, Bernstein and Taffer considered their young readers and their diverse interests and readiness. They knew they had some nonreaders and also that students could get a great deal of information from examining pictures. They decided to kick off their learning expedition by inviting students to view and ask questions about *pictures* of machines. They also read aloud an informational science book for emerging readers. This shallow dive into the topic, with visuals and teachers' voices doing most of the work of creating meaning, gave students a chance to get excited about the topic and begin to grapple with the guiding questions of the entire unit: "How do simple machines make our lives less work?" "How can I use my knowledge of simple machines to serve my community?"

Then, once students were hooked on the topic, Taffer and Bernstein asked students to use their reading muscles to dig deeper into text with no pictures. In order to balance rigor and relevance in text that would stretch students and also engage them, Taffer and Bernstein took a novel approach: they wrote their own texts (see Exhibit 2.1). The series of short passages they used for close reading lessons were crafted to include key vocabulary words and to model the writing strategies—introducing a topic with a question, supporting a statement with details—they wanted students to eventually use in their own writing.

Exhibit 2.1 What Is Work?

As second graders you work all the time! At school and at home you have work to do. But when scientists use the word *work* they don't mean the opposite of play. For scientists, work means moving something. Anytime you push or pull something to move it you have done work. You can move something a few inches like a pencil on your desk or you move something many miles if you take it with you on a long walk. Pushing a friend on the swing is work. But pushing against the wall of our classroom is not work because no matter how hard you push you can't move it. If I ask you to put your chair on your desk is it work? What about if I ask you to stand still and hold heavy books? Since simple machines make work easier, we know that simple machines make it easier for us to move things.

Crafting Challenging Learning Targets

In addition to choosing worthy texts, an important first step toward deeper literacy instruction is crafting learning targets that ask students to grapple with the complexity and nuances of text. Deeper learning requires that students do more than simply decode and restate what a text says. They must also describe what a text does (its purpose and how it achieves its purpose) and what a text means (to its particular audience). They must use the strategies of inference and questioning to ask why an author has chosen a particular diction and structure. They must infer bias, tone, and perspective, and analyze how the language and organization of a text impacts an audience. They must consider the implications and context of the information or argument. In short, they must read, think, talk, and write critically. Crafting learning targets for individual reading and writing lessons begins by teasing apart the discreet skills and concepts that critical readers employ.

Identify What You Want Students to Learn

Learning targets that highlight enduring and transferable literacy and cognitive skills empower students to be successful self-directed learners across contexts. Four developmentally appropriate learning targets from the simple machines literacy unit illustrate this precept.

1. *I can use my whole body to show a speaker I am listening to them.* This target addresses the Common Core Speaking and Listening Standard SL.2.1: "Participate in collaborative conversations with diverse partners about grade 2 topics and texts." The language of the target is student friendly, but it also articulates

that using your whole body—making eye contact, sitting knee to knee, holding your hands quiet and still—is how one listens deeply.

2. *I can learn new facts about simple machines by listening and asking questions.* This target addresses Common Core Speaking and Listening standard SL.2.3: "Ask and answer questions about what a speaker says in order to clarify comprehension, gather additional information, or deepen understanding of a topic or issue." It connects learning new facts with the habit of asking questions, which underscores why students should engage in discussion and also how one learns about any topic.

3. *I can find important vocabulary in a text.* This target addresses Common Core Reading Standard RI.2.4: "Determine the meaning of words and phrases in a text." It invites students to identify words that are important because they illuminate the meaning of the text. These are words experienced readers hang onto and return to—the domain-specific and academic vocabulary that bolster reading for a lifetime.

4. *I can find the most important facts in a text.* This target addresses Common Core Reading Standard RI.2.6: "Identify the main purpose of a text, including what the author wants to answer, explain, or describe." Implicitly this target asks students to use evidence in the text, synthesize, compare, and select facts from the text to justify how some support the main idea better than others.

Develop Text-Dependent Questions in Advance

Text-dependent questions—questions that require students to read for evidence and use the facts, quotes, and graphic information in a text to support their answers—require that students wrestle with the words on the page in order to determine the meaning of a text. Text-dependent questions serve as a scaffold to understanding—when developed thoughtfully, with learning targets in mind, they can enhance comprehension, not just assess it. The questions "can literally lift students up to challenging text, enabling them to understand more about a text than if they are left on their own" (Dobbertin, 2013, p. 55).

Planning these questions in advance, so that they strategically engage, stretch, and build students' reading muscles, is a critical component of deeper instruction in literacy. Without preplanning, it is easy to fall back on low-level questions—used to highlight or remind students of facts from the text, rather than crystallize or push conceptual understanding.

Every time we ask students, "What was the name of the town in which the characters in this story lived?" we leave less time for questions like "Why do you think the characters never left home?

—*Alfie Kohn, "Who's Asking?"*
Educational Leadership September 2015

Developing an overarching "focus question" that reflects students' purpose for reading creates an umbrella for the series of text-dependent questions that will guide students through a text (see Exhibit 2.2). Beneath this umbrella, one effective way to generate text-dependent questions is by addressing all four quadrants of qualitative complexity: background knowledge, language, meaning, and structure. Questions that help students understand these four layers of a text will lead students to the big ideas of the text.

Exhibit 2.2: Text-Dependent Questions Related to Simple Machines

Focus Question: How do simple machines make our lives less work?

Background knowledge
Why is the scientific definition of "work" different from our everyday definition?

Language
What is the scientific definition of work?

Meaning
Why is holding heavy books not "work?"

Structure
Why does the author ask the reader so many questions in this writing?

Beneath the umbrella of the focus question, organize text-dependent questions to build students' confidence and capacity as readers. Start with small "right there" questions, ones that students can find answers to directly in the text. Build up to questions that require students to infer from text clues, synthesize supporting details, or evaluate quotes or logic. Create a logical sequence of questions so that the answers to early questions accumulate evidence needed to answer later questions. Another way to make questions deeper and more complex is to start with small bites of text—words and sentences—and move to larger chunks of text or to multiple texts that students must consider as a pair or set.

Gwyneth Hagan, lead curriculum writer for EL Education's Grades 3–8 ELA Curriculum, advises teachers who are designing their own literacy-rich units to

> "write a ton of text-dependent questions that scaffold from concrete to abstract. Begin with questions that get at the gist of the reading. Then ask yourself what will make this text hard for readers—vocabulary or structure or theme? Winnow your pool down to the questions with the highest leverage points for serving your purpose in reading this text. Then keep the others in your back pocket—for when you need to slow things down or support students who feel challenged by the text."

Sequence Lessons So That Students Need to Know What's in the Text

In addition to creating questions that require students to reference evidence from the text, deeper instruction invites active participation. The interplay between kinesthetic, visual, and verbal activities increases engagement and reawakens students' enthusiasm for reading. Sketching, acting out, sorting, debating, and doing experiments are all ways of not only *applying* what's learned from text, but also *deepening* learning from the text.

Hands-on learning experiences deepened the learning for Bernstein's and Taffer's students

While planning their simple machines unit, Bernstein and Taffer intentionally linked lessons that had students mostly reading, to lessons that had students mostly doing—applying what they had read to real-world contexts. According to Taffer, "Doing hands-on experiments filled out students' background knowledge, because they saw firsthand what they had read about in the texts. Toy cars roll smoothly down an inclined plane, but not so much over wood chips on the playground." Running the experiments gave students a reason to use the vocabulary and concepts they had read about. It also drove them back to the text to find out more information that would help them explain the results of their experiments. Like students working a jigsaw puzzle, the more they learned about their topic, the more "pieces" they could fit into the puzzle, and the more they used the knowledge they gained.

Doing Worthy Work: The Task

Just as Bernstein and Taffer gave students many opportunities to *read to understand*, they also gave students regular opportunities to apply their learning through tasks that showed their understanding. For example, students wrote using the evidence from both their reading and their experiments. After close reading a text called "How Wheels Were Invented," students tried to solve the problem laid out in the text with their own inclined planes and wheels. By infusing and sequencing their lessons to address all of the literacy skills—reading, thinking, talking, and writing—and adding *doing*, Bernstein and Taffer actively engaged their second-graders. They gave students with varied processing styles equal access and motivation to read challenging text.

Bernstein's and Taffer's tasks were carefully planned and scaffolded to support the execution of high-quality work. They included short tasks, like writing thank-you letters to guest speakers that give students a chance to practice discreet writing skills. They sequenced lessons in writing topic sentences, using evidence, writing introductions and conclusions, incorporating questions into their paragraphs, the difference between revision and editing, and oral presentation. These lessons, which took place over many weeks, allowed students time to learn and focus on new skills. Each lesson directed students back to the text or to their own science experiments to grapple with evidence to support their talking and writing. Consequently, students learned to value evidence as the litmus test for any claim. They also learned implicitly that reading and writing (the text and the task) are intricately connected and that more and better evidence will make a more convincing argument—one that can move important people to action. See Appendix E: From Assignment to Assessment, for a process to support high-quality work.

Use Models to Understand the Criteria for Excellence

For both teachers and students, the learning experiences in these lessons were guided by a vision of effective persuasive letters. Taffer and Bernstein employed a high-leverage move for motivating students to create quality work: a critique lesson. In a critique lesson, students and teachers together examine high-quality (and sometimes anonymous low-quality) samples of the kind of writing students will be doing in order to collaboratively generate a list of the criteria that define high-quality writing in the genre that students are expected to produce. Such a lesson is designed to support the learning of all students, not primarily to improve the work of one. (Ideally the models a teacher uses are of student writing, but they could also be professional or teacher-created writing that exemplifies specific criteria students can describe in their own words.[1])

To launch their simple machines unit, Bernstein and Taffer each completed the assignment they would soon give their students and then analyzed their model letters with students. In Bernstein's model (see Exhibit 2.3), she has identified the elements of a good persuasive letter that she wants students to include in their own letters.

These elements (i.e., criteria for success) were helpful to students as they began planning and writing their own letters. This process also helped the teachers better anticipate the challenges students would encounter when they began writing, which helped them craft the lessons they taught to scaffold student success.

Exhibit 2.3: Model Letter Used for Analysis

February 9, 2014
Dear Board of Education:

I am a second-grade student at Centennial, a School for Expeditionary Learning. There are many students at our school who use wheelchairs. Yet, our playground is not wheelchair accessible. [*problem*] We need your help to make our playground an inclusive place where all students can play. [*something I want my reader to do*]

Play is a right that all children should have! [*exclamation*] Play helps children stay healthy. Children need to race, yell, roll, hide, and make big messes. When children play

(continued)

together, they learn to work together. Unfortunately, my friends who use a wheelchair don't get to play because our playground's surface is covered in wood chips. [*strong fact*]

If we change our playground surface to poured rubber, everyone would be able to play together. We have been studying simple machines. We found out that wheels need a low friction surface to roll well. Many people are realizing that wood chips are not accessible for wheelchairs. One judge even ruled that a school district in California had to change their playgrounds' surfaces. By just changing our playground surface, we could make our playground accessible to all children. [*restate main idea*]

I am truly sad about the fact that in 2014 children with disabilities are still excluded from the playgrounds in Denver Public Schools. [*big feeling*] Being excluded feels awful. My friends in wheelchairs are just like me. They want to play too. I want to make sure that playgrounds are a place where all children feel included. [*what I want*]

I would love to find a time to meet and discuss these important changes that we need to make. [*something I want my reader to do*] Don't you think it's time to make sure that all students have the right to play? [*question*]

Sincerely, Alison Bernstein

Motivate Students with an Authentic Audience

After analyzing models, engaging in specific writing craft lessons, practicing, and receiving feedback from both peers and teachers, students completed their letters and sent them to district officials. Students also presented excerpts from the letters out loud in the form of an informational and persuasive simple machines readers' theater. The performance blended sentences from the letters with voices that included the students with special needs who sparked the motivation for this project, many of whom were nonreaders and nonwriters. For one student with a serious behavior challenge, says Taffer, "This was a defining moment where he found his voice. Now he has become a helper in the special needs classroom and has earned the reward of assisting those students at a Special Olympics event. The presentation allowed him to find empathy and learn how to use his voice to make a difference." See Exhibit 2.4 for this student's letter.

Exhibit 2.4: Sample Student Letter

March 7, 2014

Dear Ms. Laura, Ms. Brinkman, and Mr. Liberatore,

Kids in wheelchairs can't play on the playground. We don't have enough ramps. Kids in wheelchairs can't go through the wood chips. Kids in wheelchairs can't get to the swings. I feel disappointed and depressed because kids in wheelchairs can't access our playground.

Just with a few changes to the Centennial playground, kids in wheelchairs can play so it is fair to them. We can add some more ramps to the Centennial playground. Instead of the wood chips we can have turf or poured rubber. I would feel happy and excited if we did these things to our playground so kids in wheelchairs may access our playground.

We need your help with the Centennial playground! Can the school district help us pay for this? Whose permission should we need to make this happen? Can you help us do this to our playground? This is a good idea for the Centennial playground.

Sincerely, Derek

Writing for an audience inspires, motivates, and empowers students to do their best work. Knowing that they would be presenting their persuasive letters to people with the authority to upgrade their playground motivated Taffer's and Bernstein's second-grade students to write expert paragraphs and to revise them with care. "Students came up with powerful sentences like, 'Woodchips may be my friends, but they're wheelchairs' enemies,' because it really mattered to them to have an impact on the readers. They also stayed engaged through the revision process when older students helped them peer edit. They were motivated to get the words and punctuation right."

Empower Students to Reflect on Transferable Skills

As we saw in Chapter 1, debriefing "how we learned" as well as "what we learned" enables students to name the new skills they have gained in a lesson or unit that will be helpful to them again in the future. Ali Bernstein looped with the second graders featured here into a third-grade classroom. Working with the same students who did the simple machines unit, she testifies to how the lessons they learned the previous year about a different skill—reading for and writing with evidence—transferred to their approach to reading this year. "Last year," she says, "we used T-charts to record our main ideas and evidence as we read. We had to model that over and over and it was hard for students. This year, right away a student suggested that strategy when we started reading a difficult text. This has allowed me to increase the rigor for everyone, and has been especially helpful for students who struggle. They know that if they persevere, partner up with a stronger reader, and use this tool, they will be able to get through it and understand the text. Our work has lifted everyone up. There is no opt out. We can all reach the target and we know what that looks like."

As this simple machines unit shows, determining a powerful lesson sequence and using the Four Ts to get the most out of any curriculum lays a solid foundation for deeper instruction. In the In Practice section that follows we build on that foundation to unpack specific instructional strategies, including the teaching of writing, that strengthen students' literacy skills.

IN PRACTICE

For the Love of Literacy

Ironically, because reading and writing are the daily bread of every grade level and every subject area, both teachers and students can take their value for granted. For students to appreciate how literacy sustains lifelong learning, they need to see reading, writing, speaking, and listening as powerful tools for improving their own lives. In this section, we focus on 12th-grade ELA and history classrooms at Capital City Public Charter School in Washington, D.C, where students who could be the most indifferent to reading in school are getting energized by one last booster shot of deeper literacy instruction before they graduate.

Launching the Text with Wonder

Capital City history teacher Kavitha Kasargod begins a yearlong progression of strengthening students' capacity for argument—a skill colleges frequently flag as weak—with a complex text about writing proficiency in urban high schools. In the same spirit of wonder with which the Centennial second graders began their learning about friction, Kasargod introduces Peg Tyre's groundbreaking article, "The Writing Revolution," first published in the *Atlantic* (2012) to her students. The content of Tyre's article is packed with data on what typical high school students *can't* do as writers. Provocative articles like Tyre's can be great hooks.

The article invokes students' wonder because they relate to the story of other students for whom writing an essay initially seems like an impossible task. The students in the article, who never learned the strategic calculus of stringing sentences together, learn to convey their ideas and prepare for college through persistence and incremental practice. But the article provides more than an access point for these high school readers. The structure and language of Tyre's article also provides a strong professional model of how a writer builds an argument, like a careful stonemason, by layering, fitting, and joining pieces of evidence together in defense of a claim. "I am not preparing you to leave here in June," Kasargod tells her students after they've discussed the Tyre article, "I'm preparing you to be ready for your first day of college. A big part of that is being able to independently think and access resources. We live in a world where you can Google anything. But you also need to know how to read—really read—and respond to what's on your screen." The logic of this revolution is evident to students. They know from this first lesson that they are going to have to step up and work in order to succeed.

Grappling with Meaning

Deeper instruction that challenges students provides them with enough background knowledge to feel anchored, enough scaffolding to feel supported, and enough time and intellectual freedom to wrestle with complex ideas and problems that stimulate their thinking. *Grappling* with ideas means that students are putting the building blocks together themselves. As the author of *The Having of Wonderful Ideas*, Eleanor Duckworth, has said, "You have to put them [students] in a situation where they develop that understanding—it's not going to happen from your telling them. . . . They have to put the idea together themselves, or they don't have it at all. Otherwise, it's just words" (1991, p. 30). But what does that "putting together" actually look like?

Insist That Students Do the Thinking

Kasargod begins a close reading of the Peg Tyre article by asking students first to discuss the "gist" of the opening paragraph. She points out to students that real-world reporting and scholarship, the kind they will read frequently in college and even in serious mainstream newspapers and journals from the *New York Times* to *Rolling Stone*, often don't have an obvious topic sentence or explicit thesis statement. Students' next challenge is to identify main ideas and supporting details, codifying these in a graphic organizer. Although students have read and annotated arguments in English class, transferring this skill to an authentic text in history class raises the real possibility that students won't be able to make sense of it, that in their first attempt they will "fail" as readers. Work worth doing, work that grows our stamina, our perseverance, and our understanding always contains this possibility.

In order for students to practice making meaning on their own, they need many opportunities to grapple with complex ideas—before, during, and after reading.

In a reading lesson that uses the Workshop 2.0 lesson structure (see Chapter 1 for more on Workshop 2.0), the first opportunity occurs five minutes into the lesson, when students read their first chunk of text independently, often with a broad question to guide their thinking. It's important that this does not happen *after* the teacher has read part of the text while "thinking aloud" or taught specific and explicit reading strategies that can be used to pry open the text. Instead, the teacher simply provides a short section of text for students to grapple with on their own, to see how they can make sense of it first without assistance.

The possibility of failure often scares teachers, who, understandably, want their students to succeed. We know from the literature on academic mindsets, however, that failure is in fact a prerequisite of success; we learn much more from failure than we do from easy wins. We stated the following in Chapter 1, but it's worth repeating here:

> "A well-designed opportunity for students to grapple with problems, texts, ideas, or concepts is where the rich brew of deeper instruction is most powerful. This is where asking the right questions, as opposed to giving the right answers, can give students a challenge that they can sink their teeth into. Allowing them to grapple with that question collaboratively engages them in co-constructing knowledge and empowers them as they learn that they can discover the "answers" with their own ingenuity."

Table 2.2 contains a few strategies to enable those students who refuse to try or give up easily to accept the risk of failure.

Table 2.2   Encouraging Students to Grapple with Challenges

If you're concerned that . . .	Try this . . .
Students will give up when the text feels too hard	Encourage students to re-read. Give them more time than a single read requires.
Students give up when they encounter hard or unfamiliar vocabulary	Pre-teach select vocabulary words and demonstrate strategies for determining meanings in context.
Students don't know enough about the topic to care about reading the text	Introduce the topic with photographs, a read- aloud, or artifacts that spark students' curiosity.
Students will give up because the text is long or overly dense	Break the text up into smaller chunks. Build students' reading muscles by praising effort rather than achievement.

Constructing Understanding

Once students are engaged in a challenging text, reading it again and talking and writing about it with peers allows them to take "core samples" of meaning from different layers of the text and to sift these understandings through conversation with other readers.

Give Students Ownership through Annotation

One important way that readers take ownership of a text is by literally writing all over it—annotating it with comments, questions, highlights, and other annotations. Students at Capital City get so much practice annotating text, says English teacher Justin Sybenga, that several have returned from college to show him how they've annotated college reading assignments. These students have remarked that many of their peers struggle with college reading precisely because they aren't in the habit of annotating what they read.

Kasargod requires her students to come to a discussion with their text annotated with a surprise, a connection, a comment, and a question. For students who are anxious about participating, the minimal writing they do before the discussion gives them something to say and allows them to choose their moment for chiming in. In other words, annotation becomes a vehicle for rich discussion and argument.

Kasargod's students annotated the Peg Tyre article by underlining main ideas and numbering pieces of evidence that support those ideas. Then, over multiple lessons, they teased apart the paragraphs to identify and discuss Tyre's strategic and sophisticated use of quotations from her interviews, how she explains data from scientific research, how she creates setting and plot for this real-life story with lively description, and how she attributes subclaims to experts in order to establish credibility for her argument. As the semester proceeds, students transfer those skills to primary sources they are reading about the formation of government—including the Constitution. "We close read the search and seizure amendment and break it down. We make a word wall of difficult vocabulary words. We paraphrase it side-by-side with the text. Then, we unpack its meaning in the context of what happens in students' own lives today," says Kasargod. This time-consuming but productive peeling-of-the-onion approach to text enables students to analyze at a deep level. It is also how they master academic vocabulary that unlocks the door to the next complex text. Figure 2.4 describes how teachers can augment a Workshop 2.0 lesson for the close reading of complex text.

Figure 2.4 Augmenting Readers' Workshop 2.0 for Close Reading of Complex Text

Workshop 2.0	Close Reading of Complex Text
ENGAGE Students engage with a question, quote, object, or activity that spurs thinking and engages them in the lesson's purpose/topic.	When students are closely reading a complex text, the workshop is more teacher directed because the text is harder for students to read independently. Teachers' preplanning is essential so that they can act as guides for students as they make meaning of complex texts. Very specific enhancements to a readers' workshop (see following) will help students access complex texts in order to build their knowledge about the world and their literacy skills.
GRAPPLE Students grapple independently with a text (this may mean reading silently in their heads while the teacher reads aloud).	
DISCUSS Students follow a structured protocol to discuss the reading with a peer or group, re-reading and referring to the text to support their comments.	During the FOCUS section of a workshop: • Ask strategic text-dependent questions that bring students back to particular words, sentences, or paragraphs in the text. These are not generic questions, but rather questions about this specific text (e.g., "In paragraph one, what do the authors mean by 'genetic specificity'?").
FOCUS Provide explicit instruction to "mop up" whatever students don't figure out on their own. Gradually release responsibility, enabling students to practice the task with support.	• Model only as needed to clear up misconceptions. (*Note*: It will be difficult to mop up misconceptions without asking text–dependent questions.)
APPLY Allow time for students to practice the skill or concept, providing intentional differentiation.	During the APPLY section of a workshop: • Students reread to answer strategic text–dependent questions or to complete a specific task (e.g., determining main idea and finding key details). • Students may need to reread multiple times.
SYNTHESIZE Assess progress toward learning targets, address misconceptions, generalize conceptual understandings.	• Students apply their learning, writing in response to a prompt and sharing orally.

Ask Questions Worthy of Discussion and Written Response

Launching a text with "What do you wonder?" invites students to be curious. Asking students "How do you know?" or "Why does the author think that?" brings rigor to students' process of exploring their curiosities. Text-dependent *how* and *why* questions redirect students' attention to the text itself, to the facts, quotes, argument, and explanation offered there. It pushes them to support and justify an answer to their initial question. It may also help them understand that the best questions have multiple answers. The evidence one student lifts up may be different from the evidence another student brings forward from the same text. When students talk with each other about the discrepancy, collaboratively constructing a mutual understanding, their job is to determine which evidence is most important or how the evidence works together to support a bigger concept.

Socratic Seminars allow students to lead their own learning as they engage deeply with texts and each other

Kasargod develops these analytical skills by intentionally asking strategic text-dependent questions. In one example, she has students read an essay on native communities in Chesapeake Bay, and then she leads a Socratic Seminar with a series of questions that stair-step up Bloom's Taxonomy. Her questions include the following:

- *Remember.* Who were the Native Americans in the Chesapeake region prior to European arrival?

- *Understand.* Describe the structure of the communities in which they lived? How did Native Americans assimilate into European life?

- *Apply.* The text says, "Many of the difficulties experienced by the Chesapeake Natives were mirrored over the centuries by other Native Americans as settlers moved across the continent." What does this mean? Provide examples from other time periods.

- *Analyze.* The text states, "Oral tradition was critical for preserving cultural knowledge; when elders died, it was like having entire libraries burn down." What does this mean and are there contemporary examples of this?

- *Evaluate.* Did the signing of treaties between Native Americans and the English colonists lead to a positive or negative outcome? Explain in your own words.

In the Strategy Close Up that follows we see the value of another tool—technology—for supporting students to have engaging and purposeful conversations about texts or other academic subjects.

STRATEGY CLOSE UP: Digital Discussion Motivates Students to Think and Write

In schools with reliable and accessible Internet technology, interactive discussion tools like blogs, threaded discussions, and synchronous chat applications provide a compelling way for students to talk productively to each other on the digital page. According to Marielle Palombo, an education consultant who specializes in using Web 2.0 media and other technologies to support learning, thanks to texting, many students are already experts in interacting through writing. "Students often recognize right away that online exchanges allow everyone to speak and be heard at the same time, which differs from face-to-face discussions. They appreciate the opportunity to argue in writing about ideas with real people—their peers—rather than just complying with the demand to show what they know to the teacher, which is frequently the form that traditional classroom writing exercises take." Palombo explains that these tools can meet both students' need to be social and teachers' need to get students discussing substantive ideas in accountable ways, using academic rhetoric.

> "Written conversations online are qualitatively different from classroom talk because you have time to compose your own thoughts and process other peoples' thoughts, and because multiple people can be communicating at the same time, and especially because the conversation is captured for students and teachers to revisit. With appropriate norms and discussion protocols established, the platform can encourage a diversity of responses, inclusive participation, and a safe space for intellectual interchange. Being heard in this way makes a differ-

ence for students and can increase their investment in communicating clearly and effectively."

Palombo recommends that teachers identify the specific purposes they want digital discussions to serve and choose applications accordingly. Some require more training or preparation up front than others, and some are designed with privacy and sharing features customized for educators and students. If you want students to have some breathing room and reflection time, you might try using a threaded discussion, and ensure that your prompts push students to think, use evidence, and engage with each other. If you want students to brainstorm collaboratively or participate in small-group conversations, a chat tool might work best. If you want students to draft essays that others can critique, a blog might be the best fit.

Whatever the purpose, teachers should start small with an application that is manageable, given their resources and prior knowledge. "Teachers need to see examples of using these tools that are not focused solely on the bells and whistles of what is technically possible. They need to see how specifically these tools meet the needs of students and teachers as writers, readers, and speakers." If digital communication media such as chats, blogs, and online discussions can motivate students to join academic conversations in purposeful ways, then they can become valuable tools for the classroom.[2]

Teach Conversation Norms

Students in engaging literacy classrooms become accustomed to the interplay of reading, thinking, talking, writing, and doing. They see (and feel) that they learn best when they participate, and it's more fun because the text and the talk answer their questions and give them a chance to share their own ideas. However, in order for this interplay to become the norm in a classroom, teacher and students must establish a culture of conversation that is respectful and inclusive, one in which students who speak up feel both safe and valued. This takes time and intention.

The first step is creating and holding space for classroom norms that "make it absolutely clear to everybody that the smallest comment is valid and interesting to other people" (Duckworth, 1991, p. 31). Explicit discussion norms—share the air, take turns, listen twice as much as you speak—and discussion protocols that guide students in having focused, productive and respectful conversations about text support students in learning how to participate in respectful and focused discussion.

If you want students to really engage in complex discussion, you have to make it safe to really argue. You have to have a culture that says, you come to this with your own deep context and we assume it is of value in helping us all understand things more deeply. We don't want your lip service; we want your real thinking. You are truly welcome here.

—*Sarah Boddy, school designer, EL Education*

Use Protocols to Structure Productive Conversation

We discussed protocols at length in Chapter 1. Here we focus on the Socratic Seminar (see Appendix A), which Kavitha Kasargod uses frequently to engage her students in collaborative discussion. Once students had practiced preparing evidence to support their arguments about the cultural history of the Chesapeake Bay, Kasargod expected students to apply their learning by leading a Socratic Seminar about a different text. In preparation for an investigation of their own community's history, students worked in pairs to facilitate discussion and debate about *The Urban Odyssey: Multicultural History of Washington, D.C.*

A protocol like the Socratic Seminar is an excellent example of the relatively simple instructional choices teachers can make to foster deeper learning. The act of turning desks into a circle and having students lead a text-based discussion based on thoughtful questions is a high-leverage daily instructional move that challenges, engages, and empowers students, and it's one any teacher can make.

What follows are some common questions that students or teachers might ask during a Socratic Seminar:

Sample Key Questions to Help Interpret the Text

- What is the main idea or underlying value in the text?

- What is the author's purpose or perspective?

- What does (a particular phrase) mean?

- What might be a good title for the text?
- What is the most important word/sentence/paragraph?

Sample Questions to Move the Discussion Along

- Who has a different perspective?
- Who has not yet had a chance to speak?
- Where do you find evidence for that in the text?
- Can you clarify what you mean by that?
- How does that relate to what (someone else) said?
- Is there something in the text that is unclear to you?
- Has anyone changed their mind?

Sample Questions to Relate the Text to Students' Lives

- How do the ideas in the text relate to our lives? What do they mean for us personally?
- Why is this material important?
- Is it right that . . . ? Do you agree with the author?

Sample Debriefing Questions

- Do you feel like you understand the text at a deeper level?
- How was the process for us?
- Did we adhere to our norms?
- Did you achieve your goals to participate?
- What was one thing you noticed about the seminar?

Kasargod invites her students to reflect on their participation in the seminar by measuring themselves against the yardstick of specific criteria that they've developed together. Here's the rating scale students complete at the end of each Socratic Seminar:

Circle 1 for "not yet meeting" and 4 for "exceeding"

Responding thoughtfully to questions multiple times	1 2 3 4
Using evidence to support a position or presenting factual information	1 2 3 4
Drawing another person into the discussion	1 2 3 4
Asking a clarifying question or moving the discussion along	1 2 3 4
Highlighting and marking the text with questions/commentary	1 2 3 4

Socratic Seminars are an excellent way to structure respectful, evidence-based discussion and debate. But they aren't the only way. Two previously referenced videos, "Thinking and Speaking Like Scientists through a Science Talk" from Chapter 1 and "Policing in America" from earlier in this chapter are also excellent examples. Also see twelfth-grade biology students from New York City deeply engaged with scientific texts as they prepare for a bioethical debate on TALEN gene therapy in the accompanying two-part video. Note that in each of these videos, the students' text-based preparation and established norms for conversation empower them to have rich and purposeful academic conversations.

WATCH

Video 11: Preparing for an Academic Conversation, Day 1: Analyzing a Scientific Document
Video 12: Preparing for an Academic Conversation, Day 2: Constructing Arguments Using Science Notebooks

---

Ask Students to Paraphrase, Summarize, and Defend Their Arguments with Evidence

Once students have mastered a protocol, a skillful discussion facilitator gives students additional opportunities to grapple by asking them to reread for additional evidence that fine tunes or bolsters their arguments. Particularly when the text-dependent questions that students are talking or writing about demand higher-order thinking skills like analyzing or evaluating, spirited debate about what the text means in the context of the author's purpose invites students to defend their arguments with evidence.

English teacher Justin Sybenga describes a lesson, for example, in which he asked students to decide whether Zora Neale Hurston was "poking fun" at small-town residents in her book *Their Eyes Were Watching God* or representing them fairly. Students gathered as many quotes from the book as they could find to support their position, then posted them on the wall. Peers from the opposing side then critiqued the evidence by challenging the interpretation, context, or weight of the evidence. "Students really had to defend their claims," says Sybenga, "and along the way, some students changed their minds and switched sides."

Teach Students to Say, "You're Right"

Evaluation is near the top of the ladder of complexity in Bloom's Taxonomy. To engage in scholarly debate, students must be able to analyze the credibility of the text based on sources, context, and the weight of the evidence. They must be able not only to defend their own arguments with evidence, but also to concede an argument when others have more—or more credible—evidence. This give and take is an intellectual habit that forms with much practice over time. The accompanying video features middle school students in Syracuse, New York, engaged in a protocol in which they take a stand on an issue and, most important, often change their minds based on the reasoning of their peers.

 WATCH Video 13: Take a Stand

The ability to discuss evidence productively and without prejudice, and the willingness *to change one's mind* according to the evidence presented are the fundamental aptitude and attitude for academic and career success. In an interview with the *New York Times*'s Thomas Friedman, Laszlo Bock, senior vice president at Google, describes the dispositions that are most important if you want a job at Google. These include "the ability to pull together disparate bits of information," to problem solve with a sense of ownership and shared leadership, and most important, intellectual humility. "What we've seen is that the people who are the most successful here, who we want to hire, will have a fierce position. They'll argue like hell. They'll be zealots about their point of view. But then you say, 'Here's a new fact,' and they'll go, 'Oh, well, that changes things; you're right.'"

Similarly, Edward Brown, the Brown University student who graduated from the Springfield Renaissance School, puts it this way:

> "When I first went to Renaissance, I wasn't that vocal in class, but teachers always used cold call. I knew I would get called on and that I could speak and they would listen. At first it was just giving my opinion, but as I got more comfortable, I realized that I could ask probing questions too and I had to give evidence for my opinions and be ready for other people to dissect my answers. That's what's prepared me for the level of college discussions, as well as the leadership positions I have in the Black Student Union and other organizations. I understand that my opinion and my arguments are valuable and important to others as long as I can defend them and also listen to other people. I learned that at Renaissance, and I rely on it every day here at Brown."

Writing with Purpose

Writing is fundamentally an act of communication. Different modes of writing serve different purposes. Narrative writing tells a story, joining the threads of personal experience, imagination, or history. Informational writing informs or explains a topic to the reader, reformulating an understanding gained from reading, thinking, talking, and doing, and delivering that understanding in a new package to new readers. Persuasive and argument writing attempts to influence the reader through analysis and synthesis of multiple perspectives, which the writer distills into a claim supported by evidence gleaned from texts or original research.

The purpose of all of these modes of writing is to evoke a dialogue with real readers who care enough about the writing to speak back—to tell their own stories, add their ideas, or launch a counterargument. Good writing—whether it be literary criticism, a newsletter, policy brief, technical manual, sales pitch, dissertation, museum signage, a novel, or a brochure—is an invitation to conversation. It's not simply "the task students do at the end of the unit," but also the beginning of a lifelong habit of expressing ideas and opinions and sharing knowledge.

The essential questions for writers are "Who is my audience?" "What do I hope they will learn and feel from reading my work?" "How can I engage my readers and make my work effective and memorable?" Grappling with these questions, individually and with others, is the force that shapes quality writing. Ironically, for almost all the writing students do in schools, these questions are almost irrelevant.

There is no real audience for most student work, and students are understandably more concerned with pleasing the teacher and getting a decent grade (the teacher is often the only audience for the writing) than evoking feelings in actual readers or imparting important knowledge. The intrinsic drive for quality—the reason to care—is absent for many students. The excitement of refining written work to reach real readers, the engine of quality revision, is missing. When we are discouraged as teachers that our students are not motivated to revise and improve their writing, to strive toward an ambitious vision of quality, we need to ask ourselves, "Is there a purpose for this writing that would inspire students to work toward quality?"

Deeper instruction that leads to high-quality writing helps students understand *why* they invested time in reading, analyzing, and talking about a variety of text, and *how* they can use their new understanding to tell a story, convey information, or launch a powerful argument to a real audience. Connecting reading and writing in this way involves two types of writing assignments: short on-demand tasks that build and assess students' understanding, and related authentic tasks that are drafted, revised, and polished for an audience beyond the teacher. Authentic tasks, such as researching and writing a report to present to city officials, are often the final product of a unit. Short tasks along the way—assessed formatively or summatively—can also be rigorous and provide important scaffolding for students learning to improve their craft. In other words, the short tasks allow both students and teachers to measure their progress along the way as they build the skills for the significant writing project that follows.

At Capital City seniors take an on-demand document-based, argument writing assessment in English class. They also write a lengthy research paper. In Kasargod's history class, they regularly complete short writing assignments in which they synthesize information and use evidence to support claims. These short tasks support the culminating project, in which, as ethnographers in their own neighborhoods, they gather the demographic data and histories of their neighbors and communities to explain the cultural and political significance of place to their families and communities.

One of the short tasks Kasargod assigned was to interview a neighborhood resident. She provided a model from National Public Radio's *Story Corps* that students listened to and analyzed together. Their critique focused on the kinds of questions interviewers ask and the subtleties of communication that make

So many of our kids are first-generation Americans. They are trying to negotiate what it means for them to be living in the shadow of the American government. They are trying to respect and love their parents, but also figure out how to be themselves. This project helps them discover their own neighborhoods, which are really different from what most people know of Washington, D.C. The students are at the forefront of how their place is changing, so telling their own neighborhood story is powerful for them.

—*Kavitha Kasargod, teacher, Capital City Public Charter School*

the interviewee feel comfortable, safe, and deeply listened to. Next students formulated questions and interviewed each other, practicing the skills they had learned from the model. Just as the task of conducting and writing up an interview of one neighborhood resident would scaffold the larger ethnography project, the low-stakes interviews of their peers scaffolded students' success toward high-quality interviews of their neighbors. Short tasks, then, nest successively to build a strong structure for more complex culminating tasks.

Kasargod's culminating assignment takes students weeks to complete and demands complex, critical thinking—analysis, evaluation, and creation of a product that interprets and presents a place they've lived in all their lives.

What follows are specific writing strategies Kasargod and Capital City English teacher Justin Sybenga taught, and which any teacher can employ, to support students in doing quality work on this challenging task.

Analyzing Evidence

Before they are ready to write, students must gather and analyze demographic, economic, and housing data from local agencies and exhibits at local museums. They have to graph trends in this data, for the neighborhood they are profiling, over four decades. Many students struggle with this task, stumbling over how to interpret percentages, or how to represent numbers accurately in graphs. "We talk a lot about types of evidence," says Sybenga. "Students are drawn to anecdote because it's familiar and easy, but they struggle to be critical about statistics and numbers. It's hard for them to select which numbers are most significant or to identify when statistics are being manipulated to deliver nonsense."

To help students address this challenge, Sybenga teaches lessons on the credibility of "experts." Students rank the evidence from least to most credible. "One thing students take away from those lessons is that you have to have academic training and/or work experience in something to be an expert, unless you're just talking about your own life. This counters what students' initially offer as evidence, which was all numbers and statements from popular sites they found on the Internet."

Learning the Language and Structure of Argument

Reviewing the results of the schoolwide writing assessment, teachers at Capital City noticed that although students were spirited debaters who brought passion and reason to Socratic Seminars and oral discussion, those skills didn't always translate to paper. To be successful in writing the argumentative essay component of their neighborhood project, they would need to dig into the details of how to construct an argument.

To facilitate that, Sybenga gave students a Google.doc template in outline format with places for claim, evidence, and analysis. The template mirrored graphic organizers students had used earlier to analyze arguments written by historians. In both English and history class, students shared a common language for the criteria of a strong argument:

- Is the claim supported by evidence and analysis?

- Is the evidence valid, sufficient, and persuasive?

- Does the reasoning weigh the strengths and weaknesses of the evidence and draw logical conclusions?

As they began to fill in the outline, students were also required to supplement their book knowledge with firsthand evidence. Working in teams, they toured their own neighborhoods on foot and identified places that people who live in the neighborhood would count as significant—not tourist destinations, but, for example, the 7-Eleven where day laborers hang out waiting to be offered jobs. They also attended and reported on neighborhood commission meetings. Then they formulated their claims, which, as the steps that follow demonstrate, is a rigorous cognitive process:

Forming an evidence-based claim

Step 1. Find important details.

- Students read a text and look for details that are important. They take notes, annotate the text, or record the details on a graphic organizer.

- From these details, students begin to develop questions (or the teacher may provide the questions) that inquire into the gaps or relationship between the details.

Step 2. Connect the details (trace the argument).

- Students think, talk, and write about how the details connect to one another:
  - Do all the details point to the same main idea?
  - What answers to the question(s) bubble up from the details?
  - What answers are missing from the details?
  - What new questions arise from the gaps or disconnects?

Step 3. Evaluate the details.

- Students think, talk, and write about whether the details are valid, relevant, and sufficient.
  - Is the source reliable and credible? Is the source biased?
  - Are the details accurate?
  - Do all of the details clearly support the specific claim?
  - Is there enough data to hold up the claim consistently and convincingly?

Step 4. Make a claim (induction from the evidence)

- Students draw inferences from the text based on the details.

- Students formulate a new claim (first orally, then in writing) that answers a focusing question.

Step 5: Build an argument.

- Students identify which textual details provide good evidence for their claims.

- Students determine how to organize the evidence to support an original argument.

- Students invite critique of or dialogue about their arguments. This conversation mirrors steps 2 and 3 and is essentially a collaborative evaluation of their own arguments, referencing back to the textual evidence they have brought forward in support of the claim.

- Students re-read, reevaluate, and revise their "case" based on critique and new evidence or new interpretations.

In many American schools, the challenge of teaching writing is magnified by the fact that so many students come from non-English-speaking households. This poses an especially daunting challenge when teaching something as complex as analysis and argument. The Strategy Close Up that follows offers a concrete strategy for unveiling the mystery of scholarly writing for English language learners at a Spanish-English immersion school in Oakland, California.

STRATEGY CLOSE UP: Teaching English Language Learners the Structure of Academic Writing

English language learners often know the vocabulary of nouns and verbs, but they often fail to see how analytical writing relates ideas to each other by strategically employing prepositions and conjunctions. Mark Zucker, a fifth-grade teacher at Manzanita SEED Elementary School in Oakland, California, addresses this confusion head on with a combination of writing lessons at the sentence level and reading lessons on gathering evidence from text.

The topic of recent student writing is a planet report that answers this prompt: "We want to know if life can exist on other planets like on Earth. Therefore, we will have to learn what conditions exist on Earth that have allowed life to evolve here and compare other planets with Earth. How would the conditions on the planet you are describing make life possible or impossible there?"

Zucker's sequence of writing lessons let students into a secret: "The little words writers use signal the relationship between factoids. They are a key to good writing."

(continued)

Cause-Effect (e.g. as a result, consequently, hence, due to, in order to)

_____, so _____.

_____, because _____.

_____, thus _____.

_____, therefore _____.

Because _____, _____.

Compare-Contrast (e.g., unlike, different, contrast, similar, same, both, more, -er, than)

_____, but _____.

_____, however _____.

_____, whereas _____.

_____, while _____.

Students practice using these language structures in poems, grammar exercises, and oral presentations first with information that is familiar—likes and dislikes, friends, pets. They get to practice the language structure and the thinking skill without having to learn new content.

When students get back to studying the planets, using evidence from their reading and shaping that evidence into sentences that use the language structures they've learned, the results are much more complex and well-crafted pieces of informational writing. For one student, this was the result:

> Venus is a beautiful light green planet, so people long ago named her after the Greek god of beauty. It is similar to Earth in some ways, so it has been called Earth's "sister" planet. For example, Venus is 7,000 miles across, which is just a little bit smaller than Earth, but much smaller than any of the outer planets. Also, they are the second and third planets from the sun, and we can even see Venus from Earth. However, life could not exist there like it does on Earth, and here are reasons why. First of all, because Venus is closer to the Sun than Earth, Venus is hotter than the Earth. In fact, while Earth never gets above 120 degrees, Venus is 800 degrees! This is so hot that all water would be just steam, whereas on Earth, water can be a liquid or even solid. Since life began in liquid water and there is no liquid water on Venus, life could not exist there. Also, living things need oxygen to survive, but the atmosphere on Venus is mostly carbon dioxide, so we couldn't breathe there. It's the carbon dioxide that makes it so hot on Venus, because it traps in the heat like the windows on a greenhouse. Venus is like the Earth except with way more carbon dioxide in the atmosphere, but humans keep putting more and more carbon dioxide in the atmosphere on Earth from running factories and cars, so guess what? Is it possible that Earth could become like Venus someday, and life won't be able to exist anymore on Earth? Is it possible life used to exist on Venus before it got too hot? Maybe Venus used to be like the Earth. Venus is beautiful, but life cannot exist there now because of its carbon dioxide.

Refining Quality

It's one thing to assign a complex writing task and, as many teachers know, another to get students to complete the task with quality. Once students have a purpose for writing, they need a clear vision of what defines high-quality writing for a specific assignment. That vision is nested within our broad definition of high-quality work, which we describe as follows:

High-Quality Work Is Complex

- Complex work is rigorous: it aligns with or exceeds the expectations defined by grade-level standards and includes higher-order thinking by challenging students to apply, analyze, evaluate, and create during daily instruction and throughout longer projects.

- Complex work often connects to the big concepts that undergird or unite disciplines.

- Complex work prioritizes transfer of understanding to new contexts.

- Complex work prioritizes consideration of multiple perspectives.

- Complex work may incorporate students' application of higher-order literacy skills through the use of complex text and evidence-based writing and speaking.

High-Quality Work Is Authentic

- Authentic work demonstrates the original thinking of students—authentic personal voice and ideas—rather than simply showing that students can follow directions or fill in the blanks.

- Authentic work often uses real work formats and standards from the professional world rather than artificial school formats (e.g., students create a book review for a local newspaper instead of a book report for the teacher).

- Authentic work often connects academic standards with real-world issues, controversies, and local people and places.

- Authenticity gives purpose to work; the work matters to students and ideally to a larger community as well. When possible, it is created for and shared with an audience beyond the classroom.

High-Quality Work Demonstrates Craftsmanship

- Well-crafted work is done with care and precision. Craftsmanship requires attention to accuracy, detail, and beauty.

- In every discipline and domain, well-crafted work should be beautiful work in conception and execution. In short tasks or early drafts of work, craftsmanship may be present primarily in thoughtful ideas, but not in polished presentation; for long-term projects, craftsmanship requires perseverance to refine work in conception, conventions, and presentation, typically through multiple drafts or rehearsals with critique from others.

Quality writing with some or all of these attributes responds to the needs and motivations of its audience. It is eloquent, fresh, and intelligent. It brings new evidence into the discourse of writer and reader and makes the work that students do in school meaningful beyond the schoolhouse doors and into the future.

In the Getting Started section of this chapter we saw second-grade students develop a shared understanding of the criteria for quality by critiquing a model of a persuasive letter. Older students also benefit from models that show with eloquence and grace the features of the specific type of writing they are expected to produce. Then, after they have conceived and drafted a piece, writers still need individual feedback on the particulars of organization, the relationship among ideas, style, sentence fluency, and conventions.

Effective feedback aligns with the literacy learning targets set forth for the assignment. That is, it reinforces specific strategies that have been taught and ones that will be assessed when the writing piece is turned in. Many secondary school teachers find that commenting on student papers through a shared online platform (like Google.docs) allows them to provide timely feedback that is specific, user-friendly, and actionable. An electronic dialogue also teaches students how to engage in the kind of professional exchange they will undoubtedly use in college and the workplace.

Quality feedback from the teacher or peers is an empowering way to bolster students' capacity for reflection and skill transfer. A carefully implemented protocol for providing students with specific feedback pauses the classroom action and opens a space for reflection. In that space, we ask each student to stop, look at what she's written, inquire whether it says what she meant, and dialogue with another person about how to more effectively craft the writing so that it communicates her ideas. In the accompanying video, view a unique and efficient protocol for peer feedback.

 WATCH Video 14: Using a Speed Dating Protocol to Think Critically about Writing

Providing a list of questions to guide the dialogue between peers can also support their efforts to provide specific and helpful feedback. For example, the questions that follow can support older students to help their peers improve specific aspects of their writing:

- Ideas: What is the writer's claim? What evidence does the writer provide to support the claim?

- Organization: Do the transitions between paragraphs enhance the flow of the argument as a whole?

- Voice: What words does the writer use to convey a tone appropriate to the audience's educational and vocational background?

- Style: Does the writer use a variety of sentence lengths and structures?

In the accompanying video we see how a teacher in Portland, Maine, uses a rubric to provide highly focused and descriptive feedback to each student. On the rubric she has highlighted particular areas the students need to address along with detailed written comments. Students are then invited to meet with her in mini-lessons related to each part of the rubric.

 WATCH Video 15: Descriptive Feedback Helps All Students Meet Proficiency

Giving Students a Chance to Present

A writing task that challenges students to muster their intellectual courage and work to create a polished product for a real audience also yields a deeper payoff. When Kasargod's students were working on their final presentations of the neighborhood project, she says, "They were engaging with each other and you almost didn't know that I was there. It could continue without me, because students were so passionate.

They were using multiple sources to answer questions that really mattered to them, even outside of school. And they were producing quality work that goes beyond answering cursory questions." Because students knew they would be presenting their work to their families and community members, including people they had interviewed, they had a real stake in doing a good job. Just as the Centennial second graders were invested in convincing school district officials to resurface their playground, these seniors cared about impressing the audience with their knowledge, scholarship, professionalism, and investment in their own neighborhoods.

Reflecting and Assessing

At Capital City, as we've seen, students achieve a deep understanding of how to break down and make arguments through practice and reflection. "The sheer repetition of these skills is what makes a difference," says Sybenga. For the past few years, all Capital City teachers have participated in norming and grading a schoolwide writing assessment that calls for an evidence-based argument. This structure has also developed teachers' common understanding of what good writing is. "Now students use the same organizers and language, and rubrics in all of our classes. We assess those skills as freshmen, then students reflect and set goals, and then we practice more, and then we assess them again." The result, according to Sybenga, is that students themselves can articulate the habits of scholarship that bolster effective reading and writing. "They come back to us from college and tell us their peers have never written a research paper. They put their annotations on Facebook! Our students have confidence and skills, because they've done this in high school."

What's more, students leave high school with the ability to apply what they've learned in the real world. "I want them to learn the content of my social studies standards, and they do," notes Kasargod. "But this project isn't just history out of a textbook. It's economics, political science, sociology, anthropology, ethnography. Students come to realize that reading, debating, writing, and presenting are what professionals in all of these fields do, so the skills they learn are ones they can actually use after graduation."

The Critical Moves of Deeper Literacy Instruction

Deeper learning happens when students get beneath the surface of a topic, when they recognize that speaking, listening, reading, and writing are the bedrock of the precious skills they can carry with them into the future. The instructional moves that facilitate this kind of learning engage students in topics and cognitive work that matters. As shown in Table 2.3, deeper instruction challenges students to read, think, talk, and write as members of a learning community. And it empowers students with a toolkit that opens the door to lifelong learning.

Table 2.3 The Who, What, and Why of Deeper Literacy Instruction

What Do Teachers Do?	What Do Students Do?	What's the Result?
Establish a culture of growth in which everyone is expected to work hard, learn from mistakes, and persevere.	Take academic risks, re-read multiple times, learn from mistakes, and celebrate the efforts of peers.	Students learn that hard work pays off over time and that becoming a strong reader and writer takes practice.
Use the Four Ts: Topic, Text, Target, Task to challenge, engage, and empower students.	Read as writers and write as readers in order to dive deeply into a topic and share it with others. They build knowledge and vocabulary, which accelerates their ability to read harder texts.	Students meet or exceed standards *and* they come to see reading and writing as ways to learn about the world and research their own questions and passions.
Teach literacy in all content areas, with an intentional focus on discipline-specific vocabulary and genres.	Use reading as a way to learn about science and history. They add to their toolkit for accessing difficult and discipline-specific knowledge.	Students are stronger scholars when they can synthesize concepts and skills across all subject areas.
Curate complex and compelling texts, with attention to qualitative and quantitative complexity, as well as students' needs and interests.	Build their reading muscles with new vocabulary, language structures, and themes. They want to read because texts are relevant and compelling.	Students improve their reading breadth and depth. They are exposed to a wide variety and complexity of reading that prepares them for college and careers.
Develop engaging and challenging lessons that invite students to read, think, talk, and write about texts.	Participate in rich conversation that enables them to construct and communicate meaning from their reading.	Students develop important transferable skills such as collaboration, conversation, and summarizing.
Insist on grappling. Frequently ask students to "have a go" at a text before direct strategy instruction or thinking aloud.	Persevere to make meaning from text without the teacher's instruction. They develop confidence in tackling difficult text.	Students become independent readers who can apply close reading strategies to any text.
Teach students to value evidence by using protocols for discussion and developing text-dependent questions in advance.	Value evidence as the standard for truth and credibility, return to the text to seek support for their ideas, and use evidence to support their own claims in writing and speaking.	Students are better prepared for college and careers when they use evidence to support their own claims and to analyze the claims of others.

(continued)

Table 2.3 Continued

What Do Teachers Do?	What Do Students Do?	What's the Result?
Develop engaging and challenging writing tasks in real-world formats.	Learn a variety of real-world formats to convey their ideas to authentic audiences. They are motivated to write because they have real readers.	Students connect with real readers and listeners and feel the power their own voices have to make a difference in the world. They write with purpose.
Provide models for writing. Teach students to critique and revise based on specific criteria for quality.	Use models to guide drafts and revisions. They give and receive kind, helpful, and specific feedback.	Students expand their ability to describe and produce quality writing in multiple genres.
Debrief transferable literacy skills and concepts. Help students reflect on the skills and concepts they can use in different and future contexts.	Reflect on how they've learned as well as what they've learned. They articulate the skills and concepts that can help them learn in new contexts.	When students can name the skills and processes that help them learn, they are empowered to lead their own learning.

SCHOOLWIDE IMPLEMENTATION

Supporting Literacy Instruction in Every Classroom

When it comes to literacy, the leader's most important job is to continually reinforce that every teacher—from English to science to special education—is a teacher of literacy. Providing a collaborative planning schedule and professional learning opportunities that include and involve all teachers in literacy instruction will go a long way toward sending this message. But leaders must go further to create the systems and ongoing support that teachers who have not been trained as reading and writing teachers will need to do this work. Content-area teachers in particular may need additional support and ongoing coaching to learn how to integrate reading and writing instruction into their subject areas. All teachers, including English language arts teachers, will likely need professional development in teaching informational texts, argument, and reading and writing grounded in evidence. Building trust and collaborative practices between teachers is critical.

Key Leadership Actions

Lay the Groundwork

- Provide adequate planning time and support for attending to the Four Ts: Topic, Text, Target, Task.

- Schedule ongoing collaborative planning time that allows content-area teachers and ELA teachers to coordinate their effort.

- Budget for continual acquisition of compelling, relevant, and complex texts (instead of or in addition to textbooks).

- Help teachers find compelling complex texts for their students and appropriate sets of magazines, journals, and primary sources. Appendices F and G contain online resources for finding primary sources, including photographs.

- Involve and support teachers from all departments in selecting text based on the criteria for complexity.

- Help teachers develop relationships with community partners who can serve as authentic audiences for student writing and oral presentations.

Build Teachers' Capacity

- Provide professional development and coaching on literacy instruction to content-area teachers. One good way to begin this work is a "cross-walk," or comparison, of content-area texts and tasks and standards.

- Provide professional development specifically on teaching nonfiction and reading for and writing with evidence. Our 2014 book *Transformational Literacy: Making the Common Core Shift with Work That Matters* is a good resource for helping teachers understand and address these instructional shifts.

Support Teachers to Deepen Their Practice

- When conducting observations or learning walks, pay attention to why, what, and how texts are being used to challenge and engage students in deeper learning. Are students grappling with text on their own before direct instruction? Are students using protocols to think, write, and talk about text? Are students annotating text, taking notes, and synthesizing their ideas in writing? Are teachers asking higher order questions and text-dependent questions? (See Table 1.5).

- Make time for faculty to analyze student writing samples and discuss the assignments and rubrics behind them. Develop a bank of quality assignments and rubrics that can serve as models for new teachers and teachers new to writing instruction.

- Develop a bank of quality student writing models in different writing formats. A strong set of models and resources can be found in *Models of Excellence: The Center for High-Quality Student Work* (http://modelsofexcellence.eleducation.org/)

- Document critique lessons and peer feedback protocols through video and other means to help foster the ongoing use and refinement of these practices.

COMMON CHALLENGES

Settling for Text That Is Not Worthy

A worthy text is compelling, complex, and often relevant to students' real lives. It's a text worth reading multiple times and coming back to for additional evidence, reference, or the deliciousness of its structure, language, or graphics. When teachers settle for the first thing they find on the bookshelf or on the Internet, they often shortchange students' learning. Making time to research and curate text resources is a critical part of planning. Criteria for a good text cannot be limited to the topic of the text. Worthy texts must also be beautifully written for that genre.

Failing to Align Topic, Text, Target, and Task

The alignment of what students are studying, the texts they use to learn about the topic, how they demonstrate their learning, and what you want them to know and be able to do in the end is crucial for student success. And it requires deep planning. When time is short (and it usually is), teachers can be tempted to choose a fun topic they don't have adequate texts for or one that doesn't leverage their standards. Or they might plan for an activity that students enjoy but that doesn't challenge them to apply new learning or use evidence from text to demonstrate their knowledge. Although it requires an investment of planning on the front end, it pays off in rich and coherent literacy units that push students to learn deeply and discover the joy of reading and writing.

Failing to Scaffold Close Reading Skills

Close reading is a challenging skill that requires practice over time. Insisting from the get-go that all students grapple independently with complex text can be a recipe for frustration and failure. Instead, teachers must be mindful of students' individual needs, interests, and readiness. Differentiation strategies like chunking text and previewing vocabulary, and careful scaffolding of the duration and depth of close reading, will help all students to succeed with complex text.

Teaching Literacy Only in English Class

All teachers are literacy teachers. Because reading and writing are foundational skills for all subject areas and a predictor of academic success generally, it's important that all teachers grow their understanding and practice of literacy instruction. By incorporating reading, thinking, talking, and writing about texts into every subject area, teachers send the message that strong readers and writers can unlock the door to any content area. Literacy-rich content-area instruction reflects conclusive research that shows that as students gain knowledge and vocabulary through reading their capacity to gain further understanding of the topic accelerates.

Teachers Doing More Work Than Students

To develop the skills they need for college and careers, students must practice, practice, practice. Students themselves must do the work of summarizing, synthesizing, evaluating, and making meaning from difficult texts. This means that teachers should structure the work—for example, using protocols, graphic organizers, and anchor charts—but still expect all students to grapple independently with text and engage actively in thinking, talking, and writing about text. Both the text itself and other students are important "teachers" in the classroom. Structures for collaboration teach students that reading and writing are acts of communication and shared understanding.

Lack of Models for Quality Writing

In order to understand what is good we need to see it. Models, whether created by other students, by professionals, or by the teacher help students identify and describe what quality writing in a particular genre looks like and sounds like. Schools can collect good models representing diverse formats and grade levels into a valuable resource for teachers who are developing critique lessons or rubrics.

Not Providing Enough Time for Students to Revise and Improve

Good writing takes time—to draft, reflect, revise, edit, and polish. Teachers need to balance the assignment of short, on-demand tasks with long-term authentic tasks that involve revision. Short tasks are often a good way for students to practice a discrete writing skill and to assess knowledge along the way. In the end, though, students need time to assimilate their new learning, to practice, make mistakes, and revise in response to both teacher and peer feedback. Careful calendaring will help teachers avoid the trap of low quality resulting from too little time.

NOTES

1. EL Education's online *Models of Excellence: The Center for High-Quality Student Work* includes a collection of student writing distinguished by voice, imagination, and impact (http://modelsofexcellence.eleducation.org/). Other resources for student-writing models include the *Concord Review* (www .tcr.org), which publishes well-crafted academic and research papers written by secondary students, *The Write Source* (thewritesource.com), which provides student-written models from all grade levels and in many formats, and *Achieve the Core*'s "In Common" collection of student writing samples for all Common Core standards (http://achievethecore.org/page/507/in-common-effective-writing-for-all-students).

2. *Going Online with Protocols: New Tools for Teaching and Learning* by Joseph P. McDonald, Janet Mannheimer Zydney, Alan Dichter, and Elizabeth C. McDonald is an excellent resource.

Chapter 3

Creating Scientists and Historians

OVERVIEW

Confronting Complex Questions

Science teacher Eric Beck wants two things for his eighth-grade students at Rimrock Expeditionary Alternative Learning Middle School (REALMS). First, he wants them to understand the big ideas of science that underpin his required standards and will show up on required standardized tests. Second, he wants them to engage in doing real science beyond the test, which allows them to put those big ideas into action and demonstrate critical thinking. Toward this deeper learning, Beck is constantly mining his Oregon community—whose economy thrives on the recreational use of abundant water and beautiful forests—for current scientific questions and dilemmas. "More than anything else I want my students to know that being able to support their arguments with data gets them into the conversation. There is a lot of distrust of science these days. You see it in politics and in the general public. But when students can trace the connection between a policy and the concrete facts that support it, then they are more likely to trust science as a way of understanding and solving problems in the world," says Beck.

Confronting complex questions like Beck's students are doing is also at the heart of history instruction at the Metropolitan Expeditionary Learning School (MELS) in New York City. There, ninth-grade students don't just study a textbook; they write their own. Students explore what teacher Claire Wolff calls, "The historian's craft—those skills and understandings that shape the ways in which history is written and read," including how text books infect history with bias resulting from privilege, racism, and the fallibility of the historian. Wolff's students attempt to answer the compelling question, "Is history the truth?" by learning about the famed Rosetta Stone and then analyzing and evaluating primary and secondary sources, including artifacts in a local museum. Finally, they synthesize what they've learned and take on the role of historians themselves by writing their own textbook entries. This approach challenges students to think critically about an enduring dilemma in the construction of knowledge: history is shaped not only by those who live it, but also by those who write it down.

What does it mean to teach science and history deeply? What questions should students ask? Whose answers and whose telling of history should students learn? In both disciplines the landscape of standards teachers must cover is vast, and teachers have to navigate difficult choices: "How do I balance teaching the content of end-of-course tests with teaching conceptual understanding?" "How do I divide my instructional time between experiences in the lab or investigating primary sources and surveying a textbook or delivering lectures?" While acknowledging and respecting the attention teachers give to covering their content, we emphasize that *creating* scientists and historians—nurturing young minds to be capable and curious researchers—requires a deeper approach.

Uncovering the Big Ideas in Science and History

Beneath the surface of science and history (and the reason we address these disciplines together in this chapter) is a foundational belief that knowledge is based on a cumulative gathering of evidence. The more evidence there is for a scientific or historical explanation, the more powerfully that explanation, or big idea, drives our understanding of the natural or social world. A big idea, says educator Grant Wiggins, is "a theory, not a detail. It helps us make sense of lots of confusing experiences and seemingly isolated facts. It's like the picture that connects the dots or a simple rule of thumb in a complex field" (Wiggins, 2010, p. 1).

Harvard professor David Perkins reminds us that big ideas and disciplinary frameworks are what allow students to make sense of the facts they encounter. Without these frameworks, it is like giving students lot of bricks—discrete facts—and asking them to build a house. Without blueprints—big ideas and disciplinary frameworks—all the students have is a pile of bricks. They have no idea how to build understanding with them. (Personal communication, 2015.)

Unlike standards, there is no comprehensive or definitive list of big ideas in science and history. Teachers must do the work of distilling and articulating the big ideas that emerge from their standards and/or textbooks and organizing disparate facts and details into something concrete and transferable for students.[1] For example, Wolff might simply have covered the features of ancient river civilizations and the development of writing in her study of the Rosetta Stone. Instead, by having students write their own textbooks, they uncovered a concept that endures throughout history and across the globe: *The meaning of artifacts depends on who owns them and who tells their story.* Digging into this big idea gave students an opportunity to recognize patterns in history and will help them transfer their learning to new contexts. We return to Beck's and Wolff's classrooms later in this chapter to unpack the instructional moves they make that invite students to leverage the big ideas.

Practicing Inquiry

If lifting up big ideas is the first pillar of deeper instruction in the content areas, then the second is practicing inquiry by teaching students to think like scientists and historians and to use the tools of these disciplines. To become active, informed citizen-scientists, students must investigate their own questions, develop theories, and support them with evidence. This means students need experience solving problems the way that scientists and historians do—by experimenting in the laboratory or investigating in the field; gathering, evaluating, and interpreting data; constructing explanations and arguments; and communicating information. Thus, the teaching strategies we focus on in this chapter, while addressing required content-area standards and preparing students for state tests, show how to get students grappling with the big ideas and pursuing their own questions through scientific and historical practices.

Why These Practices Matter

Deeper instruction in science and history increases the odds that American students will be able to compete (and collaborate) with graduates from other nations. In 2008, 31 percent of US bachelor's degrees were awarded in science and engineering fields, compared to 61 percent in Japan and 51 percent in China. The attrition rate (38 percent) of American students in college STEM majors (science, technology, engineering, and mathematics) encourages companies in these grow-ing fields to frequently hire from other countries because American graduates are less prepared and less available than their international counterparts (National Math and Science Initiative, 2014). Although this crisis is less urgent in the social sciences, students of history, sociology, anthropology and other social science fields are also more likely to enter a life of meaningful study, productive work, and contribution to community and civic life if they have the intellectual tools of their discipline. Deeper instruction matters because it develops in students the mindset of scientists and historians—the value of evidence, the payoff of perseverance, the worth in not finding the "right" answers, and the importance of accuracy and reliability—that will prepare them for success in college and careers and as citi-zens in a changing world.

Complex Challenges Mirror the Real World

Instruction that asks students to grapple with complex texts, debate in a com-munity of learning, and write for real audiences prepares students for similar challenges beyond high school. To succeed in college, students need to be confi-dent and critical readers who interrogate evidence, evaluate and synthesize mul-tiple sources of information, and formulate arguments supported by evidence. They also need to have the foundation of knowledge about science and history acquired through consistent, connected study in these disciplines. These compo-nents of scholarship are the engine of science and history, and of our instructional practices.

Engaging Instruction Opens the Door to Big Ideas

Instruction that engages students in real-world problems and introduces them to the big ideas of science and social studies makes learning meaningful and relevant, even beyond the schoolhouse doors. In 2007, a Carnegie Foundation commission of distinguished researchers and public and private leaders concluded that "the nation's capacity to innovate for economic growth and the ability of American workers to thrive in the modern workforce depend on a broad foundation of math and science learning" (Carnegie Corporation of New York-Institute for Advanced Study Commission on Mathematics and Science Education Executive Summary). Peter Stearns of the American Historical Association points out that while some students of the social sciences will become historians, political scientists, or psychologists, many will apply their historical habits of mind in business, activism, public service, journalism, and finance (Stearns, 1998). Deeper instruction in the content areas engages students in the practices and questions they'll one day encounter as professionals.

Deeper Instruction Empowers Students to Reflect on Their Learning and Its Impact on the World

Social studies "encourages habits of mind that are vital for responsible public behavior, whether as a national or community leader, an informed voter, a petitioner, or a simple observer" (Stearns, 1998). Instruction that develops young minds into scientists and historians invites students to consider the impact of their learning and how new skills and understandings can be employed in novel contexts. When students can describe how they learned as well as what they know about the natural world and their own communities, they are more likely to continue participating in civic debate and leading positive change in the world at large.

Models of Deeper Learning in Science and Social Studies Curricula

EL Education has created a variety of open source science and social studies curriculum modules that incorporate literacy standards from the Common Core. The hallmark of these modules is their focus on big ideas. The modules weave together science and/or social studies content, literacy skills, and "disciplinary thinking" in response to essential questions. Language arts teachers working to integrate science and social studies topics into literacy lessons, as well as content-area teachers looking for literacy-rich science and social studies lessons, will find them useful models for deeper instruction in science and social studies.

Science Curriculum

In grades 3–5, EL's successful English language arts (ELA) curriculum has been enhanced to include a science supplement comprising four weeks' lessons on the same topic, which address the Next Generation Life Science Standards. These lessons emphasize scientific discourse, eliciting student thinking, and inquiry. They are available at Commoncoresuccess .elschools.org on the following topics:

- Grade 3: Freaky Frogs: life cycles, frogs, ponds, ecosystems
- Grade 4: Animal Defense Mechanisms: structure and function in animals and plants, diverse habitats
- Grade 5: Rainforest and Biodiversity: coniferous and deciduous forests, food webs—producers, consumers, decomposers

A module for grades 6–8, appropriate for either language arts or science class (or both) explores the Earth's hydrosphere and is available from achievethecore.org.

- Water Is Life: The Earth's Hydrosphere and Its Impact on Living Systems.

Social Studies Curriculum

EL Education offers secondary curricula in social studies that address both American history and world history. Teachers are encouraged to explore:

- Grade 6: World Geography. This is a year-long scope and sequence focused on migration, education, and human rights around the world, with approximately nine weeks of daily lessons to guide instruction in the first part of the year. Available from Commoncoresuccess.elschools.org.
- Grade 8: Voices from Little Rock: Understanding the Civil Rights Movement through Primary Sources. Focused on the American context, this module provides sample lessons and an overall sequence for twelve weeks of instruction. Available from Achievethecore.org.
- Grade 9: World History. This is a year-long scope and sequence focused on change, revolution, and the concept of justice around the world from medieval to modern times. It includes approximately nine weeks of daily lessons to guide instruction on this topic relevant to medieval societies. Available from Commoncoresuccess.elschools.org.
- Grade 9–10: From Revolution to Democracy: The Complex Fight for Freedom. Through the lens of American history, this module provides sample lessons and an overall sequence for teaching the foundations of democracy. Available from Achievethecore.org.

In the Getting Started section that follows, we take a closer look at what deeper instruction looks like and sounds like in Claire Wolff's high school history classroom and Eric Beck's middle school science classroom.

GETTING STARTED

Uncovering the Big Ideas

Creating a learning environment that is rich in experience and inquiry requires, more than anything else, deep planning. In order that science and history curricula lift up the big ideas of their disciplines *and* prepare students for mandatory state tests, we promote a planning strategy that begins by aligning required standards with big ideas. Teachers can then find opportunities to make deep dives into narrow topics that can illuminate those big ideas for students and help make the learning last. The steps below describe an approach to building challenge, engagement, and empowerment into science and history instruction by using the Four Ts—Topic, Text, Target, and Task—that we introduced comprehensively in Chapter 2.

Bundle Standards into a Relevant TOPIC

The first step toward finding a compelling topic for a deep dive is to look *through* content area standards for the alignment of big ideas among time periods, geographical areas, scientific fields, disciplinary skills and disparate disciplines. (Wiggins says that big ideas are a lens rather than an object [2010].) Frequently state standards in the content areas contain a confusing catalogue of unrelated indicators and objectives. Finding the connections between them that tease out the big ideas can take some insightful thinking, as evidenced by Meg Alexander and her colleagues at Glennwood Elementary in Decatur, Georgia, in the example that follows.

When reviewing their social studies and literacy standards, these third-grade teachers identified those that would fit together into a challenging and engaging topic that captured a big idea of history: *Governments are organized around specific principles that guide how people make change over time.* Two of their history standards were:

- **SS3H2:** The student will discuss the lives of Americans who expanded people's rights and freedoms in a democracy, including Paul Revere (independence), Frederick Douglass (civil rights), Susan B. Anthony (women's rights), Mary McLeod Bethune (education), Franklin D. Roosevelt (New Deal and World War II), Eleanor Roosevelt (United Nations and human rights), Thurgood Marshall (civil rights), Lyndon B. Johnson (Great Society and voting rights), and César Chávez (workers' rights).

- **SS3H1:** The student will explain the political roots of our modern democracy in the United States of America. a. Identify the influence of Greek architecture (columns on the Parthenon, U. S. Supreme Court building), law, and the Olympic games on the present. b. Explain the ancient Athenians' idea that a community should choose its own leaders.

Looking at these standards divergently, Alexander and her colleagues realized that they have in common a theme of leadership and the impact individuals have on governing bodies through the democratic process. Teachers focused in on that theme, but they still weren't done unpacking their standards.

Next they noticed that their literacy standards asked students to do the following:

- **ELACC3R13:** Describe the relationship between a series of historical events using language that pertains to time, sequence, and cause and effect.

- **ELACC3R11:** Ask and answer questions to demonstrate understanding, referring explicitly to the text as the basis for answers.

To leverage these Common Core reading and writing standards as well as the social studies standards during a presidential election year, teachers decided to bundle the standards around the topic Democracy at Work in order to get at the big idea: individuals organize groups to affect government and social decisions. They designed a case study on reading and writing biographies of civil rights leaders, followed by an investigation of the democratic process in their own community.

A **case study** is an investigation of a person, place, institution, or event that allows students to become experts on a specific topic before they generalize their learning to broader concepts and content (e.g., an investigation of a local civil rights hero that illuminates a broader study of the American civil rights movement). Or, more loosely, it is a narrowed subtopic or example that animates and clarifies the broader topic (e.g., a focus on women's roles in the Civil War).

To engage their young historians in authentic inquiry and research, the Glennwood teaching team anchored their case study in open-ended guiding questions: "How is democracy 'of the people, by the people, and for the people?'" "How can I show my rights and responsibilities as a citizen of Glennwood?" "Why vote?" Guiding questions also narrowed the broad topic, in this case, civics, around a specific inquiry topic so that students had a purpose for the reading, thinking, talking, and writing they did in class. Students were eager to investigate.

Identify Long-Term Learning TARGETS That Illuminate Big Ideas

To scaffold students' efforts to answer the guiding questions, Glennwood teachers developed an itinerary for the learning landscape. The itinerary captured what they wanted students to take away from their learning in long-term learning targets written as student-friendly "I can" statements:

- I can describe how ancient Greece influenced our country's government and traditions.

- I can explain how and why American historical figures expanded the rights and freedoms of people today.

- I can write an opinion piece supported by evidence from my research including facts, definitions, and details.

- I can work with my group effectively to create a well-crafted public service announcement.

Then, teachers planned backward to identify the daily supporting learning targets—landmarks along the journey—where students could demonstrate proficiency in specific standards. The short-term targets (e.g., "I can name the three branches of government and describe their functions") kept students on track as they marked their progress toward the big ideas and long-term learning targets. Once the topic has been narrowed down to focus on standards-based learning targets, teachers identify compelling texts that will enhance students' reading skills and build their understanding of the topic.

Build Knowledge from Complex TEXTS

Text resources for case studies should go beyond textbooks, which sometimes take the grit and grapple out of the reading experience. Textbooks often have didactic bolded subtitles and vocabulary words. They are predigested for students, with definitions in the sidebars and questions at the end of the chapter. More authentic and complex informational text leaves the task of understanding the vocabulary and determining what's important to the reader. When a teacher gives such a text to students, and takes the time to parse the vocabulary and help students untangle the meaning, it sends the message that learning to read complex discipline-specific texts is so important that we are going to take the time to understand them together.

Scientists and historians are readers of journals, data, technical manuals, and primary sources. They read to learn about the big picture of their discipline—meta-studies, literature reviews, news articles. And they read to analyze print evidence—data in charts, tables, and graphs, as well as qualitative data in surveys, documents, and eyewitness accounts. Providing a real-world text for students gives them the kind of reading task that professionals in the fields of science and history do every day.

Third-graders at Clairemont Elementary, in the same district as Glennwood, studied the same standards in a case study called "Power to the People." To embrace the challenge of complex texts with these young readers, teachers taught close reading lessons on the *Brown v. Board of Education* court decision and created "expert folders" of articles, photos, video clips, and sound clips about the historical figures mentioned in their standards. Instruction with complex texts like these immersed students in the literature of the discipline and bolstered their expertise.

In a challenging case study, students don't just "read to read." They read to build background knowledge about their topics *and* to build their capacity as readers for the kind of reading they will do in college and beyond. As we've noted previously, many secondary content teachers are frustrated by their students' efforts to read and write effectively in their discipline. The antidote for this frustration requires a paradigm shift in which content-area teachers also become literacy teachers who focus specifically on the skills needed to read informational texts, including grappling with disciplinary vocabulary, analyzing data, and evaluating sources for reliability and credibility.

Toggle between broad coverage and deeper dives with primary sources

Many topics in social studies and science are so huge and have been studied at such depth that it's impossible for students to learn it all from their own reading without the teacher delivering some of the background in summary lectures. Toggling back and forth between strategic lectures that "cover" standards-based content and deeper dives that "uncover" historical or scientific big ideas through a compelling topic is a balanced way to prepare students for state tests as well as college and career expectations.

Claire Wolff often asks her ninth-grade students to analyze primary documents. When studying the pre–Civil War period, for example, students read a cartoon from 1856, a speech given by Frederick Douglass about the *Dred Scott* decision, the Emancipation Proclamation, and reward posters seeking fugitive slaves. These sorts of documents raise questions and build students' curiosity. Students recognize at once that these are real artifacts from another place and time, and they want to know about everything from the idioms to the images. They especially want to know the details about the people behind the posters. Still, once students are engaged, Wolff strategically builds their background knowledge by returning to the secondary sources, reviewing maps, and digesting summary articles and other resources to get an overview of the historical timeline, learn key vocabulary terms, enhance students' knowledge of relevant geography, and foreshadow major themes or concepts they will uncover in primary sources. She purposefully cycles back and forth between giving students opportunities to analyze primary source documents and helping them build the foundational narrative they need in order to understand these documents.

Digging deep into primary sources allows Wolff's students to construct their own telling of history

Based on this background knowledge, she invites students to construct their own meaning from the documents. "If we think of history as thousands of narrative interwoven strands, then what I'm doing is giving students some of the strands and the task of constructing the next one. From these documents, they can themselves begin to determine the causes of the Civil War." Historians use documents to make arguments about what happened in the past, notes Wolff. Although her students aren't doing original research on the Civil War era, the document-based questions they answer for this case study are an authentic historical task—one that involves answering open-ended questions with evidence from primary sources. By constructing meaning from primary documents, students demonstrate their understanding of change and causality during this key time period in American history.

The curricular and instructional move of toggling back and forth between covering content and uncovering concepts respects the reality of science and social studies teachers who are accountable to state requirements that students should be able to recount a myriad of facts and to explain the timeline of seminal concepts in science or key events and actors in history. We want students to succeed on these tests. Furthermore, the more knowledge students have, the more they are able to comprehend more complex texts on the same subject, adding pieces to the puzzle of an entire discipline. That's how deep understanding of big ideas happens. "Knowledge becomes a kind of entry ticket into the wider debate." (Trefil & O'Brien-Trefil, 2009, p. 32).

Furthermore, building knowledge, or surveying the field, is ongoing work for scholars, not just something that happens before students dive deep into a case study. Learning and remembering facts may be the lowest rung on Bloom's Taxonomy of thinking, but it's one that must be revisited often as students move recursively between remembering and understanding what they've learned already, applying that knowledge, analyzing and evaluating new information, and creating their own formulation based on deep synthesis. Punctuating a lecture with protocols to comprehend new information, compare and analyze perspectives, save information to memory, and assess learning will ratchet up the challenge, engagement, and empowerment of the traditional lecture format.

Curate text sets to scaffold independent thinking

Like a museum historian, Claire Wolff thinks of herself as a curator. To boost her students' literacy skills through historical content, she curates text sets that build students' knowledge of a topic and also engage them in the real work of historians—piecing together the puzzle of "What happened?" "What does it mean?" "Who cares?" and "Why?" When putting together a collection of texts, she is careful to balance text complexity to match the diverse levels of readiness among her students. Then she gradually releases primary sources and complex texts to students.

Her sets include photographs, posters, and cartoons as well as dense historical documents and letters written in archaic language. She also explicitly teaches students how to read closely, using a single common text for all students. Students collaborate in intentional groups, determined by the teacher, to read, discuss, and write about the common text. (See Appendix C for a primary source close reading guide.)

Once students have begun to see how the primary sources fit into the background narrative, she is able to release them more so that individuals and small groups become experts on different texts and use their reading as evidence for their own historical thinking—in discussion, writing, projects, and tests.

Choose texts that represent diverse perspectives

In curating texts, Wolff is evaluating her sources for credibility, bias, and validity as well as complexity. These are skills she wants students to acquire, so the first step is teaching them to analyze the evidence, perspective, and reasoning in the texts she has chosen. Doing so lifts up a big idea in the discipline of history: what's significant depends on the perspective and credibility of the source.

"If the goal is student independence in the historical process," she notes, "then students need to build foundational schema at the same time as they grapple with difficult documents presenting a variety of voices and perspectives." Eventually, students begin to curate their own texts in support, for example, of an independent research project. Now that they know the kinds of texts that historians consider worthy, they are much more likely to find and use similar texts on their own. See Wolff's students curate sets of primary source documents in the previously referenced video, "Prioritizing Evidence to Address a Document-Based Question."

In another two-part video, see fifth-graders at Polaris Charter Academy in Chicago examine primary sources on slavery written from multiple perspectives. Notice in particular how students grapple with the complexity of a nineteenth-century source, written from a historical context in which many people accepted and condoned slavery. This text challenges students to infer how the subtleties of language perniciously shape readers' assessment of slavery.

 WATCH
Video 16: Analyzing Perspectives through Primary Sources, Part 1
Video 17: Analyzing Perspectives through Primary Sources, Part 2

Engage Students with Worthy TASKS

Reading, thinking, talking, and writing about authentic texts is rigorous academic work. And it gets even more rigorous and interesting when students connect their book learning in the classroom to experiential learning outside the classroom. During their case studies on democracy, teachers from Glennwood and Clairemont invited their third-grade students to participate in the exchange of opinions that is democracy. Clairemont students wrote opinion letters to community members encouraging them to vote in the upcoming election, and they created public service announcements (PSAs) that aired on a local TV station. Glennwood students designed campaign posters and buttons for the historical figures they were studying and "picketed" the local square, sharing their learning about these important forebears with their community.

In subsequent years, when there was no presidential election to hook their study of democracy to, Clairemont third-grade teachers linked the study instead to a local school board election and a state governors' election. The processes of campaigning, voting, and making change enabled students to discover the same big idea: that individuals organize groups to make change in their communities. Third-graders interviewed school board members and legislators in their own community to find out what these elected officials do. Then they wrote PSAs promoting the qualities of great leaders to help voters evaluate candidates.

Although they couldn't vote themselves, students learned they have a stake in having qualified and diligent leaders in office. Their PSAs, which they presented to those who won these elections, say, "We are your constituents, and this is what we expect of you." By choosing a real-world task that engaged, challenged, and empowered students, these third-grade teachers made the mandated social studies topic purposeful and meaningful.[2]

In summary, a worthy task provides students with a concrete and engaging goal that helps them understand why they are learning the material, enables them to practice and polish real-world scientific and historical work, and is a culminating product that allows the teacher to assess students' mastery of skills and concepts. The task, married to an engaging topic, challenging texts, and standards-driven targets is where students demonstrate what they have learned and what they can do when they put their hearts and minds to work. In the Assessing Student Learning section of this chapter we explore how a well-chosen task is used to assess learning.

Doing School in the Real World

Like Claire Wolff's history students, Eric Beck's eighth-grade science students at Rimrock Expeditionary Alternative Learning Middle School (REALMS) begin with a big picture view, mapping the dynamic relationship among humans, flora, fauna, water, and the land in Oregon's Columbia River watershed. They read and discuss broad biology content extensively. Then Beck takes school into the field where students can learn from professionals and gather their own data.

Doing school in the real world is one way to help students see the purpose for their hard work

Photo: Jamie Schwaberow/Clarkson Creative

Often school schedules or district constraints on transportation and funding for off-campus trips make it very challenging to take students into the field. However, because the benefits of real-world investigations are so great, it is worth seeking resourceful and creative ways to overcome logistical challenges. Consider topics that can be studied through on-campus (or within walking distance) fieldwork (e.g., a science case study on disease-causing bacteria in the school, as we saw in Chapter 1's description of the Science Talk protocol; or an ethnographic study within the students' own neighborhoods as we saw in Kavitha Kasargod's classroom in Chapter 2).

Inviting experts from the community into the classroom to work with student scientists or historians (not just talking, but actually facilitating data collection or working with tools) is another way to sidestep off-campus work but reap some of the same benefits. Especially in courses like chemistry and physics, where data collection typically happens in the lab, an expert who can bump up the rigor of classroom investigations may be a strong choice.

Reach Out to Professionals

In Eric Beck's class, before engaging students in experiments or data collection, he expanded students' perspective from casual observers to apprentice scientists. Beck contacted local scientists whose daily work included measuring and analyzing river data. He knew that his students could learn to collect this same data with relatively inexpensive tools. Taking on the role of scientists, he reasoned, his students would also learn to record their experiments in a field notebook, analyze their data, and communicate them through charts, graphs, and visual representations that mirror the publications of professional scientists. These activities would invite students to see their own watershed through the eyes of scientists, deepening their understanding of what scientists do and also of the relationship among flora, fauna, water, and urban development in the changing riparian zone of their local stream: Tumalo Creek. The Strategy Close Up that follows describes how professional practices can guide students' fieldwork.

STRATEGY CLOSE UP: Using Professional Practices to Guide Fieldwork

When planning fieldwork, determining the specific methods, tools, and documentation practices that are used by professionals in the field will help guide decisions about expectations for students. Teachers can begin by researching generally, on the Internet, and specifically in their own community:

- How do professionals identify a problem or question?
- What sources, skills, and tools do they use to learn more about the topic or to investigate the question?
- How do they record and interpret data?

(continued)

- What do they do with their knowledge?
- What formats do they use to "publish" their results?
- Who do they present their findings to?
- What information or service is needed that students can help provide?

Beck contacted the Upper Deschutes Watershed Council and learned about their work with the Fish and Wildlife Service and the U.S. Forest Service restoring the banks of Tumalo Creek. Scientists from these organizations met Beck's students in the field and in the classroom to teach lessons on streambed mapping, geomorphology, riparian vegetation, water quality testing, and macroinvertebrates. Among other things, students learned how moving large boulders could change the course of erosion and how adding woody debris near stream banks could create habitat for fish.

Learning about and comparing the many variables of stream health developed students' background knowledge enough that they could begin to ask *their own* questions by looking at relationships between variables. Would colder water be better for the fish? How does development influence run off and erosion? Priming students' curiosity in this way engages them for the next step: looking for answers.

Conduct Fieldwork

When teachers can take their students off campus to do authentic fieldwork, the possibilities abound for acquiring the tools of the discipline and applying their learning through authentic tasks. Beck recognized that for students to become aquaculture scientists, they needed to go beyond the standard linear scientific method often presented in textbook labs. Real inquiry is a messier but still systematic problem-solving process that often includes dead ends, reformulating questions, improving experimental design, and drawing conclusions that contradict the original hypothesis. Beck's student-scientists began by formulating their own testable scientific questions. One student, Lukas, came up with this question: "Does the macroinvertebrate community, dissolved oxygen, and water temperature indicate poorer water quality in Tumalo Creek below the Tumalo Irrigation District (TID) diversion compared to Tumalo Creek upstream of the TID diversion?" We'll see the result of Lukas's inquiry in the pages that follow.

Then students ventured out to the creek itself to look for answers. Beck's students returned to their study site again and again to practice scientific protocols for counting macroinvertebrates, testing water quality, and monitoring changes in the stream bank and streamside vegetation. Fieldwork like this, that takes place over an extended period of time, can be particularly powerful, as students become experts. Through fieldwork (as opposed to a field trip) students are actively engaged *as researchers* in gathering information or data that they will use back in the classroom to produce high-quality work. Plus, the more students know about the issues, the more they invest in them.

> The time spent in the field collecting real data, answering real questions, replanting native species, and making a real difference locally in these restoration projects inspires students to care more deeply for these places.
>
> —*Eric Beck, teacher, Rimrock Expeditionary Alternative Learning Middle School*

Students' hands-on experience motivates them to embrace the challenge of doing real science, which isn't as clear-cut as a cookbook lab. Lukas, for example, demonstrates sophisticated scientific thinking when he says, "At first my question was too complicated. I had to narrow my question down and revise it several times before I could start. I had to select my variables so that I could really tell what was happening." To get an accurate picture of the complex interrelationships in the river, Lukas had to get smarter and more precise in order to produce valid results. Realizing that the initial design of his research methodology would yield questionable results taught him one of the most important concepts of science: that good science must be reliable and reproducible.

Deeper instruction often means letting students confront not knowing. Challenge emerges when students try to design experiments that isolate one variable, conduct tests that don't go as planned, puzzle over data that doesn't make sense, or use their data to convince stakeholders to take an unpopular action. Lukas was surprised to find that the water quality above and below a dam that diverted Tumalo Creek was not that different. "I expected the warmer water below the diversion to have less dissolved oxygen that macroinvertebrates need to thrive. So then I had to figure out why the water wasn't actually as warm as I predicted."

Meaningful academic and scientific work emerges as a result of grappling with real problems. Lukas soon realized that because the air temperature had been especially cool during the period when they were measuring water quality, the water temperature was also colder than usual, so macroinvertebrates were thriving. "But in the summer," he hypothesized, "more water is diverted *and* the air temperature is warmer, so probably the water quality differential above and below the diversion will be greater. The macroinvertebrates will get less oxygen below the dam and there will be fewer of them."

Make the Most of Museums

For science teachers, the natural world is the obvious choice for fieldwork, but for teachers in urban schools and social studies teachers everywhere, museums and other cultural and historical sites offer equally powerful opportunities for fieldwork. When Claire Wolff's students at MELS prepared to write their textbooks, they began by learning the history of the Rosetta Stone, which was an essential key to understanding ancient Egyptian hieroglyphics. They were asked to think critically about the contemporary controversy over whether or not the British Museum should return the Rosetta Stone to Egypt, where it was discovered in 1799, again raising questions about how we record history, and who "owns" history as societies change over time. Along the way, students addressed history content standards on ancient civilizations and the role of rivers and agriculture in their development. They became experts on one of the four ancient river-valley civilizations and conducted secondary source research on that civilization, focusing on the eight key characteristics that all civilizations share. Through this facet of their task, they met state standards specific to river-valley civilizations.

Next they journeyed to a local museum, New York's Metropolitan Museum of Art, where they examined primary source artifacts from their expert civilization. Students had first-hand contact with artifacts that they analyzed and interpreted apart from other historians' interpretation. And in preparation for writing their own textbook interpretation of the artifacts, they grappled with the big idea of continuity and change so that they could trace the roots of humanity from Paleolithic tribes to complex civilizations able to produce an object as technologically sophisticated and linguistically advanced as the Rosetta Stone.

In planning and conducting this case study, Wolff made a couple of important high-leverage moves. First, she built a scaffold for the museum fieldwork with clear expectations and protocols, and a note-catcher that enabled students to document their examination of artifacts with accuracy and detail. This ensured that all students returned from the fieldwork with something in hand that complemented their background knowledge from research and secondary sources, a Rosetta Stone of their own to help them translate their fieldwork experience into a high quality product.

NOTE-CATCHER: Museum and Exhibit Fieldwork
NOTES

Museum:

Expert Civilization (Exhibit):

Learning Target: I can analyze museum artifacts in order to draw historical conclusions about my expert river-valley civilization.

Today you will be gathering primary source information for your final project: a textbook chapter about your expert ancient civilization. Which **five key characteristics** of your expert civilization are you focusing on for your final project (textbook chapter)?

- ❏ religion
- ❏ writing system
- ❏ government
- ❏ social hierarchy
- ❏ cities
- ❏ art/architecture
- ❏ specialized labor
- ❏ public works/technology

Examining Ancient Artifacts

Artifact Title:	
Date:	Country of Origin:
Description:	Sketch:
This artifact connects to: Religion Art/Architecture Writing Government Social hierarchy Specialized labor Cities Public works	What can you learn about your expert civilization from this artifact?

Second, Wolff explicitly connected their case study work to the big picture disciplinary concept of how civilizations are defined and characterized generally. For students who will go on to study other time periods and culture (and to experience civilization as citizens, travelers, students, and perhaps historians) this understanding was the big take away.

Assessing Student Learning

Tests and other short-format on-demand assessments are a useful tool for assessing students' knowledge of key content in science and history. Traditional assessments, such as tests and quizzes, will help teachers know whether students have met required standards and are prepared for standardized tests in the subject area. Unfortunately, the facts students memorize for tests may not last long for students once the semester is over. To promote deeper understanding, it is valuable to include additional assessments that require students to transfer their knowledge of standards to real settings. Students can use their fieldwork data (or data collected by others in the field) to teach others key concepts in the discipline or to present their findings in a real-world format for an audience beyond their own teachers and parents.

Real World Tasks

For assessment purposes, it's important that the task students do measures whether they are meeting the long-term learning targets set forth at the beginning of the unit, including skills, literacy, and concepts. And, in order to engage and empower students to see their own work as purposeful and valuable beyond the classroom, the performance task should be parallel to one that scientists and social scientists in the real world perform.

MELS students, for example, shared their textbook with sixth-grade students in their own school whose world history curriculum spirals through the same content. In the course of their study, the students had critically analyzed the problems that all textbook writers confront—the tendency to overgeneralize when distilling multiple secondary sources and the need to define and describe concisely. After their museum visits, they had to face these challenges for themselves. Their format had the same criteria that professional writers have: bolded vocabulary terms with definitions, insets with contemporary connections, photographs of artifacts with captions, and critical thinking questions at the end.

And they had a real audience to consider whose understanding and reading level affected word choice, organization, and the selection of content. Because students had carefully examined models of professional textbooks, their own chapters were based on a deep study of the topic through multiple layers of source material. Students took the time to draft, get feedback, and revise their chapters multiple times. See Figure 3.1 for a sample textbook page.

Figure 3.1 Sample Textbook Page

WRITING:

In Ancient Mesopotamia, the first written language was created. This language was called Cuneiform. It consisted of wedge-shaped images, making the language a pictoral language. It first emerged in Sumer in the late 4th Millenium BC, and was only used by high class officials and scribes. You would not see a peasant writing out this language. As you can see from the image towards the bottom left of this page, very detailed marks were all put together to document a simple event. This is why later in history, Cuneiform evolved into a language that was not pictoral, because it took so long to write a simple message. Cuneiform was most commonly written on clay tablets, and sometimes on other materials. It was written into this clay tablets by using a blunt reed for a writing utensil. Towards the beginning Bronze age, the number of characters were 1000 and decreased down to 400 in the end of the Bronze Age. Cuneiform was first successfully deciphered in 1857, but no country actually holds it as their native language. Since Cuneiform was later replaced by alphabetic writing throughout the Roman Era, it had to be deciphered from scratch.

This shows how the character for head progressed through out the years Cuneiform developed.

Metropolitan Museum of Art

This tablet depicts an overview of the stock of barley a person or place had at that period of time. The cuneiform pictoral marks show a human, and multiple hunting animals, and an animal that is being hunted.

FUN FACT:

Between 1.5 million and 2 million Cuneiform tablets have been excavated in modern times, but only 100,000 have actually been published!

Changing the way that textbooks are organized, designed, and written can help to make future students interested in world history.

Ana, student, Metropolitan Expeditionary Learning School

The eighth-graders in Eric Beck's science class also engaged in a task that assessed their learning and mirrored the work that real scientists do. They formulated their own research question, conducted experiments, and then wrote up their field research in the format of a scholarly scientific paper.

Excerpts from Lukas's final report, shown in Figure 3.2, demonstrate that he has met the Common Core writing standard WHST.9–10.2: "Write informative/explanatory texts, including the narration of historical events, scientific procedures/experiments, or technical processes" with the organization, domain-specific vocabulary, formal style, and objective tone appropriate to a scientific paper. The report also demonstrates that he has mastered a disciplinary writing format for communicating ideas to the scientific community.

Because "research to build and present knowledge" is a new and important addition to most state standards, and important to colleges and many employers, we spend a little more time here outlining key instructional choices teachers can make to ensure that students develop the evidence-based writing skills they will need to pursue further study and work in many disciplines.

Conducting Secondary Research

High-quality research papers like Lukas's are not chance outcomes. Deeper instruction prioritizes not just what scientists and social scientists study, but also how they investigate and communicate their ideas. Previously, we've discussed how students conduct research in the field, but researching and writing up their secondary research—for either analytical or argumentative writing—is also an important and rigorous task to culminate a case study and assess learning. Secondary research—online, through print sources, or working with data— requires that students be critical consumers of information, able to identify significant sources or variables, evaluate credibility and validity, and dig deep for confirmation from multiple sources.

Figure 3.2 Excerpts from Lukas's Final Report

Question: Does the macro-invertebrate community, dissolved oxygen and water temperature indicate poorer water quality, in Tumalo creek below the Tumalo Irrigation District (TID) diversion compared to Tumalo creek up stream of the TID diversion?

Data That Will be used in Answering Question: Water temperature, dissolved oxygen and macro-invertebrate data from collection sites located upstream and downstream of the TID diversion.

Hypothesis 1: I think that water temperature will be higher and dissolved oxygen will be lower in Tumalo creek below the TID diversion than up stream the TID diversion at Shevlin Park because of lower stream flow downstream the diversion during the summer months.

Hypothesis 2: I think the macro-invertebrate abundance and diversity is less in Tumalo creek below the TID diversion than up stream of the diversion at Shevlin Park because of lower stream flow downstream of the diversion during the summer months.

Variables:

The Independent Variable: The diversion and the fact that the water flows are being manipulated by TID.

The Dependent Variables: Water temperature, dissolved oxygen along with macroinvertebrate abundance and species richness or diversity.

Background Information

Macro-invertebrates – stoneflies, mayflies and other aquatic bugs that live in the creek can tell us a lot about the health of Tumalo creek because they are sensitive to changes in water temperature, dissolved oxygen levels, turbidity and other water quality and stream habitat conditions. The macro-invertebrate community also cannot easily escape changes in water quality. Macro-invertebrates live in the aquatic ecosystem for a little over a year and either all or part of their lives depend on being in the water so their survival is directly correlated to water quality. Different types of macro-invertebrates can be classified by their different tolerance levels to poor water quality/pollution. There are three different stress level categories: intolerant, somewhat intolerant and tolerant. If one finds a high number of intolerant macro-invertebrates it means the stream is healthy. A high number of somewhat intolerant macro-invertebrates indicates the stream is somewhat unhealthy. The presence of macro-invertebrates that are tolerant of poor water quality, along with a lack of intolerant macro-invertebrates indicates an unhealthy stream.

Much like a sentinel species or a canary in a coal mine, the macro-invertebrates in Tumalo creek can be used as biological indicators to track long-term restoration effectiveness and as indicator of stream health (e.i. water quality). They also play a

Figure 3.2   Continued

Sample site located just below TID diversion:
The macro-invertebrate sample at the site below the TID diversion consisted of a total of 237 individuals. Two hundred and thirty four of those collected at this site are classified as sensitive to poor water quality. Two of the macro-invertebrates collected are classified as somewhat sensitive to poor water quality and two of the macro-invertebrates are classified as tolerant of poor water. (Figure 5).

Below the TID division we found 3 caddisflies, 100 mayflies and 130 stoneflies in the sensitive to poor water quality group. We also found 2 crane flies in the some what sensitive to poor water quality category. We found one aquatic worm and one midge in the macro-invertebrate group that is tolerant to poor water quality, which gives us a grand total of 237 macro-invertebrates.

The percent EPT below the TID diversion is 98.31%.

Discussion

I stated in my first hypothesis that I thought that water temperature would be higher in Tumalo creek below the TID diversion than up stream of the TID diversion at Shevlin Park because of the lower stream flow downstream of the diversion during the summer months. I went to the Oregon Water Resources Department website and check the flow information for October 7th and October 8th which were the days we took our samples. The flow information on the website showed between 20 and 30 cubic feet per second more water in the stream above the TID diversion than in the reach of stream below the TID diversion, where water was diverted from the stream into the irrigation canal

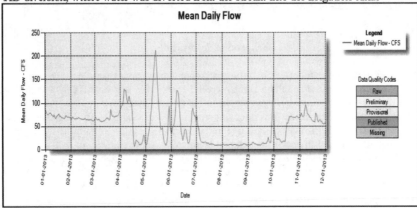

Figure 1.   : Oregon Water Resources Department Near Real Time Hydrographic Data for Tumalo Creek just below Tumalo Irrigation District Irrigation Diversion. (January 1, 2013 through December 1, 2013.)

An **analytical research paper** offers a fresh, critical evaluation or interpretation of the topic, based on analysis of primary and secondary sources. The analysis presents a new perspective, rather than defending a position. Example: An analysis of the rhetorical style of Lincoln's speeches.

An **argumentative research paper** takes a stand on a debatable or controversial question to persuade readers with strong evidence from primary and secondary sources. Example: An argument that the government should fund large-scale cricket farms, based on research comparing the nutritional and ecological benefits of eating insects versus traditional livestock.

Teaching students how to conduct secondary research begins by teaching them to search for accurate, valid, and reliable answers. Students need to know which databases and browsers are most likely to yield information that is more specific than a random Google search, and that there is a world of information beyond Wikipedia. Then they need to know how to narrow their search terms to efficiently find information on a particular topic. When content-area teachers, language arts teachers, and media specialists collaborate on lessons focused on these discrete skills, they help students connect the skills of research to the content of their learning.

Writing with Evidence

Research papers or presentations stretch students' reading and writing skills and demonstrate their ability to synthesize, use evidence, and ground their ideas in precedents from the literature. These are certainly capacities that professional scientists and historians rely on daily.

Writing a research paper or presentation about a scientific or historical topic requires students to explain concepts accurately and realistically through graphic representations, charts, graphs, illustrations, and numerical data as well as prose. This multidimensional thinking is the kind of challenge promoted by deeper instruction. In this chapter, we've shown many examples of writing with evidence. For a fuller treatment of the lessons behind this practice, see Chapter 2.

The accompanying two-part video shows students from King Middle School in Portland, Maine, engaged in a series of writing lessons that build to their creation of a high-quality final product. Students gather sources, evaluate reasoning and arguments, and marshal their evidence. As the video shows, students spend a week reading, talking, thinking, and writing briefly about a topic before they are ready to make their final product. This kind of intellectual dialogue and critical thinking mirrors what scientists and social scientists do in the laboratory, at conferences, and through the peer review process.

WATCH
Video 18: Scaffolding Research-Based Claims with Sixth-Graders, Part 1: Making Research-Based Claims
Video 19: Scaffolding Research-Based Claims with Sixth-Graders, Part 2: Staying on Track and on Target

---

Creating Products for Real Audiences

A product designed with a real audience in mind is especially empowering to students (see Table 3.1). There is nothing like seeing your audience face to face to motivate high-quality work and affirm that what we learn in school matters in the real world. Although short tasks or early drafts of work may reveal thoughtful and rigorous understanding of a topic, long-term projects that are revised or rehearsed multiple times also demonstrate the kind of perseverance that scientists and social scientists must have to make real breakthroughs on sticky questions.

Table 3.1   Science and History Products for Real Audiences

Challenge students to learn complex concepts and transferable skills	
High-quality products demonstrate a deep understanding of big ideas in the discipline	Examples:
	Informational brochures for a public health fair that require deep understanding of disease pathology, causes, and prevention
High-quality products exemplify craftsmanship, complexity, and authenticity resulting from critique and revision	Interpretive signs for public nature area that explain different ecosystems visitors will see
Engage students in using professional skills and serving real stakeholders	
Creation of the product requires students to use the tools of the discipline	Examples:
	Field guides, formal debates, maps, models, proposals or presentations of data collected through surveys or field studies
Creation of the product provides an opportunity for authentic service	Testing homes for radon (or neighborhood soils) and sharing the results with residents
	Creating stimulating "toys" for rescued animals based on the behaviors they need to successfully return to the wild after rehabilitation

Empower students to apply their own learning to inform or persuade an authentic audience	
The product requires students to become experts, explain their thinking and support their claims with evidence	Examples:
	An annotated map of the local watershed presented to a conservation group involved in land-use decisions
Students present their product to an audience beyond the teacher who needs the information or can serve as peer reviewers by asking questions	A campus energy or water use audit presented to the school board
Students can name what and how they learned by creating the product; these are concepts and skills they can use again in the future	Oral histories of community leaders presented to a local historical society

The ultimate reward for students is to have their work judged on its disciplinary merits—both its conformity to standard formats of a particular discipline and its innovation or confirmation of important ideas. Beck's students, for example, have contributed years of stream monitoring data to a regional database maintained by the Upper Deschutes Watershed Council. Several students have also participated in the Healthy Waters Institute student mentoring projects, in which students teach other students. Lukas presented his Tumalo Creek research alongside his teacher at a professional conference on stream restoration ecology. Through such experiences, students learn to defend their own ideas, and to do so with evidence. They become experts whose own data, conclusions, and findings contribute to professional and community debate. "At the conference," said Lukas, "I had to answer a bunch of questions, but I learned that when you go out and collect data and do really good work, it doesn't just benefit your own learning. You benefit the learning of your whole community."

Serving Communities

Sometimes the most meaningful task is one that allows students to provide a tangible service to their own community. In addition to conducting their own research projects on Tumalo Creek, Eric Beck's eighth-graders invest their time and energy in an ongoing stream bank restoration project overseen by the forest service. In 2014, students engaged in meaningful service learning by creating a public service announcement called *Our Rivers, Our Future, Your Choice* that debuted at the Telluride Mountain Film Festival.[3] "Our philosophy," says REALMS school director

Roger White, is that if students get their hands dirty and learn the science of their place, and also just spend time reflecting on it from their own dream spot on the riverbank, then their appreciation and intellectual understanding will generate a sense of stewardship. They will become life-long stewards of water wherever they live."

Students' reflection on the importance of taking care of their watershed and making a contribution to their own community empowers them to carry their learning forward into new places and new interests. This kind of reflection is facilitated by teachers who pause—strategically and intentionally—to mark that moment at the end of a project when "aha" echoes through the room.

The In Practice section that follows will hone in on the thinking and process skills behind the "aha" moments in science and history.

IN PRACTICE

Developing Scientific and Historical Ways of Thinking

Many educators would agree that all too often students accept as truth whatever their teacher, parents, or the Internet says. People often ally themselves uncritically with a statement or position based on politics, religion, or another affinity, regardless of the evidence behind that position. This tendency is what we might call *everyday thinking. Scientific thinking*—critical thinking—on the other hand, is quite different. First and foremost, it is thinking that weighs empirical evidence as the standard for truth.

Nobel laureate Carl Wieman, the former associate director for science in the White House Office of Science and Technology, has said, "The most valuable metric for evaluating effective teaching should be creating patterns of scientific thinking" (2012). But how do teachers who want to deepen their instruction create patterns of scientific thinking?

Building on the case study approach described previously, we encourage teachers to hone in on the particular problem-solving approaches and tools that are described in the "process standards" for science and social studies. These standards focus on the practices and ways of thinking that are particular to scientists and historians—the enduring skills students at all grade levels cultivate and carry forward through their education. The Science Process Skills (see box) include practices like classifying information, interpreting data, and creating models to explain or predict phenomena. In social studies, they include History's Habits of Mind (see second box). Giving students the opportunity to practice the process skills in order to uncover big ideas in the discipline prepares them to grapple with new questions in a changing social and natural world long after the "content" of a particular course is forgotten.

Science Process Skills Supported by Inquiry-Based Instruction[4]

The National Research Council notes that scientific inquiry involves asking questions, prioritizing evidence, formulating explanations from evidence, connecting explanations to prior scientific knowledge, and communicating explanations with justification. The science process skills that follow underpin inquiry and exemplify scientific thinking and investigating. When these skills become habits of mind, students view and interact with the world as scientific thinkers.

- **Classifying:** arranging or distributing objects, events, or information representing objects or events in classes according to some method or system
- **Communicating:** giving oral and written explanations or graphic representations of observations
- **Comparing and contrasting:** identifying similarities and differences between or among objects, events, data, systems, and so on
- **Creating models:** displaying information, using multisensory representations
- **Gathering and organizing data:** collecting information about objects and events that illustrate a specific situation
- **Generalizing:** drawing general conclusions from particulars
- **Identifying variables:** recognizing the characteristics of objects or factors in events that are constant or change under different conditions
- **Inferring:** drawing a conclusion based on prior experiences
- **Interpreting data:** analyzing data that have been obtained and organized by determining apparent patterns or relationships in the data
- **Making decisions:** identifying alternatives and choosing a course of action from among the alternatives after basing the judgment for the selection on justifiable reasons
- **Manipulating materials:** handling or treating materials and equipment safely, skillfully, and effectively
- **Measuring:** making quantitative observations by comparing to a conventional or nonconventional standard
- **Observing:** becoming aware of an object or event by using any of the senses (or extensions of the senses) to identify properties
- **Predicting:** making a forecast of future events or conditions expected to exist

History's Habits of Mind[5]

The National Council for History Education (NCHE) believes that historical thinking develops a unique capacity to comprehend human situations, challenges, and interactions. Thinking historically introduces students to the wonders of the past and fosters the ability to make judgments about the present. History's Habits of Mind articulates this distinctive approach, one that leads towards engaging with and understanding the contemporary world and serves as a foundation for lifelong, productive learning and active citizenship.

History's Habits of Mind empower and enable individuals to:

- Grasp the significance of the past in shaping the present
- Perceive past events and issues as they might have been experienced by the people of the time, with historical empathy rather than present-mindedness
- Read critically, to discern differences between evidence and assertion and to frame useful and appropriate questions about the past
- Interrogate texts and artifacts, posing questions about the past that foster informed discussion, reasoned debate, and evidence-based interpretation
- Recognize that history is an evolving narrative constructed from available sources, cogent inferences, and changing interpretations
- Appreciate the diversity of cultures and variety of historical contexts and distinguish elements of our shared humanity
- Understand the impact made by individuals, groups, and institutions at local, national, and global levels both in effecting change and in ensuring continuity
- Realize that all individuals are decision makers, but that personal and public choices are often restricted by time, place, and circumstance
- Negotiate a complex, often uncertain and ambiguous world, equipped with the appreciation for multiple perspectives
- Engage in patient reflection and constant reexamination of the past and present

In this section, we lift up six specific ways of thinking common to both science and social studies:

- Asking questions

- Conducting research (experimenting and investigating)

- Analyzing data (looking for trends and patterns)

- Designing, critiquing, and revising

- Communicating through models and simulations

- Generalizing and drawing conclusions

Each way of thinking is described and then followed by a list of key instructional moves. By focusing on these disciplinary ways of thinking teachers can create lessons that jumpstart a continuum of learning from the classroom, into the community, into the next grade level, and eventually into college and careers.

Asking Questions

A transformative shift in classroom instruction happens when teachers switch from writing lesson plans that "deliver content" to writing lesson plans that pose real questions. Lessons that begin with open-ended strategic questions—broad questions to which the enduring understandings of a discipline adhere—create a culture of inquiry that invites students to be resourceful, curious, critical, and creative. Asking questions, and teaching students to ask purposeful questions, also encourages students to engage in a scholarly dialogue that mirrors how scientists and social scientists collaborate and communicate by sharing evidence in support of their answers.

Stitching the classroom conversation together with questions gives students permission to "not know" the answer immediately, and also to seek answers that make sense in the context of a larger understanding. Microbiologist Martin Schwartz's beguiling article, "The Importance of Stupidity in Scientific Research," underscores the point that to be a good scientist, one must get comfortable with *not* knowing. The difference between traditional K–12 science classrooms and graduate programs, he suggests, is that in our schooling we are rewarded for always knowing the answers, but in graduate school, we are expected to do original research on questions that *nobody* knows the answers to. This shift is disconcerting to many promising scientists. Yet, Schwartz argues, real science requires exactly this kind of "ignorance by choice." "One of the beautiful things about science is that it allows us to bumble along, getting it wrong time after time, and feel perfectly fine as long as we learn something each time . . . The more comfortable we become with being stupid," he says, "the deeper we will wade into the unknown and the more likely we are to make big discoveries" (Schwartz, 2008).

Science education is about guiding students and asking interesting questions... Professional scientists go ask questions that the world needs them to answer.

—Megan Hall, teacher, Open World Learning Community School

Three types of questions can anchor science and history curriculum and instruction. **Guiding questions** frame a whole unit of learning and students' final products demonstrate an answer to the question posed at the beginning. For example, the guiding question *What do European explorers in the New World, astrophysicists, and sixth-graders have in common?* frames an inquiry into the "unknown" connections between Columbus's exploration of the Americas, teens' exploration of puberty, and the out-of-this-world technology of space exploration. The original riddle sparks both curiosity and strategic thinking. It points students in a direction that encourages them to discover for themselves the motivation of explorers through the ages.

Strategic questions support students to grapple within individual lessons or writing tasks. Instead of showing students the answer, the teacher (or a student facilitator) poses a question that focuses students' reading, thinking, talking, and writing in ways that are likely to yield an interesting and evidence-based answer. For example, the question, *Why did fifteenth century explorers sail to the Americas?* could be the prompt for an essay or an engaging turn-and-talk opportunity to launch a lesson with discussion and wonder.

Text-dependent questions, prepared in advance and related to a specific reading lesson, are questions that require students to be evidence-based thinkers because they must answer with evidence from the text. In a science or social studies class, the "evidence" students are using to support their answers may also be laboratory results, observations, or notes gathered during a museum tour. For example, the question, *In Columbus's journal entry, why did he say he was sailing West?* asks students to be close readers, providing the text's answer to the question—which may be one of several answers that students will need to analyze, compare, and evaluate.

Finally, students **formulate their own questions** and seek answers through debate, experimentation, and investigation. Deeper instruction fosters and celebrates the spirit of wonder. Discovery-based lesson structures, like the Five Es, described in Chapter 1, are one way to encourage students to ask questions and chase down answers. The Question Formulation Technique, discussed in Chapter 1, is also a useful tool.

In Action: Strategic Questioning

EL Education's secondary social studies module *From Revolution to Democracy: The Complex Fight for Freedom* structures instruction around a Socratic Seminar that prepares students to write their own evidence-based opinion editorials. Before the seminar, students analyze primary and secondary sources from the different perspectives of people who experienced Shays' Rebellion—an armed rebellion against the Massachusetts government by Massachusetts' farmers in 1786 that was a primary catalyst for the creation of the U.S. Constitution. Then, during the seminar, the teacher nudges students into deeper intellectual waters through strategic questions:

- How well were the ideas expressed in the Declaration of Independence upheld during the Critical Period (1781–1787)?

- What political, economic, and social factors contributed to instability during the Critical Period?

- What were the lessons learned during the Post-Revolutionary Period

Students respond to these big questions with answers backed up by evidence from their reading. Articulating their positions and marshaling evidence to support them prepares them to make persuasive arguments in writing following the seminar.

Key instructional moves for teaching questioning

- Frame a case study with guiding questions

- Give students opportunities to grapple with complex, strategic questions

- Insist that students support their answers with evidence in writing and discussion

- Prepare text-dependent questions in advance to support literacy instruction

- Teach students how to formulate and narrow testable questions

- Record and reinforce (don't answer) students' own questions; celebrate wonder!

Analyzing Data: Looking for Patterns and Trends

Scientific thinkers look for both qualitative and numerical patterns and trends. Scientists pore over their data to look for reproducible results (repetition) or anomalies that indicate a new variable is impacting the results. Social scientists look for patterns and trends in cultures, change over time, or populations. Scientists measure everything from the size of molecules to the number of invertebrates in a stream to the distance between stars. Social scientists collect numerical data on voting behavior, the incidence of poverty and wealth, mortality rates, migration patterns, and so on. Analyzing data they collect themselves or data collected by professional scientists and historians invites students to grapple with the meaning behind the numbers.

In Action: Looking for Patterns and Trends

The discovery of "discrepant events" in data can present a particularly intriguing mystery for students. Megan Hall's seventh-graders at Open World Learning Community School (OWL) in Minnesota recently took on the question, *What makes a community thrive or suffer?* In Hall's class, students explored this question by partnering with the National Park Service to conduct a case study of keystone species along and in the Mississippi River. Students inventoried species in the water, yielding some surprising data. "What scientists do," says Hall, "is make sense of data that isn't immediately logical." Her students expected the Mississippi to be a polluted, unhealthy environment because it runs right through a big city. In fact, she says, "They found evidence of river otters. That opened up a conversation about the history of the river and what developments and variables affected the river either adversely or beneficially."

By designing her lessons so that students can count, describe, or measure real things in their own environment, Hall ensures that students have to "deal with the data." Next year OWL will move to a new campus, and Hall has already noticed that the "empty" field on their campus will be a good place for students to plant milkweed and build a Monarch way station. Her students will act as citizen scientists with Monarch Watch, a group that inventories monarch habitat. Students will keep track of how many monarchs visit their way station and document monarchs and other native species with illustrations they create in language arts and art class, as well as science.

Key instructional moves for teaching students to analyze data

- Provide authentic data sets as "texts"

- Challenge students to interpret data and to recognize when data are valid, reliable and significant and when they are not

- Analyze the limitations of data

- Use authentic data in mathematics lessons that address statistics and probability

- Use graphic organizers to capture patterns and trends

- Call attention to discrepant data and outliers

- Encourage students to ask new questions based on data

- Partner with organizations that encourage data collection by citizen scientists

- Team with a mathematics teacher to catalogue, calculate, organize, and present data provided by the content area topic

Conducting Original Research: Experimenting and Investigating

In the 1993 film *And the Band Played On*, which depicts the Center for Disease Control's search for a vaccine to prevent HIV, the lead scientist begins by asking his team "What do we know? What do we think? And what can we prove?" Student scientists and historians engaged in a case study that involves original research begin by asking these same questions. These three questions allow scientific thinkers to triangulate among multiple sources and design a specific research methodology that will yield accurate and reliable results. That methodology answers further questions: *What data do I need to collect? How will I collect these data? How will I organize my data? How will I make meaning from it?* Deeper instruction challenges students to respond to these questions with a clear, specific experimental or research plan that they can manage productively in the field.

In Action: Conducting Research

At the Springfield Renaissance School in Springfield, Massachusetts, the ninth graders wondered just how much energy their schools were costing the city. To find out, they conducted an energy audit of the city's aging school buildings. "At first they just went out to local schools with blank paper thinking they would determine how much energy the schools were using," says teacher Aurora Kushner.

That approach didn't yield very accurate or analyzable data, however. If they were going to propose energy saving measures to the city, they realized, they would need to show how certain features of the schools used more energy than others. Under the guidance of City facilities manager Joe Forest and other experts, they created a data collection tool for energy use and loss from windows, lights, major appliances and heating systems. It still wasn't enough. Students had to make phone calls to compare their data with ideal usage figures from energy companies, window manufacturers, and HVAC contractors.

Forest "provided some contacts, but he also told students that they were basically like his assistants. This is what he would task an employee to do," said Kushner. "Sometimes they found out they took the wrong data in the field or didn't collect enough, so they had to go back and do it over. There was a lot of authentic, real-world learning. I remember my room being a-buzz with activity and collaboration during that project. Kids were at the helm and I was just a facilitator and connector."

With their evidence in hand, students learned how to calculate costs and benefits of different types of energy use. Eventually, they collaboratively published a polished, fifty-page report that demonstrates their knowledge of energy conservation and makes evidence-based recommendations to the city for cost and energy savings. The mayor of Springfield and Forest received the report with appreciation and respect, saying, "These students are now a part of the solution . . . The city needs a fresh set of eyes and minds to help us move forward . . . It is a win-win for the school and the city." Based on the students' report, the city dedicated $150,000 for energy renovations to schools, and within two years their efforts saved the city over $160,000 in energy costs. The city subsequently set aside $250,000 for energy retrofits of additional city buildings and asked students at the school to once again serve as "professional" energy auditors.[6]

Key instructional moves for teaching students to do original research

- Identify research that really needs to be done, and that connects to required academic standards

- Involve students in designing a research plan; allocate time for reassessment

- Invite professional researchers and scientists to lead students

- Establish teams of students with clear roles, responsibilities, and account-ability

- Evaluate research procedures for validity and reliability

- Create consistent expectations for research notebooks and templates for recording data

- Use professional formats for reporting research

- Identify authentic audiences who are interested in student research findings

Designing, Critiquing, and Revising

Closely related to conducting research is the skill of designing or engineering a solution to a problem one has investigated. The design process, familiar to engineers and popularized by many STEM (science, technology, engineering, and mathematics) initiatives, allows students to integrate science, mathematics, technology, engineering and even art concepts and to apply them to real-world problems (see Figure 3.3). The design process invites students not only to be innovators, but also to persevere through failed designs by continually critiquing and revising their plans and prototypes until the design works. Deeper instruction encourages students to take risks and learn from their mistakes.

Figure 3.3 Engineering Design Process

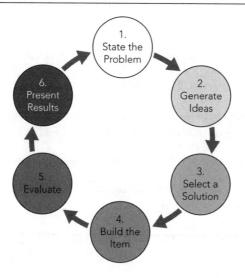

In Action: Designing, Critiquing and Revising in Action

When teachers go beyond STEM *coursework* to create inquiry-based opportunities for students to actually design and build something, students are motivated to become engineers. In Peter Hill's science classroom at King Middle School in Portland, Maine, students studying the discrepant access to electricity in the developing world relative to the industrialized world were challenged to "create a device that captures natural energy and transforms it into something that's useful in some part of the world."[7] Trying to wrap their brains around such an ambitious task, students were anxious but intrigued. Student Liva Pierce's first reaction was, "I can't do that. I don't know the first thing about electricity."

Her teachers were undaunted. They provided multiple opportunities to build robots and turbines, and guided students through a deep investigation of how wind turbines manifest the science of motors, magnets, and wires. Students designed, tested, and improved working models of wind turbines. In competition with each other to see whose design could produce the most electricity, students were determined, creative, and eager to apply the science of energy. Then, they were ready for the final challenge, creating a technical drawing for their own energy gadget. Liva Pierce successfully created a crank flashlight to attract disease-carrying insects away from people in a tropical country. More important than the particular concepts she applied in her drawing, Pierce says, she got a new understanding of science as a way of thinking. She discovered that she was as good at science as she is at reading and writing. "It's not just something in a book," she says. "Science is doing. Science is building. Science is creating."

Key instructional moves for teaching the design process:

- Establish a culture of growth in which "success is sweet, but mistakes are good food"

- Identify real problems in your community that need fixing

- Establish teams with clear roles, responsibilities, and accountability

- Provide adequate resources, scaffolding, structure and freedom for students to succeed at invention and building

- Follow and track students' progress through the steps of the design process

- Teach critique workshops and peer feedback protocols (for a fuller explanation of these practices, see Chapter 2)

- Involve stakeholders in giving feedback to students

Communicating with Models and Simulations

A hallmark of scientific and historical thinking is the ability to describe natural and human systems through models and simulations. Practice 2 of the Next Generation Science Standards, *developing and using models,* notes that "In science, models are used to represent a system (or parts of a system) under study, to aid in the development of questions and explanations, to generate data that can be used to make predictions, and to communicate ideas to others. Students can be expected to evaluate and refine models through an iterative cycle of comparing their predictions with the real world and then adjusting them to gain insights into the phenomenon being modeled. As such, models are based upon evidence. When new evidence is uncovered that the models can't explain, models are modified."

Historians similarly integrate ideas from multiple disciplines and perspectives in order to represent the connections between them in visual models or interactive simulations. Scientific models—from simple machines to complex computer-generated models of phenomena too small to see with the naked eye—are an engaging and challenging way to assess students' understanding of dynamic relationship between interacting parts or forces. In history, producing a product like something created in another culture or time period is a similarly engaging way for students to experience the perspective of another culture and to develop a deeper and more compassionate understanding. Much like a living museum shows visitors "what it was like" to live in another time or place, creating a simulation allows students to communicate their learning by taking the audience through an experience.

In Action: Models and Simulations

At Evergreen Community Charter School in Asheville, North Carolina, eighth-graders investigated the history of southern Appalachia to describe, as historians and scientists do, the relationship between the Scotch Irish settlers of the post-Civil War/early 20th century period and their rich and rugged mountain landscape. The essential questions that guided their work were: *What does it mean to be Appalachian and how has it changed over time? How are our values reflected in our relationship to the land? How do we use knowledge to make change?* These are questions that depend on seeing significant patterns of change and continuity over time.

Students developed a nuanced understanding of cultural and natural trends through an interdisciplinary investigation that involved mapping the watershed, studying land use practices, and learning about the literature, music, and food traditions of their region. They viewed the PBS documentary, *The Appalachians*, and described the key relationships between info-bites from their reading and viewing on a visual mind-map.

Taking their inquiry outside the classroom, they interviewed local people whose roots in Appalachia grow deep. Then, in partnership with the Appalachian Food Story Bank, they compiled an oral history that included how culture is communicated through preparing and serving food. Among the stories their subjects told were how to slaughter a chicken, how to forage for wild greens, and how to preserve mountain olives. The stories and recipes were archived at the North Carolina Department of Cultural Resources.

Finally, students created a living model of an old-time mountain festival. They too made apple butter, pickled beets from the school garden, and baked sweet stack cakes. A few engaged in a reflection on their own ethics of eating meat and then respectfully slaughtered a chicken using traditional practices. Then they served it all up to those they interviewed and their families at an Appalachian shindig, complete with contra dancing led by a professional caller and live traditional music.

Students' interactive simulation of cultural characteristics including language, values, and food demonstrated their deep understanding of people and place—very much like a well-researched history museum exhibit.

Instructional moves for teaching students to create models and simulations

- Teach lessons that invite students to think by analogy and to use words and pictures to describe natural or historical phenomena

- Teach students to compare and contrast parts of a system, to analyze cause and effect relationships, and to evaluate what makes things work or not work

- Identify the criteria for a "good" model by critiquing functionality, authenticity, and detail

- Evaluate the limitations of a model

- Use a model to generate data, predict results, or test a system's reliability

- Partner with individuals or organizations who can provide an authentic audience

- Encourage students to be resourceful and innovative but also attuned to the instructional purpose of a model

Generalizing and Drawing Conclusions

Both intentionally and indirectly, scientists and historians act as agents of change. Scientists generalize from the specific data they collect to draw conclusions about the natural world. Historians describe a singular perspective, a case study snapshot of the social world in a fixed place and time or by comparison over time. Taken together, their accounts, based on the data of thousands of scientists all looking at climate change, or thousands of political scientists studying immigration patterns over the last two centuries, tell an empirical "truth" about the world that drives decisions in public policy and private enterprise. These professionals add their own "two cents" as it were to a vast and continually accumulating trove of empirical evidence, the weight of which shifts over time to confirm or counter the theories of the day.

When taught to use the tools and thinking strategies of a scientist or historian, students are quite capable of using evidence to make hypotheses and decisions or to recommend action, and of adding their own data to the knowledge base of an organization or discipline. Whether a teacher has the ability to engage students in genuine research beyond the school or whether she is limited to research tasks within the classroom, she can still encourage students to develop hypotheses and she can elevate and celebrate their thinking in her instruction. When those students collect evidence about their hypotheses during their research, they can then make evidence-based arguments for what they believe.

> Some projects allows students to use science to create institutional change. They gather data, make recommendations, and present them to those in power. Often, this is what real scientists do.
>
> —*Stuart Miles, teacher, Evergreen Community Charter School*

Indeed, the Common Core standards for writing indicate that by sixth grade students in the content areas should be making arguments based on evidence and continually circling back to critically read what other people have said about a topic. The recursive process of reading, writing, and back to reading, is steeped in questions that are always front-and-center, *Is this evidence reliable? Is it valid? Does it prove my point?* "What you want," according to Megan Hall, middle school science teacher at Open World Learning Community School, "is a culture in which the question 'what's your evidence?' is the standard. It's how we think every day in every lesson."

Generalizing and Drawing Conclusions in Action

At Casco Bay High School in Portland, Maine, students tackled a topic that scientists and policy makers the world over are grappling with: climate change. Through a carefully sequenced series of lessons supported by reading scientific papers, listening to a series of radio reports, taking notes from lectures, and conducting experiments related to carbon dioxide, students developed their background knowledge on Earth's changing atmosphere. Based on their knowledge and research, they were challenged to create a comic infographic depicting an element or compound of the atmosphere as a hero or villain (see Figure 3.4).

Students with talents in drawing as well as those who like to write found this twist on the conventional "poster" engaging. They had to evaluate the positive and negative implications of their element as it relates to Earth's atmosphere or environment, and they had to persuade others of those implications through the conflict illustrated on their infographic. Through this project, said science teacher Brooke Teller, "Students are able to intricately link the impacts of our dependence on fossil fuels to the environment around them. By studying the components of the atmosphere, students can develop a model of how greenhouse gases work to insulate the planet. They can describe how even relatively small changes in the amounts of these gases can impact their world in dramatic ways."

After creating the infographic, students learned in civics class how policy is made and changed through the complex dialogue between private advocacy groups and public agencies. In English class, guided by teacher Susan McCray,

Figure 3.4 Sample Infographic

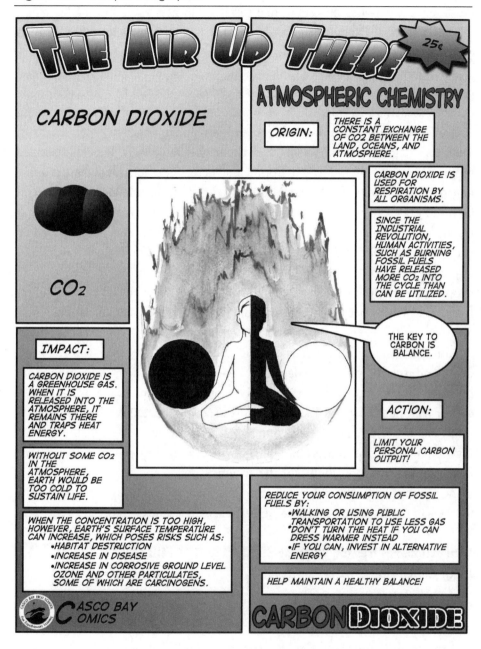

they learned to read policy documents and conduct research; they had opportunities to interview policy makers from a variety of local agencies. In mathematics, teacher Stephanie Doane taught them to analyze data and represent their own data graphically through tables and charts.

Then they put the pieces together in a "white paper" on an environmental policy related to all of their learning. In a gathering not unlike a doctoral thesis defense, students presented their proposals before a panel of experts including environmentalists, legislators, lawyers, and government agency representatives. Students had to present the science and defend their proposals. The experts asked probing questions about how environmental factors interact and about the accuracy of their research and the details of their argument that made students defend their thinking with evidence. Many students stepped up the rigor of their thinking when a real audience challenged them with questions. Afterward, experts invited students to apply for internships, partner with them on doing further research, or to present to their own stakeholders. "They are always so moved by seeing young people who are this committed and knowledgeable. They always say our future is in better hands because these students will be life-long active citizens," said McCray.

Although Maine professionals are undoubtedly moved by the Casco Bay students' enthusiasm and knowledge, they also want to hire them because they are prepared for the challenges of social science and science in the real world. These deeper learners know that they need to read, think, talk, and write in order to understand. They are purposeful in their learning and eager to apply their learning to new situations and problems. They have learned to collaborate, communicate, and take responsibility for the accuracy, detail, and implications of their work. By engaging students in scientific and historical thinking-and-doing, the teachers of these young people have created scientists and social scientists.

Instructional Moves for Teaching Students to Generalize and Draw Conclusions

- Guide students through a structured process of inferring from data—questioning the experts and drawing their own conclusions

- Provide opportunities for students to read, think, talk, and write about contemporary and controversial issues in science and social studies

- Teach the history of scientific and historical "truth," demonstrating how theories have shifted over time as evidence has unfolded or been re-examined

- Create opportunities for students to defend their thinking before authentic stakeholders

The Critical Moves of Creating Scientists and Historians

Challenging, engaging, and empowering students to think like scientists and historians requires attention to both curriculum and deeper instruction. Teaching the big ideas of these disciplines, engaging students with the tools and work of professionals, and scaffolding lessons so that students create meaningful products and participate in the debates of the scholarly world are ambitious, but manageable goals. Table 3.2 illustrates the who, what, and why of creating scientists and historians.

Table 3.2 The Who, What, and Why of Creating Scientists and Historians

What Do Teachers Do?	What Do Students Do?	What's the Result?
Plan case studies that bundle powerful standards to illuminate the big ideas and address the Four Ts: Topic, Target, Text, and Task.	NA	The case study provides students with a window into how scientific and historical concepts manifest in the real world.
Ask guiding and strategic questions that point students toward the big ideas they are researching and reading about.	Learn through a process of inquiry and searching for answers in text, experiments, artifacts, and other forms of evidence. Students sometimes formulate their own questions.	Students' discussion and writing is focused and grounded in evidence. They make defensible intellectual arguments supported by evidence.
Connect content to the underlying themes, questions, and frameworks of the discipline.	Connect facts in science and history to the broader questions that professionals grapple with.	Students understand more about how the fields of science and history operate.
Provide related complex reading experiences for all students. Teach reading in all content areas.	Read a wide variety of informational, authentic texts that correspond to the kinds of sources from which professionals extract information, multiple perspectives, and data.	Students meet or exceed standards and are prepared for the demands of college courses and careers.

(continued)

Table 3.2 Continued

What Do Teachers Do?	What Do Students Do?	What's the Result?
Seek local or immediate connections to global or social "issues." Develop partnerships with experts and fieldwork sites in the community that can contribute to students' learning.	Understand that science and social studies are anchored in real-world problems and solutions. Students engage in relevant, purposeful learning as "apprentice" scientists and historians. They acquire the skill set and intellectual habits of scientists and historians.	Students believe science and social studies are relevant to their own lives. They have a sense of agency in and responsibility toward their own community.
Plan and teach sequenced, inquiry-based lessons that focus on disciplinary process skills.	Formulate questions, gather and organize quantitative or qualitative data, interpret evidence, conduct investigations, and communicate conclusions.	Students become competent inquiry-based thinkers. They value evidence and persevere to solve problems.
Assess students' understandings and skills through multiple formative and summative measures.	Write in a variety of professional formats and also take traditional tests. Respectfully submit "work" for critique, feedback, and final evaluation.	Students come to understand that the work of scientists and social scientists is a collaborative and cumulative enterprise that relies on accurate communication in agreed upon formats.
Seek and/or provide forums for students to participate in intellectual debate beyond the classroom.	Present and invite feedback on interpretations, conclusions, and recommendations orally and in writing to other stakeholders in the school, community, and fields of study.	Students "sit at the table" with others engaged in respectful, ongoing debate based on an expanding body of evidence. They develop a nuanced understanding of "facts," "theory," and "truth."

SCHOOLWIDE IMPLEMENTATION

Making Inquiry a Priority

Making inquiry-based science and history a schoolwide practice starts with building a "let's find out" culture across the school, a mindset of inquiry. School leaders need to be the first to inquire! An inquiry-based culture is one in which educators frequently look to the research evidence as the basis for trying new things in their classrooms and afterward discuss the results with each other. Inquiring teachers "experiment," collect data, interpret their findings, and communicate their conclusions. Above all, a culture of inquiry is one in which leaders, teachers, and students value evidence as the standard for best practice. In an inquiry-based culture, for teachers and for students, the claim "this works" is supported with quality student work and consistent performance data.

Shifting a school community toward an inquiry-based culture is a process. It begins by reimagining the structures that impede interdisciplinary collaboration and connecting students to the big ideas and issues outside of the textbook. Following are the key steps for advancing this progression toward science and history instruction that is challenging, engaging, and empowering for all students.

Key Leadership Actions

Lay the Groundwork

- Help teachers unpack the big ideas of their disciplines and align them to required course standards and assessments. This includes identifying standards that have the most leverage across a discipline, that is, the standards that show up frequently in state tests and reflect the big ideas in science and social science generally.

- Infuse literacy into the content areas. Insist that every teacher supports students in using literacy skills to master disciplinary content. Make literacy the backbone of content-area instruction.

- Supplement or replace textbooks with more authentic curriculum materials, including quality nonfiction books, current journals and magazines (e.g., Time For Kids, National Geographic), newspapers, as well as brochures, newsletters, and other publications that illustrate local issues and concerns. Prioritize primary sources: provide ways for teachers to locate and purchase case-study specific, quality primary sources. Support teachers to vet and recommend credible scientific and historical websites, and ensure that all teachers and students have ready access to Internet sources that support their learning (see Appendices F and G).

- Consider using ready-made standards-aligned science and social studies curricula, such as EL's secondary modules for the content areas. Introduce teachers to Models of Excellence: The Center for High-Quality Student Work (http://modelsofexcellence.eleducation.org/) and other sources for excellent models of student work.

- If feasible, schedule classes in a way that allows for flexible blocks of time when students can leave campus to do fieldwork or have an expert come in to lead hands-on lessons. Trust teachers with the freedom to trade time blocks in order to allow for fieldwork or extended project work. In schools where multiple classes are conducting the same case study simultaneously, this may mean creating a temporary rotating schedule so that some students in a grade are off campus while others continue their studies in the classroom.

Build Teachers' Capacity

- Focus professional learning on the practices and thinking strategies of science and social studies.

- Emphasize inquiry-based instruction; teaching data collection, analysis, and interpretation. This may include providing lesson-plan templates that follow an inquiry-based structure (see Chapter 1).

- Use creative communication structures to foster interdisciplinary or multidisciplinary planning and instruction.

- If feasible, establish a part- or full-time position for a fieldwork coordinator who develops community partnerships, documents expert contact information and offerings, and coordinates transportation, scheduling, and logistics for off-campus fieldwork and expert visits.

Support Teachers to Deepen Their Practice

- Encourage teachers to identify authentic purposes and audiences for the products of student learning. Build relationships with service agencies and scientific organizations in the community by inviting members to school events or tours. Create or coordinate forums for students to participate as "experts behind the mic" in conversation with other stakeholders interested in local and pressing scientific or social issues.

- Raise funds or develop community partnerships to support printing and distributing the results of student research.

The Strategy Close Up that follows highlights how a school in Rochester, New York, calendars interdisciplinary case studies to maximize students' ability to meet their long-term learning targets and their opportunities for deeper learning.

STRATEGY CLOSE UP: Calendaring Learning Experiences to Scaffold for Quality Products

Calendaring the learning experiences that scaffold a science or history case study allows the teacher, or teaching team, to sequence and streamline direct instruction, time for reading and research, time for drafting, critiquing, and polishing writing, and other unrelated school experiences (i.e., interim testing, school assemblies). A tight calendar, closely followed, is a must if students are going off campus to conduct research or if busy professionals are visiting the classroom to present information. Rather than simply listing dates when presenters will come and completing field trip forms, actually putting the entire case study on a calendar will help teachers make the most of their instructional time.

Seventh-grade teachers at World of Inquiry School in Rochester, New York, use a collaborative method for calendaring. Based on an initial brainstorm of possible experts and fieldwork sites, and a rough sequence for what order these lessons need to follow, the four teachers divvy up phone calls to identify possible dates. The following week they come back and build a calendar on chart paper using sticky notes for each date. Field work is entered on pink sticky notes, experts on yellow, close reading lessons on blue, research and product creation on green, and so on. "Sticky notes allow us to be flexible and move things around as we need to, even after we start an expedition. But whenever we have collaborative planning, we start by making sure we're 'on calendar' so that students have the chance to meet their learning targets successfully," says Chris Widmaier.

After adding learning targets that reflect science and social studies standards as well as deadlines and due dates for drafts, revisions, data sets, homework, and other assessments, teachers can step back and evaluate whether students have enough time to do quality work, and whether teachers have enough time to prepare quality instruction. The end result of this time-consuming but beneficial process is a comprehensive long-term plan for a deep and relevant case study in the content areas.

COMMON CHALLENGES

Trying to "Cover" All Standards Equally

Identify and teach what's most important. Some states' standards seem to require the study of all time periods, continents, and scientific disciplines each year. Instead of trying to do it all, toggle back and forth between "surveying" the field (building the bedrock of facts that students need to know to satisfy state tests) and diving deep into a case study.

Doing Science and History without Reading First (or Second)

Critical reading is fundamental to critical thinking. Lab experiences, experiments, and firsthand investigations engage students, but teachers should avoid the temptation to jump right in without establishing a foundation of essential knowledge. The ability to read critically and support writing with evidence from the text is emphasized in the Common Core literacy Standards for History/Social Studies, Science, and Technical Subjects (National Governors Association Center for Best Practices, Council of Chief State School Officers, 2010). These standards set the expectation that students:

- reason with evidence
- consider multiple perspectives
- collaborate with others
- use technology effectively
- attend to task, audience, and discipline

Students of both science and history need many opportunities to analyze text, evaluate evidence, dialogue with other readers and thinkers, and write in response to reading. These opportunities prepare students for the intellectual heavy lifting of authentic research in the classroom or community.

Relying Too Heavily on Dry Textbooks or General Overviews

Be sure to include compelling and provocative primary and secondary sources. Evaluate them first for complexity, disciplinary and academic vocabulary, and relevance to students and to standards. Texts that engage students are more likely to build their literacy skills and their disciplinary comprehension.

Scheduling That Doesn't Allow for Collaborative Planning

Collaborative planning builds on multiple strengths and perspectives. In departmentalized high schools or large institutions with more than four teachers in one subject area at a grade level, scheduling can drive curriculum and instruction. Creative solutions to this cart-before-the-horse dilemma include: Teaming teachers so that they work with the same groups of students and share planning time; expecting (and supporting) collaboration between teachers for at least part of the school year; reserving early release days or schoolwide professional development for collaboration; and developing high-quality, inquiry-based but single-discipline units of study that can be shared electronically.

Scheduling That Doesn't Allow for Fieldwork

Fieldwork promotes engagement in real-world learning. The cost, logistics, and safety requirements of taking students off campus to conduct authentic fieldwork pose a particular challenge for large schools and underfunded programs. When such hurdles arise, consider designing lessons around issues that meet standards but can be studied *on campus*, such as recycling, water or energy use, bullying, or immigration. Enlisting parents, non-instructional staff, and community partners to help supervise and pay for fieldwork may also be an option at some schools.

Not Involving Authentic Audiences and Community Partners

Take advantage of learning opportunities beyond the classroom walls. When designing projects and products students can do for real audiences, identify community partners who express a real need, perhaps one that will take years to address. For example, habitat data collection or stream restoration might involve multiple classes or multiple grades of students contributing their collective efforts over time. While students will not get the immediate gratification of finishing a task, they will get a more realistic and valuable experience of how scientists and social scientists make change over the long haul—by working together and staying the course!

Prioritizing the Demands of Standardized Assessments and Not Also Including Authentic Assessment

Performance-based tasks assess more than facts and give students a reason to persevere in the habits of scientists and social scientists. Careful calendaring and deep planning allow time for students to both acquire the generalized knowledge needed to succeed on mandated multiple-choice exams and to apply that knowledge through projects and presentations. Teachers may need support for and feedback on long-term plans and the development of performance assessments that measure progress toward standards and clear learning targets.

Notes

1. The notion of big ideas as a hallmark of deeper instruction is supported by recent formulations of standards promoted by professional organizations. The National Research Council in partnership with the National Science Teachers Association, the American Association for the Advancement of Science, and Achieve have put forward the Next Generation Science Standards. The National Council for Social Studies endorses the College, Career, and Civic Life C-3 Framework for Social Studies State Standards.

2. You can see the Clairemont third graders' PSAs on vimeo: https://vimeo.com/113646188.

3. You can view the video here: www.youtube.com/watch?v=gcD8TqkRqqg.

4. Learning Standards for Science, Copyright 1996, New York State Education Department, used with permission.

5. National Council for History Education. Retrieved from www.nche.net/habitsofmind.

6. You can view the students' report, *Greenprint*, in *Models of Excellence: The Center for High-Quality Student Work* (http://modelsofexcellence.eleducation.org/search?search_api_views_fulltext=greenprint)

7. For more on the ReVolt project see http://modelsofexcellence.eleducation.org/resources/revolt-illuminating-standards-video

Chapter 4

Reimagining Mathematics Instruction

OVERVIEW

A Different Mindset for Mathematics

Two Rivers Public Charter School, in Washington, D.C., gets mathematics results that are remarkable. Two Rivers is an urban K–8 school with a diverse student population drawn from a lottery. Its mathematics achievement in 2013 was 24 percent above the city average. In every grade, student scores were not only far above other city schools but have also shown consistent, significant growth for years. Reading scores are similarly strong, and a visit to the school reveals a place of great joy in learning. It's not surprising that the school has the longest waiting list in the city: more than 1000 families.

When people hear about the school's success in mathematics, they often ask what they believe to be the key question: "What math program are they using?" Our fixation on this question reveals a central problem for teaching and learning mathematics: we often expect a packaged curriculum to be the answer.

The questions we should be asking instead are more complex:

- What are they doing at Two Rivers to build a new mindset for mathematical learning—to build excitement in teachers and students to dig into, embrace challenging problems, and work hard at fluency and conceptual understanding?

- What structures, strategies, and routines have they found to be most effective in raising mathematical understanding and achievement—at the whole-school level, the classroom level, and the lesson level?

The secret at Two Rivers is that they have built a schoolwide culture of mathematical literacy and achievement. The bad news about this is that if we are looking for a quick fix, this offers no answer. An effective culture is not easy to build and maintain, and it doesn't happen overnight. The good news, however, is very hopeful: Two Rivers shows us that this is possible anywhere. The students and teachers there are not privileged in the usual sense of the word; this is not an exclusive private school in a wealthy suburb. The privilege at this school is something very different: students and teachers are compelled and supported to take mathematical thinking seriously and to work together on mathematical challenges.

This chapter describes what it takes to reimagine mathematics instruction and build a culture of mathematical literacy and achievement in a school—the structures, content, strategies, relationships, and most important, change in mind-set about mathematics. Almost every school in America is filled with teachers and students who declare, without apparent shame, "I am just not a math person," or "I just don't get math; I've never been good at math." What teacher would glibly say, "I'm just not a reading person" or "I just don't get writing?" Somehow we have decided that it acceptable to be "bad at math"—even if you are a teacher! That culture needs to change, especially in schools.

Stanford researcher Carol Dweck, author of *Mindset: The New Psychology of Success* (2006), would say that many teachers and students have a *fixed mindset* about their ability in mathematics: they assume that it is just not an area of strength for them. The biggest difference in the culture at Two Rivers is that teachers and students there have a *growth mindset* about mathematics: they believe that if they study and practice, they will—all of them, students and teachers—get smarter in mathematics.

The elementary and middle school teachers at Two Rivers spent three years in professional development guided by mathematics expert Jeff Heyck-Williams, a founding school leader. Year 1 was spent entirely studying mathematical content. They were not studying *how to teach mathematics*; they were studying *mathematics*. They were learning the mathematical concepts and skills that they had forgotten over the years, or more likely, had never really understood fully in the first place when they were students. Together, they built their own mathematical growth mindsets and capacity, and grew excited about mathematical challenges.

The students at Two Rivers have a different mindset about mathematics, and about learning in general, than students in many schools. They describe their primary work in school as "learning to solve hard problems." They explain that "the harder the problems, the more our brains grow." Mathematical lessons, and all major lessons, assignments and projects, are problem based. Students expect to begin each lesson by struggling, individually and collectively, to solve hard problems.

Building a culture of mathematical achievement is a deep and long-term investment. This chapter offers structures and resources to support a teacher or a school in launching and sustaining the foundational work of deeper mathematics instruction. It provides structures to make mathematics more challenging, engaging, and empowering for students and teachers as well.

Transforming the Culture of Mathematics

We do not promote the purchase of a new curriculum as the starting place for transforming the mathematical culture of a school. Different schools and districts have often already committed to a particular program, and no curriculum in itself is perfect or even sufficient. There are many different strategies that could be used to catalyze the improvement of mathematical culture and achievement in a school. We elevate two of those strategies in this chapter as paramount.

The first and most important change for a school to make to improve mathematical achievement is a shift in the adult professional culture in the building toward one that embraces mathematical learning. This takes a willingness of the faculty to address their own mathematical strengths and weaknesses and to commit to improving their own mathematical content knowledge—which goes hand in hand with learning new teaching strategies. It means that faculty members must marshal their mathematical courage to take risks together, grapple with problems together, and get excited about learning mathematics together.

Building schoolwide commitment to such an initiative may seem implausible, but it is actually common in the realm of literacy. Many schools have adopted a literacy-across-the-curriculum focus in which all teachers of all subjects work together in professional learning settings on concepts of literacy and literacy instruction. There is no reason for mathematics to be different. At a primary and elementary school level, almost all classroom teachers are explicitly teachers of mathematics, so the wisdom of such an initiative is clear to everyone. At a secondary level, most teachers do not consider themselves teachers of mathematics, and they often feel they have no need to be robust in their mathematical understanding. There are many ways in which schools pay a price for this perspective (e.g., teachers of other subjects rarely integrate mathematics into their lessons; teachers often model for students a fixed mindset about mathematics; teachers often avoid helping students during study halls, advisory or crew sessions, breaks, and before and after school times when it comes to mathematics).

Because shifting the faculty culture of a school is a big and holistic undertaking, we come back to it in the Schoolwide Implementation section of this chapter. Here we begin with the second strategy we advocate as a powerful starting place for improvement: remodeling the basic lesson structure for mathematics. Although a switch to a new lesson structure is most effective when it is done across a faculty so that teachers can share their learning—challenges, modifications, and promising practices—it is still possible for individual teachers to adopt efficacious changes in their lesson structure, at an individual pace. This can be a great place to start shifting toward deeper instruction in mathematics.

A shift in lesson structure can help address the biggest shifts demanded by new and more challenging standards. All the new standards require students to grapple with more difficult problems and explain, defend, and critique their mathematical reasoning. There is no divide between conceptual depth and computational fluency: agility in both is necessary for efficient problem solving and cogent mathematical arguments. "These standards are not intended to be new names for old ways of doing business. They are a call to take the next step" (p. 5), ". . . stressing conceptual understanding of key ideas but also by continually returning to organizing principles . . . There is a world of difference between a student who can summon an mnemonic device to expand a product such as (a + b)(x + y) and a student who can explain where the mnemonic comes from" (National Governors Association Center for Best Practices, Council of Chief State School Officers, 2010, p. 4).

A new mathematics lesson structure is needed that can prioritize this focus. Workshop 2.0, introduced in Chapter 1, is a highly effective lesson structure for meeting these new demands. Workshop 2.0 has a clear and simple structure that can be followed exactly, but it can also be customized. Therefore, we present it descriptively, rather than prescriptively, in the Getting Started section of this chapter and unpack individual elements and strategies more fully in the In Practice section. The elements as a whole or in part can challenge students with higher-level problems and presentations of understanding, engage them with more interesting problems and classroom discourse, and empower them to be more independent mathematical thinkers.

Why This Practice Matters

It is easy to understand why many educators and national leaders consider mathematical literacy to be the most important educational issue of our time. It is a cornerstone of the future of our national and global economy. The United States is currently ranked twenty-seventh of tested countries in mathematics scores on the latest PISA test (Programme for International Student Assessment)—in the bottom-half of participating countries. When businesses and organizations within and beyond the United States are recruiting top mathematical thinkers, these data present a grim picture of the potential of American students.

New standards for mathematics create a unique opportunity to move forward as a nation to address this problem. For the first time in history, states can work together with common resources and assessments toward a common standard for mastery of mathematical skills. We must be clear, however, that the standards assure nothing about student growth. They simply define what we are aiming for. Unless the conceptual understanding of our teachers and the instructional practices used in classrooms change profoundly, we have little hope of getting there.

Deeper Instruction Challenges Students to Understand Mathematical Concepts

New and ambitious standards require students to think critically and understand the concepts and underlying principles of mathematics. Students must be able to articulate these concepts and apply them to novel settings. Lesson structures that compel students to grapple with challenging problems and present mathematical arguments in ways that demonstrate deeper understanding of concepts—not just application of algorithms—are necessary to help students reach this higher bar.

Deeper Instruction Engages Students in Building Their Growth Mindsets about Mathematics

There is no academic discipline more plagued by a fixed mindset than mathematics. Even teachers will voice a fixed mindset (i.e., "I'm just not good at math"). The research in this area is compelling. In a study of students entering seventh grade with similar achievement records in mathematics, those whose survey responses indicated a growth mindset showed much stronger success in mathematics (Blackwell, Trzesniewski, & Dweck, 2007). Similarly, growth mindset interventions have been shown to dramatically narrow the gender gap in mathematics (Good, Aronson, & Inzlicht 2003).

But students do not develop a growth mindset from a teacher telling them to have one. They build a growth mindset through seeing themselves improve in ways that are unexpected and seeing that the process of productive struggle with challenging work makes them smarter in mathematics.

Deeper Instruction Empowers All Students to Succeed in Higher-Level Mathematical Work

Mathematical literacy is at the center of our struggle as a nation to promote equity and close the educational attainment gap. When schools begin to sort students in ways that determine their educational futures, mathematics is the most important factor in that sorting process. Mathematics placements in sixth grade often determine when algebra will begin, what high school mathematics classes will be, and whether it is even possible to go on to calculus. Mathematics is a gatekeeper. A student's math profile sends an important message to colleges—a fact that college-educated, wealthier parents understand. For low-income families, the implications of this sorting process are often not clearly understood, and education prospects for their children are often constrained before anyone understands what has taken place.

The potential of deeper instruction in mathematics to address this issue is made clear by the groundbreaking work of mathematician and educational leader Uri Treisman (Treisman, 1985, 1992; Fullilove & Treisman, 1990; Treisman & Asera, 1990). Treisman's work provides a new paradigm for what is possible. At University of California-Berkeley, Treisman examined the almost universal poor performance of African American students in college calculus classes. Treisman found that people's stereotyped suppositions of why this poor performance was happening were totally wrong. People assumed that African American students were lacking in ability, were primarily from families and a peer culture that did not value success in this realm, or that they lacked the internal motivation to succeed academically. He found just the opposite. African American students who studied calculus were almost always high-achieving, hard-working students from families who valued academic achievement. Typically they were "math stars" in high school, sometimes valedictorians. Their mathematics SAT scores equaled or exceeded those of white and Asian students. Why were they failing?

What the African American students lacked was the right mindset and support. When they encountered mathematics work that confused them, they lost confidence and withdrew individually, assuming that they were not as smart as they had always believed. They had never struggled in mathematics before, and now that they were struggling they got discouraged, got poor grades, and often dropped their courses and their mathematics major. Treisman began a program to address this problem. It was not a remedial program or support program—it was an honors program. The students he convinced to join this program, most of whom were students of color, were given problems that were *more challenging* than typical problems. The difference was in the mindset and the collaborative work with peers. The students were *expected to struggle*. This was made clear as a goal, not a sign of weakness. They were compelled to work together in study groups to critique each other's work and to build understanding collaboratively. They were required to explain their thinking to peers and in front of the full group. Treisman's program embodied the vision and elements of Workshop 2.0 that we describe in the pages that follow.

The students in Treisman's program not only showed a dramatic difference in grades—going from a D average to an A or B average—they performed better on average than the white students taking calculus. Treisman brought this program to the University of Texas, Austin, and it then spread across the country and resulted in dramatically increasing the national percentage of minority students receiving higher degrees in mathematics and sciences.

The need for an improved approach to mathematics instruction is clear. In the Getting Started section that follows we describe how Workshop 2.0 can challenge, engage, and empower students to do more than they think possible as they develop their mathematical skill and courage.

GETTING STARTED

Identifying the Problem

Picture this: A middle school principal is sitting in the back of a classroom on a blue plastic chair with a clipboard, ready for a classroom observation.

Mathematics period is just beginning. Students enter the room and sit at desks, pull out their textbooks, notebooks, and pencils. They know what to do: everyone is on task and quiet; students have their supplies and homework. They look up at the white board and see their list of "Do Now" problems—review problems—and begin to work on them.

After eight minutes, the teacher stops the students and asks for the answers to each of the Do Now problems. A few students raise their hands and offer the answers to each problem as they move through the list. The teacher nods, checks off the answers, and occasionally asks follow-up questions for which a few students raise their hands. She gives verbal reminders about the vocabulary and algorithms used in the problems, and gets into brief discussion with one student who has further questions. Fifteen minutes have now passed.

The teacher then asks students to take out their homework. Before they review the answers she reminds them to make note of any wrong answers as they go so that they can return to those problems and clear up confusions. For each problem a few students raise their hands to give their answers. Most answers offered aloud are correct. Wrong answers are corrected by calling on another student who raises his or her hand. At the end, the teacher asks for any problems that a student would like to see explained on the board. Two students have a question, and the teacher solves each problem on the board for them and then collects homework. Twenty-five minutes have passed.

The teacher then begins her new lesson for the day at the whiteboard. She presents a few new vocabulary terms and a new algorithm to learn. She puts a few problems on the board and solves them for the group, using the new process. She then puts a problem on the board and asks for a volunteer to solve it. She calls an eager student up front and leads that student through the solution for the class to hear. At each step in the process, she prompts the student with the next step: "And what should you do to each side now?" "And what should you bring over here?" With her guidance, the student gets the correct answer. Forty minutes have passed.

She now asks the students to open their textbooks to the correct page and begin a problem set similar to the problems she has presented on the white board. As they work on the problems, she walks the aisles, looking over their work and offering help. Fifty-two minutes have passed.

She now announces to the class, "Please finish these two pages for homework" and "Gather your materials for the bell." At fifty-five minutes, the class ends and students exit.

The principal looks over the boxes on her district *classroom observation rubric*:

- ❑ Lesson begins in an orderly fashion.

- ❑ Students are polite and focused.

- ❑ Students are prepared.

- ❑ Lesson routines are clear to the group and followed efficiently.

- ❑ Goals for the lesson are clearly stated.

- ❑ Goals for the lesson fit the district curriculum.

- ❑ Students stay on task during work times.

❑ Individual student needs are met.

❑ Closure and homework fit the lesson.

The principal checks all of the boxes. Only one box is a question for her: "Individual student needs are met." This was hard for her to judge. But that's a small point. In every other way, this was a good lesson—clear, orderly, focused, well delivered. It's puzzling to her why standardized test scores have been weak for so many of these students.

Let's look at this very same lesson from a different perspective:

Brittany, a shy and distractable student, enters class and sits at her desk at the back of the room near the window. She tells her friends she "hates math," but that isn't really true. She doesn't actually hate the subject. She doesn't even think her teacher is mean. But she feels bad about herself as math student. Generally she is a "good student," and she can't figure out how she became a bad student in math. In elementary school she started out fine in math, but she is very aware that she has not been "proficient" in math for three years in a row on state tests. She feels dumb, and she knows this is going to hurt her future. But she doesn't understand what to do.

She passes almost all of her tests in class because she can memorize how to solve the kind of problems they are working on at the time. But when the state tests come, they are a mess of problems of all different kinds. She doesn't even know where to start on many of them. For some problems, she is asked to explain in writing how she solved them.

Brittany takes out her things and sighs to herself. She works listlessly on the Do Now problems, but those are just review problems and they don't count and the teacher doesn't even collect them, so it doesn't matter if she tries. She knows that it will be half an hour before she actually has to do some work that will be looked at, so there is no need to focus yet. During homework check, she sees that her answers are correct after the first few, so she stops paying attention. Each homework problem is essentially the same problem, just with different digits. Once she has memorized the algorithm, she can solve them; it's just a matter of putting in the time to do them all.

After 30 minutes of doodling and drifting in and out of attention, she wakes up and realizes the teacher is starting the lesson. She focuses closely on the teacher lesson on the white board. She tries to memorize the six steps that the teacher is explaining. She listens intently for a few minutes and succeeds in remembering the steps. She is happy because she knows her work is essentially done. After this, she simply applies those steps to the problems in her textbook set, the same steps for each problem, and begins her homework. If she is lucky, she can finish it at lunch and not have to take her book home tonight. She hates taking her math book home.

This is a fictional lesson. But it is fair to examine it as a model of a pervasive problem in mathematics instruction. It mirrors the lessons that international researchers found across the United States when they videotaped hundreds of lessons in various schools as part of the Third International Math and Science Study (TIMSS).

In 1995 and again in 1999, the TIMSS video study showed mathematics lessons in various schools across a group of countries at different points during the year. In 1999, researchers filmed and analyzed almost 700 mathematics lessons in seven different countries. The preceding fictional lesson was typical for mathematics lessons across the United States. Of the seven countries in the study, the United States scored the lowest on the TIMSS math assessment of student performance (Stigler & Hiebert, 1999).

Although there was some variation in the look of classrooms in the United States—for example, some had students facing forward in rows of desks; some had groups of students working together at tables—certain qualities were almost present, or absent. In a comparison of the lessons in the seven countries, mathematics lessons in the United States were characterized by:

- Focusing on review of old material more than working on new material. US lessons were, on average, more than 50 percent review.

- Avoiding challenging problems. The United States had the smallest percentage of high-complexity problems: 6 percent. By comparison, Japan had 39 percent.

- Missing the connections among facts, procedures, and concepts. Class discussions about problems that actually connected these three pillars of understanding took place in US classrooms less than 1 percent of the time. Other countries were typically 40–50 percent.

Schools that are concerned about mathematics performance are often inclined to "double-down" on mathematics time—lengthening or adding extra mathematics periods or offering classes outside of school time. This makes good sense, especially for students who are behind. Having more opportunities to engage with mathematics is important. However, to get better results we need to impact the dynamic relationship within the instructional core where the teacher, the content, and students interact every day. We need a new model of what a mathematics lesson can be.

Introducing Math Workshop 2.0

The idea behind this new lesson structure—beginning lessons with intriguing and challenging problems and using these problems as a motivation and structure to learn facts, procedures, and concepts—is not new. Many leaders in mathematics education have been promoting such an approach for a long time.[1]

Math Workshop 2.0 is a simple framework that provides the clear and concrete structure that allows teachers to focus on the content and teaching. We have field-tested and refined this relatively simple lesson structure in K–12 classrooms across the country. However, we know well that Math Workshop 2.0 may look simple on paper but is anything but "simple" in the classroom (see Table 4.1 for a full description of Math Workshop 2.0). Using this lesson structure effectively means making smart choices about problems, managing time efficiently, and being willing to tackle messy questions of what students actually understand.

Table 4.1 Math Workshop 2.0

Component	Purpose	Students . . .	Teachers . . .
Engage and grapple 5–15 minutes	Build students' curiosity and need to know linked to the purpose of the lesson. Build students' self-reliant problem-solving skills. Grapple with an interesting, complex problem or problem set related to the learning target(s).	Work independently Demonstrate perseverance and self-reliance	Choose an interesting, complex problem or problem set, connected to the real world or other disciplinary content when possible Circulate to observe students; offer limited support (only enough to ensure that students can access the task) Set a positive tone for learning May share the learning target now or later

Component	Purpose	Students . . .	Teachers . . .
Discuss 5–10 minutes	Build students' skills to be metacognitive about their own approaches, justify their mathematical reasoning, and consider others' mathematical reasoning.	Follow a structured sharing protocol to share their mathematical reasoning in pairs or small groups Present arguments and critique one another's reasoning in pairs, small groups, or with the whole class Use accountable talk	Pre-plan strategic questions to pose for discussion Group students intentionally but flexibly Structure sharing with protocols Observe and listen to note patterns of thinking, great ideas, and misconceptions (but do not interject at this time) Track individual understanding (e.g., by using a running record or note-catcher) Ensure that students are following discussion protocols and class norms
Focus 10 minutes *It is essential that this component be focused and brief to allow time for other components; the bulk of class time is for students to do the mathematical thinking and work.*	Provide explicit instruction if needed to "mop up" whatever students don't figure out on their own, focusing on a particular skill or concept. Respond to gaps in understanding, misconceptions, or good ideas from students. Gradually release responsibility. Create a "safe space" for students to practice the task with support; give students experience with success.	Demonstrate active listening Analyze other students' and/or the teacher's thinking Focus on one skill or concept at a time	Discuss the learning target(s) with students Model their thinking processes through a mini-lesson; may analyze models of strong or confused student work about a particular skill or concept Make connections from student reasoning to mathematical and academic vocabulary and underlying mathematical structures Provide closure related to the problem students grappled with unless students will continue to work with the same problem when they apply.

(continued)

Table 4.1 Continued

Component	Purpose	Students . . .	Teachers . . .
Apply 15–20 minutes	Time for students to practice the particular skill or concept in a collaborative learning culture. Options: May return to original problem Analyze models of student work—strong and weak Rotate through stations Work on one or more additional problems, focusing on the learning target	Work individually or in small groups, supported by intentional grouping, roles, and/or graphic organizers Look at, ask questions about, make predictions, and/ or participate (with tools, manipulatives, specimens, events, objects, etc.) May return to some of the actions in "Discuss" during this time	Provide differentiated support as needed Confer with individuals or groups Continue to assess "Catch" small groups or the whole class as needed for brief clarifications
Synthesize 5–10 minutes	Clarify the learning target(s), assess progress, and identify next steps/set goals. Address misconceptions, generalize conceptual understanding, and build lasting understanding through synthesis.	Share their thinking and work (from above) in small groups or with the whole class, following protocols and class norms Reflect on their progress toward the learning target(s), perhaps revisiting the original problem/ concept (*What*); Make generalizations re: mathematical concepts and structures (*So what*) Discuss transference (to other concepts, real-world applications, next steps) (*Now what*)	Craft debrief questions to help students synthesize understanding of both content and process Facilitate protocols to assess student understanding Collect work and/ or reflections from students to determine next instructional steps Assign homework

In this section, we describe the structure and purposes of the elements in a Math Workshop 2.0 lesson. Schools and teachers may choose to customize Math Workshop 2.0 rather than use it exactly as presented here, such as adjusting the time for each section. For teachers who must use a different mandated lesson structure, we suggest that different parts of Math Workshop 2.0 can be integrated to augment those lessons. This is also not the only structure we recommend for mathematics lessons and mathematics work: review days, test days, game days, project days, presentation days are also important. And outside-of-class tutorial support in mathematics for individuals and small groups is important as well.

Finally, we acknowledge that many schools use additional individualized mathematics programs or structures that allow students to progress through mathematical content at different paces and depths. Those are structures such as menu math, math stations and math centers; Judo Math and similar badging programs; flipped classrooms that use online tutorials such as Khan Academy; or online fluency programs. We see great merit in many of these programs and structures and have seen schools that use them effectively. Even with these individualized programs, however, group and whole-class conversations and problem solving remain important elements to an effective mathematics education for most students, and the elements of Workshop 2.0 can enhance both individual and group work.

In summary, we suggest that Workshop 2.0 can become a new "regular" routine for mathematics lesson in *many* schools, and elements of the structure can be useful in *every* school.

Engage and Grapple

The lesson begins, as many mathematics lessons do, with a problem or set of problems for students to work on as soon as they enter the room. There is a subtle but important difference, however, with the problems presented to students in Workshop 2.0 than in a typical American classroom. In most classrooms, students begin with a problem set called a "Do Now," "Warm-Up," or "Bell Work." These problems are usually review, used to activate brains and keep students busy at the start of class.

The grapple problem or problem set that begins Workshop 2.0 is not a review problem, though it must connect to previous learning and represent a logical next step from their past work. It is, by design, a new and challenging problem that will intrigue and confound most students and require productive struggle to solve. The students don't have a solution or quick algorithm in mind when they see it, and there is no sense that there is a single "right way" to solve it. Most important, the concepts and skills embedded in the problem connect to the conceptual and skills goals for the day—the learning target for the lesson.

It is not assumed that all students, or even most students, will be able to fully solve the problem right away. Confusion and mistakes are expected and respected; they are part of the focus of the lesson. Students grapple with the problem on their own before they get help and confer with others. The teacher is able to observe the work of students as she circulates, noting the levels of understanding and the strategies students are using.

Discuss

After the engage and grapple portion of the lesson, students then join into pairs or small groups in which they explain and discuss their solutions—or the ideas they have toward a solution—and refine their thinking. Students learn the skills to describe and justify their thinking, using words and visual representations, in this low-stakes but accountable setting. For small groups to be effective, the class explicitly builds, refines, and regularly assesses criteria for positive and useful group discussion. These guidelines include norms for respectful peer interaction and also standards for explaining one's own thinking and critiquing the thinking of others in kind, specific, and helpful ways.

The teacher circulates during group discussions, noting both patterns of thinking and interaction, and particularly noting common understandings and misconceptions. She then leads a whole-class sharing session of student thinking about how to solve the problem. Rather than call on every group to share their thinking in turns, which can be time consuming and repetitive, she strategically picks groups or individuals to share their thinking to illuminate correct or incorrect assumptions. She often asks students to come to the front to explain their thinking to the group.

She does not make clear which students are "correct" or not. She particularly chooses to have certain students share misconceptions that she feels are prevalent, and maintains a neutral, nonjudgmental tone in highlighting those ideas. She asks provocative questions. She is patient to allow the misconceptions to be clarified by the logical realizations of the students themselves, ideally with very light guidance from her.

Focus

In this part of the lesson, which is a teacher-directed mini-lesson, the teacher typically reveals the learning target(s) for their collective work—the conceptual or skill goals they are aiming to achieve. She addresses the problem they have been grappling with—perhaps affirming or clarifying appropriate solutions to it, or perhaps intentionally leaving things unresolved so that students can continue to work on the problem. Although this mini-lesson is planned ahead of time, it is also responsive to what the teacher has observed and heard in student thinking up to this point in the lesson. Much of what was planned ahead of time to address the learning target may be reframed by the teacher to directly relate to what students have been saying or thinking.

The goal of this mini-lesson is not to tell students what is correct (i.e., so that they can stop their questions and thinking because "here is the answer") but rather to describe and acknowledge the thinking they are doing now and to put that thinking into the context of traditional mathematical frameworks and vocabulary. If there is a standard algorithm traditionally used to address a part of the problem, she may affirm and explain this, and explicitly describe it as "the standard algorithm."

She is aware of the importance of standard algorithms as efficient procedures, ones that students should learn and may choose to use, and she is equally aware that when those algorithms are memorized without conceptual understanding, students often can only apply them in familiar, repetitive contexts (e.g., textbook problem sets, but not novel word problems or real-world problems).

This mini-lesson prepares students to grapple more deeply with the targeted concepts and skills, with more clarity and some new frameworks and vocabulary.

Apply

Students work individually or in small groups, returning to the original problem or problem set, or working on a related problem or set. The teacher circulates and confers with individual students or groups, or convenes a subset of the class whom she feels could be pushed further with an enhanced challenge, or a subset whom she feels could benefit from further clarification of concepts or procedures.

During the apply portion of Math Workshop 2.0 students often collaborate on problems

As she circulates, the teacher works to closely understand students' thinking through observation of their work or strategically placed questions. The teacher may choose to interrupt small groups or the whole class to examine and critique, as a group, the thinking of individuals or groups that she feels is provocative and helpful to clarify concepts or raise important questions.

The work during the Apply section of the lesson may be identical for all students or may be differentiated for different levels of complexity. The differentiation can be done through rotation to stations, teacher-selected, short-term focus groups on different skills or concepts, or student-selected problem choices. Although review and remediation are built in to conferring with individuals and small groups and offered during supplemental sessions for students who need it, none of the differentiated problem offerings for students during the Apply section should be remedial practice. In every school there are plenty of students who need more time to memorize foundational math facts (e.g., times tables) or math vocabulary. That need must be addressed, but not during the Apply section of the workshop, where all students should be solving problems that are at least at grade level. The conceptual gaps that can undermine students in that grade-level problem solving (e.g., an unclear grasp of foundational concepts such as fractions, negative integers, variables, geometric proof logic, factoring) are the very things that can and should be addressed by peers and teachers during this part of the lesson. They may not be fully solved as conceptual gaps during the session, but they can ideally be clarified so as to make subsequent support or tutoring more focused and useful.

Synthesize

In many mathematics classes the lesson ends with students working on a textbook problem set. When the bell rings students scramble to gather supplies and dash to the door. The teacher may call out a reminder over the chaos: "Homework is on the board! Page 88, even numbers!" This is such a common scenario—it's the way lessons end in every movie with a classroom scene—that we often do not consider if there is a more effective way to end things.

The final part of Workshop 2.0 is a time to synthesize learning. The time allotted in most schools for a mathematics lesson often seems too short already (to teachers; not necessarily to students), and giving up 5–10 minutes of that time for a strong closure may seem unwise or even impossible. However, smart structures for synthesis can help students and teachers achieve two main goals. First, the synthesis helps to crystallize the learning in the minds of students before they leave class. When students identify in concrete terms the things they learned together it helps make that learning last. The second goal is for the teacher to get a sense of what students did and did not understand from the work of the day in order to inform next steps for subsequent lessons, and for students to reflect on their growth and process.

The synthesis portion of the lesson can give teachers time to reinforce the context of the learning—where the concepts and skills being learned fit into the broader terrain of mathematics or where they are used in the outside world. Often the discoveries and theories that students make in class can be generalized into mathematical frameworks that are broad and significant, and students can leave the class with a memorable sense of achievement.

Synthesis can permit students to reflect individually or in pairs or small groups on their progress toward the learning targets, how much they now understand and can do, and how close they got to what they set out to learn. It allows them to set goals toward what they need to work on to better reach the target.

Using exit tasks and exit tickets (brief problems and response cards), the synthesis can allow teachers to collect short responses for each student that can give an indication of which students can solve a diagnostic problem; what students self-report about what they understood about the lesson, what they did not, and what questions remain; and to learn about how students are feeling about their progress and their confidence.

As we've noted in other chapters, deeper instruction begins with strategic planning for deeper learning outcomes. Teachers want students to be engaged, not just compliant. They want students to be challenged and to grow intellectually. And they want students to be empowered with the tools for learning that they can apply in novel settings. Math Workshop 2.0 is a powerful lesson structure for realizing these goals. When it is used effectively in classrooms, teachers have reported the following shifts:

- Students do more of the mathematical thinking and the teacher does less.

- Students do more speaking, writing, and risk taking, and less passive listening.

- Students work on more challenging problems, and do less review and repetition.

- Students often lead their own learning.

- Students and teachers are clearer about what students understand.

In the In Practice section that follows we lift up and describe some of the strategies that will support these outcomes for students and enhance mathematics instruction in any classroom.

IN PRACTICE

The Power Practices of Math Workshop 2.0

Whether or not you are interested in using the full Math Workshop 2.0 lesson structure, customizing it for your classroom, or just borrowing ideas and elements from it, the five parts of the structure are built around strategies that can engage students in problem solving, challenge their mathematical thinking, and empower them with the tools and language of mathematicians.

Before any lesson begins, it is important to pre-assess students' skills and understanding of concepts. It is tempting (and sometimes mandated) to follow a set curriculum, whether or not it corresponds to what students in any particular group actually need. Unfortunately, the work provided may be too basic for the majority of the group, or too advanced. In order to meet the needs of all students, we also need to know who the outliers are, which students need more practice, review, or more advanced work. Quick pre-assessments or systematic adaptive tests (like NWEA's Measures of Academic Progress [MAP]) provide an indication of whether students are ready to dig into grade-level standards. Comprehensive assessments (e.g., giving the equivalent of an end-of-chapter test as a pre-assessment) can clarify whether students have already met some of the learning targets set forth in a unit.

Finding, Choosing, and Using Strong Problems (*Engage and Grapple*)

Whatever the grade level—from prekindergarten through postsecondary mathematics—one challenge is the same: finding worthy problems that will engage students and reinforce and elevate their understanding and skills. There is no shortage of banks of problems—in textbooks, workbooks, and websites—but finding, choosing, or creating *worthy* problems at the *right level* of challenge is no easy task.

One of the challenges for teachers of mathematics in the United States is that many of us were raised on a diet of "super-sized" problem sets. We remember being given dozens and dozens of almost identical problems, all of which we were expected to solve in the same way, by applying the same algorithm, over and over. It's not surprising that we often require the same thing of the students we teach today. Many textbooks are set up that way, and it is easy to assume that big sets of repetitive problems are simply the way mathematics is best taught.

However, countries leading the world in mathematical achievement choose a very different approach. Students spend a great deal of time with a single, challenging, generative problem, or a small problem set. Class time challenges students to understand different approaches to problems, making sense of both novel and standard algorithms. This approach is described by John Van de Walle and colleagues (2013) as teaching mathematics *through* problem solving, as opposed to the traditional US approach of teaching mathematics by presenting an algorithm to memorize, then afterward using that algorithm to solve a problem.

In these high-achieving countries, teachers tend to obsess about the quality of problems, and about building teacher skills to use problems effectively with students. Elizabeth Green's 2014 book *Building a Better Teacher*, which uses mathematics instruction as the case study for how all teaching can improve, presents compelling descriptions of Japanese educators studying problems with peers to determine how to choose, create, and improve the best problems. Teachers continually observe each other's instruction, often in formal Lesson Study protocols with master teachers, to learn how to unpack problems effectively with students. (For more on the Japanese Lesson Study, see Chapter 1.)

Green describes a remarkably thoughtful, collaborative process of teachers and textbook companies experimenting to find the best initial problem to teach the regrouping process of subtraction to young students. It seems like it would hardly matter: Why would 12 minus 7 be any better or worse that 15 minus 8? But they discovered that 13 minus 9 was superior to all other configurations of numbers because it was the most generative in leading students to consider different approaches to solving the problem. In Japan, finding just the right problem was a national obsession, and, judging by the high achievement of students, a very productive one.

Switching class and homework time to delve more deeply into a single deep problem or small problem set—rather than the standard textbook problem set of dozens of problems—can raise concerns for mathematics teachers, and with good reason. We know that mathematical literacy includes fluency, and that fluency requires practice. We understand that if students don't practice math facts, such as memorizing their times tables or the definitions of geometric terms, they will struggle to recognize patterns, to understand relationships, and to solve problems efficiently. But we can make the mistake of assuming that this means that memorization and rote practice is what is needed *all* the time, *every* class, *every* homework assignment.

Focusing on students practicing and learning foundational skills and definitions such as times tables is a vital part of mathematical fluency. It is essential. But it is not the only element of fluency. Fluency also requires facile mathematical thinking—solving problems that require more than repeating the application of a single memorized fact or algorithm. Many students who can recite math facts or definitions capably and can solve big problem sets of near-identical problems correctly are lost when a problem does not look familiar to them. They are only fluent when the conditions are narrowed down so much that the task is perfectly clear to them.

We don't have to choose between the essential features of "old math"—building a strong base of foundational skills—with the essential features of "new math"—building deep understanding of concepts and facile, independent problem-solving skills. This presents a false choice. For memorizing foundational facts, traditional approaches make good sense: flash cards, practice sets, games, timed quizzes, personal tracking systems for growth. *And* students also need to learn how to grapple, independently and collectively, with challenging problems such as those they will encounter on high-stakes tests and in their lives outside of school. That requires regular opportunities to get off the treadmill of long problem sets in order to grapple with a small group of more complex and nuanced problems.

Seek Out Good Problems

Ideally, just choosing the "right" mathematics curriculum would provide all the problems and the guidance one needs. And many mathematics curricula do offer a thoughtful sequence of strong and useful problems; however, most experienced mathematics teachers know that they can't rely on a single curriculum to provide this. They supplement and customize the curriculum they use continually through finding, sharing, and trying out new problems gathered from a range of resources, and they continually improve the way they use problems by monitoring their efficacy with students.

Most mathematics textbooks and supplementary textbook materials include optional deeper problems that typically go unused. They are often presented as extension problems or challenge problems for students who are ahead. Those problems can often be used or customized for the whole class. In addition to textbooks, there is a range of strong books and online resources for teachers on mathematics instruction that also offer strong problem examples. John Van de Walle and colleagues offer multiple books and Marilyn Burns and Dan Meyer have useful websites.[2] In addition, Appendix H suggests many Web-based and print resources for finding challenging mathematics problems.

When evaluating a problem for use, particularly in the grapple and discuss portions of your lesson, consider the following questions:

- Does it focus sharply on the concepts you want students to grapple with at this time?

- Does it have multiple entry points—different ways one could approach solving it?

- Is it the just right level of difficulty—challenging, but an appropriate next step for students thinking?

- Does it have multiple solutions (so solving it is not just a race), or, does it allow for different representations and justification of the solution that are equally valid?

One of the important characteristics of a generative problem—one that can promote broad understanding of concepts—is that students across the class are interested in grappling with it and believe that they have a chance to contribute something to the class understanding of the concepts in the problem. This is not the classic "brain teaser" that the teacher presents and students race to get the single correct answer. In that case, most students assume the "smart kids" will get there first and they don't even want to be in the race. One student may call out the answer before other students have even organized their approach. In contrast, a generative problem may allow for a range of different correct solutions, which compels students to share and justify their responses. Or, if there is a single correct answer, the focus of class analysis is on the different approaches that yielded the correct answer and those that did not, and why.

Table 4.2 shows how generative problems that begin a grapple session are distinct from typical Do Now/Warm-Up/Bell Work problems.

Generative problems can be rich, interdisciplinary, and connected to the real lives of students, and they can also be basic and purely symbolic. Van de Walle et al. (2013) gives the following simple example: when working with a fourth-grade class on multiplication, one could give them three numbers and ask them to find the product of those three—a fast race for some, a losing race for most; done in a

Table 4.2 How Grapple Problems Differ from Do Now Problems

Grapple Problem	Traditional Do Now Problems
Focused on the concepts and skills of the lesson	Review problems
Challenging for every student	Easy enough for students to complete independently
May take the entire lesson or more to solve fully	Can be solved in a few minutes
Is worthy of rich analysis and student presentations	Have simple answers

minute. Or, alternately, one could ask them to find three numbers whose product is 108. Suddenly the problem is interesting. It has different approaches and solutions, and the discussion of what students came up with can unpack important concepts of factors, multiples, and problem-solving approaches.

One strategy can turn almost any challenging problem into a powerful generative one: give students a problem that is accompanied by a set of sample solutions to that problem created by other students. The task now is much more complex and powerful than just solving the problem, and it is not a race. Students must analyze and understand the approach to the problem that each sample student took, evaluate his or her solution, and explain what they think this student was thinking in his or her approach, if they think the student was correct or not, and why. Ideally the student samples represent a range of approaches to solving the problem and to representing their thinking, with some correct and some incorrect in the final solution. Think back to the cognitive rigor matrix introduced in Chapter 1 (Figure 1.3). This approach to problem solving falls in the *Evaluate* category of Bloom's Taxonomy and the *Strategic Thinking/Reasoning* category of Webb's Depth-of-Knowledge levels. It's an elegant way to elevate the cognitive demand of the task and engage students in high-level academic discourse, and it is highly engaging for students.

The Strategy Close Up that follows describes another source (and approach) for finding good grapple problems.

STRATEGY CLOSE UP: Formative Assessment Lessons from the Math Design Collaborative

The Mathematics Assessment Project (part of the Math Design Collaborative) created an open source set of Formative Assessment Lessons for Grades 6–12 that provide a strategically curated set of actual student solutions for each problem. The Formative Assessment lesson sequence (like Math Workshop 2.0) requires students to grapple with the problem themselves first, then analyze the sample student solutions in small groups to evaluate them. The problems on this website can be excellent grapple problems (http://map.mathshell.org/lessons.php). This resource also provides a model that all mathematics teachers can use to create their own version of this resource. Rather than using the same problems year after year, teachers can collect interesting student solutions to those problems and copy them (with the student name redacted). Over time it is possible to create a sizable bank of sample solutions for future students to analyze and evaluate. Few experiences are more powerful for building student understanding than this.

Test-Drive Problems Yourself

Just as we believe that it is essential that every teacher read a book before they teach it, we believe that it is equally important for teachers do the math before they give problems to students. This important step gives teachers a sense of what is clear, what is confusing, where things could go wrong, and how long it may take. By working the problem in advance, teachers can develop insights into approaches their students may take in class.

It is tempting for teachers to skip the step of "test driving" the problem ahead of time. Teachers already know how to solve it; why should they waste time doing all the steps when they have so much other preparation to do? But test driving problems provides insights that cannot be predicted: it previews for the teacher the pathways their students are about to take, and all the wrong turns and confusions they could encounter along the way. Finally, test driving enables teachers to see how the problem can generate student thinking, revealing multiple entry points and ways of approaching a solution.

Use Problems from Real Life

Students often have a disconnect between the concepts and skills in mathematics class (beyond simple arithmetic) and their lives within and outside of school. If we can create genuine connections between mathematics and life for students by choosing problems that relate to the content of other academic classes, or relate to school, community, or national and world issues, student engagement and purpose can be ignited. However, when these connections are not a genuine fit for the mathematics, the integrity of the mathematical learning is compromised and the connection can be a distraction. Therefore, choosing problems from real life is recommended, but only if it is done carefully and strategically and is not a force fit.

If a chosen problem is a real-life problem, or a simulation of a real-life problem, Jeff Heyck-Williams of Two Rivers Public Charter School reminds us that it is important to strip away the complex extraneous information to focus on the targeted mathematics. For example, if students are planning a school fund-raiser, there is a good deal of rich mathematics that can be involved, with high student interest. However, if students are planning the fund-raiser during mathematics class, much of the time may be spent discussing non-math issues (e.g., logistics, marketing), or on mathematics that is not relevant to what students need to learn (e.g., reviewing the balance of the student fund, counting change). Instead, with smart teacher planning, mathematics class can focus on particular concepts and skills for the project that also fit the concepts that students need to learn (e.g., profit margins under different scenarios of ordering and pricing). Heyck-Williams advises, "Put the thinking you want kids to do on the table. Take everything else off. Make sure that the time is spent grappling with the important concepts and skills."

The case study that follows describes a real-life problem and its power to engage first graders at Two Rivers.

CASE STUDY

Challenging, Engaging, and Empowering Very Young Mathematicians with a Real-World Problem

It is a sunny February morning, and Anne Simpson's first-grade class at Two Rivers Public Charter School is bursting with excitement. Students are diving into a mathematics problem that will span multiple days and push every student's thinking and understanding. They can hardly sit still on the carpet. Two Rivers uses its own custom version of Workshop 2.0, part of its problem-based task approach to mathematics. Their grapple problems spark class investigations that can last for a single lesson or for multiple lessons. In this case, the problem before students is to create proposals to spend money to purchase supplies that will enrich their classroom, using real prices (rounded off to whole dollar amounts) for real items. Because their class store raised $400 in profit, this is not a simply an academic exercise—students have real money to spend!

Simpson designed the problem and the lesson sequence collaboratively with the school's mathematics leader, Jeff Heyck-Williams, to meet Common Core mathematics standards and to build on the current level of student understanding and skills in mathematics. There are a number of first-grade mathematics content standards that the problem can address effectively: *Represent and solve problems using addition and subtraction; Add and subtract within 20; Count to 120; Work with addition and subtraction equations; Understand place value; Represent and interpret data.* Additionally, the problem addresses many of the Common Core's Standards for Mathematical Practice. Simpson and Heyck-Williams have constrained the choices for items to purchase to reflect amounts and approximate prices that will compel students to work right in the center of what the standards require.

Simpson kicks off the grapple with a KWI chart—standard practice at Two Rivers—in which students read and listen to the problem and then collectively brainstorm *"what do you KNOW, WHAT do you need to find out, and what IDEAS do you have for solving the problem?"* In older grades at Two Rivers, the grapple problem is typically done with the whole class at once. In kindergarten and first grade, however, Simpson has modified the process to help the younger students stay focused—she introduces the problem to

(continued)

a small group, typically just four students. During the time that Simpson is working with each small group, other students in the class are simultaneously working on a weekly problem that has differentiated versions, or they are working at centers that support the same skill development. For some problems, Simpson combines students who have similar levels of current understanding and skill. For other problems, she creates a group with a balance of levels. In this case, most groups had two students whom Simpson judged as currently strong in numeracy, and two students who are currently more challenged.

After the launch of the problem, students begin to attack the problem using pencils and paper and, for many students, manipulatives, including base-ten blocks with "longs" and "singles." Students begin plans to distribute $100 wisely among a range of supplies and books that are listed on a sheet provided. Students work together at tables to explain their thinking and computation and the representation of their thinking on the page. They critique each other's work and some make adjustments.

After this phase of the work, Simpson uses a gallery walk protocol for the whole class in which students leave their work out on desks and tables and circulate silently around the room, looking at the solutions of other students. They carry sticky notes and leave comments—affirmations, questions, or suggestions—on the work of at least three or four other students as they circulate. Sometimes Simpson uses a gallery walk protocol with the work of *all* students and sometimes she strategically selects a few solutions for students to consider for their understanding and critique—solutions that the class will then discuss together. At the beginning of the year, many students left feedback on sticky notes that were largely drawings and mathematical symbols with few words, but now, in February, with stronger literacy skills, the notes left by students consist mostly of written text. A number of students exclaim with joy and interest at the different approaches and representations used by fellow students.

Following the gallery walk, Simpson calls the whole class over to the carpet. She has strategically chosen four solutions from different students to analyze together. The first two solutions are projected for the class to see and each is explained by the young mathematician who created it. Other students ask questions and give feedback. Simpson intentionally chose students with a variety of approaches to the problem and methods for representing their thinking in order to push the understanding of the class. Some of the solutions are correct and some have mistakes in understanding or computation. Some of the visual representations are clear and helpful. Some are not. Simpson keeps her face and judgment neutral—there is no sense that she is approving of certain students' "correct" answers. During the course of the discussion, sparked by student observations, insights, and conclusions, the class develops a collective understanding of what constitutes a valid solution to the problem and what a clear representation can look like.

There are many aspects of this lesson that demonstrate wise planning and facilitation. The problem itself is engaging and real for children, it is challenging for all, it is perfectly aligned to standards, and there is no single right answer, allowing every student to aspire to a unique, correct solution at their own pace. The individual and group grapple and discussion times give Simpson time to work with individual students on adding and subtracting skills, place value, and on representing their thinking. There is a good deal of peer support and tutoring taking place throughout the lesson. This particular lesson does not have a synthesis because the problem will continue the next day, but students leave even more excited than when they began the work, ready to refine their solutions toward a final draft tomorrow.

You can see Simpson lead a similar lesson with kindergarten students in the accompanying video.

 WATCH Video 20: Going Deep with Kindergartners through Problem-Based Math

Of course, good problems are the just the starting place. The same problem that can appear dead or inscrutable in one classroom may come to life in another. Next we explore the instructional moves that make the difference and put good problems to good use in the Discuss portion of a math workshop.

Building Rich Mathematical Discourse (*Discuss*)

Effective mathematics classrooms have one feature in common, no matter the curricula, textbooks, configuration of desks, or how "traditional" or "progressive" the classroom culture. That feature is rich mathematical discourse. In all successful mathematics classrooms, whether in preschools or high schools, students can discuss mathematical concepts and patterns with sophistication.

For students to develop the skills to engage in high-level mathematical discourse, they must have frequent opportunities to reflect on their thinking and work and to present it to their peers—in pairs, small groups, and whole class— and to critique each other's thinking. This should take place both in speaking and in writing. The Math Workshop 2.0 lesson structure builds this into the second phase of the lesson, requiring students to share their work from the grapple problem. Whether using Workshop 2.0 or another lesson structure, making student thinking public is key to helping them develop deeper understanding of the concepts and making the learning last.

Cultivate Mathematical Courage through Curiosity and Questions

The capacity of students to discuss mathematics deeply and insightfully is almost never dependent on the innate ability of the students themselves. It is a product of deliberate structures, strategies, and mathematical culture established by the teacher. For most of us, it means changing our patterns of questions, directions, and affirmations to build students' mathematical courage and language. Mathematical courage means students are willing to take risks in their thinking and their work, willing to take risks in asking questions, proposing hypotheses, explaining their thinking and critiquing the thinking of classmates. A growth mindset is essential—students must believe that we all will get smarter in mathematics if we try hard things, make mistakes, persevere, and practice.

For that mindset and culture to flourish, teachers must establish a classroom culture that is an emotionally and socially safe place to ask questions and suggest ideas without fear of looking "dumb." This means that teachers must be vigilant in promoting norms of respect in all communication. It also means we have to change our own patterns of responding to students. Without meaning any harm, it is natural for teachers to get excited by "smart" questions and correct answers, and to be discouraged by comments that suggest confused thinking. Our faces make this very clear, even if we are careful with our words.

Students pick this up quickly and are reticent to offer ideas that will cause us to frown or roll our eyes in frustration. If our reaction to student ideas is a more neutral curiosity (e.g., "What makes you say that? Can you explain your thinking a bit?" "Very interesting. What brought you to that solution?"), everything changes. First, the student asking the question or proposing the solution feels encouraged and honored for trying, and second, the rest of the class has to pay attention now, because they are not sure if you are suggesting that the student is right or not.

Being neutral about the correct answer does not mean being dispassionate. The best mathematics teachers are continually excited by student thinking and ideas, and they model this (e.g., "Wow, I would never have thought to set up the problem that way! Tell us what you were thinking"). But it is important not to telegraph, through your words and facial expressions, when a student is "right." It means nodding appreciatively as students explain their theories and solutions, correct or not, so that other students, watching you, have to do their own thinking and analysis because they cannot depend on you to do the thinking for them.

A growth mindset in the classroom means that discussions can't always be rushed and should not be limited to the most confident and outgoing students. Efficient use of time in a classroom is important, but allowing thinking time for all students is equally important. Some students need more wait-time than others to consider their thoughts and responses. Having a system to share speaking time for students is helpful (e.g., when calling on students, randomizing by using cards or popsicle sticks with their names on them; for open discussion, a checklist on the board or magnetized names to show who has commented). When choosing sample student ideas and solutions to analyze together with the class, however, the goal is not equity. You only have time to unpack a few ideas and solutions as a whole group, so it is key to choose the student work strategically: choose work from students—correct or incorrect—that represent a variety of issues you want to highlight and will move the collective thinking forward. Be respectful and thoughtful in working together to make sense of those sample solutions.

When teachers model respect, patience, and curiosity in drawing out students' thinking with probing questions, and model the use of mathematical vocabulary, students get a picture of what strong mathematical discourse can be.

What follows are examples of probing questions to build mathematical discourse.[3]

Questions and Prompts for Developing Mathematical Thinking

Taking Students' Ideas Seriously

- Explain how you solved the problem.
- How did you figure that out?
- What in the problem made you use addition? (subtraction, multiplication, division)
- Why did you use this method?
- Who knows what the presenter is going to do next?

Encouraging Multiple Strategies

- How is your strategy similar to/different from this approach/model?
- Can you solve this problem using a different/more advanced way?
- Does anyone have a different way to explain this?
- How could you organize the information more efficiently?

Pressing Students Conceptually

- How do the numbers relate back to the problem context?
- Does this approach always work? How do you know?
- For what types of numbers does this approach work?
- How could you rewrite this problem to make it more challenging?

(continued)

- Is there an example where this doesn't work?
- What is the pattern?

Addressing Misconceptions

- Would this idea work in all situations?
- When does this idea work and when doesn't it?
- Why doesn't this approach work?
- How could you avoid this mistake next time?

Focusing on the Structure of Mathematics

- What does this idea/symbol mean in the problem/model?
- What assumptions are you making?
- How would you convince someone else that this is correct?
- How does this approach work for more difficult numbers/problems?
- What are the key mathematical ideas that come out of solving this problem?

The accompanying video, from a third-grade classroom, illustrates what it looks like and sounds like to build a strong mathematical discourse in the classroom. It is also a great example of a teacher asking neutral questions to push students' thinking.

 WATCH Video 21: Teaching Students to Prove their Mathematical Thinking through Questions, Charts, and Discourse

Model Mathematical Vocabulary

The other role that the teacher has in promoting high levels of mathematical discourse is in introducing conventional mathematical vocabulary to the discussion once students understand a concept. Whether rephrasing a student's comment with a mathematical term or introducing vocabulary in the mini-lesson, teachers elevate the complexity and precision of students' discourse when they model mathematical vocabulary. Students feel a sense of ownership and power when they are able to use the technical language of mathematics.

A commercially produced poster of mathematical vocabulary words on the back bulletin board is unlikely to grab much student interest. However, when students share ideas and then see those ideas honored and reframed by the teacher to connect to the vocabulary of the field, then they can get excited about learning these new terms. When the teacher celebrates a student's approach to a problem by naming it for that student (e.g., "Jabari's method") and also explains that there is an official mathematical name for that approach, it is a memorable event. When students learn new mathematical terms that they can immediately use to discuss each other's work, and those terms are posted prominently and referred to regularly on class-built anchor charts (e.g., "Jabari's method" = Create a table of multiples for each of your different denominators), the learning is more likely to last and students build an identity as young mathematicians.

It is also useful to have students take notes during class discussions so that they have a record of their learning of concepts and vocabulary. Those notes can be stored on note-catchers created by the teacher or in mathematics notebooks that every student keeps and refers back to in order to refresh understanding and memory.

Provide Opportunities for Students to Reason and Argue about Mathematics

In addition to modeling rich mathematical discourse with the whole class, teachers will need to prepare students to be effective contributors in small groups. The questions and vocabulary from whole-class discussions are directly transferable to small groups, with the goal being for students to follow the teacher's model and explore each other's work—asking probing questions and trying to make sense of each other's thinking—before rushing to judge each other's solutions. Keep in mind that the social setting of small groups is very different for students. It will be important to support effective group work by establishing group norms with students, monitoring them closely and consistently, using discussion protocols with clear steps and assigned roles, and using a timer to keep discussions crisp. It can be useful to model small-group discussion at first by using a Fishbowl protocol, in which an inner ring of students engages in conversation while the rest of the class watches and offers critique of the process.

Educator Brian Meyer, when researching high school mathematics discussion groups at High Tech High schools, focused on the important question of whose ideas are listened to during small-group conversation, and why. Students were asked to try to differentiate when a mathematical idea or solution is listened to with respect in the group. Is it because: (a) The student has social status; (b) The student has mathematical status; (c) The student has a compelling mathematical argument; or (d) The student presentation is intimidating. Simply by analyzing their conversation patterns with this lens, the students had new insights into how to improve their discourse.[4] In the Snapshot that follows, we see high school students defending their solutions to their peers and their peers, in turn, respectfully evaluating their thinking. This is what the Common Core Mathematics Practice Standard 3—"Construct viable arguments and critique the reasoning of others"—looks like and sounds like.

SNAPSHOT: Fostering a Culture of Mathematical Discourse

In Steve Jenkin's high school mathematics classroom, the pressure to explain and defend mathematical thinking is powerful. "I was afraid to speak on the carpet for the first few months of class," a student explained. "Everyone seemed so smart. It was intimidating. But now I offer comments. I even present my solutions sometimes!" "The carpet" refers to the carpeted space close to the whiteboard, where Jenkins regularly convenes a highly charged discussion forum, as in, "It's time for *the carpet.*"

On a table near the carpet are three piles of problem handouts, labeled "Hard," "Extra Hard," and "Seriously Hard." It is telling that there is no "Easy" or "Medium" pile; it is like a salsa bar with only hot and extra-hot sauces available. A student shares that she used to take only the "Hard" problems, until her friends were working on an "Extra Hard" and she took the plunge. Sometimes students grapple individually with these problems, and other times they work on them collaboratively, with Jenkins circulating to ask provocative questions, observe thinking, and provide tutoring where appropriate. Regardless of which problem students choose, every problem is valued when students present their work toward a solution to the class on the carpet.

The room grows quiet as everyone puts down their pencils and walks over to the carpet, weighing in their minds how confident they feel about making their thinking public for class consideration and critique. Unlike some younger students who sit on the floor for sessions like this, these high school students sit facing the board on chairs in the front rows, with a back row of students sitting elevated on the edge of tables. It is a semicircle of intensity. By choice, students came to the whiteboard and explain their work toward a solution to a problem, justifying their thinking verbally and symbolically with diagrams, tables, and equations. There are norms for respect and kindness, but no hesitation to question the mathematical thinking. It is a "be easy on the people, tough on the ideas" classroom.

Most striking in the discussion on the carpet is what is not present. There is no sense of "smart" kids showing off their knowledge by being harsh in critique. There is no evident hierarchy about which problems are shared, or which students share them. Errant reasoning or computation is questioned and cited, but there's an equal amount of pleasure and compliments for keen ideas and thoughtful presentation of thinking on the board. Students clearly tailor their critique to encourage students of all levels, while at the same time, there is no room to be evasive and unclear in one's explanation. "How did you derive that?" "How can you make that assumption?" are frequent questions. The entire forum is training ground for mathematical thinking and understanding.

Mini-Lessons That Illuminate Concepts *(Focus)*

After students have grappled with a problem, discussed solutions, and raised questions, a mini-lesson allows teachers to affirm the importance of students' ideas, focus their thinking on the targeted concepts, and equip them to work on their own. When using Workshop 2.0, the mini-lesson happens during the Focus portion of the lesson. No matter the lesson structure, however, it is important that the mini-lesson occur *after* students have had a chance to grapple with a problem and you have had a chance to observe their thinking. Because we want students to do most of the thinking in class, the mini-lesson should be genuinely *mini*: we suggest about 10 minutes. Often the mini-lesson flows seamlessly into an extended collaborative teacher–student time in which students are working, presenting their thinking, and returning to work.

Keys to an Effective and Engaging Mini-lesson

- Focus sharply on the learning target(s).

- Plan everything ahead of time: main points, vocabulary, examples, visuals.

- Be ready to adjust the plan to connect to student ideas, language, and questions observed during the grapple and discuss sections of the workshop.

Connect New Concepts to the Grapple Problem

Be sure to create a learning target (or a few learning targets) for the lesson that describe exactly what you hope students will be able to demonstrate by the end, whether it is a single-day or multiple-day lesson (e.g., I can change a fraction to a decimal; I can graph a linear equation based on two ordered pairs). Unpack the target with students so that you are clear that they understand the language and the goal.

The mathematical concepts and strategies you present in your mini-lesson should connect to the ideas and questions students raised while grappling with problems. It is empowering for students to learn that their mathematical thinking parallels established conventions and algorithms. If you label the ideas of students by their names (e.g., "Alicia's approach"), not only does it make Alicia feel proud and invested, but it pulls in the other students as well, as they consider how their approach to a problem is similar or different to hers, and consider whether they believe her approach will work or not. If there is an assertive student who has prior knowledge of an effective algorithm to solve a problem (typically a standard algorithm learned from a parent or sibling), it makes sense to acknowledge his or her approach along with the others, but not to celebrate it as the "right way."

If your mini-lesson includes the explanation of a standard algorithm for solving a problem, allow students to explore the problem(s) and come up with a range of approaches before giving them what may be seen as the single "right" method. Although it may feel frustrating to allow students to struggle before giving them a simple process to solve a problem, it is from this productive struggle that students learn to understand and appreciate what an algorithm does, once it is introduced, rather than memorizing it without understanding.

Memorization of foundational facts and definitions (e.g., times tables; geometric terms) can often be accomplished effectively by rote; however, when algorithms are memorized by rote, without understanding their derivation, students can easily become lost if they forget or confuse a step. Most students have learned to divide fractions by following a standard algorithm but struggle with word problems where this could be applied because they don't understand why it works. Most adults have forgotten the mathematical algorithms they memorized in high school, and because they never understood the underlying mathematics, they become lost when confronted with problems beyond elementary mathematics.

Standard algorithms are important for students to learn—they are effective and efficient approaches to solving problems, and they are the procedures that most students' parents understand. However, the most capable mathematical learners— not just professional mathematicians but also students who excel on mathematics assessments in accuracy and speed—are not constrained by algorithms, but rather use a variety of approaches to problems. Ideally, all students will understand the mathematics behind standard algorithms, so that they can use them if they wish, shorten them to save time, and use a different approach if it works better for them.

Giselle Isbell, a fifth-grade mathematics teacher at Anser Charter School in Boise, Idaho, explains that she "purposefully begins with the least efficient method of solving a problem, and then moves along to the more efficient method." That way, students get the conceptual understanding that they need and have ample time to practice it in the Apply part of the workshop. You can view Isbell in action in the video, "Grappling with New Concepts during a Common Core Math Workshop," which was first referenced in Chapter 1.

In the Strategy Close Up that follows, and in another accompanying video, we see how a fourth-grade teacher guides her student to "discover" a standard algorithm.

STRATEGY CLOSE UP: Don't Start with the Standard Algorithm

Jessica Proffitt, fourth-grade teacher at Two Rivers Public Charter School, asks students to "grapple with the ideas behind the math and figure out for themselves why the math works." So that all students have the same access to the problem, she also reads the problem aloud and makes sure students understand the note-catcher they are using to capture their thinking as they work. On this day, the problem asks students to calculate the number of vegetables that a garden will yield if each mound produces 2 ears of corn, 20 bean pods, and 9 squash; there are 20 rows in the garden, each row with 6 vegetable mounds.

The problem is challenging, and students aren't given an algorithm for solving it. They do use the problem-solving strategy KWI (*what do you KNOW, WHAT do you need to find out, and what IDEAS do you have for solving the problem?*) which helps them connect the new problem to what they already know.

Once Proffitt is certain that students have at least one idea for how to begin the work, she asks students to choose a partner with a similar idea with whom they will work on the problem. Proffitt gives them 30 to 40 minutes—fully half of the class period—to

The KWI helps students approach new problems

(continued)

work out their solution. During this time, she prompts their thinking by listening and asking strategic questions.

For the last 15 minutes or so of the class, Proffit invites students to present their visual representations with the entire class. They don't all get the right answer, but Proffitt notes that, more important, they see common patterns in how they approached the problem and recognize that mathematics involves a great deal of thinking and double checking.

In this lesson students also see that a systematic use of addition may not be the most efficient way to solve this complex problem. Discovering this reason for becoming fluent in the new language of multiplication is the big idea behind this lesson. And because students have discovered this principle of mathematics themselves, they leave the lesson with a need to know what's next. The lesson has engaged them and certainly challenged them. What's more, using the trusted strategy of the KWI, they can dig deeper into the next problem and persist until they find the answer.

 WATCH Video 22: Using a Problem-Based Task with Fourth-Graders to Create Deep Engagement in Math

Individual and Group Practice (*Apply*)

Independent or collaborative application time can be structured in a variety of ways, most of which allow the teacher to circulate and meet with individual students or small groups for clarification and teaching. In a Workshop 2.0 lesson, this portion is often the longest.

Structures for Independent or Collaborative Work Time

- A whole-group session in which students are working individually or in small groups on a single problem or problem set, interrupted at frequent intervals by selected students explaining their thinking to the whole class, with teacher facilitation

- Students working individually or in small groups on the original *grapple* problem or problem set, or a related problem that extends the challenge, with no interruptions from the teacher

- Students working individually or in small groups on differentiated problems. Those problems can be differentiated by:

- Complexity
- Extensions and connections
- Visual layout (to accommodate different learners)
- Topics (all related in some way to the learning targets)

- Students working at self-selected mathematics stations related to the learning targets

If the work is differentiated, it can be self-selected from a range of options provided by the teacher, or it can be assigned by the teacher based on her assessment of mathematical needs and learning styles. If work is differentiated by complexity, all of the problems should be at least grade-level in challenge. To use the approach of mathematics teacher Steve Jenkins, if students are choosing from different problems, those categories could be Hard, Extra Hard, or Seriously Hard; none are Easy. Differentiation can be also related to extensions and applications of the mathematics. It can be based on visual and textual modifications to support English language learners or students with special education needs; again, the mathematics in these cases is not remedial, but the visual presentation and teacher support may be different.

Solidify and Assess Understanding *(Synthesize)*

The final section of a mathematics lesson may be the most important, but, unfortunately, it is the section that is most often cut short or eliminated. Even when we plan ahead to leave time for a debrief and synthesis of learning at the end of class, things almost always run long, the bell is about to ring, and time disappears before we can close things properly. It is important, however, to keep this part of a lesson—in mathematics and in all subjects—sacrosanct. It means creating a new habit of vigilance in how we use time.

The Multiple Purposes of Synthesis

- to review and solidify what was learned before it dissipates

- to assess what was learned (i.e., did we reach our learning target(s)?)

- to inform the planning of subsequent lessons

- to ground the day's learning in the broader terrain of mathematics

- to reflect on our work as mathematicians and teammates

If there are only 5 or 10 minutes for this section, it is not possible to address all of these purposes with integrity every day. If you can hit the first three purposes every day, the last two can be addressed intermittently.

There is no single best way to use the final 10 minutes of a mathematics lesson, but returning to the learning target(s) for the day to assess students' progress is a good way to begin. That assessment can be a self-assessment, shared with a partner or small group verbally, or a written self-assessment on an exit ticket collected by the teacher. These strategies can be combined.

At Two Rivers, teachers spend the synthesis portion of their lessons having one or two students share their learning from the grapple problem. Sometimes that is focused on a particular approach they took to solving the problem, a particular way of modeling the mathematics, and occasionally a place where the student or a group of students got stuck in the problem solving process. Ultimately, it is up to the teacher to make informed decisions about who shares during the synthesis. This is an important decision. She picks students who will provide fresh perspectives and insights to the class, reveal confusions or illuminate effective strategies, and move everyone closer to the lesson's target.

Capture Student Thinking for Assessment

The other key practice that teachers at Two Rivers have identified as essential in the synthesis is providing all students with a graphic organizer to capture the thinking that is shared during the closing discussion. This graphic organizer is a place for accountability as students record what they learn from each student that shares. And it is a space for identifying how the synthesis has reinforced or changed their thinking.

Beyond self-assessment, exit tickets can also be a mini-assessment task: a single short problem, a quiz, or a question about conceptual understanding. Often, a single problem or question posed for the exit ticket can clarify for a teacher which students concluded the lesson with clear understanding and which students did not.

Exit tickets and paired, group, or whole-class discussions can also track other issues:

- What questions were raised for you by today's work?

- What is still confusing for you?

- What connections are you making to other mathematical concepts?

- How do you rate your effort today? Your collaboration?
- What other student's ideas or help did you appreciate?
- What can I do more effectively as a teacher to help your learning?
- How are you feeling about yourself as a mathematician? Why?

We suggest that exit tickets are a standard part of every lesson, and the structure and use of them be varied to keep things fresh, and to meet different needs. For example, one day the exit ticket may check on a student's level of mathematical confidence through written reflection; another day, it may be a mathematical problem to check their understanding. It is not essential to check on every student's self-image as a mathematician every day, but checking on it occasionally is helpful. Not every lesson requires that students demonstrate their understanding of a concept to you by solving a representative problem or giving you a written description, but many lessons would be stronger with this assessment. And, of course, exit tickets are only valuable if teachers make time to read and analyze them so that they can adjust instruction to meet the needs of students.

The Critical Moves of Reimagining Mathematics Instruction

Reimaging mathematics instruction is a heavy lift. Most teachers have years of traditional mathematics instruction under their belts by the time they enter their professional careers. Believing in students and believing in oneself is the first step. After that, following a new lesson structure like Workshop 2.0 is a high-leverage next step to challenge, engage, and empower students to be skilled and facile mathematicians. Table 4.3 describes the who, what, and why of reimagining mathematics instruction.

Table 4.3   The Who, What, and Why of Reimagining Mathematics Instruction

What Do Teachers Do?	What Do Students Do?	What's the Result?
Model mathematical courage and foster a culture of growth. Continually build mathematical content knowledge and instructional strategies.	Embrace mathematics challenges with determination. Be willing to make mistakes, analyze patterns of error, and try again. Build mathematical courage and grit.	Teachers and students see themselves as continually growing in their mathematical confidence and skill; the harder they work, the stronger they get.

(continued)

Table 4.3 Continued

What Do Teachers Do?	What Do Students Do?	What's the Result?
Engage and challenge students with problems that generate deep understanding; test-drive them to analyze how students might solve them; assess the efficacy of problems with students and adjust problems as needed for maximum learning.	Work fewer problems but with greater purpose. Evaluate information and think critically to discover the concepts behind standard algorithms. Demonstrate their thinking by showing their strategies for solving problems.	Students acquire conceptual mathematical knowledge and develop the habits of computational thinking and perseverance. They don't just know standard algorithms—they understand why they work. They are facile, accurate thinkers whether using algorithms or not.
Give students time to grapple, individually and collaboratively. Students have the opportunity to take on challenging problems themselves first, and to analyze solutions with peers.	Do more of the cognitive work in the classroom. Spend most of their classroom time actively solving meaningful problems, rather than reviewing or taking notes.	Students have confidence in their ability to struggle productively on difficult problems. They are prepared to encounter confusing problems in high-stakes tests and in real-life settings.
Foster rich mathematical discourse: model mathematical vocabulary, ask open-ended questions, and use protocols to guide student collaboration and discussion.	Regularly respond to questions with explanations rather than "answers" to problems. Present and critique mathematical arguments (in writing and verbally).	Students know how to discuss mathematics effectively and can use peers and teachers in the future to advance their own learning—in college and in life.
Connect new concepts to prior learning or grappling: teach mini-lessons that matter, give students time to practice new skills and understandings in meaningful ways.	Articulate mathematical concepts clearly and are able to apply them in novel problem sets or revise their thinking/problem solving based on new understanding.	Students see mathematics as a cumulative and coherent rather than as a series of arbitrary and disconnected facts. They can work independently and collaboratively.
Synthesize learning by debriefing at the end of lessons, to imprint under-standing of concepts; to transfer to other contexts; and to connect to the broader field of mathematics.	Articulate what they know and how they learned it. Be aware of what they are trying to learn and can name their next steps for reaching their goals, and where their learning fits in the big picture.	Students understand how their mathematical understanding can be used and transferred. They can articulate where the concepts they learn fit into the field of mathematics.
Assess student thinking and skills in multiple ways: use student-engaged assessment practices, exit tickets, and well-designed performance assessments.	Demonstrate their thinking in multiple ways. Expect to be held accountable for demonstrating their mathematical understanding. Use feedback from formative assessments to revise their thinking.	Students see assessment as something done *with* them rather than done *to* them. They connect their academic habits with results. Students know that learning is the result of effort and strategic practice.

SCHOOLWIDE IMPLEMENTATION

Creating a Culture of Mathematical Thinking

When educators marvel at the mathematical success of students at Two Rivers Public Charter School, they often look for the magic ingredient: What is the special difference there? The difference at Two Rivers is the schoolwide growth mindset and passion for the challenge of mathematics, and a commitment to using problem-based tasks. Changing culture begins with leadership and requires bringing the same awareness to the culture of mathematics throughout the school that many leaders bring to the culture of literacy (e.g., schoolwide silent reading times when even the principal and custodian are in the hallway reading; bulletin boards of what faculty members are reading in their spare time; reading awards; library celebrations, schoolwide literacy events).

At Two Rivers, and at other schools with a strong mathematical culture, leaders bolstered teachers' belief in themselves as mathematicians with concrete professional learning in mathematics and in teaching mathematics. Teachers learn mathematical concepts themselves, and then learn how to motivate and support students in grappling with concepts themselves. The following steps describe key leadership moves that make this work possible.

Key Leadership Actions

Lay the Groundwork

- Build a growth mindset around mathematics. Acknowledge with empathy that mathematics is challenging for many adults as well as students, but that all of us can grow and succeed at mathematics with effort and focus.

- Examine the mathematics curriculum for alignment with standards that focus on conceptual understanding. Identify and test-drive strong problems and problem sets that can anchor lessons.

- Build structures to support fluency and remediation outside of regular class. To enable classroom time to be devoted to problem solving and challenging work for all students, create structures to support students who are behind with foundational concepts and skills outside of regular class time:
  - Tutoring programs using students, volunteers, or paid staff
  - Extra classes with individualized support time

- Online fluency practice programs, and websites (e.g., Khan Academy) with in-school support for using them
- Study groups with staff support and dedicated meeting times

Build Teachers' Capacity

- Lead professional learning on Math Workshop 2.0. Unpack the elements of this model for purpose and the specific instructional moves, structures and resources that make it effective.

- Create time, structures, and resources for all teachers to develop and deepen their own conceptual understanding of mathematics. Support teachers to observe master mathematics teachers and debrief what works and what does not.

- Develop a common language for norms and accountable phrases students can use to discuss mathematics and to critique each other's problem solving strategies (e.g., "I am not sure I understand how you got that solution. Can you explain your method?").

Support Teachers to Deepen Their Practice

- Collaborate with teaching teams to develop formative and summative assessments that measure conceptual understanding of mathematics.

- Assess students' conceptual understanding by looking at student work not for answers but for mathematical explanations. Collaboratively identify common misconceptions and multiple strategies for working problems that demonstrate conceptual understanding.

- Encourage teachers to share mathematics with the broader community through newsletters, schoolwide mathematics events, and displaying and celebrating mathematics publicly on the walls and at community meetings.

- Make improvement in mathematics and problem solving a schoolwide focus for staff as well as students. The case study that follows details how Two Rivers Public Charter School made mathematics the focus of a three-year professional learning sequence.

Case Study: Improving Teachers' and Students' Conceptual Understanding of Mathematics

At Two Rivers Public Charter School, the transformation of mathematical culture began with a full year of building staff culture and capacity in mathematics, with no direct focus on application of mathematics instruction in classrooms. Led by school cofounder and mathematics guru Jeff Heyck-Williams, the faculty began the journey with surveys about their mathematical backgrounds, skills, and attitudes, which helped them create differentiated teacher groups. Over the course of the year, the staff was involved in a series of seven three-hour workshops on mathematical content, working as a whole staff and in differentiated groups.

The series began with the faculty spending three hours creating, sharing, and critiquing their personal "math stories." Although some teachers found only pleasure and success with mathematics in their youth, for most teachers this was not the case. In fact, mathematics educator Deborah Lowenberg Ball (2003) reminds us that "teachers—like all other adults in this country—are graduates of the system we seek to improve." Math stories impelled the Two Rivers staff to be candid with each other and begin the journey of pushing and supporting each other. There were many "math scars" left on the psyches of teachers that left them less than confident, unwilling to take mathematical risks, and with a propensity to cover up areas of mathematical confusion. Some of them referred to this collaborative work as "math therapy." As they worked together that year to gain deep understanding of content, they would have to step up and show *mathematical courage*: the ability to admit when they were confused, and the willingness to take risks, ask questions, and propose ideas.

As Heyck-Williams taught the Two Rivers staff, he modeled the kind of mathematical instruction that he wanted teachers to use with students. The sessions modeled the types of problems and discourse that is the goal for all classrooms. The mathematics that teachers were learning was primarily mathematics that they had "learned" themselves years ago as students, except that, for the most part, they had never really understood it deeply back then, and they needed to refresh their understanding or, in many cases, build it solidly for the first time.

In addition, most teachers had never experienced learning mathematics in a way that required them to grapple with concepts. By reconnecting with their own experience as mathematics learners, they developed greater empathy and insight into the learning process. As they developed new and deeper understanding of mathematics concepts, they also were learning how to structure experiences for students to do the same thing. Heyck-Williams used Suzanne Chapin and Art Johnson's book *Math Matters: Understanding the Math You Teach* (2006) as an anchor text during this year.

In the second year, teachers and leaders at Two Rivers identified the elements of good mathematics instruction and reconceptualized how units of mathematics instruction were

(continued)

organized and delivered. Through professional learning sessions as a whole group, and through ongoing cycles of trying out strategies in classrooms, observations, coaching, sharing, and critiquing progress as a whole staff, Two Rivers staff began organizing units of instruction around the big ideas of specific strands of mathematics and integrating those with a focus on the Common Core Standards for Mathematical Practice. With this shift, the faculty reviewed textbook series and switched their core textbook to one that was easier to customize.

In the third year, teachers focused sharply on teaching problem-based tasks (PBT). The Two Rivers PBT framework is similar to the Math Workshop 2.0 framework, with some details that are distinct. Problem-based tasks at Two Rivers are used in all grades, preK–8, and they range from single-day tasks to full-week challenges (with most lasting for a day or two). Teachers focused on many of the same topics covered in this chapter: how to find, customize, or create good problems; how to support students to solve them individually and in groups; how to build strong thinking and discourse catalyzed by those problems; and how to synthesize learning. The Two Rivers PBT sequence also has an added step not explicitly in Workshop 2.0: after the grapple problem is introduced, the teacher leads a discussion using a KWI chart (*what do you KNOW, WHAT do you need to find out, and what IDEAS do you have for solving the problem?*). The "Learn with Two Rivers" website offers further description and resources about their approach to problem-based tasks.[5]

When students at Two Rivers saw their teachers getting excited about mathematics, learning new things and taking risks as a faculty, the energy and mathematical courage was infectious across the school. Teacher Jes Ellis described her own mathematical journey at Two Rivers: "At first I felt that this was impossible. Crazy even. I wanted my textbook back. Now we are using multiple resources and texts to plan lessons. By the end of the year I felt that I could actually create these experiences for students. And the students' perceptions of math are transformed . . . They make it work with challenging material; they have new thinking routines."

Beyond the professional learning sequence, the school also embraced a celebratory schoolwide culture of taking on mathematics challenges. Whole-school community meetings feature mathematical problems, shared by the "Mathemagical Wizard" (Jeff Heyck-Williams in a wizard costume), that students, families, and teachers can work on individually or in groups. The Mathemagical Wizardry Prize, as the weekly problems are called, has galvanized the community at Two Rivers by getting everyone, from students to the crossing guard, engaged in challenging mathematics problems. Students and adults are thrilled to have their names called out to the community for solving these problems. In addition, Two Rivers has hosted Math Coffees for parents, at which teachers and leaders share with families how to support their children with mathematics, and an annual community-wide Math Festival at which students and families engage in an evening of games and problem solving. Most significantly, students in the school, whether in kindergarten or middle school, consistently try to "grow their brains" by taking on difficult mathematics challenges.

COMMON CHALLENGES

Deeper Instruction Sounds Great but My Students Don't Even Know Mathematics Basics

Support all learners with strategies and time for the basics, which may include extra time for mathematics classes, extra classes, individual or small-group tutoring, online practice, and family support. Some foundational facts and definitions (e.g., times tables) are well suited to rote memorization through different formats (e.g., flash cards, songs, chants) that are not connected to deeper, problem-based instruction. However, all students also need and deserve to be grappling consistently with challenging problems and building their math courage, resilience, and acuity. In the short term, they need challenge in order to succeed on the new high-stakes tests; in the long term, they need challenge in order to succeed in life.

We Can't Start This Kind of High-Level Work Until Our Test Scores Look Good

Don't assume you have to "fix" all the basic skills first before you offer challenging, engaging problems for students. Challenging problems create the motivation for learning basic skills. In addition, by learning to persevere in the face of challenge and the underlying concepts behind algorithms, students will improve their test scores. As a case in point, fourth-grade students in Jessica Proffitt's class at Two Rivers took a network standardized interim assessment that required that they use division before they had been taught the unit on division. However, they had already had a unit on multiplication and understood that operation deeply and its general relationship to division. Students persevered on the challenging division problems applying what they knew about multiplication to a new class of problems. They outscored their peers in other schools even on these problems that they hadn't been directly taught. They had developed the mindset and the mathematical practices to tackle any problem.

We Can't Do This Kind of Work Because We Have a Curriculum and Textbook to Follow

Almost all schools that are using Math Workshop 2.0 or a similar problem-based approach to mathematics also have a textbook and curriculum that they are, to some degree, following. It may be possible in your setting to follow the basic content and sequence of your curriculum and textbook, even to use required assessments, if needed, and still customize the way lessons are structured. Unless there is a requirement that lessons are delivered exactly as prescribed in a teacher's edition of the textbook, including required problems and pacing, then you should be able to stay on the basic flow of the textbook content while still creating rich, problem-based experiences and challenging deeper lessons.

My Students Are at Widely Divergent Skill Levels. How Could I Possibly Find a "Challenging Problem" That Is Right for All of Them?

There is not a single answer here but, instead, a variety of strategies. First, you can choose problems that will challenge every student, but have multiple entry points. Often those problems have multiple solutions and prevent students from racing for a single right answer. Include sample solutions from prior students to analyze; in that case, the task is not just to solve a problem but also to analyze and critique the thinking of other students. That structure allows for entry points and discussion for everyone, and the task is not simply to solve, but to understand. Another approach is to create related, differentiated versions of the grapple problem: all are challenging, some more than others.

Our School Faculty Is Not Strong in Mathematical Content and Skills

This is a difficult challenge that is true in many schools, both elementary and secondary. For elementary schools, where most teachers are also teachers of mathematics, the approach used by Two Rivers, described in this chapter, makes good sense: establish a sequence of collaborative professional learning to support math confidence, identity, and content growth for all teachers. For secondary schools, despite the fact that most teachers are not technically charged with teaching mathematics, all teachers should be math literate and integrate mathematics where possible. Many schools have chosen to focus on literacy as a professional learning topic across the full faculty. Taking the same approach with mathematics simply makes good sense. When a faculty tackles mathematical learning together, the mindset for mathematics changes throughout the school.

Notes

1. John Van de Walle and colleagues' books:

   Van de Walle, J. A., Lovin, L H., Karp, K. S., & Bay-Williams, J. M. (2013). *Teaching Student-Centered Mathematics: Developmentally Appropriate Instruction for Grades Pre K–2*. Pearson.

   Van de Walle, J. A., Lovin, L H., Karp, K. S., & Bay-Williams, J. M. (2013). *Teaching Student-Centered Mathematics: Developmentally Appropriate Instruction for Grades 3–5* (second edition). Pearson.

   Van de Walle, J. A., Lovin, L H., Karp, K. S., & Bay-Williams, J. M. (2013). *Teaching Student-Centered Mathematics: Developmentally Appropriate Instruction for Grades 6–8*. Pearson.

2. Marilyn Burns's website: mathsolutions.com; Dan Meyer's website: blog.mrmeyer.com

3. © 2009 Jonathan Brendefur and Sam Strother. Initiative for Developing Mathematical Thinking, Boise State University. Developed under a Mathematics and Science Partnership (MSP) grant from the U.S. Department of Education.

4. Explained to the authors by Lilian Hsu, director of High Tech High Chula Vista.

5. http://www.learnwithtworivers.org/problem-based-tasks-in-math.html

Chapter 5

Teaching in and through the Arts

OVERVIEW

Art at the Heart of Deeper Instruction

Fifth-grade teacher Kathy White works with some of the nation's poorest students at the Alamo Navajo Community School in Alamo, New Mexico. Although many of her students have a keen eye for the flora and fauna of the desert landscape, she wants them to "see" that landscape with the eyes of artists, the voices of writers, and the minds of scientists.

"Our first language is pictures," says White. Marginalized and low-performing students are often more inclined to visual, tactile, and kinesthetic learning styles. "Building on these strengths provides a means for students to become leaders of their own learning." To narrow the gap at Alamo in science and literacy achievement, White engaged her students in an art product based on the process described in Beth Olshansky's *The Power of Pictures*. White's students then wrote and illustrated a book called *Day in May* that describes the biological diversity of their desert environment in both "silver-dollar words" and rich watercolor paintings.

The high-quality book students created built their academic confidence and commitment (see Figure 5.1). Furthermore, in the course of their learning journey, students did much more than paint a watercolor and memorize biology facts and vocabulary words. From close observation, art lessons, and scientific research, they learned to be precise and evidence-based in their thinking, writing, and drawing. From analyzing models and participating in critique and revision

Figure 5.1 Sample Book Pages

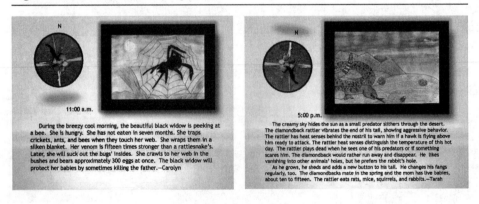

11:00 a.m.

During the breezy cool morning, the beautiful black widow is peeking at a bee. She is hungry. She has not eaten in seven months. She traps crickets, ants, and bees when they touch her web. She wraps them in a silken blanket. Her venom is fifteen times stronger than a rattlesnake's. Later, she will suck out the bugs' insides. She crawls to her web in the bushes and bears approximately 300 eggs at once. The black widow will protect her babies by sometimes killing the father.—Carolyn

5:00 p.m.

The creamy sky hides the sun as a small predator slithers through the desert. The diamondback rattler vibrates the end of his tail, showing aggressive behavior. The rattler has heat senses behind the nostril to warn him if a hawk is flying above him ready to attack. The rattler heat senses distinguish the temperature of this hot day. The rattler plays dead when he sees one of his predators or if something scares him. The diamondback would rather run away and disappear. He likes vanishing into other animals' holes, but he prefers the rabbit's hole.

As he grows, he sheds and adds a new button to his tail. He changes his fangs regularly, too. The diamondbacks mate in the spring and the mom has live babies, about ten to fifteen. The rattler eats rats, mice, squirrels, and rabbits.—Tarah workshops, they learned craftsmanship and perseverance. From an innovative approach that prioritizes listening to the language of pictures, they learned that their cultural value of revering the natural world complements scientific and literary endeavors. From their hard work and an attuned audience, they learned they have something of beauty to give to the world beyond the reservation, and something to celebrate within their own community.

Across the country in Boston, Massachusetts, students at Conservatory Lab Charter School, a high-performing and diverse urban school, are gearing up for their Spring Fling. The event will include a showcase of music played by six student orchestras and one ensemble from this school of nearly 400 students in grades pre-K–8. Music is at the core of Conservatory Lab's mission and is the heartbeat that drives its unique culture and pedagogy. Every student learns to play in an orchestra through a powerful and proven approach, *El Sistema*, based on a world-acclaimed classical music education and social change program founded in Venezuela. Founders of *El Sistema* and teachers at Conservatory Lab believe that every child has the ability to strive for excellence, to contribute to the broader community, and to learn to experience and express music deeply.

El Sistema's approach emphasizes group learning, peer teaching, and a commitment to the joy and fun of musical learning and music making. This is exactly what you hear and see when you walk through the doors of Conservatory Lab. The sounds of violins, cellos, flutes, trumpets, drums, and singing ring through the classrooms and hallways.

At Conservatory Lab, music is not taught in isolation from other academics. In addition to direct music instruction with *El Sistema* resident artists, students in each grade participate in music-infused interdisciplinary learning expeditions in science and social studies, as well as listening projects that promote active listening and deep appreciation for musical genres from folk to blues to classical. Teachers believe that interdisciplinary teaching that includes music is more engaging than teaching each subject in isolation.

First graders, for example, participate in a project called "Building with the Three Little Pigs," which culminates in an original musical that integrates literacy, science, and engineering knowledge and skills. Students build close reading skills through a comparison of seven different versions of the Three Little Pigs folktale. They use their new reading "smarts" in science class to investigate the properties of matter through books and hands-on experiments. Students observe and manipulate synthetic and natural building materials; they use new vocabulary words to describe the strength and flexibility of wood, straw, plastic, glass, and concrete.

The drama escalates when three anxious pigs show up at the door seeking assistance from the first-grade scientists and engineers. The pigs are actually adult staff members dressed in costume who come by to tell the story of how their own houses keep getting blown down by the big bad wolf and to challenge students to design something stronger that will keep them safe. For the next few weeks the worried pigs return again and again to check on the students' progress designing houses, bridges, and fences for the piggyplex. What they discover is that when the wolf is near, first graders are very motivated to solve the problem!

Soon students come up with the idea of bundling the straw to make it stronger. They learn how to mix concrete and mold it into bricks. They build a bridge out of wood so that it won't fall. And all along the way, they critique and reflect on the important work of civil engineers.

Conservatory Lab students designing their "piggyplex"

Photo: Toni Jackson

The Conservatory Lab three pigs project parallels their listening project on Broadway musicals, in which students learn about how songs, costumes, sets, and script combine to make a quality production. To communicate their learning about the science of matter and the engineering design process to a broad audience, first graders decided to put on their own musical featuring an original Three Little Pigs story. With the help of a local theater organization, teachers and students collaborated on a script and songs that express the theme of community and cooperation ("When we work together, there is nothing we can't do!"). And, to connect all the dots of their multidisciplinary learning, students create playbills that document each phase of their learning process.

"What students really discover," says teacher Jovanne Buckmire, "is that just like in an orchestra, you really have to help each other and learn from each other in order to build a piggyplex. Students have to grapple with the problem and work in partnership. They discover the same idea all over again when we practice the musical. If one person forgets their lines, someone else has to help them out. We sing best when we listen to each other too. A musical is a group effort and by the end students feel so empowered to be part of the cast that creates this amazing performance."[1]

Both Conservatory Lab and the Alamo Navajo Community School recognize that the arts—dance, media arts, music, theater, and visual arts—teach character skills as well as academics. They teach discipline, cultural sensitivity, integrity, and teamwork, as well as history, mathematics, and physics. They believe that art is the heart of high-quality student work and student achievement across the disciplines. Instruction in and through the arts challenges, engages, and empowers students to work toward quality and artistry in all things.

Three Ways of Doing Art in School

A common debate today pits teaching art for its own sake against teaching art for the purpose of learning in the core subject areas (mathematics, reading, science, and social studies). The false dichotomy draws a hard line between doing art to learn problem solving, planning, and perseverance and doing art to express truth, beauty, and joy.

What we see in schools that teach art deeply is that high-quality art instruction is all of these things. It dispels the debate entirely. It can take place in art class with a focus on learning artistic history, stylistic components, and technique while creating high caliber work and for an authentic audience. It can also take place at the intersection between two or more subjects and be focused on learning artistic control in order to gain and communicate greater insight into a topic outside of the discipline of art. This chapter describes effective practices in *both* of these arenas. What it doesn't do is describe "arts enhancement" or the practice of using art as a fun activity to get students through an otherwise disengaging subject. This practice, defined in the box that follows, can be a useful tool for teaching necessary skills, but it is not the focus of this chapter.

Whether art is taught as its own subject or integrated with another, we believe that it should be taught as an intellectually valuable and rigorous subject in its own right, as well as a vehicle for discovering new perspectives in topics like history and science. In both approaches, art must also be recognized as a deeply engaging and emotionally fulfilling practice worthy of teachers' time, resources, and professional learning.

The Kennedy Center for the Arts Definition of Three Approaches to Arts Education[2]

Art as Curriculum

If a school has a music, art, drama, or dance teacher, his or her approach is most likely Arts as Curriculum. Students develop knowledge and skills in a particular art form. Often referred to as "arts learning" or "art for art's sake," the programs are guided by national, state, or local standards for each of the art forms. For example, in visual arts, students learn the content, processes, and techniques for two- or three-dimensional work. They learn how the visual arts developed and changed throughout history, and engage in creating and analyzing works created in a variety of media.

Arts-Enhanced Curriculum

When the arts are used as a device or strategy to support other curriculum areas, but no objectives in the art form are explicit, then the approach is called Arts-Enhanced Curriculum. For example, students sing the ABCs as a means to other ends—remembering the letters and sequence of the alphabet. However, students are not usually expected to learn about melody, song structure, or develop specific singing skills.

Arts-Enhanced Curriculum acts as a "hook" to engage students in learning content. Additionally, teachers need little or no training in the art form. Arts-Enhanced Curriculum is often mistaken for Arts-Integrated Curriculum, or a distinction is not made between the two.

Arts-Integrated Curriculum

In Arts-Integrated Curriculum, the arts become the approach to teaching and the vehicle for learning. Students meet dual learning objectives when they engage in the creative process to explore connections between an art form and another subject area to gain greater understanding in both. For example, students meet objectives in theater (characterization, stage composition, action, expression) and in social studies. The experience is mutually reinforcing—creating a dramatization provides an authentic context for students to learn more about the social studies content and as students delve deeper into the social studies content their growing understandings impact their dramatizations. For Arts-Integrated Curriculum to result in deep student understanding in both the art form and the other curriculum areas, it requires that teachers engage in professional development to learn about arts standards and how to connect the arts to the curriculum they teach.

By definition, *arts integration* implies a deep collaboration between classroom teachers in different subject areas. Art, music, drama, dance, and core academic teachers plan both what and how students will learn. In schools where art is both a means and an end to understanding important things about the world, teachers design curriculum for the greatest learning leverage. In Rochester, New York, for example, teachers at the Genesee Community Charter School break "arts integration" down into three subcategories: literal, historical/cultural, and conceptual. The goal of a literal art product, explains principal Lisa Wing, is simply to express understanding of a topic through art, for example by singing blues songs in music class when studying African American history. The focus of a historical and cultural integration is to develop a deeper understanding of social studies content by studying the music, dance, and visual artwork of a particular historical period or culture. In contrast, the goal of a conceptual integration is to link both the art content and the academic content to an overarching abstract "concept" that underpins both curriculum areas. For example, when studying the cycle

> Arts integration is incorporating beautiful and meaningful projects into the academic curriculum. Final products are hands on, artful pieces that also reflect the students' learning.
>
> —*Matt Newsum, teacher,*
> *Santa Fe School for*
> *the Arts and Sciences*

of metamorphosis in insects, students might also learn about and create music that contains cycles—noticing how the pattern of repetition runs through both nature and human-made art.

Why These Practices Matter

Deeper instruction in and through the arts is important for several reasons. Foremost, arts are the pathway through which cultures and individuals express what it means to be human: our hopes and dreams, our sorrow, our questions, and our ideas. Arts are at the center of what we value about civilizations: when we study other cultures and other historical eras, it is their art that is enduring. And arts are what often sustain us as people: when we find joy in our leisure time it is often because we listen to music, watch videos, dance, draw, or write.

The pressures of tight budgets and high-stakes test preparation have compelled districts, schools, and teachers to cut back on arts—in arts faculty and arts classes offered, and in the flexibility and support for teachers to integrate arts into their curriculum and lessons. This is disproportionately true in schools that serve low-income students. Americans with economic privilege—business leaders and the legislators who determine public school budgets and policy—almost always send their children to elite independent schools or well-appointed suburban schools that are rich in arts opportunities. If people who can afford the best education for their children make this choice, it is a moral imperative for us to make sure all students have this opportunity.

A rich arts-infused education balances and complements deeper instruction in "high-stakes" subjects like language arts and mathematics. Like the other practices in this book, deeper instruction

> Ninety minutes a day [doing art, and] not doing core academics is a hard choice for any school. But it's a choice we make because we believe art is a means to success in math and reading. We reject the assumption that low-income students will underperform. To prove that assumption wrong, we offer high support—materials, time, really professional teachers, well-funded programs—and we have high demands of students too. And they are showing that they are up to it.
>
> —*Emily Stainer, head of school, Alma Del Mar Charter School*

in the arts is one part of an education that leads to a well-rounded, intellectual, expressive, and profoundly human experience in the world. And arts provide a powerful framework—for many students the most powerful framework—to cultivate skills of inquiry, creativity, problem solving, collaboration, perseverance, and craftsmanship.

Artistic Skills and Ways of Thinking Provide Students with Complex Challenges

Deep arts instruction is not about hooking kids with hands-on activity, or providing them with a window-dressing product that makes classwork look pretty for parents. It is intellectually challenging and complex in its own right. A ceramics artist, for example, must understand the chemistry of clay and the physics of gravity and mass. She studies the history of artists whose work punctuates the evolution of this functional art form and envisions new manifestations, variations, and applications for old techniques and materials. Art is complex intellectual work, and deeper instruction scaffolds students' knowledge and skill building through a strategic series of rigorous lessons.

Moreover, deeper instruction underscores specific cognitive and executive skills like problem solving, synthesizing, and planning that are critical to producing successful works of art. In art class and through integrated subject area and art projects, students learn to observe, listen, analyze, compare, interpret, and evaluate the artistic products of individuals and cultures. These are skills and ways of thinking that support students' growth across the academic enterprise.

Teaching in and through the Arts Holistically Engages Students and Honors Their Diversity as Learners

At its core, art instruction recognizes and values the multiple intelligences and diverse learning styles of students. Because the arts tap into visual, auditory, and kinesthetic ways of thinking, students with particular strengths in one of these areas are engaged by the opportunity to apply their natural inclination to an academic subject and have greater access to the complex and sophisticated ideas embedded in art. Visual learners in Kathy White's classroom at the Alamo Navajo Community School found vocabulary-building lessons for precise and poetic descriptions of the natural world more compelling because they began with pictures.

Similarly, students with a musical bent or an athletic bent may be more likely to attend and achieve in mathematics or music classes that involve composition and movement. Some schools that use this approach have discovered they give fewer referrals for misbehavior and see improved academic performance in reading and mathematics (McKibben, 2015; Schwartz, 2015). The jury is still out on whether there is a broad transfer of skills from arts education to other academic proficiencies and whether the relationship between studying the arts and performance in other areas is causal (Hetland & Winner, 2004). Nevertheless, some studies in brain development and neuroscience suggest there is at least a strong correlation between music education and students' language processing, reading and mathematics achievement, and even graduation and attendance rates (McKibben, 2015).

Within our own school network, the correlation between artistic focus and academic success is compelling. Arts-rich schools like Genesee Community Charter School in Rochester, New York—where academic units are co-planned by classroom teachers along with visual arts, music, and movement teachers—show remarkable academic success. It may be difficult to scientifically determine that the artistic instruction directly causes the high academic achievement, but a visit to any of these schools makes the connection hard to ignore.

Creating Art Is Empowering and Joyful Work!

Teaching that highlights artistic thinking and understanding can inspire students to discover new talents and aptitudes. Interacting with and learning from professional artists and performers can introduce students to a world of beauty and meaning beyond their previous experience, allowing them to glimpse—as artists do—the extraordinary in ordinary life. Great art teachers inspire wonder in students. In fact, they make a habit of soliciting wonder and of visualizing the impossible, bringing it into being on the page, the canvas, the dance floor, or the performance.

Creating something new, which often requires learning a proven technique or artistic style, is the essence of innovation and the engine of life-long learning. As Christine Marmé Thompson, Penn State professor of art education says of the shift from STEM (science, technology, engineering, and mathematics) to STEAM (which also includes art), "We are at a critical moment, when decisions are being made against the best advice of people who have devoted their lives to understanding children, teaching, and learning," says Thompson. "I believe this is a time when we need to listen to children, to parents, and to teachers, and to realize that the things that make children happy and proud and confident matter a great deal, and belong in schools. Every child deserves to have diverse educational experiences, including in the arts, so they can determine what they love to do and who they hope to be. That is supposed to be how America works" (Beattie-Moss, 2015).

In schools across America, art classrooms and performance spaces bring students from all walks of life together to engage their bodies, hearts, and minds in creative pursuits. Without the arts in school, many students wouldn't find these opportunities anywhere else. Teaching in and through the arts has real power. In the Getting Started section that follows, and in the accompanying video, we explore what it takes to create a culture of art and its power to challenge, engage, and empower students.

 WATCH Video 23: Teaching in and through the Arts: Three School Case Studies

GETTING STARTED

Bolstering Creativity in and through the Arts

In his provocative exploration of creativity titled *A Whack on the Side of the Head,* Roger Von Oech describes the artist as someone who "looks at the same thing as everyone else and thinks something different" (1998, p. 11). In order for our schools to produce students who are creative, artistic, and inventive, we need teaching and learning practices that invite all members of the school community to think differently. Let's explore what schools as different as the Alamo Navajo Community School and Conservatory Lab Charter School do to bolster creativity in and through the arts.

Create a Culture of Art

Standing in the lobby of the Alamo Navajo Community School, you are indoors, but you are nevertheless surrounded by the soft colors and spare landscape of the high desert. The indigenous language of the Navajo people, the Diné, graces the walls above panoramic shadow boxes that display student-created dioramas of landscapes and traditional sheep farming in the Rio Grande Valley.

Photo: Rayna Dineen

In the adjoining hallways, student work hangs alongside luminous murals of the night sky punctuated with the constellations of Navajo legend. The traditions of this tight-knit Navajo community, striving for survival against the pressures of modernization, assimilation, and poverty, are displayed with pride here. By creating an entryway that honors students' own culture and work, educators convey to students that each one is valued, each one belongs, and each one is supported by the strong hearts and minds of their elders and clans.

In fact, when rival sports teams come to the school, students turn off the florescent hallway lights and let the glow-in-the dark images of the murals do the talking. It's intentionally intimidating, but letting the walls speak—and even brag a little—is one way this tiny remote school creates leaders, thinkers, and students who are proud of their school and own their own learning.

When you walk in the front doors of Conservatory Lab, you are likely to hear music. If you peek into classrooms, you'll see students working together; they make art collaboratively and perform as a group regularly. Conservatory Lab incorporates two hours of music instruction and a full complement of academic courses into every student's academic day. Teachers often partner with musicians to integrate music into mathematics, literature, history, and even science. While this focus on music as the core of learning at Conservatory Lab is unusual and not something every school can adapt, the culture of art at the heart of school is something any school can build over time.

At both Conservatory Lab and the Alamo Navajo School, a culture of art emerges in part from the thoughtful use of space filled with student work to show that the school values students' expression and understanding of the world. These schools also consistently communicate the vision to all stakeholders of how art benefits students and arts achievement is recognized equally with other academic achievements.

Conservatory Lab is planning a permanent building that will house all grade levels in one building as well as performance and rehearsal spaces that will serve both students and the community at large. Meanwhile, when families enter the current primary school, they are greeted by self-portraits created by the previous year's K–1 class. "They are really impressed by the quality of the work," says Community Outreach Coordinator Toni Jackson.

> "They quickly learn that the long hours of the school day, celebrations of learning, Friday assemblies, and afternoon concerts are all part of joyful learning and excellence that makes school engaging for their children. Every year, all K–2 families come in on a Saturday to help their student create a life-size model from papier-mâché of the string instrument she or he will play. There are always brothers and sisters, grandparents and friends in addition to parents helping to glue and getting their hands sticky with paste. Each family activity is both a window into the classroom work students are doing and an opportunity for families to feel pride in their child's accomplishments."

Conservatory Lab students carry the culture of art with them when they go on the road too. This year the K–1 portraits were on display at a local library, where there was an opening night reception for families. Students performed the Three Little Pigs musical at a center for seniors. Older students performed original songs created for social studies projects at Paul Revere's historic home, the Old North

Church, and at the House of Blues in Boston. "Each of these events provides another opportunity to share students' work with a wider audience and that, in turn, helps students understand the role and value of the arts in the community," says Jackson.

A culture of art also illuminates intentional practices that teach craftsmanship, artistic style, and discipline, both as skills and as character traits. Jill Mirman, an EL Education coach who works with teachers at Conservatory Lab, describes, for example, how early childhood music teachers use hand signals to tell students what to do, who to work with, where they are in the lesson, and whether they are playing correctly. They believe that less teacher talk encourages students to listen more, and "when they are talking, they are really whispering and students tune in intently. Their classrooms don't have a regimented silence," says Mirman. "Instead, students are learning to listen the way artists do, to how the music moves and speaks as much as the people. When they are listening to Vivaldi, they become trees leaning in for the sound, and when they enter and leave the classroom, it's a quiet dance conducted through hand signals."

A culture of art goes even deeper when it comes to teachers' interactions with individual students. Kathy White tells the story of one fifth grader in her class who was already an excellent artist. "He could draw anything, and he always wanted to draw. But he struggled with perseverance. He was already so much better than his peers, so it was a waste of time to redraw." Because the higher purpose of teaching through art was to help her students acquire a growth mindset—a commitment to continuous improvement—White challenged her student to draw his tarantula wasp from different perspectives. "How could you draw it flying or on a flower?" she asked. "We found all kinds of different scientific photos as models. His perseverance developed by drawing it different ways. Students need to know that when artists do different drafts, they might not draw the exact same thing each time. Sometimes a drawing just needs tweaking. Sometimes it needs a really good eraser. The goal is to start with one product and get to a final high-quality product, but the path to excellence might be different for different kids."

One way to help students learn the artistic skills they need to complement the mathematics, reading, or content skills they have is to bring in experts from the community or take students out into the community to work alongside mentors. Schools make these arrangements in a variety of innovative ways, through partnerships with local or state arts councils, by inviting parents who are artists into the classroom, or by building on connections staff have with community artists. The point, says coach Jill Mirman, is that "regular classroom teachers have to buy in and commit themselves to learning artistic strategies alongside a capable art teacher or artist so that they can continue to support their students in the same kind of learning. Everyone in that partnership gets better together—the artist learns her role in education, and the teacher and the students learn that to create an excellent product, they have to learn some art fundamentals too."

In summary, schools create a culture of art by being intentional about and investing resources in what teaching and learning looks like, sounds like, and feels like from day to day. They make school a beautiful and welcoming place where diverse voices and songs are celebrated and where each student is encouraged to create, improve, perform, and grow as an artist. Such schools value students' unique gifts and imaginative efforts as contributions to a community worth showcasing, improving, and sharing with the world.

Plan with the Product in Mind

Non-art teachers can sometimes be hesitant to integrate the arts when they feel that they don't have adequate artistic skills themselves. At the same time, art teachers are sometimes reluctant to support content-area teachers because they have so little scheduled time with each class of students already, and art takes time.

The solution to both of these dilemmas is planning with the product in mind, well in advance, and often with deep collaboration between teaching colleagues. For the non-art teacher who is concerned about being judged a novice by his students or simply unsure of the steps to create a quality artistic product, the first question is simply, "What can students make that matches our topic, learning targets, and available resources (including time and expertise)?"

At the Santa Fe School for Arts and Sciences, there is dedicated arts instruction by art teachers, but most artistic work is done in non-art classrooms by regular classroom teachers. Every teacher infuses his or her lessons with art. Matt Newsum teaches fifth graders, and he doesn't have a background in art. So when he started thinking about how to teach wetland science and integrate that topic with art, he wasn't completely sure where to go. "The first thing I had to think about was what do scientists do? They observe, they research, and they draw what they see. So I knew our project would have to involve recording and drawing something in the field."

Newsum also looked for models of scientific drawings that he and his students could learn from. He discovered the stunning artwork of Ernst Haeckel, the biologist who discovered microscopic *protista* in the ocean. After showing students some of the artwork and a biographical video about Haeckel, Newsum asked his students, "If you discover something, what can we make to help teach other people what we've learned? What would be the best way to communicate our discoveries and findings?" Students themselves chose the format of a field guide. With Haeckel's intricate drawings to guide the style and dozens of published field guides to guide the form, creating artistic scientific drawings seemed much more feasible. Haeckel's drawings demonstrated a key concept: that scientific work must also be detailed and accurate, not just beautiful. With a wonderful model to exemplify this concept, Newsum could focus on developing lessons to teach the science and the art.

Map Out the Four Ts: Topic, Target, Text, Task

The Four Ts, described fully in previous chapters of this book, also provide a helpful framework for planning a high-quality study in art or integrating an art project into the content areas. Key questions teachers should ask at the beginning of their planning include:

What TOPIC provides an umbrella for my subject area standards and the art standards in my grade level?

For Newsum the topic of wetland science fit nicely with fifth-grade standards in life science: "Understand the properties, structures, and processes of living things and the interdependence of living things and their environments."

Specifically, the topic "A Microscopic World of Wonder" would address Benchmark III: "Understand the structure of organisms and the function of cells in living systems" and the New Mexico fifth-grade art standard 1 A: "Identify the principles of design in works of art and the environment." The principles of design guide both Haeckel's artwork and the students' field guides.

In other classes, and particularly in high school curricula where teachers are more specialized, choosing a topic that allows you to emphasize big ideas and powerful standards can be more challenging. Elyse Rosenberg, the high school art teacher at Metropolitan Expeditionary Learning School (MELS) in

New York City, sees her class as a place where students synthesize all of their learning through art. "Art is a means of deepening understanding about what different media can do and how messages can be conveyed through composition, imagery, and symbolism," she says. Choosing a topic that engages students and is something they want to talk about gives them a reason to work hard on the art.

In ninth grade, for example, teachers landed on the topic "Times They Are a' Changin'," because the connection between standards in history, language arts, and art intersected in the product students would create: a mixed-media collage to address issues of social justice. Rosenberg notes that at the high school level and when working with students from different grade levels, the national Core Arts Standards (Table 5.1) provide an excellent framework for identifying anchor standards across the grade levels (National Coalition for Core Arts Standards, n.d.).[3] These anchor standards underlie the key skills of every grade level and every art form, so they are great touchstones for planning a project that all students can learn from.

Working from these anchor standards in visual and media arts, Rosenberg's students were able to craft profound ideas responding to their learning in science and history into creative projects their audience could connect to. See Figure 5.2 for one example.

Table 5.1 The Core Arts Standards

Creating	Generate and conceptualize artistic ideas and work
	Organize and develop artistic ideas and work
	Refine and complete artistic work
Performing, Presenting, Producing	Analyze, interpret, and select artistic work for presentation
	Develop and refine artistic work for presentation
	Convey meaning through the presentation of artistic work
Responding	Perceive and analyze artistic work
	Interpret intent and meaning in artistic work
	Apply criteria to evaluate artistic work
Connecting	Synthesize and relate knowledge and personal experiences to make art
	Relate artistic ideas and works with societal, cultural, and historical context to deepen understanding

Figure 5.2 Sample Student Collage Work

"Re-Sorting"

What learning TARGETS—in content, art, and character—will I focus on in my lessons and assessments?

Learning targets are the bull's eye of skills and understanding that your students are aiming for. Deeper instruction in and through the arts enables students to reach or exceed these targets. Students are more engaged and more successful in any project if they can "see" the bull's eye clearly, that is, they know what the target is, they understand it deeply, and they have many opportunities to check their progress relative to the target.

For this reason, it is important for teachers to invest in writing carefully crafted targets that are student friendly, measurable, and clearly aligned with the most important skills, ideas, and habits of mind in the topic. (Learning targets are discussed in more detail in Chapter 1.) Rosenberg's long-term targets for visual arts included, for example:

- I can declare the change I want to see in the world in the form of a mixed media collage.

- I can explain the way(s) I used symbolism, media, and composition to visually declare the change I want to see in the world.

- I can provide respectful, critical feedback to my peers using art vocabulary and rubric standards.

What TEXTS—about the content or the art—will help my students build background knowledge and challenge their thinking?

As a rigorous discipline in its own right, art has a rich and varied history, as well as a vast library of texts about the craft of various art forms. Students who read the history of art, biographies of artists, and articles about an art form have a better background knowledge upon which to build and innovate in their own craft.

Many art forms themselves are also "texts" broadly defined. Students can "read" and interpret dance, music, drama, or photography. (We include a protocol for conducting a close reading of artwork later in this chapter.) They can study the relationship among text, images, and other forms of mixed media. They can explore and learn from the writer's craft as well as the content of a poem or story.

With so much to choose from, teachers must plan carefully to align the purpose of reading the text with students' need to know so that they can meet targets and accomplish the creative task they are working on. Reading the literature about art as social protest or about the craft of collage may require literacy lessons (e.g., unpacking the vocabulary of the art form or the time period) and time for discussion and application. Adding written text to an art project creates multiple opportunities for integrating literacy, content, and craft in ways that really challenge students to think critically.

Before creating their guide book, students in Matt Newsum's class watched and discussed a biographical video about Ernst Haeckel, as well as Haeckel's own book of illustrations, *Art Forms in Nature*. These texts provided inspiration, understanding about why scientists draw, and motivation for students who hadn't previously thought of themselves as artists. They also read articles about the wetlands and researched wetlands flora and fauna in scientific texts to gain understanding in context of the animals they drew for the guidebook. In addition, they explored dozens of guidebooks to analyze the form, organization, and relationship between text and illustrations. Each of these texts and tasks allowed students to meet short-term learning targets in biology (reading for understanding the role of organisms in the ecosystem) or art (reading for understanding the characteristics of scientific illustration).

What creative TASK will allow students to demonstrate what they know and can do?

The task or artistic product, as discussed previously, needs to fit the topic, targets, and text. Moreover, effective planning for an artistic task will also consider time, expertise, resources, and audience. A calendar is a good place to begin, especially if a project is being taught across more than one class. The opening conversation between team members might include these questions:

- How much time will it take students to draft, critique, revise, and polish their art?

- What expertise does each member of the team bring to the project?

- Who will teach the various components of the art process? And when?

- How do the parts of the project—learning about the topic, generating ideas, learning about the art, drafting, crafting, presenting—fit together?

- How will we support students who work at different speeds with "work time" for the art and keep them all on task and engaged?

- What materials will students need to do the art? Where will we get them, and how will we pay for them?

- What skills do we need to teach students besides the art and the content (e.g., how to clean brushes, frame pictures, or build a theater set)?

- Who will students share their art with? How will it be evaluated?

> Teaching in and through the arts is "not just telling the art teacher what you're doing in class, and then telling her what you want her to create. It's not just illustrating. It's deeper than that. It's a back and forth that deepens student's learning and understanding of classroom content as well as art content."
>
> —*Anna Loring, teacher, Downtown Denver Expeditionary School*

The answers to these questions are, of course, as varied as the arts themselves. In the sections that follow, we share examples that illustrate some important through-lines in teaching deeply in and through the arts.

Balancing Content and Form, Models and Creativity

Perhaps the greatest challenge of teaching art as curriculum or as integration is the juggling. You want to keep all of your priorities under control and airborne all of the time. You want to teach your history content and motivate students to produce a fantastic museum-quality display of their learning, or write and produce an original historical play. You want to show them how to analyze models of excellent paintings or musical performances, pressing home the message, "You can do this!" And, you want them to choose their own inspiration, direction, and execution of the project so that they can be original and own their learning. All of these truly are priorities of effective deeper instruction. In this section, we explore instructional practices that enable both art and content-area teachers to keep all the balls in the air.

Engage Students with Inquiry

For students to see and value artistic expression and art as a way of communicating ideas, they need to feel like Ernst Haeckel, seeing a microscopic ocean creature for the very first time in human history. The engagement engine of art is fueled by discovery. An engaging art lesson plan or unit of study provides students with opportunities to engage the senses—to see, move through, make music about, or, in culinary arts, even taste the world around them.

Matt Newsum, for example, started his field guide project by taking students out into the wetlands for a discovery experience.

> "I took them to a pond at the Leonora Curtain wetlands. We hiked around and I asked them to write down all of the living things they thought lived there. They wrote down the obvious things like trees, rabbits etc. Then I had them collect mud and water samples and asked them if they thought anything was living inside. They had some thoughts that maybe there was, but they didn't really know.
>
> Then back at school we let the samples sit and reproduce while we learned how to use the microscopes and read about the basic building blocks of life. That's how we introduced the kingdom of protista and how

there are thousands and thousands of living things that they'd never heard of or seen—and a lot of them have not even been discovered yet! The protista is the least known-about kingdom. Then it was time to look at our samples with the microscopes. Some of the students actually started screaming with excitement and awe, while others were a bit sad at first because they couldn't see anything under the microscope. Then they started helping each other adjust the focus. I'll never forget the look on Berke's face and the squeals and screams that came out of her mouth after her first sighting of a squirming creature under the microscope. She had been a student who wasn't that interested in anything like this and didn't think she was capable. Suddenly she was so fascinated and excited and after that she really opened up and engaged in the whole project."

Newsum's experience illustrates that the first step toward getting students to engage in art is simply teaching them to "see" the world from a new perspective, to discover patterns, nuances, and design that they hadn't seen before. See Figure 5.3 for a sample page from the students' field guide.

Figure 5.3 Sample Protista Field Guide Page

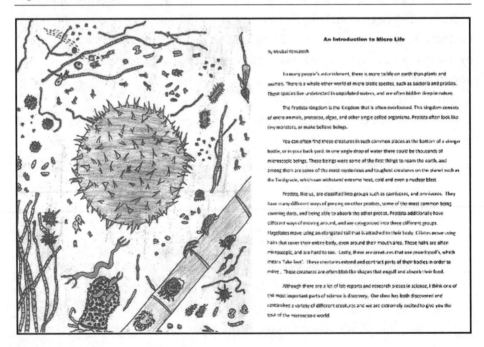

Challenge with Choice to Meet the Needs of All Students

In Newsum's classroom, giving students choices and affirming their own keen understanding of how they learn and perform best is the key to giving all students access to the complex ideas embedded in an arts-integrated unit. Like many content-area teachers, Newsum rarely has a special educator in his classroom, but he does have students with physical and cognitive disabilities and attention deficits, as well as English language learners. To accommodate the range of needs during instructional time, he provides text resources at different levels on the same topic—audiobooks, picture books, video, or chunked text, for example—and sometimes modified scientific instrumentation, like a digital microscope. He also encourages students to make thoughtful choices about where, with whom, and how they want to work. Some choose to work independently while standing up at a desk. Others choose to work with a partner on the floor, or with a group at the corner table.

More important than the modifications or the choices themselves, says Newsum, is how the culture of diversity and inclusion in his classroom mirrors the culture of diversity and creativity in the arts themselves.

> "We all start with the same criteria for excellence that we've determined from critiquing models, but we work toward those criteria in different ways. It's not about kids doing perfect work. It's about them doing their best work and demonstrating growth through effort. So, I often ask a student who's struggling, "What do you need to do your best work?" He can usually tell me, and I try to accommodate that. We problem-solve every challenge, and when students know that they are free to try different things without a penalty, then students respectfully take care of themselves and each other."

Build Knowledge: Research and Investigate

The next step is to challenge students to wrap their brains around a complex topic with complex implications for their artwork. The cross-grade, interdisciplinary arts integration at MELS was ambitious in its scope and complexity. The broad theme, "Times They Are a' Changin'," allowed for each discipline to take a unique perspective on social justice and change. In global history, for example, students studied the history of the caste system and social classes. In living environment

The tenth-grade team at MELS planned together for interdisciplinary integration of "Times They Are a' Changin'" across all subjects.

Photo: Claire Wolff

class, students researched ecosystems and interdependency in Jamaica Bay. In mathematics, students calculated the rates at which plastics pollution in the watershed increased over time. In language arts, students read and wrote about power, leadership, and racial profiling.

Challenge Students to Imagine, Evaluate, and Analyze

Deeper instruction in the arts invites students to grapple with complexity by thinking symbolically and metaphorically about how to represent abstraction within the concrete. Rosenberg wanted her MELS students to choose an issue they felt passionate about, but also one they were deeply knowledgeable about from their social studies, mathematics, and language arts courses. To push this kind of synthesis around the "Times They Are a' Changin'" theme, she had them record the issues and big ideas they had learned about in each class. They made connections between them and identified the issues and ideas they felt most strongly about. From these, students wrote statements about the change they wished to see in the world.

Then, with their message in mind, students studied the mixed-media collage artwork of master artists such as Jaune Quick-To-See Smith, Romare Bearden, and Robert Rauschenberg. They read these artworks closely (as texts) and followed protocols to debate questions including:

- What do I see?

- What is the message this artist is communicating?

- How did this artist communicate that message?

- Why did the artist choose this strategy?

Examining and discussing professional artists' renderings of ideas—art as representation—enabled these student artists to articulate the relationship among ideas, images, textures, and composition choices in preparation for creating their own mixed media collages (see Figure 5.4). Like literary criticism or historical interpretation, this is the intellectual work that parallels creating art.

Figure 5.4 Sample Collage

Provide Opportunities for Feedback and Revision

Frequently the key difference between the novice artist and the professional is the openness to critique and the willingness to revise. Students will sometimes say, "If I like it this way, it's art for me" or "Art is purely subjective, so you can't really criticize it." Consequently, one of the greatest challenges in advancing students' understanding and practice of art is getting them to value and apply critique. All of the teachers whose practice we've featured in this chapter spend many lessons analyzing models with students and use various strategies, including peer, teacher, and expert critique of students' work, followed by laborious revision. We explore some specific protocols for art critique lessons in the In Practice section of this chapter.

Share and Reflect

The process of critique is rooted in reflection. Students who reflect on the quality of their work and can articulate how they have achieved (or not achieved) quality are empowered to replicate the same effort and strategies in another setting. Sharing one's artwork—through display or performance—similarly fosters celebration, reflection, and empowerment. Art is meant to have spectators. When students present their art to an authentic audience, especially one beyond parents and teachers, they are motivated to do more than they thought possible.

The fifth graders at the Alamo Navajo Community School were excited to share their Day in May book with their parents, elders, and their community. "The first thing students do when they get their book is find their own work, and then they look for classmates work," says Kathy White. "There is giggling, and a lot of 'Oh, look at this' as it hits them that they are really published! Then when parents see the book, they ask their child, 'Did you draw this? Is this your writing?' and the students respond 'Yes!' with pride in their voices and the newfound confidence of artists."

At Conservatory Lab, Buckmire echoes the sentiment that when students share their work with others, they discover something important about themselves. Buckmire recounts the experience of a Spanish-speaking student who worked so hard to learn his songs for the musical in English. "Then when he started to sing on stage, everyone's jaw just dropped. He was very small physically, but he had the most amazing voice. That student and his parents never knew he had that hidden talent. Singing changed the whole way he saw himself and what he was capable of."

Empower Students with Confidence and Competence

Beyond the sense of ownership students feel when they present their work to real audiences is the sense of efficacy they develop from collaborating, practicing, polishing, and seeing themselves improve. Persisting through multiple revisions and then rehearsing and polishing a presentation by themselves or with others is a planned part of deeper instruction. Teachers set character learning targets as well as content area and art targets. They assess these targets with equal vigor, emphasizing for students that artists succeed through effort not innate talent.

Taking imagination to the canvas, the stage, the dance floor, or the concert hall takes emotional and intellectual courage. The artist must often go out on a limb to express her truth or persuade an audience of its value. Some students spend a lot of time finding a medium they are secure and accomplished in, while others are more willing to take risks. Often students need to learn the give and take, push and pull of collaboration as well as the elements of their art form. Regardless of the medium, says Rosenberg, you want students to take pride in the planning, problem solving, and craftsmanship of the project. "Students want to be heard," says Rosenberg. They are eager to express their opinion and vision through their artwork as long as they believe someone will try to understand it. "And they are willing to work and problem-solve in order to find that audience."

With a culture of arts firmly established, we turn our attention to some of the more advanced instructional practices for teaching in and through the arts in the In Practice section that follows.

IN PRACTICE

Museum-Quality Learning

Our definition of achievement includes not only mastery of knowledge and skills, but also character and high-quality student work. In the arts, deeper instruction aspires first and foremost to have students make something that has value, beauty, meaning, and purpose in the real world. In this sense, deeper instruction embraces the same work as any museum: to be educational and inspirational by documenting, archiving, and publicly sharing the culture and history of a community.

When Northwest Opportunities Vocational Academy (NOVA) in Milwaukee connected with Arts @ Large, a nonprofit organization that partners with schools, history teacher Kelly DiGiacinto discovered a whole new way of teaching in and through the arts that inspired and motivated her previously disengaged students during the school year and well beyond graduation. Working with Linda D'Acquisto, author of *Learning on Display: Student-Created Museums that Build Understanding* (2006), DiGiacinto's students collaborated with Arts @ Large to create an exhibition for their public gallery. They spent weeks conducting a case study of local events, people, and places involved in the civil rights movement of the 1960s in Milwaukee. Then they constructed an exhibit of their own called "March to Equality," combining images, words, and documents into displays and performance pieces for a real audience. When the exhibit opened, students served as docents and participated in interactive exhibits, bringing the time period and culture of Milwaukee's protests to life for a large audience.[4]

The project had a lasting impact on students, even those who hadn't initially signed up for the class. One student came to DiGiacinto on the day of the museum opening; he'd caught the buzz from others students and wanted to participate. DiGiacinto posted him at the door as a greeter. Afterward he said, "I guess I didn't think they let people like me into places like this." Once in, he was hooked. "He admitted that he had ruined his college chances with such bad grades up to that point," DiGiacinto says, "but the next semester he enthusiastically joined the bus tour the class did after the gallery opening and began to really improve. He went on to the Milwaukee Area Technical College, and he's taking business classes now."

Inspiring Engagement

Teachers working from prescribed standards can tap into students' curiosity by asking a question or creating a storyline that intrigues students enough to ask for more. DiGiacinto started her project by dipping into spoken word poetry. "I noticed that lots of kids will say they have no outside interests at school, but then they write poetry on their own. It's a way for students to process the world around them. Their vocabulary is better in poetry than in everyday speaking or academic writing. So I introduce them to the work of Russell Sims and Dasha Kelly and other youth poets." Then students begin to see that performing poetry is performing history, and they want to be a part of the project.

Reach Out to Community Partners

Involving community partners in students' education penetrates the membrane between school and the real world to help students feel that their education is relevant. It also allows teachers to borrow on the expertise of scholars, activists, artists, and others beyond their teaching colleagues.

DiGiacinto is a history teacher and her first expectation is to have her students gain proficiency in Wisconsin history standards. But she also wants her students to *feel* a personal connection to their local history and a personal responsibility for educating and enlightening others through their own academic work. She initiated the partnership with Arts @ Large to help her use the arts as a vehicle to explore academic topics and connect students with artists, educators, business leaders, community organizations, and museums. Taking students out into the community and bringing experts from the community into the classroom magnifies and multiplies educational resources. Now there are lots of teachers in the room, and "the room" includes museums, public spaces, universities, and private businesses as well as the classroom and its virtual counterparts.

DiGiacinto collaborated closely with D'Acquisto throughout the project. Using the planning process outlined in D'Acquisto's book, they identified a big idea: individual activists organize and strategize to mobilize change on social justice issues. Then they visualized a museum exhibit as a product that would allow for lots of students to take part, employing diverse strengths and abilities toward a variety of art forms. Planning backward with those products in mind, they came up with three guiding questions that could be answered through many art forms:

1. What were the key issues addressed by the Milwaukee civil rights movement?

2. Who were the key leaders in the Milwaukee civil rights movement?

3. Why did they choose the strategies they chose to mobilize change?

Given a question that turned their gaze outward into community history, and inward to their personal history and identity, students' academic work became engaging and challenging.

Challenging the Artistic Intellect

DiGiacinto's next step was to challenge students to think in complex ways about the relationship between history and communicating history through words, pictures, and performance. Right away, she directed students to the primary sources that are the raw material of a museum curator's art.

Students began their inquiry with the rich digital archive *March on Milwaukee* at the University of Wisconsin-Milwaukee. There they gained access to unedited audiotapes, photos, video footage, documents, newspapers, and interviews with activists, bystanders, and police on the scene during Milwaukee's turbulent and sometimes violent marches for housing and economic equity.

Next, students interviewed local historian, Jasmine Alinder, an expert in the Milwaukee civil rights movement who was instrumental in creating the archive. Talking with Alinder about the role photographs played in instigating and escalating activism helped students understand how art can galvanize a community around an issue. An important instructional move for teachers is to consider what art forms have been used, or could be used, to move an audience toward action. Introducing this connection to students early in a project will motivate them to engage deeply with both the issue and the art.

The instructional steps to teach analysis and interpretation of primary sources, from a historical or scientific point of view, were described more fully in Chapter 3. When connected with an art project, these thinking skills also apply to artistic primary sources: photographs, poetry, fiction, visual art, music, drama, dance. Looking at art itself as an artifact of its time and culture, and thus a primary source, creates an opportunity to teach the connection between art and ideas.

Teach the Connection between Art and Ideas

In addition to interviewing activists and historians, DiGiacinto's students interviewed and learned from poet and activist Margaret Rozga, as well as from photographers and other artists who could speak to the artistic intention and design behind historical artistic work. Students also worked with drama and music experts, Sherri Williams Pannell and Pat Bridges, to create performance pieces for their opening night celebration. These lessons encouraged students to begin to think about how artists choose which stories to tell and how best to tell them through their art.

Even in the youngest grades, students can begin to look at art as a medium for expressing and communicating both ideas and feelings. Second-grade teacher Michele Morenz and art teacher Anna Loring at Downtown Denver Expeditionary School in Colorado collaborated on a project that combined memoir writing and mixed-media self-portraits. They wanted students to create self-portraits that were not just images of what students look like, but also images of students' thinking, doing, and feeling. To get "character" into the portraits, the teachers created lessons where drawing and painting facilitated writing, and writing facilitated drawing and painting.

"This was the beginning of the year," says Morenz, "and we wanted to find a way for the second graders to tell the people in the community about themselves." Students started the year by drawing self-portraits in art class. Then, in the regular classroom, they listened to a read-aloud of a model memoir, Cynthia Rylant's *When I Was Young in the Mountains*. Noticing and discussing the details of Rylant's illustrations and how they elaborated on the setting and characters in the story pushed students to think about descriptive details in their own memories.

"Then the kids used oil pastel and water color to create the setting of their own memoirs. Drawing and painting helped solidify their writing," notes Morenz. "Painting the scenery in the background of their cover self-portrait gave them the opportunity to think deeply about the smells, sounds, and colors in the memoir. When they wrote, they were able to elaborate with more detailed information, since they had already thought about it."

As students wrote, they continually went back and forth between the "word pictures" in model memoirs and the actual pictures artists used to illustrate them. Loring used a variety of models, graphic organizers, and prompts to show students how writers zero in on a significant small moment that blossoms with meaning.

Then Loring photographed students in poses that complemented the small moments students were writing about. At this point students had painted the backgrounds for their portraits and written their memoirs. Finally, Loring modeled for students how she picked out important/juicy words or images from Morenz's model memoir that told the story and/or painted a picture in the viewer's mind. She highlighted how the words connected to the art in Morenz's self-portrait.

Students then got to work selecting from their own writing important words and phrases to illustrate the photographs. This back-and-forth between writing and creating images resulted in collages that tell the story of who students are from the inside out, not just what they look like (see Figure 5.5).

Figure 5.5 Mia's Self-Portrait

Compel Students to Grapple and Synthesize

The Denver second graders and the Milwaukee high school students all grappled with the artist's dilemma: how to make art that is provocative and meaningful and is beautiful in its own way. To do so, they had to process ideas, images, and words and put them together, or synthesize them, into a new creation. The Milwaukee students synthesized primary sources from history, images from artistic models and professional exhibits, and a common understanding of the purpose of their museum exhibit. The Denver students synthesized their own memories and personal histories with photographs and paintings.

Although this process may seem like a kind of mental alchemy, it is exactly the kind of deep thinking that yields new and lasting understanding. It's what students do when they summarize or synthesize the main points of a lecture. It's what doodlers do when they are listening and "visualizing the connections they make while thinking," an "artistic" process that also fosters long-term memory (Drabowska, 2015; Mueller & Oppenheimer, 2014).

In addition to synthesizing images or sounds and ideas, student artists are also grappling with multiple and complex perspectives that enhance empathy and emotional connection. Analyzing art encourages students to consider how others represent and express ideas and emotions based on their own experience or understanding. Creating their own art gives students an opportunity to express their own perspective. Perspective seeking and perspective taking are markers of empathy and emotional engagement in a topic and the project associated with it; arts education builds perspective and the capacity for empathy toward those who are different from us. "The arts tap into deeply cultural and expressive aspects of peoples' lives that are at the center of what it means to be human" (National Association of State Boards of Education, 2003, p. 7).

Empower Students with Strategies to Improve Their Work

At any grade level, and particularly if a similar project has been done in the past, conducting a critique lesson using professional or student work models will result in more focused and more effective work time toward high-quality products.

Before writing their own text panels for the March to Equality museum exhibit, DiGiacinto's students studied professional museum exhibit artifacts and the captions and written documents that accompanied them. The purpose of examining these models was to norm the common vision for what the final product would look like. The lessons started by selecting high-quality work from local museums that the students' own exhibit would parallel. Students then named and described the artistic strategies the artists used to be successful. For example, when they analyzed the museum caption copy, students pointed out fundamentals like the number of words in a typical caption, the size of the font, and that there weren't any spelling or grammatical errors. But they also commented on more nuanced characteristics like how the captions zeroed in on big ideas, encouraged the reader to do an activity, quoted a primary source, or asked a question.

Armed with these specific criteria, represented in the Kid Curators Rubric in Appendix I, students were both more confident and more capable of creating their own works of excellence.

At any grade level, and particularly if a similar project has been done in the past, conducting a critique lesson using student work models will result in more focused and effective work time toward high-quality products. There are many online resources on museum and educator sites that provide rubrics and questions to guide students in productive critique (see, for example, incredible@rtdepartment, at www.incredibleart.org). Students, like professional art critics, also need that common language in order to be kind, specific, and helpful in peer critiques. The lesson plan that follows show how one teacher prepares middle school students to think critically about a model piece of art, and then critique each other's first drafts.

Lesson Plan: Critical Thinking in Art (50 min)

Learning Target(s): I can categorize and discuss open-ended critical thinking questions.

Formative Assessment: Question activity and debrief

Table 5.2 Lesson Plan: Critical Thinking in Art

Component	Description
Engage and Grapple 2 min	Explain: "Today we are going to be doing an art critique. Turn and talk: What do you think "critique" looks like and sounds like?"
Discuss 5 min	Pairs share out with the whole group. Brief discussion of how "critique" is not just your own opinion, or what you "like," but an evaluation supported by analysis of the detail in the artwork and understanding of what the artist's purpose and method is. The definition of "critique" is: "a detailed analysis and assessment of something"

Component	Description
Focus Mini-lesson 15 min	Explain: "When we critique something, we need to focus on the artwork, not the artist. Our critique should describe the artwork and use specific language that shows we are looking for the artist's intent.
	To help us get better at critiquing art—professional artwork, and then our own and each other's—I have a bunch of questions (see Exhibit 5.1). Today, I'd like you to organize these questions by the types of thinking that art critics do. These are also types of thinking that you do every day and they lead to what we call 'critical thinking.' The interesting thing is that just being able to describe something carefully is a building block for being able to evaluate it accurately. The types of thinking are: Describe, Analyze, Interpret, Evaluate"
	Assign each table ONE of these words and note that they are going to "unpack what they mean." Model with "Describe." Explain: "To describe something is to name what it actually looks like and sounds like. So, an analogy would be to present a realistic and detailed photograph of it."
	Have group members discuss/list synonyms or analogies for what their assigned word means, then share out to the whole group. Facilitate a brief discussion to make sure that all students understand how these types of thinking are different. (5 min)
Practice with Guidance 5 min	Explain the modified four corners protocol:
	"You will each get a question. Notice that I've put our four categories up in the four corners of the room. You'll have three minutes to decide which category your question goes into. Think carefully about this, because you'll need to be able to explain why you put your question there."
	Model this with one or two questions.
Apply 15 min	Students each go to the corner that matches their question.
	Students circle up within each question category; they each in turn explain to each other why they chose that category.
	Call on two students in each category to share out with the full group which question they had, and why they located it there.
Synthesize Debrief 10 min	Circle up the whole group. Invite students to respond to the question:
	How will answering these questions about a piece of artwork allow us to better evaluate whether it's good?

Source: Adapted from a lesson written by Heather Kabot, art teacher at Franklin School of Innovation, Asheville, NC, 2015.

Exhibit 5.1: Art Critique Open-Ended Questions for Visual Art

Description: What do you see?
- What is the subject matter of this artwork? Are there recognizable images?
- Describe the artist's use of color. (e.g., bold, delicate, contrast, emphasis)

(continued)

- Describe the composition of the piece. (e.g., foreground, middle ground, background)
- Describe the artist's use of line. (e.g., thick, thin, hard, soft, implied)
- Describe the sense of light in this piece.
- Describe the artist's use of value. (e.g., shading from light to dark range, mid-tones, contrast)
- Describe the technical properties of the artwork. (tools, materials, medium)

Analysis: How did they do that?
- How does the artist create points of emphasis in this piece?
- What leads your eye around from place to place?
- What are the relationships between parts of the artwork?
- What is interesting in the background or corners of the piece?
- Where do you see balance? Rhythm?
- Where do you notice texture? Is it real or implied?
- How does the title relate to the piece?

Interpretation: What does it mean? How does it feel?
- How does it make you feel? Why does it do that?
- Does this art remind you of anything you have experienced?
- What meanings or message do you imagine the artist intended in this art?
- What does it mean for you?
- What seems important? Why?
- What subthemes are hiding in this composition?
- What do you wonder about?

Evaluation: Opinion. Is it any good? Is it successful?
- How does this work reflect the artist's cultural values?
- What is the most original or creative thing you see?
- How is this artwork similar and/or different from other artwork you have seen?
- What about the work makes you feel you have something in common with the artist?
- What could the artist revise to further express his or her ideas?
- What could the artist revise to create a stronger composition?
- How easily were you able to see the artist's intent in this piece?
- What is the purpose of the piece? Is the purposed achieved?
- How does work relate to other ideas or events in the world?
- How does this work impact its audience?

In the lesson following this introduction to critique, students ask the same questions about a model piece of art (that none of the students created). Then they aim these questions at their own artwork and respond in writing to their teacher. This gives students practice explaining their own efforts using the language of art *before* they have to do so with real critics. They'll use their answers later as notes to write a formal artist's statement.

And finally, working in trios, students describe, analyze, interpret, and evaluate each other's work, providing kind, helpful, and specific feedback based on the answers to these questions. In the peer critique sessions, the discussion always begins with pure description, and the remainder of the session is balanced between what is successful in the work (praise) and what can still be revised to improve the composition and the communication of the message (suggestion).

At MELS in New York City, students used a protocol for critique called Praise, Question, Polish for their "Times They Are a' Changin" mixed media collages. Using a rubric that normed class expectations for their work as a guide (see Table 5.3), students used the following questions to hone their feedback to their peers:

- *Praise:* What has the artist done well?

- *Question:* What question arises when you view the piece?

- *Polish:* What could the artist do to strengthen the piece?

Figure 5.6 is an example of a completed feedback form used during the Praise, Question, Polish protocol.

Table 5.3 MELS Art Rubric for the "Times They Are a' Changin" Mixed Media Collages

	Above and Beyond 4	Got It 3	Getting There 2	Not Yet 1
Communication of "Change"	The artist displayed specific imagery that serves as visual clues to *clearly* indicate the change the artist wants to see.	The artist displayed imagery that indicates the change the artist wants to see.	The artist displayed imagery that *vaguely* indicates the change the artist wants to see.	The artist displayed imagery that *has no relation* to the change the artist wants to see.
Media Choices	Artist *clearly* considered the special properties of each medium in order to best convey his or her message.	Artist considered the special properties of most media in order to best convey his or her message.	Artist considered the special properties of some media in order to best convey his or her message.	Artist selected the media at random, not considering how each medium would best convey his or her message.

(continued)

Table 5.3 Continued

	Above and Beyond 4	**Got It 3**	**Getting There 2**	**Not Yet 1**
Unity	Artwork is unified, as all of its parts fit together in a cohesive whole through specific placement of images and use of color.	Artwork is unified, as most of its parts fit together in a cohesive whole through specific placement of images and use of color.	Artwork is somewhat unified, as some of its parts fit together in a cohesive whole through specific placement of images and use of color.	Artwork is not unified, as placement and color were not considered in creating a cohesive whole.
Craftsmanship	There are no accidental tears, wrinkles, or smudges. The lines, coloring, and cutting are done neatly and with care.	There are few accidental tears, wrinkles, or smudges. The lines, coloring, and cutting are done neatly and with care.	There are several accidental tears, wrinkles, or smudges. The lines, coloring, and cutting are done somewhat neatly.	There are many accidental tears, wrinkles, or smudges. The lines, coloring, and cutting are done somewhat haphazardly.

Figure 5.6 Sample Praise, Question, Polish Critique Form

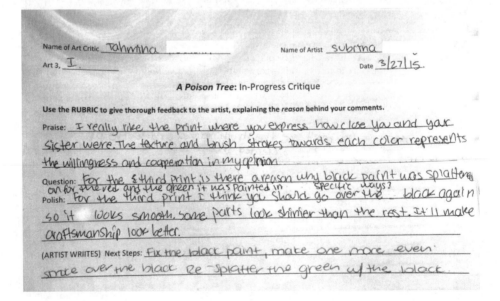

Name of Art Critic: Tahmina   Name of Artist: Subrina

Art 3, I.   Date 3/27/15.

A Poison Tree: In-Progress Critique

Use the RUBRIC to give thorough feedback to the artist, explaining the *reason* behind your comments.

Praise: I really like the print where you express how close you and your sister were. The texture and brush strokes towards each color represents the willingness and cooperation in my opinion

Question: For the 3 third print is there a reason why black paint was splattered on for the red and the green it was painted in specific ways?

Polish: For the third print I think you should go over the black again so it looks smooth. Some parts look shinier than the rest. It'll make craftsmanship look better.

(ARTIST WRIITES) Next Steps: Fix the black paint, make one more even smice over the black Re-splatter the green w/ the black.

Build on the Culture of Critique to Revise . . . Again and Again

Formal critique lessons begin to establish a culture of critique in which specific feedback from teachers and peers, and revision based on that feedback, becomes the daily, ongoing, and informal modus operandi of the classroom.

Teachers often lament the lack of time in their schedules for careful revision. But what we've noticed is that once a culture of critique is the norm, students want to show their work to teachers and peers. They ask for feedback. And they see revision as an opportunity to excel rather than a waste of effort. When both teachers and students are invested in the outcome of all that effort, the time to revise actually feels quite efficient.

Four components of revision underscore its value:

- *Rehearsal.* Even professional artists "rehearse" regularly in order to improve and maintain their skills. Critique and revision are the daily and continual rehearsal that leads to polished performance or presentation.

- *Evidence-based reflection.* Critique is most helpful when it comes in the form of evidence-based specific words, rather than evaluative words. "These colors suggest a dark mood that makes me feel sad" helps the artist determine whether he's conveying the message or emotion he intends. "I don't like the dark colors" expresses the viewer's opinion but is not very helpful to the artist.

- *Persistence*: "Artists throughout history have left behind sketches and notebooks, giving us glimpses into their artistic processes. These artifacts can provide a valuable lesson in persistence . . . Examining early drafts of master works can illuminate the revision process for students . . . and provide insight into perseverance and diligence."

I use the phrase "Praise, Question, Polish." Students are familiar with that format and get used to critiquing professional work and each other's work, as well as receiving PQPs. They know that providing and receiving respectful critical feedback is actually a learning target they will be assessed on.

—*Elyse Rosenberg, teacher,*
Metropolitan Expeditionary
Learning School

- *Practice*: Besides working toward a final, finished high-quality piece, students learn from the revision process that practicing revision itself establishes a habit of artistic scholarship that will serve them well in the long run. "Practicing revision in multiple art forms allows students to build their revision 'muscles,' making them more powerful" (Kennedy Center ArtsEdge, n.d.).

We've discussed the value of inviting in or going out to work with experts who can guide students' understanding, drafting, and revision process. For large schools and particularly high schools, this sort of real-world experience can be a particular challenge. The following Snapshot, an example of arts as curriculum, demonstrates how one school provides students with mentors and time to create and revise without disrupting the daily schedule.

SNAPSHOT: Teaching Performance Arts through Week-Long Intensives

Three times a year, students at Polaris Expeditionary Learning School in Fort Collins, Colorado, sign up for week-long intensive courses taught in collaboration with community artists, musicians, and craftspeople. Students choose these small-group courses and each course includes students of varying abilities, interests, and age groups. The school invites professionals to teach topics from cooking to fly fishing, construction to photography. In one intensive, students learned to write songs, play them, and perform them for an audience—in one week!

Professional musicians (Kathryn Mostow, Justin Roth, and Danielle Anderson) from the local community volunteered their time throughout the week to help lead short workshops, critique sessions, and group instruction. The musicians supported students to write great songs by giving them permission to take risks and inspiring them with models and a rich storehouse of their own professional experiences including "stumbling and bumbling to figure things out." Some students wrote songs from poems they hadn't previously thought of as material for music. Others started from the grist of experience or memories.

According to Polaris middle school teacher Matt Strand, "What students really learned is that artists fail over and over and over again before they finally succeed. Practice and persistence are the big takeaways." Elizabeth, a high school student who wrote a song with a less experienced middle school student, describes learning a new language for talking to herself and her partner. "You have to say 'I'm good, but I'm not there yet,' instead of saying 'I'm bad or you're bad at singing and we can't do this.' You're complementing yourself in a way that you're leading yourself to do something better."

At the end of the intensive, the students performed their completed songs in the Poudre School District's Channel 10 studio. That authentic audience and the opportunity to perform in a professional environment motivated students to perform like professionals.[5]

Require Students to Perform and Present

We have all felt the tangible booster shot of self-esteem we get when our work is applauded or noted by others who find it meaningful or inspiring. Students need that booster too! When we celebrate students' art in a public way through dialogue with an audience, students beam with pride and take ownership in their work. Ownership and pride drive further achievement. The more often students experience doing more than they think possible, the more willing they are to take academic and artistic risks that will lead to future innovations and success.

What's more, the spark of connection between students and a real audience empowers them to "archive" their learning for future projects and new audiences. DiGiacinto's Milwaukee students spent hours learning presentation skills for their various roles at the museum. Docents learned to walk backward while speaking to museumgoers, how to project their voices, and how to listen to and answer questions effectively. Other students practiced for dramatic reenactments, musical performances, or mock protests. They memorized until they could say their lines flawlessly, attended to accurate costumes, and practiced their tone of voice for authenticity and impact.

These presentation skills are ones they can also use in job interviews, college classes, or leadership positions. Like the student who realized that he had not only a right to enter but also a role to play at the museum, DiGiacinto's students are better prepared to succeed at anything because they have internalized their presentation skills. The following Snapshot describes another important real-world connection. Projects that connect art and mathematics encourage students to apply academic skills to artistic problems, and artistic skills to academic challenges.

SNAPSHOT: Connecting Art and Mathematics

Twelfth-grade digital art and mathematics students at High Tech High in San Diego, California, were asked to find the beauty, humanity, and intrigue behind mathematics in history, philosophy, and the applied arts. The goal was to promote mathematics awareness through art, media, and story. They explored the inventions of Leonardo da Vinci, the art

(continued)

of M. C. Escher, and the formulas of mathematician Fibonacci, and then represented the ideas of these historic thinkers through their own art.[6]

On the other end of the schooling spectrum, pre-K and kindergarten students at Capital City Public Charter School in Washington, D.C., worked together to connect their learning about number sense with patterns in nature. Through many visits to a local park, they captured photos of numbers zero through ten. Students then used the pictures as the class addressed standards related to number sense, combining them to understand addition and place. They then turned their learning into art by writing, typing, and illustrating a book with their photos.[7]

In both of these examples, students were challenged to connect the dots between academic disciplines and to make sense of both art and mathematics through visual representation. That kind of thinking expands their understanding of both subject areas and is foundational for the kind of visual and spatial thinking that engineers, artists, designers, and craftspeople do in the real world.

Curate School Space for Impact and Meaning

Finally, although an individual artistic presentation lasts only as long as the event or the gallery showing, many schools sustain a culture of art and creativity by attending carefully to how school spaces—like public and private spaces outside of school—showcase beauty and meaning.

At High Tech High, the display of student learning and student work go hand in hand. Hallways, classrooms, and the school lobby continually showcase student work that is regularly rotated to educate and inspire parents, educators, and visitors. High Tech High integrates technical and academic instruction with the aim of preparing students for postsecondary careers, citizenship, and education. Toward that end, students themselves are charged with designing and implementing the artistic display of their own work—something professionals often do in technical fields.

"Making student work public is a great driver of student achievement," says Chief Academic Officer Ben Daley, because it inspires both teachers and learners to see what's possible and to reach for a higher bar. To make displays beautiful as well as inspiring and informative, art teacher Jeff Robin suggests three criteria: symmetry, repetition, and surprise. These elements attract the viewer's eye and raise provocative questions that generate deep thinking about the ideas and the process behind the art.[8] The message at schools that create beautiful spaces for learning is clear: school is a place where we see, create, and value art. Teachers bring "control" to the work, tying academic purpose to artistic design problems that stretch students' capacity. These conditions invite students to become makers of beauty and meaning. By teaching in and through the arts, such schools challenge, engage, and empower students to be art-full learners in and out of the classroom.

The Critical Moves of Teaching in and through the Arts

Teaching in and through the arts requires attending to the design of curriculum as well as the instructional strategies that challenge, engage, and empower students with tools for learning. Table 5.4 describes key teaching moves that sustain powerful learning for students.

Table 5.4 The Who, What, and Why of Teaching in and through the Arts

What Do Teachers Do?	What Do Students Do?	What's the Result?
Plan with the product in mind. Identify the content and skill standards addressed by the product, as well as the texts and lessons that will scaffold student success.	Read and investigate to build background knowledge on the topic. Practice skills in order to prepare for success on the product.	Students see the relevance of the artistic product and recognize that art is a way to communicate ideas and express emotions.
Engage students through active teaching in and through the arts. Teach lessons based on artistic and content area learning targets.	Grapple with ideas they want to represent through art and with artistic design problems.	Students discover that the artistic process is a way to synthesize, symbolize, and realize new understandings of the world and diverse perspectives.
Analyze and critique models with students. Teach the vocabulary of artistic mediums by using it with students. Develop rubrics based on the critique session.	Articulate criteria for quality in their own words and assess their own and their peer's work against that criteria.	Students are empowered by having a language for talking about art and having strategies for getting to quality through revision.
Reach out to experts, mentors, and community partners who can augment artistic understanding.	Learn from a diverse group of adults. Connect artistic expression to community needs and issues.	Students build relationships with people, places, and issues in their community. They discover their own efforts can make a difference in their community and experience art as a purposeful profession.

(continued)

Table 5.4 Continued

What Do Teachers Do?	What Do Students Do?	What's the Result?
Differentiate for diverse academic and artistic interests, abilities, and processes.	Use different doorways into art content and process. They build on academic and artistic strengths to learn new skills and content.	Students' artwork demonstrates individuality and creativity. It has "voice" as well as craftsmanship. Students are empowered by the knowledge that different is good.
Find authentic audiences for artistic products. Teach performance and presentation skills.	Persist through multiple revisions and polish with a vision of professionalism for a real audience. They focus on presentation skills as well as content.	Students understand that artwork and schoolwork have meaning beyond grades and beyond the school. They see that how a product is presented matters as much as the product itself.
Curate school and community spaces for impact and meaning. Cultivate a culture of art.	Contribute to the aesthetics of their learning spaces. They become stewards of the spaces in which they learn and are inspired and engaged by beautiful surroundings.	Students value beauty, and see how aesthetics impact quality of life. They are empowered by seeing their own work in the gallery that surrounds them at school and in the community.

SCHOOLWIDE IMPLEMENTATION

Leading School Improvement through a Focus on the Arts

Prioritizing art in schools is no easy feat. In our current educational climate the arts are often seen as a perk that many schools feel that they can't afford, in terms of time, personnel, and budgets. Leaders who help teachers and other stakeholders connect the dots between academic learning and aesthetic learning and expression take a big step toward overcoming these hurdles. What follows is the story of the Maplewood Richmond Heights (MRH) school district, a small, diverse urban district in St. Louis, Missouri, that successfully and courageously connected those dots for their community.

In 2000, after decades of decline, the state Department of Education threatened to retract the MRH district's accreditation because of low performance. Typically in this situation, a state takes over a district and installs a strict, narrow test-focused curriculum, perhaps eliminating arts entirely. Instead, district and school leaders did just the opposite. They responded with a bold move that began by conscientiously searching for a vision that would counter the common metaphor of school as factory turning out products (students). They asked themselves, "What model would motivate our students to want to come to school, to achieve, and to be proud of their school and community?" More than ten years later, families are moving into the district in order to attend the MRH schools. The district is both high-performing academically and also resplendent in arts learning. The case study that follows, originally written by Linda Henke, former MRH superintendent, and Louise Cadwell, an educational consultant, tells the story of the district's elementary school's approach to improvement, teaching in and through the arts.

CASE STUDY

Maplewood Richmond Heights Elementary: School as a Museum

The metaphor for the elementary school emerged from an article by Linda D'Acquisto (Koetsch, D'Acquisto, Kurin, Juffer, & Goldberg, 2002) about students producing museum exhibits. I sent a copy of the article to the elementary principal and asked her to discuss the piece with her staff. The article outlined the experience of a school where students created displays of their learning for other students and the community. A number of teachers were interested in exploring the metaphor, and so we arranged for D'Acquisto to begin to work with a small team of volunteers. The results of the first museum opening were infectious. Parents, teachers, and children all had something to talk about—and parents came to the opening at their children's insistence. It was the biggest parent event anyone could remember. Clearly we were on to something.

Within two years, the entire school was involved in producing exhibits as part of students' inquiry education incorporating science and social studies. When we passed a bond issue that allowed us to build a new elementary school, we approached the design with the idea of a museum in mind so that every grade level has an exhibit area. As visitors enter the foyer today, they are greeted with a sign that welcomes them to MRH Elementary School and Museum. A brochure announces the exhibits that are available for viewing and how to secure a personalized tour with a student docent.

Dan Lyons has been a teacher in the district for fifteen years and currently serves as the elementary gifted teacher and chair of the Museum Board of Directors, a group of students who manage the operation of the museum. Dan was in the original group that experimented with museum exhibits and now supports students and teachers in learning in this way. Dan notes that both students and teachers in the museum school think much differently about their work than when he first started at MRH.

"Thinking about our school as a museum opened up so many ideas of what is possible. We used to teach the American Revolution as a series of facts. Now we do an object study, visit to a local museum, and create a perspective wall. More and more, we are feeling comfortable investigating where students' interests are in the topic. We're no longer driven by the textbook."

This kind of teaching, Dan acknowledges, requires teachers to be both skillful and collaborative. He remarks, "When you aren't following a textbook you have to get very clear about what you want children to learn." He also emphasizes that this work has become much more collaborative for teachers and students. "You can't be at the elementary school and stay in your classroom. You are expected to be planning with your team and helping your students learn from the exhibits other grade levels are producing."

The work at MRH elementary school strikes Dan as more authentic now that it is guided with the museum metaphor. "Kids are much more aware of 'other' because they are constantly thinking about how well we are communicating with our audience. Do we need graphics or charts or an experience to help little kids understand our exhibit? What about our grandparents? And the conversations have deepened." He reflects, "The openings give children opportunities to have rich conversations with adults. Parents, grandparents, neighbors—they all come to openings because the kids are excited to tell them about what they have learned. Kids really like being experts."

The journey of a school exploring a new metaphor is now over a decade old. MRH is a very different district now, considered one of the most innovative in the county. People move into town because they want their children involved in this kind of learning, and our student population has grown by almost 20 percent. While there have been lots of bumps along the way as with any school reform, the metaphor of museum is deeply embedded in the way children, teachers, and parents think about elementary education. Today as we wander through the amazing student-constructed exhibits, it is impossible not to sense the joy of creating and the deep pleasure of learning that is now a part of the everyday life of the school.

Short of a district-wide commitment, like we see in the Maplewood Richmond Heights case study, the key leadership actions that follow describe how leaders can initiate structures and professional learning that will deepen all teachers' capacity to teach in and through the arts.

Key Leadership Actions

Lay the Groundwork

- Rally community support. A first step toward creating a culture of art is communicating the vision for teaching the arts to parents, school or charter board members, and community stakeholders. Leaders should come to a consensus about the "elevator speech" for why and how the arts will be taught and integrated into other subject areas. Getting the teachers fully on board and giving them the tools and know-how to realize the vision will result in the best publicity any new initiative can garner.

- Schedule for collaboration. Seek input from classroom teachers about their needs for collaboration, then create a schedule that allows for group development of projects, lessons that build on team members' diverse strengths, and monitoring the progress of a project so that changes can be made to improve instruction and outcomes. The schedule may also need to include time for students to collaborate with mentors or community partners, or to present their work to outside audiences.

Build Teachers' Capacity

- Provide strong professional development. Deeper instruction in the arts is complex work. Teachers will need professional development and coaching to learn new strategies for planning, implementing, and integrating artistic concepts, especially through content area instruction. With respect for teachers' unfamiliarity or discomfort with teaching art, leaders may want to provide art lessons for teachers themselves first, then reflect together on the failures and successes they can also anticipate in their students.

- Model, reflect, and revise. Professional development, staff meetings, and school-wide traditions are all opportunities to do art together, modeling the deeper instructional practices described in this chapter.

Support Teachers to Deepen Their Practice

- Budget and fund-raise with intention. Providing materials for arts education and hallway or lobby galleries, and staffing for trips to museums or music or dance performances is an ongoing expense that leaders must commit to (many private and public arts agencies also provide grants that support the arts). It's also important to remember that art and design materials don't have to be exotic or expensive.

COMMON CHALLENGES

Using Art as Enhancement Only

Infuse the curriculum both with arts as curriculum in its own right and as a subject integrated with other subject areas. Deeper instruction includes teaching both the concepts and the skills of artistic media, with attention to process, ideas, and quality results. All students should have access to explicit quality instruction in visual arts, music, drama and movement, and in addition, art teachers and community experts should be supporting integration of the arts.

Neglecting to Treat the Artistic Components of Interdisciplinary Work with Integrity

When a history project requires students to create a poster, podcast, or play, it can bring history to life for students, making their study more engaging and enduring. However, if the focus (and assessment) of the project is limited to historical content and neglects to focus also on artistic integrity, it can result in work of poor quality. If their posters, podcasts, or play are supported by artistic lessons and critiqued by artistic experts, students will develop an ethic of craftsmanship and will produce work of much greater value and impact.

Adding Art Projects at the Last Minute

Artistic products require time, instruction, and differentiated scaffolding for students with diverse strengths. Teachers should plan backward with the product in mind to be sure that all of these elements are attended to carefully and that art products address and assess required standards in both art and, often, content areas.

Teaching Art by Formulas

Throw away the cookie cutter and teach the arts through an authentic creative process. Engaging lessons to support artistic work include building background knowledge, researching ideas and artistic strategies, learning from models, and experimenting in maker spaces. Encourage students to learn from experts and also to take creative risks with permission to fail, try again, and revise to achieve their vision. Challenge students to synthesize and communicate big ideas from other subject areas through a blend of traditional academic work (e.g., essays, infographics) and artistic expression.

Neglecting to Use Models

Provide students with models that help them develop a common understanding of quality and expectations. Be clear that you don't want them to "copy" the model, but rather to articulate and apply the strategies and qualities the artist has used to generate the exemplar.

Limiting Resources

Art is about big ideas! When planning and implementing art lessons or subject area lessons that support an art product, consider texts, community artists or experts, parent volunteers, the classroom recycling bin, the art, music, or technology teacher, your home workshop, and any other repository of materials and knowledge that can be repurposed as a resource. Encourage students to be resourceful as well, and to connect the big ideas of their artistic message with the matter they use to present the message.

Overlooking the Power of Audience

Remember that an authentic audience motivates students to work toward excellence. Artwork produced only for the teacher is likely to be pedestrian and mediocre. Inspire students to learn professional techniques and to see the real-world applications of art by arranging for or encouraging students to identify a real audience for their work. Presenting and celebrating works of art empowers students to persist and transfer their learning to new environments.

Notes

1. A video of the *Three Little Pigs* musical can be viewed at www.youtube.com/watch?v = fRF0894y5NA

2. The Kennedy Center. (2015). What Is Arts Integration? May 19. https://artsedge.kennedy-center.org/educators/how-to/arts-integration/what-is-arts-integration

3. Adapted from National Core Arts Standards. www.nationalartsstandards.org/

4. More information on D'Acquisto's process can be found at kidcurators.com

5. You can see the whole performance and reflections from the students and their artist mentors in Models of Excellence: The Center for High-Quality Student Work: http://modelsofexcellence.eleducation.org/projects/songwriting-intensive

6. You can see videos of their projects, which were showcased at a California gallery, at Models of Excellence: The Center for High-Quality Student Work. http://modelsofexcellence.eleducation.org/projects/illuminated-mathematics

7. You can view this project at Models of Excellence: The Center for High-Quality Student Work. http://modelsofexcellence.eleducation.org/projects/nature-numbers

8. You can view a narrated tour of High Tech High's inspiring building at www.teachingchannel.org/videos/make-student-work-public-hth>

Chapter 6

Differentiating Instruction

OVERVIEW

Letting Every Learner Lead

By and large, everyone in the United States goes to school. As Carol Ann Tomlinson, leading expert on differentiated instruction, points out, "Over the past half century or more, the student population has changed dramatically. Today, all children are expected to come to school whatever their gender, socioeconomic status, or physical or mental challenge" (1999, p. 20). In a keynote address at EL Education's national conference in 2011, Tomlinson described the difference "great teachers" make. They "see humanity in every child; model a world that dignifies each child; and make decisions to support the welfare of each child." Today more than ever, we possess the knowledge and tools to create classrooms and whole schools that allow us to see and treat each child as an individual and a success.

According to Merriam-Webster's dictionary, to differentiate means "to make (someone or something) different in some way"; and "to see or state the difference or differences between two or more things." Both definitions strongly apply in an effective classroom. In differentiated classrooms teachers are able to recognize and describe the differences among the learners in front of them and apply that knowledge to instruction. Teachers select different instructional approaches and paths depending on the varying needs of the individual students in the classroom. This approach allows each student to work toward the same high standards in ways suited particularly to him or her.

Differentiation applies to all students—those with disabilities and special learning needs, those who are learning English, and those who advance quickly through their studies and need additional challenges. Effective differentiation requires that teachers meet all students where they are. As this chapter makes clear, differentiated instruction is, in many ways, a partner to deeper instruction. Meeting students where they are as learners and helping them understand their own strengths and struggles supports teachers' efforts to challenge, engage, and empower all students.

The need for differentiated approaches to students' learning needs cannot be overstated. It is seen most clearly in the voices and stories of individual students struggling to make progress and find a place in school. "My understanding was that my son could learn well using specific interventions geared towards how a dyslexic brain functions. But the inclination of his teachers was more to give him lots of extra attention and encouragement so that he could plow through the 'regular' way," one parent states about her son, who struggled throughout his education.

> "In other words, they just made him work harder instead of working smarter, which was exhausting for him, although it did get him through more of his schoolwork than not having that attention. I got an image in my head that school was a foot race and my son had one leg tied up so he was hopping, instead of running. The teachers were right next to him saying, "Hop, hop faster, don't give up, you can do it," so that he sort of could keep up, but it would have been much more useful for them to help him untie his other leg so he could run instead of hop."

Effectively addressing differentiation is a very complex endeavor in a typical school classroom of twenty to thirty unique individuals. For efficiency, want of resources, and tradition (i.e., "the way we've always done things"), schools have long been organized as a one-size-fits-all model of education. At the same time, however, there is also a long tradition of teachers recognizing and supporting individual students. In many schools and classrooms, teachers are discovering the value and challenge of differentiation as they develop the skills to group students flexibly according to their needs, assess all students' understanding and progress, and create appropriate scaffolds and supports.

The Principles of Differentiated Instruction

The principles of differentiated instruction described in Table 6.1 can guide schools and teachers embarking on this critically important area of practice.[1] As the principles reflect, effective differentiation happens in the process of daily teaching and learning. Some students, for example, may have more drafts or a scaffolded graphic organizer in place to help them get to the end goal of an essay. Texts might be broken into manageable chunks to give students who need it support to access content. In mathematics, students may be given multiple options for how to tackle a problem. But teachers who are carefully differentiating ensure that the overall learning target remains the same and include strategic entry points that give all students an opportunity to learn the same content. More or less of the same, in other words, does not serve our students well. Differentiation does.

Figure 6.1 summarizes the principles of differentiated instruction and layers of differentiated support that schools should have available. As the graphic shows, the majority of students can be served in a heterogeneous classroom, working towards the same standards. This chapter delves into the specific strategies that will help teachers meet their students' diverse needs within that heterogeneous classroom.

Table 6.1 Principles of Differentiated Instruction

Principle	Definition	Example
Understand student learning strengths and weaknesses	This is the complete picture of a student's learning preferences, strengths, and challenges. It is drawn from a range of data, including the student's reflection.	Maria is an English language learner who is fluent in her native language, Spanish. Her family speaks both English and Spanish. She is able to focus on her work for long periods of time and finds learning her new language relatively simple, but she is challenged in mathematics. This makes her quite different from Jose, even though he is also a new English language learner. Jose is not yet literate in Spanish and his family speaks only Spanish at home. He is nevertheless good at mathematics, especially when manipulatives are available.
Get to know student interests	Interest is a student's particular inclination toward a subject or activity. Interest motivates students naturally and can be a doorway into challenging work.	Following the building background knowledge phase of a second-grade learning expedition about snakes, students were able to choose a specific snake that most interested them to research more deeply.
Identify student readiness for a particular concept, skill, or task	Readiness is not "ability" or intellectual capacity. Rather it captures the "entry point" a student needs. Readiness may reflect experiences, previous learning opportunities, emotional states, social skills, and mindset, as much as cognitive ability.	Some students are ready to organize their information independently, while others benefit from using a teacher-prepared graphic organizer to arrange information prior to writing.

Principle	Definition	Example
Develop respectful tasks	Respectful tasks motivate and challenge all students in the class. While the work may not be identical, it does not create a sense of "unfairness" in the amount or type of task required. The work should challenge students just enough to stimulate them with new learning, but not be so challenging as to overwhelm.	As part of a recent study of Romeo and Juliet, ninth-grade students were given the choice of three projects with the same learning targets. One project appealed to strengths of visual learners, another to auditory learners, and a third to kinesthetic learners.
Use flexible grouping	Students work in a variety of configurations at the appropriate level of challenge. At times they are grouped by readiness, interest, learning style, or choice. At times they work in small groups, pairs, or individually. The groupings are determined to match the purpose of the activity.	A teacher makes two pieces of text on the same content available to her class: one at grade level, and the other above grade level. One day she creates groups based on their choice of text. The next day she mixes groups so that students who've read different texts can learn from each other.
Embed ongoing assessment and adjustment	Ongoing assessment enables the teacher to determine students' entry points, their confusions and misconceptions, the speed at which they are grasping new ideas, and their overall attainment of new skills and concepts. She then uses the information to guide her next instructional steps.	Students complete an entry ticket that assesses material taught in the previous day's class. The teacher reviews (or invites students to share out) the entry tickets before deciding what material needs to be reinforced and/or extended in the current class and for whom.
Differentiate the process, not the content or product	Differentiating the learning *process* includes all of the varied instructional strategies, activities, tools, and resources that help students meet required standards—knowledge, skills, concepts, and habits—that teachers want all students to learn. A common final product allows students to demonstrate mastery of those standards. Unless a student has an individual education program (IEP) that states differently, all students need to meet the same standards, preferably with the same end product.	All students are required to write an analytical essay on the play *Pygmalion*, discussing the internal and external changes of its main character over the course of the play. Some students are given partially filled in graphic organizers, sentence starters, and academic word banks to assist them. Others are given less "up-front" scaffolding and are provided additional time in teacher conferencing and peer review. Still others are encouraged to extend their drafts and make explicit connections to other literature they have read and studied, beyond the initial prompt.

Figure 6.1 The Terrain of Differentiated Instruction

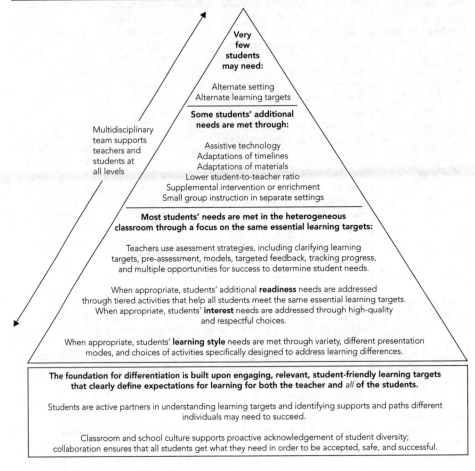

Why This Practice Matters

As described in the introduction to this book, deeper instruction that challenges, engages, and empowers students is the path to deeper learning for all. The principles of differentiated instruction and those of deeper instruction go hand in hand. Although effective differentiation is not a panacea, it improves students' experiences in school in many ways.

Differentiated instruction Provides Students with Productive Challenges

Differentiation is rooted in the principle of the "respectful task": one that is not too easy, nor so challenging as to be overwhelming. Tasks that provide a *productive* challenge for students lead to new levels of learning and promote higher-order thinking and conceptual understanding. Effective differentiation increases students' investment in taking on academic challenges because they are able to see the pathway to success. All students deserve to be intellectually challenged. When struggling students are given "alternative content" or required only to practice basic skills, they are denied deeper instruction that can enrich their intellectual lives. Teacher support and scaffolds may be needed; however, thorough understanding of students' needs and strengths allows teachers to support them in a way that doesn't take away their opportunity to grapple with complex ideas, problems, texts, and concepts and to participate in rewarding and engaging higher-order discussions.

Differentiated Instruction Engages All Students in Worthy Work

Many of the basic principles of differentiation (Table 6.1) support students' deep engagement in their learning. Flexible grouping strategies, for example, help students develop communication skills and foster the collaboration that is so important for engaging them in deeper learning opportunities. Structures that allow students to talk to and learn from each other as they work together to create new knowledge are deeply engaging. Most importantly, teachers' commitment to differentiating the process of learning and supporting all students to work toward the same compelling, purposeful final products allows all students to feel that their work has value. Students who may struggle with certain academic skills don't have to feel that their classmates get to do all of the "interesting stuff" while they are stuck working on basic skills.

Differentiated Instruction Empowers Students to Understand Themselves as Learners

There is perhaps no better feeling for a student than having his needs and strengths recognized and being seen as a unique individual who is full of potential. Differentiation not only requires that teachers understand students' strengths and needs, but that students understand them as well. Intentionally building a culture of differentiation in the classroom and fostering a growth mindset in every student, along with continual embedded student-engaged assessment, empowers students as they develop metacognition and advocate for their learning needs.

In the Getting Started section that follows we explore what it takes to build a culture of differentiation that is rooted in knowing students, knowing standards, and closely monitoring student progress.

GETTING STARTED

Building a Culture of Differentiation

Effective differentiation takes place in the context of a classroom and school culture that recognizes and respects differences and enlists students as full partners in the teaching and learning process. It is important to take the time to teach this mindset regarding learning and learning differences—it won't happen automatically. A differentiated mindset—one that values respectful tasks and individuals' needs—becomes the fertile ground for challenging, engaging, and empowering students with deeper instruction.

> I have had lots of conversations this year with kids about how we all learn differently and need different supports. When you take time to explain it, they are okay. All they want to know is that it's fair.
>
> —*Sydney Chaffee, teacher,*
> *Codman Academy Charter*
> *Public School*

Differentiation may be a very different classroom approach from what students have typically experienced. Group work, differing assignments, and genuine levels of academic challenge may flummox both the learner with academic needs and the advanced learner. Emphasizing the following points, in conversations, materials, and classroom space, will smooth the way toward a shared understanding and commitment to differentiation.

- *"Fair" doesn't mean "same."* Discuss a scenario with students in which fair treatment is not the same treatment: for example, providing sugar-free dough for a diabetic friend so she can participate in a cookie-baking party, or giving a blind student a Braille or audio version of a book you want to share with him. Differentiating in the classroom operates on the same principle:

everyone is aiming for the same academic goals, but will take different roads to get there.

- *Everyone brings something valuable to the table.* Students should be familiar with the concept that they are valued as individuals, with unique gifts. Conduct a brief journaling exercise (anonymously or not) in which students list the strengths and gifts that they bring to the table as learners in your classroom. Publish this list in a prominent place. Emphasize that everyone deserves a learning environment in which they feel safe and valued.

- *Intelligence is malleable, not "fixed."* As discussed in Chapter 1, consider conducting a discrete lesson or mini-lesson or engaging students in research on the topic of growth mindset. Many students will find this approach a surprise, particularly if they are used to thinking of themselves as "always bad at math" or "a terrible writer." Remind them that just as their intelligence grows and changes, so your teaching needs to grow and change with them through differentiation.

- *Collaboration is key.* Ask students if they've ever had the experience of a lesson going "too fast" or "too slow" for them because it was being taught in the same way to all the students in the class. Emphasize that this phenomenon is exactly what differentiated group work avoids. The better a student "fits" with the learning, the more successful he or she will be in learning it.

- *All learners should feel challenged—otherwise they aren't learning.* This principle helps students understand that productive academic struggle is a goal, not a failure. It is aimed particularly at advanced learners who may have gotten into the habit of defining academic success as "easy work." Having to put forth genuine effort in a differentiated classroom may be a new and uncomfortable situation for them. Help students understand that if they have to sit back and think, make mistakes, and try again, they are right where they need to be. Becoming accustomed to this feeling is key to deeper learning.

See Appendix J: Initiatives that Build a Positive Classroom Culture of Differentiation for concrete ideas for building a positive culture of differentiation in your classroom.

Knowing Students: Who They Are and What They Bring

Hand in hand with creating a culture of differentiation is understanding students' learning strengths and needs in as much rich detail as possible. Teachers know the importance of this instinctively; as the first step toward building a strong, trust-filled relationship with students, they often solicit information about their students' families, hobbies, hopes, and dreams. Effective differentiation requires that teachers build upon this foundation by expanding their knowledge of their students as learners.

Consider the Brain

Many of students' strengths and needs are neurologically based, "wired" from birth into their brains. Additionally, brain research has contributed a great deal to understanding how flexible and open to development the mind and intellect are. Understanding both our students' neurological profiles and their capacity for further growth is a powerful tool for deeper instruction.

Key Findings on Brain Research and Learning

- The brain is capable of developing and adding neural connections throughout one's life, called "neuroplasticity." The ways in which one is taught can enhance this neurological potential.
- High levels of stress or anxiety limit the flow of information in the prefrontal cortex, which controls judgment, reason, and emotion. "Teachers who understand this neurological consequence of the brain's programmed response to stress can change the educational and life outcomes for students who have been blamed and punished for unintentional acting out or zoning out" (Willis, 2012).
- Working (short-term) memory is enhanced by linking prior knowledge to new information. Opportunities to make predictions, receive timely feedback, and reflect reinforce these connections.
- For something stored in working memory to last it requires multiple opportunities for use. The memory is even more durable when it is connected to other memories—through recognizing patterns, similarities, and differences. Finally, "concept memory networks" require the application of something stored in memory to a novel situation or problem. "Pattern recognition facilitation and opportunities for knowledge transfer extend the brain's processing efficiency for greater access to and application of its accumulated learning. These teaching interventions will prepare graduates for future incorporation and extension of new information as it is becomes available" (Willis, 2012).

Consider Student Learning Preferences and Strengths

Thinking broadly and creatively about the strengths students come with is vital to differentiation. Previous experiences and learning add up as students' progress through their lives and through school, resulting in a different accumulation of concept memory networks for each child. Someone's athletic ability, fine motor coordination, cultural traditions, or family connections may be key levers for their growth as learners. There is not one standard for intelligence, and intelligence in any form is not fixed.

Tapping into students' varied skills and abilities supports deeper learning

Photo: Toni Jackson

Displayed side by side in Table 6.2 are two different frameworks for thinking about the wide range of ways to be "smart": Gardner's Multiple Intelligences and Sternberg's Triarchic Theory of Successful Intelligences.[2]

Frameworks like this are useful for teachers when thinking about entry points for students' learning that can make a topic more engaging. Students are offered multiple ways to "enter into" a study. What follows are possible entry points for teachers to consider when planning differentiated tasks. Following each entry point is an example that will help students meet the learning target: "I can gather and synthesize background information about the impact of the Great American Dustbowl."

Table 6.2 Two Frameworks for Thinking about Intelligence

Gardner's Theory of Multiple Intelligences	Sternberg's Triarchic Theory of Successful Intelligence
Howard Gardner, developmental psychologist and professor of Cognition and Education at Harvard Graduate School of Education, believes "intelligences" are the diverse ways in which we learn and process information and our interests in the various "contents" of the world.	Robert Sternberg, former head of the American Association of Psychologists, believes that there are three types of intelligence called upon to succeed in life:
	Analytical intelligence: "School smarts"
Linguistic intelligence: Sensitivity to spoken and written language, the ability to learn languages, and the capacity to use language to accomplish certain goals. This intelligence includes the ability to effectively use language to express oneself rhetorically or poetically; and language as a means to remember information.	Creative intelligence: "Unique insight"
	Practical intelligence: "Street smarts"
	Researchers are also now exploring a fourth facet: "wisdom," defined as the capacity to meaningfully use what you've learned for the common good.
	Analytical learners like:
	Analyzing characters and situations
	Comparing and contrasting
Logical-mathematical intelligence: The capacity to analyze problems logically, carry out mathematical operations, and investigate issues scientifically.	Criticizing their own and others' work
	Judging behavior
	Explaining difficult problems to others
Musical intelligence: Skill in the performance, composition, and appreciation of musical patterns. It encompasses the capacity to recognize and compose musical pitches, tones, and rhythms.	Sorting and classifying
	Inferring and concluding
	School!
	Creative learners like:
Bodily-kinesthetic intelligence: The potential of using one's whole body or parts of the body to solve problems. It is the ability to use mental abilities to coordinate bodily movements.	Designing
	Coming up with ideas
	Playing make-believe
	Thinking of alternatives
Spatial intelligence: The potential to recognize and use the patterns of wide space and more confined areas.	Thinking in pictures and images
	Supposing things were different
	Composing/drawing/writing
Interpersonal intelligence: The capacity to understand the intentions, motivations, and desires of other people. It allows people to work effectively with others.	Acting and role playing
	Practical learners like:
	Real-world applications
Intrapersonal intelligence: The capacity to understand oneself, to appreciate one's feelings, fears, and motivations.	To use and solve real or meaningful problems
	To know "why" they are learning something
	To interact with people—to "read" them
Naturalist intelligence: The ability to recognize, categorize, and draw upon certain features of the environment.	School is oriented toward analytical learners. However, Sternberg's research shows that students make gains on the analytical measures reflected on standardized tests when they are taught and work *in all three ways*.
Under consideration: Existential intelligence and moral intelligence.	

Narrational entry point: Through stories and words; read or tell a story or narrative

- Example: Read selections from *The Grapes of Wrath* focusing on the impact of the Dust Bowl on the displaced people.

Logical-quantitative entry point: Through numbers or measurement; provide data, use deductive reasoning, examine numbers, statistics, musical rhythm, logic, narrative plot structure, and cause and effect relationships

- Example: Examine a variety of Dust Bowl data for the environmental and economic scope of the disaster.

Foundational entry point: Through philosophy, background, root systems, rationales; ask big questions about life, death, philosophy, meaning, and our place in the world

- Example: Examine the role religion played in the psyche of the "Okies" by listening to recorded sermons and reading letters.

Aesthetic entry point: Through sensory means; emphasize sensory and/or surface features, and activate aesthetic sensitivities

- Example: Examine a collection of Dust Bowl photography and music. How does the style of photography and music at this time reflect the impact of the Dust Bowl?

Experiential entry point: Through personal encounters or experiences of others; use a hands-on approach, dealing directly with materials (physically or virtually), simulations, and personal explanations

- Example: Record (or simply listen to) the oral history of a Dust Bowl survivor. How was this person's life changed or shaped by this event?

The following examples are some other ways in which students bring their personal strengths to their learning. This list is not exhaustive by any means.

- *Skill sets.* As reflected in the multiple dimensions of intelligence in Table 6.2, students come to us with different skills. Some students are stronger at reading than mathematics. Others play instruments, program software, are strong at a particular sport, can give an effective speech, or make something useful with wood and nails. Understanding and affirming the array of skills students possess can boost their confidence and sense of worth, and bolster their learning of new or undeveloped skills.

- *Cultural and language backgrounds.* Students bring their home languages and cultures with them to the classroom. With culturally sensitive instruction, teachers recognize the strengths in the differences and make room for students and their families to feel safe and respected.

- *Home environments.* Effective family engagement in learning starts with the principle that whatever difficulties they are facing, parents and caregivers care about and want to support their children's learning. No matter their economic status, families have unique resources to offer their children. Making space in the classroom to include and support families can greatly enhance learning.

Develop a Broad Understanding of Students' Needs and Challenges

Students also bring a wide array of needs that may be neurologically based and/or derive from past and current negative experience (e.g., trauma, grief and loss, chronic poverty, hunger, homelessness). The challenges students face often lead to difficult behaviors as well as learning difficulties, and addressing behavior requires as much differentiation as other forms of instruction. The four categories that follow overlap, but it helps to think about them distinctly when considering students' learning backgrounds and how they might interact with the goals of deeper instruction.

1. *Cognitive skills.* The medical definition of *cognition* is "the mental faculty of knowing, which includes perceiving, recognizing, conceiving, judging, reasoning, and imagining." It makes sense then that "cognitive" strengths and challenges include the full range of academic skills as well as many that fall outside of those typically addressed by schools.

2. *Linguistic skills.* Students differ widely in their exposure to language: oral and written, social and academic, English and other languages. This in turn has a profound impact on the academic skills they bring to school.

3. *Emotional and social skills.* One's resilience in the face of obstacles, ability to manage emotions and moods, connect with peers, and empathize with feelings are just a few of the most critical emotional and social qualities and skills. There is ample research to suggest that the skills found in this domain are just

as crucial to deeper learning, long-term success, and well-being as cognitive skills. This skill set also includes the capacity to navigate successfully among what may be several cultures represented in a student's life.

4. *Physical skills.* At times physical skills and capacities are very obvious, but at other times difficulties may be missed or overlooked. For example, is a student's tendency to tune out during a large class conversation a result of difficulties with attention or an undiagnosed hearing problem? Being attuned to students' physical challenges is an important part of creating an effective differentiated learning environment.

Use Student Data

In our data-driven world, educators have a number of sources of quantitative information about students and their academic performance. Educators also have qualitative data in increasing amounts of quantity and quality. Using this information in regular data-based inquiry helps paint a clear, robust picture of students' needs and strengths.

Data from programs like Response to Intervention (RTI) or Positive-Based Intervention and Supports (PBIS), summative exam results broken down by standard, benchmark reading and mathematics assessments, learning backgrounds of advanced students, individual education programs (IEPs), 504 plans, and other behavioral and academic plans all constitute rich data sources from which to determine effective differentiation for our students. Collaboration with other educators is essential; instructional specialists, former teachers, coaches, and counselors can provide this valuable data and help interpret them through the lens of differentiated instruction.

Knowing the Standards: What Do Students Need to Learn?

A next crucial step in effective differentiation is to understand the standards. New standards call for deeper, more rigorous learning for everyone, and they require instructional shifts to ensure that all students meet them. Teachers must become experts in the standards they are responsible for. Differentiated instruction effectively creates different pathways for students to successfully meet the standards required at their grade levels.

It is important to remember that meeting standards should be considered a base-level goal for teachers. Challenging, engaging, and empowering students through deeper instruction and strategic differentiation is the higher goal we should strive for whenever possible.

Develop Supportive Versions of Learning Targets

As discussed in Chapter 1, we promote the use of learning targets: goals for lessons, derived from standards and written in student-friendly language beginning with the stem "I can." Learning targets empower students to identify where they are headed with their learning and track their progress in any given lesson or arc of lessons. One of the principles of differentiation that bears repeating is that teachers should differentiate the *process* of learning but not the *content*. This means that learning targets remain consistent for all students (with the possible exception of students working toward an IEP-based diploma that calls for curriculum modifications, or for those participating in other alternative pathways). In some cases, however, teachers will need to differentiate by creating more supportive versions of the learning targets in order to scaffold all students for success. Consider this example:

> **Most students** will read and text-code (i.e., annotate) grade-level or above-grade-level materials and take notes on a recording form.
> - *Learning target:* "I can gather historical data from multiple sources in order to demonstrate my understanding of Irish emigration events."
>
> **Some students** will meet the learning target by reading a shorter chunk of text and completing a more structured recording form that prompts them to find three ideas on each of the following: people's feelings, living conditions, and how emigrants made money.
> - *Supportive learning target for some students:* "[Using shorter chunks of text and a more structured recording form] I can gather historical data from multiple sources in order to demonstrate my understanding of Irish emigration events."

The bracketing in the preceding example represents teacher decision making and implementation of differentiated activities and tasks. The teacher does not share the bracketed portions of the learning target with the entire class, only with those students who need it. Likely, many students will come to notice that their peers are receiving additional support. When implementing differentiated instruction, therefore, it is essential to first establish a classroom culture that emphasizes that all students get what they need in order to learn deeply and meet learning targets; all students deserve the opportunity to be productively challenged.

Consider another example of supportive learning targets. In this classroom, the teacher has already determined that all students can appropriately sequence events for a timeline. However, some will struggle and some are more advanced in gathering historical data, both in terms of both their note-taking proficiency and their reading skills. The teacher decides all students will create timelines, but she will differentiate the *process* of how students will gather historical data. In this case, some students' learning targets offer additional scaffolding and others offer additional challenge:

All students will participate in a whole-class critique of a model timeline in order to generate criteria for quality, receive feedback on their timelines from the teacher and peers, and use that information to revise.

- *Learning target:* "I can gather historical data in order to sequence events important to Irish emigrants."

Most students use their class notes, textbook, and a graphic organizer to gather and select information and construct a final timeline.

- *Supportive learning target for some students who need scaffolding:* "I can gather historical data to create a timeline of events and inventions important to Irish emigrants [using four events provided by my teacher and three that I find on my own] and/or [by using a timeline graphic organizer with a few key events already filled in]."
- *Supportive learning target for some students who need extension:* "I can create a timeline of events and inventions important to Irish emigrants [using a challenging article provided by my teacher and without the structure of a graphic organizer]."

Note how the students receiving the challenge-level work are not given additional work to complete but are provided with more complex work that invites them to stretch. By ensuring that all students are productively challenged, teachers maximize learning for everyone.

Providing supports for students to meet the same learning targets as their peers allows every student to participate in the learning environment in the classroom and, importantly, to meet standards. Just because a student struggles to read doesn't mean she struggles to *think*. She shouldn't be disengaged from the opportunity to contribute to rich conversations about important academic content because of lowered expectations. She should have the opportunity to meet the same expectation with a different pathway if necessary. A different set of expectations is likely to leave her unchallenged, disengaged, and unempowered and her opportunity for deeper learning may be denied.

Focus on Grade-Level Standards

A natural question to ask when considering differentiation is whether using lower grade-level standards (for students who need support) or higher grade-level standards (for advanced students) is appropriate. In general, we do not recommend this approach: despite best intentions, using lower grade-level standards can devolve into lower expectations for students. Using higher grade-level standards can cause a systemic problem: unless a school is deeply experienced in extending learning across all grade levels, focusing on above-grade-level work in one classroom can result in uneven and misaligned instruction when an advanced student moves to a different teacher or school.

We instead encourage teachers to differentiate and/or extend instruction by modifying the levels of complexity within the grade-level standard. In the case study that follows and the accompanying video, we see a third-grade teacher challenge her students in just this way as they read a complex text. Close reading strategies, such as annotating text, rereading multiple times for different purposes, and answering text-dependent questions, along with differentiated scaffolding and extensions support all students to read challenging texts and engage with their peers around important content. The teacher ensures engagement by working with a text that is part of a high-quality, compelling curriculum and grouping or pairing students to work collaboratively toward shared understanding.

CASE STUDY

A Differentiated Third-Grade Close Reading Lesson

Kerry Meehan, third-grade teacher at World of Inquiry School in Rochester, New York, feels a strong sense of mission in using differentiation in her classroom. "As a critical thinker, I'm compelled to adjust the lessons to meet the needs of my students," she says. In order to make a plan for a differentiated lesson, Meehan considers three things:

1. the data that she has on her students
2. the learning target and basic structure for the lesson that she has on hand
3. her menu of strategies for differentiation.

On this particular day her class is working on a close reading lesson from EL Education's grades 3–8 ELA curriculum. They are reading *Waiting for the Biblioburro*. Meehan always begins the lesson by unpacking the learning targets. In this case the targets are "I can identify the main message by reading the text closely"; and "I can discuss how the main message is conveyed through key details."

Meehan guides her students through a close reading of the text, engaging the whole class in the same text and differentiating for groups of students at similar levels of readiness and reading skill:

1. First, Meehan reads the book aloud to the class and students read silently.
2. Next, students work individually to annotate the text, underlining key details and circling words they do not understand. This is where Meehan's differentiation begins. In preparation for the class she had placed each child's materials in a "seat sack" hung on the back of the chair. This allows her to give different amounts of text to different groups of students without drawing attention to the differences. Some students are given one paragraph to annotate, some two or three. It is the amount that varies, not the text itself.
3. Students then share their annotations in pairs and make corrections. Meehan pairs students at similar reading levels, but comments, "Even when students are on a similar reading level they bring a different subset of skills." In this way they are able to help each other with different things. During the work time, Meehan circulates and targets the students who are having the most difficulty. Her co-teacher, a special educator, works with another group of students who require additional support.
4. Students read the text again and write down the gist (what the text is mostly about).
5. Finally, they answer text-dependent questions. Again, depending on their needs, some students' recording forms offer more support (sentence starters) and some offer less (just single cueing words instead of sentence starters).

Meehan ends this lesson by having the students fill out exit tickets instead of having a whole-class discussion. In this way she gets a piece of work from each student that can help her assess how well each student understood the text.

(continued)

Meehan has developed an approach that feels efficient and doable. Using ready-made, high-quality curriculum modules gives her more time to spend on purposefully differentiating, rather than developing the entire lesson from scratch. Her students' progress is clear to her. "They don't need the same differentiation and scaffolding at the end of the year that they did at the beginning."

Summary of Strategies Used in Meehan's Close-Reading Lesson

- **Seat Sacks:** Materials that can be tailored to students' readiness and distributed without singling students out (can also use folders for older students).
- **Chunking Text:** Students read the same text but some initially read less of it. This ensures that they can complete a close-reading activity without getting frustrated.
- **Sentence Starters:** Prompt some students' thinking and writing without giving it all away.
- **Pair-Share by Mixed-Skill Level:** Strategic pairings of students to check each other's work.
- **Targeted Feedback:** Individual and/or small-group support provided by the teachers during work time to those students who need it the most.
- **Exit Slips:** A quick assessment at the end of the lesson that provides information on each student's understanding.

 WATCH Video 24: Adapting Curriculum to Learners' Needs

Scaffolding and Extending Instruction

Scaffolding and extensions are tools for teachers to develop "respectful tasks" that meet students' specific needs and build upon their specific strengths. Scaffolding and extensions allow students to learn in a supported, yet energized way; students understand how the tasks make learning accessible, purposeful, and retainable for them.

Scaffold to Lift Students Up to Challenging Content

A *scaffold* is simply a way to support all students with specific learning needs with additional supports that help them meet learning targets. Scaffolds are distinct from *accommodations* or *modifications*.

An **accommodation** is similar in concept to a scaffold, but is usually a legally mandated instructional requirement. For example, many states give the accommodation of "extra time" for English language learners (ELLs) or students with disabilities on summative tests.

A **modification** goes deeper than a scaffold or accommodation and changes the actual content and/or learning standards for students. For example, a student may require an individual education program that mandates modifications to the curriculum, such as an eighth-grade student who needs direct instruction to help him or her master elementary-level multiplication facts.

In special cases students receive *accommodations* or *modifications*. However, in general, the most accurate term to describe differentiated supports that are applicable to all students is *scaffolds*; this is the term used from this point on in.

Scaffolds should be *sensitive* to student strengths and needs. They should be *standards based* in content. And they should be *scholarly*: rooted firmly in the content tasks of the curriculum. Scaffolds also can occur outside of the curriculum: for example, students may require small-group guided literacy instruction, explicit sociocultural support, or instruction to address other needs. Strong collaboration with specialists ensures that all the instructional resources available to a student are brought to bear on the differentiation process, both inside and outside of the classroom.

Successful instructional scaffolding lies at the intersection of instructional tasks, the grade-level standards, and the needs of individual students. We divide scaffolding strategies into two groups: "front-end scaffolding" and "back-end scaffolding." Some strategies may benefit the whole class while others will be used only for certain students. The strategies in the Strategy Close Up that follows are designed to support students' different literacy readiness needs, but they may be adapted for use in other content and skill areas.

STRATEGY CLOSE UP: Front- and Back-End Scaffolding Strategies for Reading Complex Text

Front-end scaffolding: The actions teachers take to prepare students to better understand how to access complex text before they read it. Traditionally, front-end scaffolding has included information to build greater context for the text, front-loading vocabulary, summarizing the text, and/or making predictions about what is to be read. Close analytical

(continued)

reading requires that teachers greatly reduce the amount of front-end scaffolding in order to offer students the opportunity to read independently and create meaning and questions first. It also offers students the opportunity to own their own learning and build stamina.

Examples of front-end scaffolding that maintain the integrity of close reading lessons include, but are not limited to:

- Providing visual cues to help students understand learning targets. For example, using a + symbol to help students understand the concept of synthesis across texts.
- Identifying, bolding, and writing in the margins to define words that cannot be understood through the context of the text.
- Chunking long readings into short passages (literally distributing sections on index cards, for example), so that students see only the section they need to tackle.
- Reading the passage aloud before students read independently.
- Providing an audio or video recording of a teacher read-aloud that students can access when needed (such as SchoolTube, podcasts, ezPDF, or GoodReader).
- Supplying a reading calendar at the beginning of longer-term reading assignments, so that teachers in support roles and families can plan for pacing.
- Pre-highlighting text for some learners so that when they reread independently, they can focus on the essential information.
- Eliminating the need for students to copy information—and if something is needed (such as a definition of vocabulary), providing it on the handout or other student materials.

Back-end scaffolding: What teachers plan for after students read complex text to help deepen understanding of the text. When teachers provide back-end scaffolds, they allow students to grapple with hard text first and then provide help as needed.

Examples of back-end scaffolds include, but are not limited to:

- Providing "hint cards" that help students get "unstuck" so they can get the gist. These might be placed on the chalkboard tray, for example, and students would take them only if they are super-stuck.
- Supplying sentence starters so all students can participate in focused discussion.
- Simplifying task directions and/or creating checklists from them so that students can self-monitor their progress.
- If special education teachers, teachers of English language learners, or teaching assistants are co-teaching or "pushed in" to the ELA block, they can teach in stations so that students can work with them in smaller groups if necessary.
- Designing question sets that build in complexity and offering students multiple opportunities to explore the answers:
  - Students discuss the answer with peers, then write answers independently and defend answers to the whole class.
  - Students have time to draft responses before being asked for oral response
- Identifying and defining vocabulary that students struggled with while reading.
- Providing partially completed or more structured graphic organizers to the students who need them.

- Providing sentence or paragraph frames so students can write about what they read.
- Examining a model and having students compare their work to the model and revising if necessary.
- Providing a teacher think-aloud to demonstrate how the teacher came to conclusions and having students revise based on this additional analysis.

Extend Instruction to Push Students Further

Extending the instruction is the mirror image of scaffolding: it allows students who learn quickly and/or who have well-developed background knowledge to move through the instruction in a way that respects their advancement.

It is an unfortunate truth that advanced learners are often overlooked in classroom instruction. Overwhelmed by the practical challenges of their work, teachers rejoice in the presence of students who soak up knowledge, get "right" answers, and earn 100's and A's, but the same teachers may not know how to challenge these learners. As a result, advanced students are not served well when they are consistently isolated from their peers to work on other materials, relied upon as tutors for other students, asked to "do more of the same work faster," or simply left alone.

Advanced learners are labeled in many ways in schools: "gifted," "talented," "accelerated," or "highly ready." No matter what the label, it is important to think of advanced learners in the same respectful way that we think of students who need more support: not as "high" or "low," "better" or "worse," but simply "as students with specific academic needs." All students, even advanced students, require and deserve a rich, relevant, challenging learning environment that supports their growth and helps them learn not just more, but more deeply.

Consider the following basic ways to address the needs of advanced learners in the heterogeneous classroom. We draw several of these ideas from the work of Carol Ann Tomlinson (1997).

Remove scaffolds

This is a very simple way to address learners' more advanced capabilities. If a task has been scaffolded in any way, enact the reverse process and take the scaffolds out. Vocabulary can be left undefined, asking students to use their word study strategies to find their meanings. Concrete text-based questions can be de-emphasized, requiring students to dive into text immediately at more complex levels of understanding. Writing graphic organizers can be used only partially, or even eliminated altogether.

Adjust the degree of difficulty

"In the Olympics," Carol Ann Tomlinson reminds us, "the most accomplished divers perform dives that have a higher 'degree of difficulty' than those performed by divers whose talents are not as advanced. A greater degree of difficulty calls on more skills—more refined skills—applied at a higher plane of sophistication" (1997). Academic tasks with adjusted degrees of difficulty may require deep insight and broad pattern recognition, require less structure, and sometimes (though not always) may be addressed with more learner independence. Instead of simply analyzing a poem for a theme, for example, an advanced learner might be asked to determine how a theme changes from an author's earlier work to his later work. Or, as we explored in Chapter 1, asking students to explain key disciplinary concepts (like why we have seasons) can challenge them in new and deeper ways. Adjusting the degree of difficulty of a task is addressed more fully in the In Practice section.

Understand "supported risk"

Advanced learners have often had a very easy time in school. They are used to expending little effort and getting big results. Consequently, error is not normal to them. When genuinely challenged by a task for the first time, advanced learners may react with fear, sadness, annoyance, or confusion: their self-image of success has been challenged as well. They may not have developed the tools of perseverance, good humor, and academic courage to be able to deal successfully with that challenge.

"A good teacher of gifted students," says Carol Ann Tomlinson, "understands that dynamic, and thus invites, cajoles, and insists on risk—but in a way that supports success. When a good gymnastics coach asks a talented young gymnast to learn a risky new move, the coach ensures that the young person has the requisite skills, then practices the move in a harness for a time. Then the coach 'spots' for the young athlete. Effective teachers of gifted learners do likewise" (1997).

Using Flexible Grouping Strategies

Creating collaborative learning groups that are flexible and purposeful is an important part of designing effective differentiated lessons. Groups not only make implementation of differentiation manageable, but they activate the strong social component important for deeper learning. There are few things more challenging and engaging in a classroom than a focused group of peers who are synthesizing knowledge, working collaboratively, and encouraging one another to complete an instructional task. At times, as we saw in Kerry Meehan's class, it makes sense to have students of similar skill levels working together in a group. At other times, mixing students by skill level or readiness, point of view, or learning preference is called for. In general, the success of group work requires that educators put thought into how students' interactions with each other will affect their learning. Saying "Get into groups of four" may not produce the desired result.

Grouping students should be just as carefully planned as any other part of the lesson. It can't be an afterthought. And, once students are in groups, the expectations for the ways in which they work together must be taught, practiced, and assessed—and often re-taught—just like any other routine. What follows are some of the ways teachers can thoughtfully group their students.

General Group Types

- *Homogenous grouping* allows groups of students with similar abilities, aptitudes, first languages, or interests to work together. We do not suggest that these groups be yearlong "ability groups," but ad hoc groups convened for a certain need.

- *Heterogeneous grouping* allows students who possess certain academic strengths to assist and model for those who may have different academic strengths (and vice versa). Strategies for mentoring and support must be taught.

- *Social/relational grouping* takes advantage of students' social relationships to strengthen social bonds, honor already established friendships, or encourage new friendships. Strategic group assignments can be used intentionally to help support students who are new, shy, or fragile or to push cliques of friends to branch out.

- *Free grouping* honors the individual preferences and interests of the students.

Grouping Support (for students learning how to work in groups)

- Form "strategic pairs" or match partners with complementary skill sets.

- Monitor and give support to specific students more strategically (e.g., seat them closer to the teacher).

- Create norms for group collaboration, ideally involving students in the creation process; check on those norms regularly and use them to debrief group work.

- Provide and model structured roles for group members (such as "note taker," "time keeper," or "task manager").

- Have a teacher (either you or another adult) work directly with some small groups.

- Use protocols to set up collaborative groups. For more information on what protocols are and how they work in the classroom, see Chapter 1.

Embedding Regular Assessment

As teachers differentiate instruction to meet students' diverse needs, it is critical that they have effective ways to determine what students' learning needs are prior to planning instruction and to continuously assess student progress and understanding. It is also critical that students are not left on the sidelines of this process, but instead invest completely in the assessment and help determine what to do with the results. This is a vital component of deeper instruction—empowering students with the tools to understand their learning.

> One of the keys is figuring out where your students are now through pre-assessment and data analysis. Ideally formal pre-assessments should be by department and normed. An initial pre-assessment at the beginning of the year covers more material (broad and shallow). Then I use a daily exit ticket to help me make modifications after each lesson.
>
> —*Liz Butler, former teacher, Codman Academy Charter Public School*

Pre-assess Students

When differentiating, teachers should carefully pre-assess for what students do and do not already know, and what they are and are not able to do prior to embarking on a new area of study. Teachers should also explore how students might feel about the upcoming study, what students will likely be challenged by, what they are most interested in, and what they will find the easiest to learn.

Following are some examples of pre-assessing students' backgrounds, readiness, and interests:

Readiness surveys. Ask students to rate how comfortable/ready they are to engage in a task.

Interest surveys. Surveys can capture each student's learning preferences as well as interests and are helpful for supplementing a teacher's understanding of the individuals in her class. Sample items might look like this:

- I like to solve problems by talking out loud.
- I sound out new words and I am a good speller.
- When I hear directions out loud, I can follow them easily.
- I would rather participate in sports than watch them.
- I prefer going to museums where I can touch the exhibits.
- My handwriting gets worse when space becomes smaller.

A brief on-demand task. Use this to assess current level of content knowledge/skills: for example, a two-question math quiz, or a short response to a small amount of text.

Independent KWIs. When introducing a new content area, ask students to individually fill out the first two columns of a KWI chart: *"What do you KNOW, WHAT do you need to find out?"* After the lesson or period of study, have them fill out the final column, "What IDEAS do you have? This will provide discrete information for each student.

Assess the Effectiveness of Scaffolds and Extensions on a Regular Basis

Implementing differentiated instruction in the classroom is only half the battle: the other half is shaping differentiation to reflect the growth of students. It is essential to remember that differentiation's primary purpose is to assist students in reaching a particular learning target. "Assistance" is not meant to be permanent. Once a student has grown enough in their learning to no longer need a particular scaffold, the scaffold should be removed. The only way to determine the appropriate time and place for this removal is through consistent checking for understanding and formative assessment.

Teachers can proactively plan periodic reviews of student scaffolds and extensions, using multiple forms of data and taking advantage of the collaborative insights of colleagues who also teach their students. The best data, however, come from the reflection of the students themselves. Exit tickets, reflections on summative assessments, interviews, or reflections on learning targets invite students to be metacognitive as they determine directly whether their scaffolds are helpful, neutral, or ineffective. Teachers can then adjust accordingly.

In the In Practice section that follows we dive a little deeper into some of the key differentiated instructional moves and how they benefit all students.

IN PRACTICE

Diving Deeper into Differentiation

As differentiation deepens, so does learning. Students come to expect tasks that are appropriately challenging, and find greater satisfaction in their learning. They engage fully in work that is meaningful and interesting to them. And they continue to broaden their knowledge about how and why they learn.

As skill with differentiating lessons improves, the following sections on tiering assignments, engaging student choice, using technology, and supporting all students with special needs, suggest ways in which teachers can take differentiation to a more advanced stage.

Tiering Assignments

Students come to school more or less ready for different types of reading, more or less fluent with math facts or problem solving, with more or less background in historical documents, or more or less ready to participate in the scientific process. Tiered assignments involve parallel tasks at varying levels of complexity so that students can work toward the same learning targets in a way that is responsive to their readiness. Tiered assignments are developed using varied levels of scaffolding and extension for students who are ready for an additional "push," and for students needing additional support. By creating tiered tasks, teachers ensure that all students get appropriately challenging work—work that is challenging enough to push learning to new levels, but not so challenging that it is overwhelming.

Apply the "Equalizer"

The "equalizer" (Figure 6.2) is Carol Ann Tomlinson's visual representation of the various layers of complexity in lessons or tasks that teachers can tier. Focusing on one

Figure 6.2 Tomlinson's "Equalizer"

1. Foundational — Information, Ideas, Materials, Applications — Transformational

2. Concrete — Representations, Ideas, Applications, Materials — Abstract

3. Simple — Resources, Research, Issues, Problems, Skills, Goals — Complex

4. Single Facet — Disciplinary Connections, Directions, Stages of Development — Multiple Facets

5. Small Leap — Application, Insight, Transfer — Great Leap

6. More Structured — Solutions, Decisions, Approaches — More Open

7. Clearly Defined Problems — In Process, In Research, In Products — Fuzzy Problems

8. Less Independence — Planning, Designing, Monitoring — Greater Independence

9. Slower — Pace of Study, Pace of Thought — Quicker

or more layers of the equalizer when planning lessons and tasks will help teachers create responsive, tiered lessons. For example, some students may be given a writing assignment with a structured template that will help them organize their main points, while others, who are ready for more independence, may be given only a prompt—the expectation is that those with just a prompt are more ready for the challenge of organizing their writing independently. Or, all students may read the same short story, but they are given different reading response activities depending on their readiness to respond to abstract or concrete questions. Along the various axes, teachers can slide the equalizer toward more or less complexity to meet students' needs

It is important to note that we make a key departure from Tomlinson's equalizer. Whereas she suggests varying the *level* of text based on student readiness, we would suggest instead varying the *amount* of text based on readiness levels so that all students are challenged to read grade level or above texts. It is important not to think of these levels on a continuum of "high ability" to "low ability." Rather, each level simply represents the reality of what a student currently needs in order to do his or her best.

Focus on Equity When Creating Tiered Assignments

- *Establish clear learning targets.* Generally, all students are working toward the same learning targets on tasks that vary in complexity, abstractness, number of steps, concreteness, and independence. In order for tiered assignments to be effective, it is essential that they be designed with the same core learning targets in mind.

- *Introduce all tasks with the same level of enthusiasm and interest.* All students should feel that the work they have been asked to complete is respectful. It helps when the tiered activities "look" the same, including labeling the activity with the learning target so that students see that they are all working toward the same goal.

- *Ensure that all students are equally involved and active.* Take care to give different work, not simply more or less work, for different tiers, as well as activities that are equally appealing and desirable.

In the following Strategy Close Up, teacher Sydney Chaffee applies tiering to a variety of lesson components.

STRATEGY CLOSE UP: A Tiered Assignment in a High School Humanities Class

Sydney Chaffee, ninth-grade humanities teacher and department chair at Codman Academy Charter Public School in Boston, teaches a heterogeneous class. She says, "I am differentiating all the time. My students come into ninth grade with widely varying skill levels. This year someone was at a fourth-grade reading level sitting next to someone at a college reading level. I have students who came to this country a year ago and those who have been here their whole lives. One student was in a substantially separate classroom and received one-on-one instruction last year, and now he is in my full inclusion classroom."

Chaffee uses a variety of structures for creating tiered writing assignments. Beginning with the same final writing product, she offers some students optional scaffolding. For others, she requires it. This year she has begun to track which students receive which kinds of scaffolding with the explicit goal of moving them more intentionally toward needing less support. "I keep track of all of these iterations on a spreadsheet so I can see whether a student mastered the learning targets after I offered a certain scaffold, or whether pulling a scaffold caused a student's scores to drop." She explains, "I want to be able to phase out the scaffolds over time and be more intentional with what I'm doing—to ensure the most appropriately challenging set of scaffolds for each student."

She uses several strategies to decide which version of an assignment each student gets.

"I look at their IEPs to see who needs legal access to accommodations like graphic organizers. I also consider any previous writing assignments or assessments they've done for me. (For example, if on a previous essay a student was able to write a basic essay but included no transition sentences, I might give him/her the checklist as an initial intervention to see if that helps.) I conference with students after they write essays; we review the rubric and my comments together, and they make notes about what they should do during the revision process. These conversations can help me see if my scaffolds are helping them or if I need to give them more structured support.

Finally, if I believe a student is able to meet the learning targets, skillwise, but is struggling with test or writing anxiety, I might offer them some supports on the next essay to build their confidence, and then remove those supports the next time through."

An example follows of one of Chaffee's tiered assignments. In this example, students are developing and writing an argumentative essay on the topic of Puerto Rico. The prompt is: *Write a five- to six-paragraph argumentative essay responding to the following prompt: What should Puerto Rico's relationship with the United States be: a state, a territory, an "enhanced commonwealth," or an independent nation?*

A graphic organizer, which identifies the purpose of each paragraph, is required for some students and made optional for others (see Figure 6.3).

An assessment checklist is also required and/or made optional, depending on student need. All students are welcome to use it and some are required. The checklist follows.

Double-Check This List Before You Turn Your Essay In!

❑ My essay is either 5 or 6 paragraphs long.
❑ My essay starts with an introduction paragraph that has:
  • a hook (choose from: quotation, personal story, statistic/shocking fact, or imagery)

(continued)

Figure 6.3 Five-Paragraph Essay Template

Introduction Paragraph
Hook (grab the reader's attention with imagery):

Hook:

Thesis (respond to the prompt and add three claims):

Thesis:

Body Paragraphs
Claim #___ (from your thesis):

Claim #___ :

Evidence #1 (an example or detail to support Claim)

Evidence #1:

Evidence #2 (an example or detail to support Claim)

Evidence #2:

Evidence #3 (an example or detail to support Claim)

Evidence #3:

Transition (smoothly move from paragraph to paragraph):

Transition:

- context (background information about the topic)
- a thesis statement
- ❑ My thesis statement has parallel structure.
- ❑ My essay contains body paragraphs. Each body paragraph:
  - starts with a clear claim
  - includes 3 pieces of evidence
  - ends with a transition sentence that leads into the next paragraph
- ❑ My essay includes a counterclaim and rebuttal in each body paragraph.

    or:

- ❑ My essay includes a counterclaim and rebuttals in a separate paragraph.
- ❑ My essay ends with a conclusion that:
  - summarizes my claims
  - leaves the reader thinking (choose from: return to hook, make it bigger, make it current, predict the future, or challenge the reader)
- ❑ My essay includes at least 8 Words of the Week. (These are listed on the back of the rubric)
- ❑ I used a semicolon somewhere in my essay.

As Chaffee assesses her students, she is continually reconsidering her approach and assignments. She says, "The thing I've become more comfortable with is the need to constantly innovate, tinker, and go back to the design of the assignments. In much the same way I ask kids to work on their writing, what works and doesn't work, I need to do the same thing with my teaching. Is the wording of an assignment clear, is it visually overwhelming?"

Above all, she advises not to shy away from doing what is right for a particular student. "Sometimes when we're just starting out [with differentiation], we're scared [the work we assign] is going to be too easy. The level where someone needs lots of support will look very different than the place where you will eventually take that student. It's okay if their first step is really simple. Be comfortable figuring out where this kid is now. It's not where he will stay forever."

In another example of tiering, first-grade students at Delaware Ridge Elementary School in Kansas City, Kansas, are working toward the same learning target: "I can sort shapes by their common attributes." Their task, however, is tiered in complexity based on student readiness. Their teacher, Joy Marts, has prepared three kinds of baggies full of different kinds of shapes. Some baggies have simple shapes of varying colors that the class has been working with already (e.g., circles, triangles, squares); others have these same shapes plus a few more complicated shapes; still others have an assortment of these shapes, plus dominoes, pencils, and other classroom objects.

Students are challenged to create a "rule" and sort their shapes in their baggie by that rule. The range of complexity in their rules mirrors the complexity of the shapes in their baggies and meets each student at their level of readiness for the task. Some examples of the rules they create include:

- shapes that are orange and have four sides.
- shapes that are fat.
- shapes that have sharp points.

At their tables, which are arranged for this lesson so that students with the same type of shapes are working together, students collaborate to figure out their peers' rules for how they sorted their shapes. At the conclusion of the class, students self-assess, from 1 to 5, how successful they feel sorting shapes by common attributes.

Engaging Student Choice

Giving students the right kind of choices within a differentiated classroom can be tricky. The key to making choice worthwhile is "limited, well-structured choices that enable students to meet essential learning targets" (Dobbertin, 2013, p. 114). Limiting or shaping student choice allows us to make sure that students have access to appropriate materials and that each task or learning activity will allow them to make progress toward the learning targets. Choice is also one of the most efficient and powerful paths to deeper learning. Students instantly engage when they are given autonomy in their learning and feel a strong sense of ownership in their work. Their stamina to produce quality work increases when they feel they have had some choice and control. The previously referenced two-part video, "Reading and Thinking Like Scientists," offers a nice example of a science teacher collaborating with an ELL teacher to provide two different versions of a note-catcher (one that is separate from a complex text and one that is embedded within the text) so that students can have a choice of the form that will best meet their learning needs.

Try Task Cards

If teachers are just starting out incorporating student choice into their classroom differentiation, task cards (one-page explicit directions that are different for the different tasks at hand) are a great place to start. Offering students options and defining what each of those options looks like on a task card changes the dynamic of a classroom dramatically. Work time becomes purposeful. Students are more responsive and able to participate in instruction because their needs are being met. And teachers can structure each choice to give the appropriate levels of challenge to all students.

Learning targets should be printed on each task card (they should be the same or very similar on each task card) and should be the basis for planning meaningful differentiated tasks. Differentiated tasks can be written on different colored cards, and can vary based on readiness (to what degree students are ready to dive in or need some additional practice or review before diving in), interest (researching and reporting out facts about a topic of their choice), or preference (work alone or in a group).

The Strategy Close Up that follows focuses on student self-assessment of readiness tied to various choices of activities using task cards.

STRATEGY CLOSE UP: Choosing the Level of Challenge

Before becoming a math/science coach at Codman Academy Charter Public School in Boston, Liz Butler taught physics. The experience helped her understand how to successfully differentiate mathematical concepts for students. "A lot of my differentiation was in the math vein . . . skill building, word problems, etc. In working with challenging problems, I am a big fan of letting students differentiate themselves. I had students rate themselves on a scale of 1–10 on how comfortable they are with a given problem or concept."

Butler had students work on a problem as a pre-assessment and then rate themselves on how difficult it was for them (see Figure 6.4). She calls it a "comfort-level rating"—basically each student's readiness for the type of problem. Butler explained, "If

Figure 6.4 Comfort-Level Rating

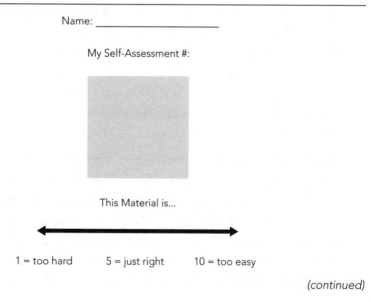

Name: _____

My Self-Assessment #:

This Material is...

1 = too hard   5 = just right   10 = too easy

(continued)

I like it—it makes me feel I'm a step ahead. It makes me feel I can learn more and be less bored than if I did something I already knew.

—*Student , Codman Academy Charter Public School*

you did it perfectly the first time, you're a ten. If you got it after we talked it through, you're a five. If you are still totally confused, a one."

After collecting the assessments (which are kept confidential), Butler puts students into groups based on the ratings. "I group them either with mixed or similar ratings. It allows me to create their groupings with their input and then have different work on task cards available for different groups. Different levels of challenge means different problems that students can move through at their own pace." In this way the self-assessments and choice of challenge become a vehicle for tiering.

The goal is that everyone is challenged at an optimal level. "I also appreciate that I can change their pace as they go," Butler adds. "I hold a set of challenge cards. Because I know the students well, I can use them to accelerate their challenge level. Someone might identify herself as a '4,' but if I think she's really a '7,' I can move her along."

Explore Other Strategies for Structuring Choice

Student choice can also be effective when the focus is on student interest, rather than academic readiness. What follows are possible strategies with interest as a focus:

- *Think-tac-toe.* This strategy involves nine commands or questions, arranged like a tic-tac-toe board. Students choose three to complete, creating a row vertically, horizontally, or diagonally. Student choice allows for differentiation by interest and/or learning style. Think-tac-toe boards for different levels of readiness can also be created and given to different groups of students. Students may also be given choices as to which board they complete during a particular class period. Students who choose the same board may form a small group for that day.

- *Menus.* Menus ask students to choose among several options with well-defined common conditions (such as learning target, deadline, and essential components.) For example, in a menu for a research project on Elizabethan England, "Living in Shakespeare's World," students choose a "lifestyle" (e.g., knight, peasant, nobleman) and then conduct research on the same subtopics: basic needs, economics, work, religion, entertainment (Dobbertin, 2013). Students work toward the same learning targets and focus on the same skills, but student

Menus empower students to take their own path toward meeting common learning targets

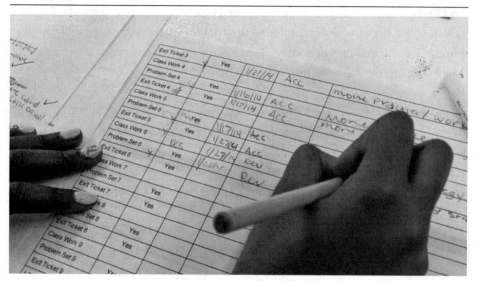

preferences and interests are taken into account. Teachers may guide students to the choices they feel are the best fit or simply let students choose independently. To see a math menu in action, view the accompanying video.

 WATCH Video 25: Developing Content Mastery and Self-Reliance through Menu Math

Using Technology Effectively

Explore the possibilities but remember the basics. Technology offers increasingly promising tools to support differentiated, deeper instruction: for tremendous inherent engagement; for respectful, targeted challenge; for flexible instructional strategies that appeal to different learning styles and preferences; for practice that yields immediate feedback and reflection on learning. From interactive games to instructional videos to voice recognition software, the variety of technological tools is almost limitless and is changing all the time.

No matter what software or hardware you choose, however, the basic premises that we outlined in the Getting Started section still apply: Know your students and know your standards. You'll see these premises echoed in the following box, which offers ten tips for differentiated instruction using technology developed by Forest Lake Elementary School in South Carolina, a school renowned for its successful incorporation of technology.[3]

Ten Tips for Personalized Learning via Technology

1. **Deliver instruction through multiple forms of media.** You now have at your fingertips far more than just the old standbys of words and still pictures. Teachers at Forest Lake use computers and whiteboards to access oodles of instructional videos, audio clips, animations, and interactive games, some through software and some available online.
2. **Gather and use immediate feedback on students' understanding.** Teachers here routinely use remote-response systems (clickers), colorful little gadgets that allow each child to enter her answer to a practice question so that the teacher can instantly see who got it right or wrong.
3. **Give students options.** All students shouldn't be required to show their learning the same way. Digital media opens up a host of possibilities beyond the traditional essay, poster, report, or quiz.
4. **Automate basic skills practice.** Educational computer programs (Study Island and EducationCity are Forest Lake favorites) can identify specific weaknesses in a child's skills, such as understanding analogies or adding fractions. Teachers can review these outcomes daily, then assign lessons to each student according to her needs—for the next time she logs on.
5. **Practice independent work skills.** Differentiating instruction often means setting up kids to work alone or in groups that are not directly supervised by the teacher. The solution for second-grade teacher Tamika Lowe is "practice, practice, practice."
6. **Create a weekly "Must Do" and "May Do" list.** Give a classroom of students an array of different, personalized tasks to do, and they'll inevitably finish them at different times. That's a tricky part of differentiation. Forest Lake teachers tackle this by assigning a weekly list of "must dos" and "may dos," so kids who finish first can always find something to do next.
7. **Pretest students' knowledge before each unit.** Before starting each unit of study, grade-level teams at Forest Lake brainstorm how to assess prior knowledge so they can tailor lessons effectively to each child—from simple questions that the class answers with a thumbs-up or thumbs-down to rigorous one-on-one conversations.
8. **Be flexible when plans go awry.** Computers don't always perform the way you wish or expect, especially if the teacher in command is new to digital technology. So as you embark on this journey, expect the unexpected.

9. **Let students drive.** If you've got the tech tools, put them in kids' hands. These opportunities allow students to work at their own pace, capitalize on their skills, and discover ways to work around their challenges.
10. **Share the work of creating differentiated lessons.** To ease the burden of planning lessons for students at diverse levels, Forest Lake teachers often divide up this task. When they plan each unit of study, different members of each grade-level team design the activities for higher-skilled kids, lower-skilled kids, and so on.

Consider Flipping

In a "flipped" classroom, teachers assign short videos to review a concept outside of class, so they can use class time to coach student practice based on the concepts the video taught. Well-known examples include the videos of Khan Academy and Crash Course. Flipping the classroom in this way can give teachers more time to provide differentiated instruction when meeting with students. Instead of spending time teaching a central concept to the whole group, teachers assess student retention of the video content and then create flexible groups and/or individual instruction based on how well the students mastered the concepts in the video.

Additionally, the videos lend themselves to a very flexible model of differentiation. A student watching an instructional video at home can do so in a myriad of ways suited to his learning preferences: turning off the sound, taking notes, rewinding and reviewing multiple times, or fast forwarding through content already mastered. If the video is situated within a bank of videos with related concepts, students can look at other videos to review fundamental concepts they need to strengthen, or move onto more advanced concepts.

Flipping requires that students have the means and motivation to view the videos outside of class time. All technological differentiation that depends on out-of-class access involves this challenge: the more socioeconomically diverse your classroom population is, the more likely it is that the students in it will have disparities regarding what technologies they have access to (Kang, 2013). The advantages of technology must always be balanced with equity of access. Some schools use a variation of the flipped classroom in which the viewing of videos actually happens in school, during particular designated class times or study times, when viewing videos at home is challenging for many students. The class lesson time remains the same.

Supporting Students with Special Needs

As illustrated in the terrain of differentiated instruction in Figure 6.1, the primary purpose of differentiation is to support all students to succeed in heterogeneous classrooms. Most students' varied academic needs can be met with well-planned scaffolds and extensions that challenge them appropriately. Some students, however, will need more specialized support. Here we will explore some of the unique considerations for students with learning disabilities and English language learners who may need additional support, accommodations, or modifications to the curriculum.

Both schools and educational law use the terms "special education," "disabilities," and "special needs" to cover a broad range of student challenges: ADHD, autism, Down Syndrome, emotional disturbance, and hearing and visual impairment, to name only a few. Additionally, students such as English language learners may have "special needs" for instruction, but may not have "disabilities." Some students, such as those who identify as part of Deaf Culture, prefer not to have their difference labeled as a "disability"; they see it as distinction that has both challenges and advantages. That perspective can be useful with many kinds of "different" learners.

To help clarify these muddy waters, we deliberately narrow our focus in this section to address two groups of students: students with learning disabilities and English language learners, because it is most likely that these students will be present in a typical heterogeneous classroom.

Though it is important to define these special groups of students, it is important to bear in mind that our recommendations here are likely to benefit all students. Differentiation works best when using approaches that are not limited to addressing one or two specific types of needs, but that can be expanded and used fruitfully in a variety of academic situations, for a variety of students. Similarly, we continue to stress holding all students to the same high standards of performance and achievement. With the best of intentions, teachers can form erroneous opinions about the abilities of their students with special needs. Yet decades of research and educational history confirm that students of all ranges of ability will rise to the occasion when we honor them by expecting their best. They all deserve and benefit from deeper instruction.

As always: *Know your students and know your standards.* This foundation of knowledge will enable you to determine which interventions and supports are best suited for your students. In this sense, there are actually no "special needs"—there is only the unique, individual child in front of you, wanting to learn and grow.

Support Students with Learning Disabilities with a Strengths-Based Approach

"Learning disabilities (LDs) are real. They affect the brain's ability to receive, process, store, respond to, and communicate information. LDs are actually a group of disorders, not a single disorder. Learning disabilities are not the same as intellectual disabilities (formerly known as mental retardation), sensory impairments (vision or hearing) or autism spectrum disorders. People with LD are of average or above-average intelligence but still struggle to acquire skills that impact their performance in school, at home, in the community and in the workplace. Learning disabilities are lifelong, and the sooner they are recognized and identified, the sooner steps can be taken to circumvent or overcome the challenges they present." [National Center for Learning Disabilities Editorial Team, n.d.]

Under the Individuals with Disabilities Education Act (IDEA), students with learning disabilities are guaranteed a free, appropriate public education, in the least restrictive environment that adequately prepares them for continued education, employment, and independent living. If a student does not qualify for protection under IDEA, they may still qualify for educational protections under Section 504 of the Rehabilitation Act of 1973.

Students with learning disabilities have differing capabilities. Often they show extreme strengths in some domains and struggle with other discrete skills and academic content areas. A strengths-based approach leverages the power of students' abilities while focusing on specific scaffolds to ensure that all students can succeed. The more challenging the learner's needs, the more important his strengths, interests, and learning styles become in planning for his learning. To put it simply: focus on what the student can do. To do this, we recommend an approach firmly grounded in (a) the legal obligations teachers have to students with disabilities; (b) high, standards-based expectations; and (c) the appropriate level of intervention.

Follow the Individualized Education Program or 504 Plan

Many students with learning disabilities have either an IEP or a 504 plan in place (see following box for more information). These legally binding documents are the first word on what differentiated supports should be put in place for students with disabilities. They are not abandoned, changed, or overridden by differentiated approaches: in fact, they should determine the primary means by which teachers differentiate for students with learning disabilities. They should be adhered to at all times.

What Is an IEP?

An "individualized education program" (IEP) is a plan or program developed to ensure that a K–12 student who has a disability identified under the law receives specialized instruction and related services.

What Is a 504 Plan?

The 504 plan is developed to ensure that a K–12 student who has a disability or medical condition identified under the law—*but does not need specialized instruction*—receives accommodations that ensure access to the learning environment.

IEPs and 504 plans often look quite different from state to state, district to district, and school to school. Regardless, the plans should be read with two guiding questions in mind:

1. What accommodations, modifications, scaffolds or supports are required by this plan for my student's success?

2. What strengths of my student are indicated or outlined in this plan?

These two vital pieces of information should form the foundation of all differentiation for students with disabilities.

Remember, however, that although you are legally bound to follow the IEP or 504 plan, the plans do not necessarily mean that you can't put additional differentiated scaffolds into place. Unless indicated otherwise on the plan, consult and collaborate with leaders and special education teachers to design individualized interventions and keep track of your efforts. As we mention in the Getting Started section, you will want to proactively review the results of any differentiation with a student to determine what is needed, what is effective, and/or what has been outgrown. Your informed input will be vital when the plans are revisited and revised.

Know the Intervention Tiers

Response to Intervention (RTI) is a federally recommended program that many schools across the country have adopted to help them identify and support students who are at risk of developing academic and/or social-emotional difficulties. Our terrain of differentiated instruction (Figure 6.1) is based on RTI's primary, secondary, and tertiary interventions. Through ongoing data-based inquiry in professional teams, students' diverse strengths and needs are identified early and interventions are assessed for their efficacy. Tiered interventions, also known as "levels," allow teachers to tailor instructional access so that it is "least restrictive"—that is, it builds strategically on students' strengths to keep students with disabilities included fully in educational settings.

- *Tier I/Primary-level interventions* are high-quality instructional practices that meet the needs of most students and occur within the regular classroom setting. This level includes ongoing assessment, differentiated learning activities, accommodations to ensure all students access to the curriculum, and problem solving to address behavioral challenges. Tier I/Primary-level interventions make room for the "grappling" that occurs in Workshop 2.0 lessons: teachers should be mindful of the dangers of "over-scaffolding" for students at this level.

- *Tier II/Secondary-level interventions* are evidence-based practices that usually take place in small groups for specific periods of time outside of the regular classroom. They are focused on addressing students learning and behavioral challenges that did not respond to the primary interventions. Tier II interventions may be used, for example, to extend instruction on vocabulary or phonemic awareness or to make time for a higher volume of independent reading.

- *Tier III/Tertiary-level interventions* are the most intensive and are individualized for students who do not respond to secondary interventions. Students who do not progress at this level are then considered for an evaluation of memory, intellectual processing, speech, sensory-motor, or other disorders that may qualify them for special education services under IDEA. The information collected during the Tier I and II interventions is used to assist in making decisions regarding special education services in Tier III.

The RTI program is not only based on differentiated responses to levels of student need, but also builds differentiated classroom instruction into its recommendations for Tier I/Primary-level interventions. In this way, RTI ideally works in tandem with classroom-based differentiation to provide efficient, effective, and accurate emotional and academic support to students with special needs.

Support English Language Learners by Understanding Their Context

> "Some reports portray English language learners (ELL) as a new and homogenous population. Actually, ELLs are a highly heterogeneous and complex group of students, with diverse gifts, educational needs, backgrounds, languages, and goals . . . In the largest sense, all ELL students are learning English, and each ELL student falls at a different point on the spectrum of experiences" (National Center for Teachers of English, 2008, page 1–2).

English language learners, regardless of their immigration status, are guaranteed full and equal access to public education under what is currently Title III of the Elementary and Secondary Act of 1965 and the 1982 US Supreme Court case *Plyer v. Doe*.

English language learners have particular needs that require specialized attention. The growth of the population of English language learners in the United States over the past decade is unmatched in our history. More than half of states have experienced a growth rate of more than 100 percent in their ELL numbers (National Clearinghouse of English Language Acquisition, 2011). It is highly likely, then, that even in schools where ELL instruction has been minimal or unnecessary, teachers will now find ELLs in their classes.

To understand the context of an ELL's learning and apply differentiation appropriately, we recommend pre-assessing the student thoroughly; considering his or her learning standards through the lens of second-language acquisition; and scaffolding for language, content, and cultural learning.

Pre-assess ELL Backgrounds, Strengths, and Needs

In the case of ELLs, it is even more critical than usual to have a full picture of the students' academic, cultural, and linguistic histories. Because of the huge variation in the population of ELLs—from US-born children of first-generation immigrants, to children of highly educated and advantaged immigrant families, to refugee students who have never set foot inside a school—nothing can be assumed about an ELL student. We strongly encourage deep collaboration with ELL families, cultural interpreters, language translators, former teachers, ELL specialists, and/or school social workers or counselors to accurately assess the strengths and needs of ELLs.

"What are the students able to do? Who are they linguistically?," asks Lubía Sánchez, an ELL teacher at Melrose Leadership Academy, a dual-immersion EL Education school in Oakland, California. Sanchez believes that the critical first step, as we assert in the Getting Started section of this chapter, is to thoroughly assess students. "It forces you to think about what the language demands of a task are," says Sanchez. "In terms of functional language, what will students need to know? The analysis is through the eyes of a language learner."

Consider Learning Standards through the Lens of Second-Language Acquisition

As Sánchez implies, learning standards must be considered through the lens of ELL language acquisition. The instructional shifts called for by the Common Core literacy standards—building knowledge through context-rich nonfiction; reading, writing, and speaking grounded in evidence from literary and informational text; and regular practice with complex text and its academic language—are meant to enhance the rigor and applicability of schooling, preparing students more effectively for college and careers. The shifts provide a useful lens for creating effective scaffolding of curricula for ELLs (described in Table 6.3).[4] In addition, states now are taking steps to link the new standards to standards specifically regarding English language proficiency development (ELPD). One such initiative is the World Class Instructional Design and Assessment Consortium (WIDA).

Scaffold for Language, Content, and Cultural Learning

Finally, differentiating for ELLs involves considering the specific academic tasks ELLs must undertake. We recommend the following overarching scaffolds for ELLs:

- *Clear expectations (targets), both content based and language based.* No matter what aspect of language you are working on with your ELLs, being clear about your academic goals is key. ELL-friendly targets not only allow ELLs to understand the purpose of the classroom work, but also to see what language objectives they must master to access the content (Himmel, 2012). Consider how you might communicate or scaffold targets in a way your ELLs can comprehend.

Table 6.3 Scaffolding Curricula for English Language Learners

Building knowledge through content-rich nonfiction	Reading, writing, and speaking grounded in evidence from both literary and informational text	Regular practice with complex texts and its academic language
Assess and build ELLs' background knowledge about the content and structure of nonfiction texts.	Build on students' backgrounds and cultures; build background where necessary on using evidence from different types of text.	Analyze complex texts and make ELLs aware of academic language found in complex texts.
Integrate ELLs' background knowledge and culture into instruction.	Create appropriate text-dependent questions for students at different levels of English language proficiency.	Choose and adapt supplementary texts in English and/or ELLs' first language based on ELLs' reading level, English language proficiency level, background, and culture.
Teach ELLs differences between structures of informational text and literary text.	Teach ELLs the academic language necessary so that they can use evidence from literary and informational text in reading, speaking, listening, and writing.	Teach ELLs strategies to guess at unknown words (e.g., cognates, prefixes, roots, suffixes).
Know and use ELLs' first-language reading literacy skills as a support when appropriate.	Provide ELLs with linguistic structures so that they can use evidence, cite sources, avoid plagiarism, synthesize information from grade-level complex texts, and create argumentative/persuasive speeches and writing.	Teach the meanings of words with multiple definitions, idiomatic expressions, and technical terms.
Adapt/supplement grade-level complex texts for ELLs at lower levels of English language proficiency.	Create and use scaffolding and supports so that ELLs at different levels of English language proficiency can take part in meaningful conversations and writing using complex text.	Explicitly teach the academic language necessary to comprehend complex texts so that ELLs can draw upon these texts to speak and write across content areas.
Collaborate to share effective strategies for teaching ELLs using nonfiction.	Design appropriate classroom assessments for ELLs at different levels of English language proficiency.	Collaborate to share effective strategies for teaching ELLs the academic language they need to access complex texts.
Scaffold and support instruction using nonfiction for ELLs.	Collaborate to share effective strategies for teaching ELLs to cite evidence when writing and speaking.	Use English language proficiency standards to support instruction.
Design appropriate classroom assessments so that ELLs can demonstrate what they know and can do.	Use English language proficiency standards to support instruction.	
Use English language proficiency standards to support instruction.		

- *Small-group work.* In particular, direct and explicit small-group instructional intervention in all aspects of reading is recommended for ELLs who struggle with reading in the elementary grades. Small-group work, in peer groups or with a teacher, is also recommended for ELL secondary students who struggle with literacy and English language development (Baker et al., 2007; Baker et al., 2014). The U.S. Department of Education's Institute of Education Sciences (IES) also recommends pair and group work for integrating oral language development for all ELL students across content-area teaching in the secondary grades. In the accompanying video, watch seventh-grade English language learners productively working through a complex text and its vocabulary with their peers.

 WATCH Video 26: Scaffolding Literacy Instruction for English Language Learners

- *Opportunities for student-driven listening and speaking.* Research confirms that classroom listening and speaking is often teacher-dominated (Ellis, 2012). Teacher-dominated discourse, if conducted thoughtfully, does not necessarily impede second language learning. However, across all instruction, providing opportunities for ELLs to authentically communicate in their second language has obvious implications for increasing their listening and speaking abilities. Pay close attention to the implications of "teacher talk time" and "student talk time," deciding what would be most appropriate to the learning at hand. Overall, it is essential to recognize the importance of oral language development for ELLs: ELLs with oral proficiency in English possess more language learning strategies and are better at engaging in academic uses of language (Genesee et al., 2005). The deeper instruction practices highlighted throughout this book, particularly those that involve students collaboratively engaged in purposeful work, are highly supportive of ELLs' oral language development.

> It's really important for us to get the same text. We get to know the same vocabulary. We get to share the same ideas. It helps us—people who are learning English—to be comfortable talking in class.
>
> —*Nicole, student,*
> *King Middle School*

- *Honoring the home culture and language.* Successful differentiation can occur when teachers don't have access to the first language of ELLs; in fact, that is the most typical situation in most classrooms. However, it is important to note that there is strong evidence that ELLs thrive in schools and classrooms that have an "intercultural orientation" (Freeman & Freeman, 2011) in which the school culture overtly honors the cultural backgrounds, traditions, and perspectives of ELL students.

  Studies show that encouraging literacy in the first language facilitates literacy in the second language—whether through the teacher's use of the first language, or through peers speaking the same language with each other. Teachers can also use the first language to help them connect personally with students, acquire vocabulary of all kinds, and help students meta-think about their language instruction (e.g., using the first language to work through the proper position of a verb in a sentence) (Ellis, 2012).

  There are obvious dangers in over-reliance upon the first language in ELL instruction (e.g., in small-group work with ELL peers), and it is important overall to expose ELLs to their new language as much as possible in the classroom setting. Bearing this in mind, however, we strongly support thoughtful and targeted use of the first language in all ELL scaffolding wherever possible.

- *Decreasing anxiety.* ELL research is clear that student anxiety about producing correct second language can have a profound negative affect on second language acquisition. This may be especially true in the secondary grades, where students naturally enter a period of identity formation and questioning that is potentially difficult to navigate (Leki, Cumming, & Silva, 2008). ELLs can also come from personal situations of high stress, such as the recent high influx of unaccompanied immigrant children across the Mexican border (Maxwell, 2014). Whatever scaffolds you choose, give strong consideration to the levels of comfort or anxiety they can induce in your ELLs.

Addressing Behavior and Social-Emotional Learning

For all students, differentiated instruction needs to take account of student behavior and social-emotional learning as well as academic learning. The students most in need of differentiation often exhibit the most challenging behaviors. "One size fits all" has left them out, and yet they often do not yet have the skills to engage productively in independent or collaborative activities without significant support. A more flexible and nuanced approach is needed to reach students who have trouble engaging in classroom learning.

Deeper instruction that engages students in compelling, purposeful work with opportunities for meaningful collaboration with peers is a great way to build students' academic mindsets—"I belong in this learning community," "I can succeed at this," "My ability and competence will grow with my effort," and "This work has value for me"—that can mitigate behavior issues caused by disconnection, boredom, and frustration. We saw this in Chapter 2 when a young student in Ali Bernstein's and Fran Taffer's second-grade class found purpose in his work advocating for an accessible playground for his classmates. The challenging behaviors he had exhibited all year lessened as he channeled his energy to worthy work.

Take a Data-Based Approach

Challenging behavior is complex and can be hard to understand. It calls for data-based inquiry: collecting data, looking for patterns, and selecting appropriate strategies. Different groups of students will need different strategies, just as they do in literacy and mathematics learning. What seems appropriate intuitively—for example, being directive, giving stern feedback, setting an inflexible consequence—may actually make the behavior worse.

Adopt a Skills-Based Mindset

First, teachers should begin by adopting the mindset that behavior is a set of skills that can be taught. "Challenging behavior in kids is best understood," writes child psychologist Dr. Ross Greene (2008), "as the result of lagging cognitive skills in the general domains of flexibility/adaptability, frustration tolerance, and problem solving." As a result, it's important to believe that "kids do well if they can." Rather than intentionally disturbing others or sabotaging his own progress because he "doesn't care," a misbehaving student is most likely trying to solve a problem or communicate distress. This change of mindset can have a profound effect on the responses of adults who are responding to the child's behavior by neutralizing anger and power struggles, and recasting the interaction as a quest to understand, founded in empathy.

For many students, then, social skills need to be taught as explicitly as other skills; it's not enough to model them. Examples of key skills may include

- managing transitions: shifting from one activity or group to another;

- mustering energy to persist on challenging or tedious tasks;

- managing one's emotional response to frustration in order to think rationally.

Differentiating one's approach to students' varying social skills may also involve developing individual plans or contracts, creating varied seating plans, or providing small group instruction. The Strategy Close Up that follows offers some tips for supporting this kind of social and emotional skill development.[5]

STRATEGY CLOSE UP: Supporting Social and Emotional Learning

Types of primary interventions supporting social and emotional learning to incorporate into the classroom as part of differentiated instruction (Minahan & Rappaport, 2013) include:

- **Environment:** Using breaks, calm space, approaches to lunch and recess
- **Executive functioning:** Implementing visual representations of time, previewing schedules, teaching "reading the room"
- **Curriculum aids:** Using pictures to help students think of and maintain a topic while they write, chunking texts to make them less overwhelming for a struggling reader
- **Replacement behaviors:** Teaching a student to ask for a break instead of disrupting the class
- **Teaching underdeveloped skills:** Including regulation of self and self-monitoring; depending on the child, rewards can help reinforce the student's use of the skills
- **Interaction strategies:** Using concise language, working on explicit relationship building, providing positive descriptive feedback
- **Response strategies:** Avoiding responses that would reinforce escape such as time-outs or removal from class if it seems that a student wishes to escape a task

---

The Critical Moves of Differentiated Instruction

The best differentiated instruction takes planning, thought, and practice, with much of the work occurring before students ever step into the classroom. So that students can benefit the most from differentiation, deeper instructional planning must meld individual student needs and strengths, learning standards, and curriculum tasks systematically and with collaboration and care. Table 6.4 illustrates the who, what, and why of differentiating instruction.

Table 6.4 The Who, What, and Why of Differentiating Instruction

What Do Teachers Do?	What Do Students Do?	What's the Result?
Build a culture of differentiation within the classroom.	Embrace a growth mindset and support each other, understanding that everyone has unique gifts and strengths, everyone should be productively challenged, and everyone is working toward the same goals.	Differentiation does not feel strange or unique, but becomes the default mode of learning and growing in the classroom.
Gather detailed information about students' learning backgrounds, strengths, challenges, readiness, and interests, collaborating with other school professionals to do so.	Share information about themselves via self-reflection, surveys, and pre-assessments.	Students feel known, safe, and supported by their teachers.
Develop standards-based student-friendly learning targets that all students work toward.	Discuss the targets and understand how they direct and influence the learning. Recognize that though paths to the target differ, the target remains the same for all.	Students and teachers know the purpose of their learning and what they need to do to achieve that purpose.
Develop appropriate scaffolding or extensions to challenge, engage, and empower students. These might include technology that enhances differentiation.	Come to understand and expect that they and their peers can take different paths to the same learning targets.	Students who need extra support and students who need extra challenge are equally considered and planned for proactively, resulting in equitable levels of challenge.
Form flexible learning groups to maximize the level of challenge and engagement.	Learn the skills and protocols needed to work successfully in groups. Understand that flexible groups meet diverse learning needs.	Students recognize the value of working collaboratively in groups that honor the needs and strengths of all students.
Embed student-engaged assessment at all points of the learning process.	Learn how to accurately assess their own progress. Articulate where they're going and how they'll get there.	Students become leaders of their own learning as they become increasingly metacognitive.
Tier assignments.	Starting from "where they are," students meet the learning target at their own pace and/or with work at varying levels of complexity.	Students are challenged, engaged, and empowered by work that is well paced and appropriately complex.

(continued)

Table 6.4 Continued

What Do Teachers Do?	What Do Students Do?	What's the Result?
Offer students a choice of tasks based on their readiness and/or interests.	Feel invested and engaged. Learn how to choose learning options that fit best with their academic needs and interests.	Students put forth genuine effort for learning that is accurately matched to their strengths and interests. Learning is deeper and more meaningful.
Differentiate classroom management and socio-emotional learning.	Understand that they are in control of their behavior. They see that they make choices about their behavior and can also make changes if needed.	Learners become full partners in making the appropriate decisions to manage themselves in the classroom.

SCHOOLWIDE IMPLEMENTATION

Creating a Differentiated School

Differentiation is not simply a classroom instructional approach; it is a philosophy that permeates a school. From building in extensive planning time for teachers, to creating disciplinary structures that honor students' individual needs, an overarching approach is required in order to foster a culture of differentiation.

When schools take on differentiation at the building or district level, both students and teachers feel respected and valued as individuals. All members of the school community recognize and build upon strengths and encourage students by meeting them "where they are."

Key Leadership Actions

Lay the Groundwork

- Build a vision and mindset for differentiation and develop schoolwide goals. School staff should understand that differentiated instruction for students with special needs in particular is the responsibility of all.

- Reinforce the connection between deeper instruction and differentiated instruction. Emphasize that the goal is for all students to be challenged, engaged, and empowered by their learning experiences, no matter what their strengths and needs might be.

- Resist "tracking" students into fixed ability groups. Provide alternate models of flexible grouping (e.g., offering an "embedded honors" option in which students can choose to do additional complex assignments, not just "more work," to exceed the standards; offering supplemental or extended day courses). Similarly, emphasize groupings in which students receiving special education services are included in the general education classrooms and have access to both content and special education expertise.

Build Teachers' Capacity

- Provide teachers with significant time and structures that help them plan together to meet a variety of student needs. This includes consistent planning time with special education and ELL partner teachers, regular grade-level meetings with counselors, and/or time for "data teams" to meet to review a variety of sources of assessment information, such as from Response to Intervention.

- Provide usable data and professional development focused on data-based inquiry so that teachers can make reliable decisions about differentiation. Collaboratively analyze results and the impact on student achievement. Ensure that policies, procedures, and protocols help struggling learners in particular meet academic and/or behavioral expectations.

Support Teachers to Deepen Their Practice

- Select a set of priority practices (e.g., tiering, flexible grouping) and work collaboratively with faculty members to develop a common practice rubric and criteria for success.

- Develop structures for support and feedback including coaching, peer observation, learning walks, and so on to ensure that teachers have many opportunities to learn and deepen their practice. The case study that follows shows how one school improved differentiation practices schoolwide.

CASE STUDY

Building Student Confidence with Schoolwide Differentiated Instruction

Kettle Falls Elementary School, a preK–fourth-grade school in rural Washington state, was struggling to meet the needs of its special education and Title I students in the context of their learning expeditions—long-term curricular units based on in-depth case studies, fieldwork, and service—which are a key part of the curriculum at the school. "Special education (and Title I) students didn't always have enough schema to access expedition content and were often letting other students do the work for them," says principal Val McKern. Although the school had tried to get teachers to differentiate instruction (Tier 1 intervention) to help all learners access higher-level expedition texts, they realized that additional support was needed.

The school wanted to maintain its belief that all students could meet grade-level learning targets and have access to the same rich deeper learning opportunities that would challenge, engage, and empower them. But to do this well they recognized that they needed to "preload" expedition content for some students in order to help them access the needed background knowledge, or schema, to participate in class and take responsibility for their learning. The school made a commitment to coordinating pull-out front-loading opportunities for all special education and Title I students (Tier 2 intervention). Grade-level teams communicated upcoming expedition content and specific texts to the special education teacher, Teresa Hill, who adjusted texts as needed and helped students build schema through pre-loading content. Hill also collaborated with colleagues to create minute-by-minute plans to pass on to the teachers or paraprofessionals who worked with the students.

Pull-out time, or "target time," took place four times a week for 45 minutes, in a ratio of one instructor to five students. During target time, Hill or a paraprofessional met with students to preload content by engaging in activities such as reading aloud and reviewing vocabulary. Target time was built into the schedule; there was a schoolwide understanding that students wouldn't miss expedition content or mathematics instruction during this time. Students remaining in the regular classroom setting engaged in book clubs or independent reading.

"We don't compromise the complexity of the text," Val McKern and Teresa Hill emphasize. "Preloading means there's more access: shorter, more illustrations and photos, larger fonts, bigger space under each paragraph for text coding and reflection. The complexity of the text itself, however, doesn't change." Students then go back to their classrooms, prepared to engage with the texts and with their peers.

Teresa Hill has seen the difference in her students. "There's a clear transition between target time and their classroom learning: they never have that lost feeling. When they pull out those articles we've worked on, their level of confidence is really significantly higher than when we didn't do preloading. A little bit of confidence goes a long, long way. It's not that often that those kids get to be leaders of their class. They're cognizant of the fact that they're learning earlier and that they may be called upon as experts, and that really helps them engage."

COMMON CHALLENGES

Classroom Culture and Mindset Are Weak

Don't skip or shortchange the process of building a strong classroom culture for differentiation—one that values difference, recognizes the variety of strengths and skills students bring, and teaches a growth mindset. A focus on classroom culture and growth mindset are the cornerstones of the self-reflective learning process that allows deeper learning to flourish in the classroom and empowers students with tools for learning.

Grouping Is Rigid

Be flexible. In traditional classrooms, students often find themselves in consistent groups. We need to shift this paradigm and move away from "high-level, on-level, and low-level" ability groups. The reality is that students have strengths and weaknesses, and are rarely able to be categorically placed in a group based on ability. The possibilities of flexible grouping are endless, inherently engaging, and have a dramatic impact on student achievement and deeper learning.

Student Engagement Is Low

Don't forget deeper instruction. Although differentiated tasks generally improve the engagement of students, it is not wise to assume that simply because a task has been differentiated, it will be compelling and purposeful for students. Ask yourself:

- What is the value of this task for my students? Is that value obvious?

- What have I done to hook students into the work?

- Are the materials I am using—the texts, the artifacts, the tools—worthy and compelling?

Remember that engagement is not a side effect. It must be planned for and is key to deeper learning and achievement.

Pre-assessment Is Neglected

Teachers and students should make informed decisions about differentiation. Taking the time to carefully assess student readiness and progress before and during instruction will allow for the most effective differentiation. When in doubt, don't be afraid to empower students with "challenge by choice."

There Is Not Enough Independent Experience

Create the right balance between group and individual learning experiences, including assessment. Eventually, all students need to build their capacity to work and learn independently. For example, although students may have highly differentiated classroom experiences, they are usually expected to work independently—and without differentiated scaffolded support—on traditional summative assessments. We highly recommend that teachers embed regular independent on-demand assessments into their long-range instructional planning to determine progress toward targets/standards. Allowing students to demonstrate their progress without support gives teachers, students, and their families a truer measure of progress and clarity about when they might be "over-differentiating." Remember that deeper learning depends on respectful tasks that are not too easy and that challenge students productively.

I Don't Know the Best Time to Differentiate a Lesson

When is it appropriate to step in with extensions and scaffolds? As you grow in your understanding of differentiation and feel more comfortable planning differentiated lessons, a key consideration is not just what to differentiate during a lesson, but exactly when to differentiate it. We believe that generally the best time is after students have given their best effort to absorbing new learning on their own. Many lesson structures—such as Workshop 2.0 and discovery-based lessons (described in detail in Chapter 1)—ensure that lessons don't take away students' opportunity to make sense of challenging problems, texts, or concepts on their own without too much front-loading.

The Amount of Individual Need Is Overwhelming

Group students according to common, if not identical, needs. Teachers who are most experienced with differentiation think about clusters of needs and grouping students together flexibly. They might plan two to four groups of differentiated activities, not twelve.

Technology Glitches Bog Down the Learning

Get the most from technology. Avoid falling into various traps such as over-reliance (e.g., thinking it's enough to challenge the highly ready or support the struggling by steering them to the computer), expense, or distraction.

Notes

1. Based on the work of Carol Ann Tomlinson.

2. Gardner, H. (1985). *Frames of mind: The theory of multiple intelligences.* New York, NY: Basic Books; Sternberg, R. J. (1984). *Beyond I.Q.: A triarchic theory of human intelligence.* New York, NY: Cambridge University Press.

3. Originally published April 6, 2010 © Edutopia.org; George Lucas Educational Foundation.

4. Diane Staeher Fenner (2013). *Overview of the Common Core State Standards Initiatives for ELLs.* Alexandria, VA: Author. Used with permission.

5. For more information on social and emotional skill development and building a positive classroom culture see: Berger, R., Strasser, D., and Woodfin, L. (2015). Management in the active classroom. New York, NY: EL Education.

Conclusion

We wrote this book with a few guiding questions: If the quality of classroom instruction is the greatest predictor of achievement, then what can we offer to help teachers *deepen* their instruction so that students are more challenged, engaged, and empowered? How can we support teachers to get their students grappling with more rigorous material in order to build deeper understanding? How can we promote *learning that lasts*? Our goal was to provide a practical guide that was accessible to all teachers: the novice teacher just trying to figure out what the state standards mean and the veteran teacher seeking new ways to deepen her students' learning. We also wanted the tools in this book to be powerful for all students regardless of setting, learning profile, or background.

At about the same time that we started this book, groundbreaking research on academic mindsets and noncognitive skills was just starting to ignite a national conversation about the attitudes students must have to succeed not just in school, but in life. What we at EL Education had long put at the center of our work—focusing on student character and habits of work as an integral part of instruction—burst onto the national stage as a critical component for student achievement. For the next two years as we gathered the stories of teachers, students, and school leaders in schools across the country, we were not surprised to find that the most effective teachers we encountered were those who deliberately stoke their students' academic courage and perseverance by instilling the habits that allow students to invest in and succeed at challenging learning.

It's easy to focus on what's *wrong* with education. To discover what's *right* with education requires looking hard at what happens between great teachers and their students. Great teachers like those described in this book plan and teach strategically to challenge, engage, and empower their students. They focus on all three of our dimensions of student achievement: mastery of knowledge and skills, character, and high-quality work. They embody the dispositions that they hope to teach. They model passion for learning, respect for others and diverse ideas, academic courage, and a growth mindset. The many great teachers whom we introduced in the pages of this book would be the first to tell you that they didn't necessarily start out that way. Through their own continuous growth in content knowledge and teaching skills, however, they showed themselves and their students that all of us grow with effort, collaboration and practice.

Writing this book has revealed the silver lining within the gray cloud over public education in America. The silver lining is the potential of teachers. We don't need to reject the institution of schooling or dismantle the whole system of teaching and learning. We need only to pay attention, deep detailed attention, to how teachers plan and carry out the lessons they teach, and to how good school leaders support this valuable work. This means also paying attention to, and learning from, teachers and leaders themselves. By focusing on practices that challenge, engage, and empower students, teachers and leaders can do more than they think is possible.

Sample Protocol-Based Lessons

SOCRATIC SEMINAR

Purpose

Socratic Seminars promote thinking, meaning-making, and the ability to debate, use evidence, and build on one another's thinking. When well-designed and implemented, the seminar provides an active role for every student, engages students in complex thinking about rich content, and teaches students discussion skills.

Materials

- Provocative question for discussion, chosen beforehand

- Associated text(s)

- Anchor Chart for protocol norms

Procedure

- Select a significant piece of text or collection of short texts related to the current focus of study. This may be an excerpt from a book or an article from a magazine, journal, or newspaper. It might also be a poem, short story, or personal memoir. The text needs to be rich with possibilities for diverse points of view.

- Develop an open-ended, provocative question as the starting point for the seminar discussion. The question should be worded to elicit differing perspectives and complex thinking. Students may also generate questions to discuss.

- Students prepare for the seminar by reading the chosen piece of text in an active manner that helps them build background knowledge for participation in the discussion. The completion of the pre-seminar task is the students' "ticket" to participate in the seminar. The pre-seminar task could easily incorporate work on reading strategies. For example, students might be asked to read the article in advance and to text-code by underlining important information, putting question marks by segments they wonder about, and exclamation points next to parts that surprise them.

- Once the seminar begins, all students should be involved and should make sure others in the group are drawn into the discussion.

- Begin the discussion with the open-ended question designed to provoke inquiry and diverse perspectives. The teacher may pose follow-up questions.

- The discussion proceeds until you call time. At that time, the group debriefs their process; if using a Fishbowl style Socratic Seminar (see Variations), the outer-circle members give their feedback sheets to the inner-group students.

- Protocol norms: Students . . .
  - Respect other students. (Exhibit open-mindedness and value others' contributions.)
  - Are active listeners. (Build on one another's ideas by referring to them.)
  - Stay focused on the topic.
  - Make specific references to the text. (Use examples from the text to explain their points.)
  - Give input. (Ensure participation.)
  - Ask questions. (Clarifying questions, and probing questions that push the conversation further and deeper when appropriate.)

Variations

- Conduct the Socratic Seminar as a Fishbowl. When it is time for the seminar, students are divided into two groups. One group forms the inner circle (the "fish") who will be discussing the text. The other group forms the outer circle; they will give feedback on content, contributions, and group skills. (*Note:* "Fishbowls" may be used with other instructional practices such as peer critiques, literature circles, or group work. If the number of students in the seminar is small, a Fishbowl does not need to be used.) Each person in the outer circle is asked to observe one of the students in the inner circle. Criteria or a rubric for the observations should be developed by or shared with students in advance: see the following example.

Did the Student . . .	Consistently	Occasionally	Not This Time	Notes/Comments
Respond to other students' comments in a respectful way?				
Listen attentively without interruption?				
Make eye contact with peers?				
Exhibit preparation for the seminar?				
Reference the text to support response?				
Participate in the discussion?				
Ask clarifying or probing questions?				

- Provide sentence stems that allow students to interact positively and thoughtfully with one another: "I'd like to build on that thought . . ." "Could you tell me more?" "May I finish my thought?"

Reference

Israel, E. (2002). Examining multiple perspectives in literature. In *Inquiry and the literary text: Constructing discussions in the English classroom*. Urbana, IL: National Center for Teachers of English.

BUILDING BACKGROUND KNOWLEDGE WORKSHOP

Purpose

This protocol demonstrates how quickly people can become interested in a topic, build knowledge, and use that knowledge to become better and more informed readers of complex text. The protocol adapts easily to content in many disciplines, and the design ensures that all students read, think, and contribute. The protocol is particularly useful when introducing a topic because it fosters curiosity and builds in immediate feedback about learning. A Building Background Knowledge (BBK) workshop, especially if it includes close reading of a common text, may include an entire class period or even multiple class periods (introducing different texts on successive days). When conducted and debriefed for educators, the protocol heightens awareness of key instructional and grouping practices.

Materials

- Chart paper
- Colored markers
- Various texts on a related topic

Procedure

- Choose a topic and find several texts as described in the following steps.
- Use a grouping strategy to shift students into groups of four or five.
- To each group, give a set of four different-colored markers, a piece of chart paper, texts, and loose-leaf paper.
- Share a "mystery text" with the whole class. Choose a relevant short text, poem, political cartoon, photograph, song, graph, map, and so on, that sparks students' curiosity about the topic. Display or provide copies of the text (remove the title if it gives away the topic).
- Activate and share background knowledge:
  - Ask students to write down what they know about the topic of the mystery text.
  - Ask students, in their small groups, to number off, then share what they know about the topic, being sure that each person has a chance to speak.

- Ask students to create a web or visualization of their collective knowledge or understanding of the topic on a piece of chart paper using just one of the colored markers. Number 1 in the group is the recorder for this part.

- Provide a "common text"—an article or essay on the topic that is interesting, offers a solid introduction to the topic, and provides multiple perspectives. All students read this article.

- Ask students to text-code (use symbols, letters or numbers, and shorthand to annotate) the article with "*N*" for new information.

- Ask students to add their new knowledge to their web using a different color of marker. Number 2 in the group is the recorder for this part.

- Distribute "expert texts": Hand out a different text on the topic to each member of the group. This is an ideal time to differentiate texts if needed.

- Again, ask students to text-code for new information.

- After everyone has read, have each student share new knowledge with his or her group and capture key points on the chart paper using the third color. Number 3 is the recorder for this part.

- Have on hand extra texts or additional media (drawings, maps, photos, graphs, etc.) for those who finish early.

- Return to the mystery text. Re-read the initial text or display it again.

- Ask students to return to what they had initially written about the mystery text; have students discuss what they now think about the mystery text, then record their new thinking on their web. Number 4 is the recorder for this part and uses a fourth color of marker.

- Contrast the first and second reading or showing of the mystery text: "What was it like to hear the mystery text the second time?" "What made the experience so different?"

- Ask general questions about what the process was like to read successive articles. Did students know much about the topic before? Had they been curious about the topic? What inspired their curiosity? If time, consider asking a question with four possible responses and having students with like responses group together in the four corners of the room. Ask follow-up questions for the groups to discuss together.

Variations

- Boxing (see graphic below): Draw a box to create a fairly wide frame for the poster. Draw a smaller box inside the first and another inside that. The boxes will create three spaces for representing learning. In the frame, have the group write their prior knowledge, or possibly what they want to learn about the topic. Next, read and discuss to build knowledge. Inside the second box, write about new learning. Finally, in the middle, either write a summary of the learning or create a graphic illustration that synthesizes the groups' understanding of the topic.

- Combine this protocol with a Poster Session in which groups share webs or boxes with other groups.

- Assign a "Roving Reporter" role to one or more students, having them view and report on group ideas to the rest of the class.

Boxing

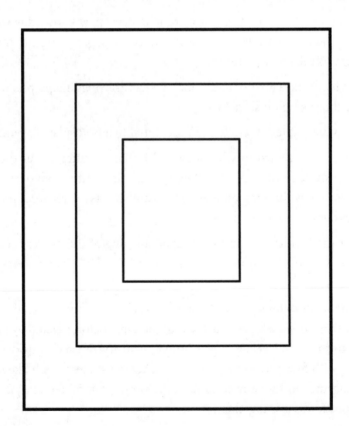

SCIENCE TALKS

Purpose

Science Talks are discussions about big questions. They are appropriate for any grade level, but they are particularly useful for elementary students. Like Socratic Seminars, Science Talks deal with provocative questions, often posed by students themselves. Science Talks provide space for students to collectively theorize, to build on each other's ideas, to work out thoughts, and to learn about scientific discourse. Most important, they allow all students to do exactly what scientists do: think about, wonder about, and talk about how things work. These talks provide a window on student thinking that can help teachers figure out what students really know and what their misconceptions are. Armed with this insight, teachers can better plan hands-on activities and experiments.

Materials

- Guiding question for the Science Talk, determined beforehand

Procedure

- Choose the question. The best questions are provocative and open-ended, so as to admit multiple answers and theories. Often, students generate great questions for Science Talks. Teachers can also generate questions based on their own wonderings.

- Introduce Science Talks to students. Gather students into a circle on the floor. Introduce the first Science Talk by discussing what scientists do.

- Then ask, "What will help us talk as scientists?" Record the students' comments, because these will become the norms for your Science Talks. If the students don't mention making sure that everyone has a chance to talk, introduce that idea, as well as how each person can ensure that they themselves don't monopolize the conversation. Stress how each student's voice is valued and integral to the success of a Science Talk.

- Set the culture. Students direct their comments to one another, not to the teacher. In fact, the teacher stays quiet and out of the way, facilitating only to make sure that students respectfully address one another and to point out when monopolizing behavior occurs. In a good talk, you'll hear students saying,

"I want to add to what Grace said . . ." or "I think Derek is right about one thing, but I'm not so sure about . . ."

- Another good question to pose is, "How will we know that what we've said has been heard?" Students will readily talk about how they can acknowledge what's been said by repeating it or rephrasing before they go on to add their comments. This is a great place to add (if the students don't) that talking together is one way scientists build theories.

- A typical Science Talk lasts about 30 minutes. Take notes during the talk about who is doing the talking and to record particularly intriguing comments.

Variations
- With young students, do a movement exercise that relates to the Science Talk. For a talk on how plants grow, students may be invited to show, with their bodies, how plants grow from bulbs. Not only does this give students a chance to move before more sitting, it also gives them a different modality with which to express themselves. Sometimes the shyer students also find acting something out first helps them to verbalize it.

- Have students prepare for a Science Talk by reading and annotating pertinent texts. Combining Science Talk with a Jigsaw or another text-based protocol could work well here.

- Pair a Science Talk with a writing activity on the same topic.

- Record the talks. Replaying the tapes later helps to make sense of what at first hearing can seem incomprehensible. Students also love hearing the tapes of Science Talks.

The What, Why, and How of Protocols

WHAT ARE PROTOCOLS?

A protocol consists of agreed-upon guidelines for reading, recording, discussing, or reporting that ensure equal participation and accountability. When everyone understands and agrees to using the procedures of the protocol, participants are able to work more effectively both independently and collaboratively, often in ways they are not in the habit of doing. Protocols hold each student accountable and responsible for learning.

WHY USE A PROTOCOL?

Text-Based Protocols for Reading and Annotating

Protocols for reading and annotating hold all students accountable for building background knowledge about a topic and for analyzing what they read by annotating the text with questions, comments, paraphrasing, or summary statements. These protocols also allow the teacher to assess which students are struggling with the text and may need further support for comprehension. Finally, these protocols allow students to gather their thoughts prior to discussion or writing about their reading.

Protocols for Collaboration and Discussion

Protocols for collaboration and discussion invite students to value different perspectives and new insights. These protocols make room for listening as well as contributing to discussion. Following guidelines for timekeeping, turn-taking, and focusing on the topic are essential for productive discussion. These are not skills that come naturally to many students. Sentence stems for accountable talk and asking questions, norms for honoring diverse perspectives, and procedures for synthesizing contributions to a discussion hold individuals and groups accountable for pushing their thinking further. Discussion protocols can be embedded in a workshop or daily lesson, or, in the case of a Socratic Seminar or Building Background Knowledge Workshop can be the entire lesson for the class period.

Protocols for Consultation and Decision Making

Protocols for consultation and decision making make it safe to ask challenging questions, to take intellectual and emotional risks, and to problem-solve difficult situations. Such protocols build trust as participants learn from each other and devise strategies and solutions collaboratively. In groups facing difficult challenges or struggling with conflict, protocols are an essential tool for mediation, embracing diversity, and overcoming fear.

Protocols for Sharing and Presenting

Protocols for sharing and presenting focus on fairness and equity. They enable all members of a group to see or hear the work done by individuals or small groups in an efficient way. Time-keeping and turn-taking norms must be reinforced in order to maximize equity of sharing.

Protocols for Critique

Protocols for peer critique are essential for teaching students how to offer and receive kind, helpful, and specific feedback on writing or problem solving. Critique protocols often take an entire class period; in that sense the protocol is the lesson for that day. It is important for the teacher to model following the critique protocol with a student's writing or with their own to demonstrate specific phrases for offering critique and the role of the author in receiving critique. A procedure for students to record their critique, plan for revision based on critique, and reflect on the value of the critique also improves this protocol.

HOW DO I ESTABLISH PROTOCOLS FOR DAILY, ACTIVE PEDAGOGY?

The skeleton that holds up any protocol includes:

- organized steps for the procedure (what participants must do);

- time frames for each step (when participants do each step and for how long);

- norms for participants (who participates and how they treat each other).

This skeleton must be explicitly taught and rehearsed the first time a protocol is used. During successive uses, it will likely need to be reinforced multiple times. Teachers are often most successful when they choose and focus on three to five protocols that anchor their instruction. Providing table tents or an Anchor Chart with the bulleted steps of the protocol and/or "role cards" that describe each person's role in the protocol will help students stay on task and do the protocol with fidelity. Using protocols as the routine of every independent reading time, discussion, or collaboration will allow students to learn more effectively and, equally important, to develop the habit of taking responsibility for their own learning and for contributing to the collective understanding of the group.

Primary Source Close Reading Guide

Created by Jill Clark, these materials draw on the work of Sam Wineburg and his colleagues at the Stanford History Education Group (sheg.stanford.edu) as well as Chauncey Monte-Sano, Susan De La Paz, and Mark Felton's forthcoming book, *Reading, Thinking, and Writing about History: Teaching Argument Writing to Diverse Learners in the Common Core Classroom, Grades 6–12.* New York, NY: Teachers College Press.

Directions and Questions for Students	Teaching Notes
First read: Determining source and context for the text Sourcing: • Who wrote or created this document? • When? • Why might this person have written or created this document? • Is this document likely to have a particular point of view? If so, what?	1. Distribute the document to students and allow them to initially engage with the text without too much mediation. 2. If the text is short, they should read the whole text. If it is longer, it may make more sense for them to read the sourcing information and the first few paragraphs. 3. Depending on the complexity of the text, you may wish to support students by reading all or part of the text aloud as they read silently. You may also wish to provide definitions, either orally

(continued)

Continued

Directions and Questions for Students	Teaching Notes
Contextualization: • Where was this document created? • Given the time and place, to which historical events might it relate? • How might this affect the content of the document?	or by writing them on the text, of words that meet *all* criteria: i. Are central to the meaning of the text ii. Are likely to be unfamiliar to students iii. Cannot be determined from context 4. After students have read the text, engage them in questions of sourcing and contextualizing the document, using the questions in the left-hand column. In order to contextualize a document, students will need to have and draw on some background knowledge. Consider referring them to a specific text or lesson. 5. Depending on student independence with these skills, you might choose to do one or more of the following: i. Model, either by thinking aloud or by having the class help you ii. Use think-pair-share iii. Have students work with partners and then call on several groups to share out iv. Have students work individually and then lead a class debrief 6. Until all students are proficient with this, all options need to include a class check-in so that students who are not on the right track recognize this and correct themselves. 7. This type of questioning is closely related to Common Core Literacy in History/Social Studies Standard 6, because considering author and context is an important step in determining an author's purpose and noticing how that purpose shapes a document.
Second read: Getting the big picture Read the whole text, one chunk at a time. As you read, mark parts of the text that do the following: • Help you understand more about the source and context of this piece • Help you answer the focusing question For each chunk of the text, circle words you don't know. Use context clues and word parts to try to figure out what those words mean and write your ideas in the margin next to the word.	1. For a longer or difficult text, chunk the text for students. The more complex the text, the shorter the chunks should be. 2. Set a purpose for students' reading with a focusing question that this document will help them answer. 3. In addition to marking vocabulary and thinking about gist, encourage students to underline phrases that relate to their focusing question. They may also want to mark parts of the text that help them add to their thinking about source and context. You may need to model this for students, so they know what an annotated document looks like.

Directions and Questions for Students	Teaching Notes
For each chunk, try to figure out what the gist of this chunk is. What is the text about? What is it saying? Write your ideas in the margins next to each chunk.	4. Students can do this work alone or with a partner; they can read silently or partner-read. If the text is long and very complex, consider reading each chunk aloud as students follow along and then releasing them to discuss vocabulary and gist. You may also consider having most students work with partners or alone on this step while you work with a smaller group of struggling readers and support them with a read-aloud and more frequent guidance about the meaning they are constructing. 5. Consider making and posting a list of words whose meanings you'd like students to generate from context as they read. List words that are central to the meaning of the text and whose meaning can be determined from context or word parts. 6. As students work, circulate and listen in, noticing any common misunderstandings. Ask students, "What in the text makes you say that?" 7. Debrief this work. Depending on the text and your students, you may wish to do this one chunk at a time (in the case of a very complex text, in which a misunderstanding early on will make it difficult for students to make meaning of the subsequent text independently), or you may wish to do it after students have grappled with the whole text. A significant portion of this conversation should be about vocabulary and how students determined the meanings of words from context. 8. Complete this step by asking students to explain what the text as a whole is mostly about. Note: This step relates closely to Common Core Literacy in History/Social Studies Standards 2 and 4.
Third read: Text-dependent questions	1. Ask students to complete a task that requires them to go back to the text and look closely at specific sections or at the text as a whole. Students should dig deeply into those aspects of the text that are most relevant to the purpose for which they are reading (i.e., the focusing question). 2. Options: a. Text-dependent questions, especially those focusing on claims an author is making, how

(continued)

Continued

Directions and Questions for Students	Teaching Notes
	an author uses details and evidence, or how point of view is apparent b. Specific note-taking task (gathering evidence for a particular question) c. Annotating the text with what they notice and wonder in regard to a particular question *Note:* This step relates closely to Common Core Literacy in History/Social Studies Standards 1, 2, 4, and 6. It could relate to other standards, also, depending on the text-dependent questions you ask.
Final read: Evaluate the source Look again at your ideas about source and context. Now that you have read the text carefully, how might you revise your original ideas? How does the author and purpose of the document affect its content? • What have you learned about the point of view of the author and his or her purpose for writing? • What information or opinions does this document include about the historical event to which it is related? How does this connect to what you know about the author and his or her purpose? • How did reading the document closely help you refine your original ideas about sourcing and context? How does this source compare to other sources that are related to this event or time period? • What information or ideas have you also found in other sources? What information or ideas are only in this source? Why might that be? • What evidence in this document is most believable? Why? • What did this source add to your understanding of the historical question you are investigating?	1. Now that students have read the document closely, they should revisit their original ideas about source and context, and they should also be able to evaluate the source more holistically. In this step, they should consider how the author and purpose of the document affects its content. 2. First, direct students to revisit and revise their sourcing and context notes. Consider doing this alone, in partners, or as a class, depending on student independence with this skill. Students should revise their original notes to reflect their new thinking. Support them in noticing how the author and his or her purpose affected the content of the document. 3. Next, help students evaluate the source by corroborating it with other sources. Consider doing this alone, in partners, or as a class, depending on student independence with this skill. It may be useful to return to the question of corroboration several days later, after students have read more documents. 4. Finally, make sure students reflect on how this source helped them address their focusing question or topic of historical inquiry. *Note:* This step relates especially to Common Core Literacy in History/Social Studies Standard 9.

Factors to Guide Your Selection of Text

What follows is a list of criteria against which teachers can analyze texts. Keep in mind: no text is perfect. As you and your team plan, ask: "What are all the things we need this text to do for us?" Keep iterating until you have landed on a text that is worth your time to analyze and plan from, and worth your students' time, effort, and intellect to understand and appreciate.

Content: Is the text aligned to grade-level content standards? To what extent will this text help students learn something important and enduring about the big ideas of an academic discipline? How can the text help to build students' knowledge about the world? If a literary text, what topics can it still teach students about? To what extent does this text provide sufficient information, so students can successfully respond to an evidence-based writing task?

Example (grade 8): *Inside Out & Back Again* by Thanhha Lai (a fictional account of a Vietnamese girl whose family flees during the Vietnam war) offers an opportunity to teach about the universal refugee experience, aligned with social studies themes such as the role of social, political, and cultural interactions in the development of identity.

Interest: Is the text compelling for students? Will students love digging into this text? Why? Is the text developmentally appropriate—will it sing to students of this age and background? Is it high interest in terms of content or format? Is it particularly beautifully written or illustrated?

> **Example (grade 5):** *The Most Beautiful Roof in the World* by Kathryn Lasky (about rain forest researcher Meg Lowman) has rich scientific information about biodiversity and the rainforest, and includes gorgeous photographs of her in the canopy and stories about her son's adventures in the rainforest that will hook kids.

Complexity: Is the text appropriate in terms of qualitative and quantitative measures of complexity? What makes this text challenging? Based on qualitative measures, in what ways will the concepts, structure, language, and so on give students something worth grappling with? Based on quantitative measures, is this text sufficiently demanding in terms of syntax and academic vocabulary? Does this text provide sufficient complexity to ensure that students have to work hard and get to build their literacy muscles as they work through this text? In unit, how will this text be paired with texts of greater or lesser complexity?

> **Example (grade 5):** *Esperanza Rising* by Pam Munoz Ryan has a Lexile text measure of just 750, somewhat low for fifth grade. Yet it provides quite a challenge for fifth-graders based on qualitative measures—the concepts (identity formation of the main character and human rights violations experienced by migrant farm workers in the 1930s) as well as the metaphorical language and symbolism.

Reading standards: Does the text offer opportunities to teach grade-level literacy standards? What opportunities does this text afford you to teach standards at a specific grade level of rigor? If the reading standard requires students to infer, is the text sufficiently rich to require such inferring or are the ideas all right there? If the reading standard requires students to interpret information presented visually, orally, or quantitatively, does the text include the types of diagrams and charts that would make this work possible? Usually, a complex text will provide opportunities to address all the reading standards. But some texts may provide a particularly elegant fit for addressing a given standard at a given grade level.

Example (grade 7): *A Long Walk to Water* by Linda Sue Park (fiction set during the Second Sudanese Civil War) traces the perspectives of Salva (from the Dinka tribe) and Nya (from the Nuer tribe). Though the language is simple for seventh-graders, the concepts related to tribal conflict, personal identity, and loss are intense. This novel affords a perfect opportunity to address Common Core standard RL.7.6: Analyze how an author develops and contrasts the points of view of different characters or narrators in a text, because each chapter opens with a section told from Nya's perspective and then provides a longer section told from Salva's perspective. And by pairing this novel with articles about the Second Sudanese Civil War and websites with information about the "lost boys" of Sudan, this historical fiction also provides an opportunity to address RL.7.9: Compare and contrast a fictional portrayal of a time, place, or character and a historical account of the same period as a means of understanding how authors of fiction use or alter history.

Writing standards: Can this text serve as a mentor text and model of author's craft? To what extent is this text a strong model of written arguments, informative writing, or narrative writing? Can this text—or sections of this text—serve not only as a context for students to build knowledge but also as an example of author's craft that students can emulate in their own writing?

Example (grade 8): *Unbroken: A World War II Story of Survival, Resilience, and Redemption* by Laura Hillenbrand is literary nonfiction. Through this text, students learn about Japanese-American relations in WWII. But they also see a master storyteller at work. Consider this review from the book's endorsements: "The author's skills are as polished as ever, and like its predecessor [*Seabiscuit*] this book has an impossible-to-put-down quality that one commonly associates with good thrillers" (Roland Green, *Booklist*). Students are sucked in as readers and inspired as writers. Hillenbrand's work serves as a mentor text when students craft their own narratives.

Source: This material was originally published in *Transformational Literacy: Making the Common Core Shift with Work That Matters* by R. Berger, L. Woodfin, S. Plaut, & C. Dobbertin. Copyright 2014 by John Wiley & Sons, Inc. All Rights Reserved.

From Assignment to Assessment

This sequential process supports students to produce high-quality work.

1. **Teach Content and Skills**

   Build background knowledge through reading, thinking, talking, writing, and doing.

2. **Assign the Task**

   Provide a clear written assignment with learning targets that guide both teacher and students.

3. **Analyze Model Work with Students**

   Choose models that show exactly what you want students to observe about the genre and quality of the assignment. Models can be student, teacher, or professionally created.

4. **Identify and Post Criteria for Excellence**

   Be specific and create an anchor chart of the criteria.

5. Design the Rubric

Be specific and use student language whenever possible.

6. Analyze Work That May Not Meet the Criteria for Excellence

This step is essential. Students need to see and debate many examples of poor- and high-quality work.

7. Practice and Teach Additional Skills Lessons

Guide students through multiple drafts of their work and remind them of the importance of a growth mindset.

8. Facilitate Peer Critique

Model the process and use a protocol to help structure student discussions— remind them to be kind, specific, and helpful.

9. Provide Students with Descriptive Feedback

Confer with students. Reference specific criteria for excellence. Challenge students to revise, not just correct.

10. Evaluate the Final Product

Assess learning targets using the product as evidence of complexity, authenticity, and craftsmanship.

Informational Text Resources

Thanks to Steve DelVecchio, Lauren Mayer, and Cindy Spruce for compiling this list of recommendations.

Resource	Description	Link
General		
Library of Congress	The largest library of manuscripts in the world, with millions of books, recordings, photographs, and maps in its collection	www.loc.gov
America's Library	Explore US history using primary sources from the Library of Congress; geared toward kids	www.americaslibrary.gov
National Geographic Kids	A great way for kids to explore animals and places on our planet	http://kids.nationalgeographic.com/kids
The Field Museum	A history and science museum, full of great resources	http://fieldmuseum.org/explore/our-collections
Scholastic Teacher Resource	A wide array of teaching materials that support students; all resources owned by Scholastic (e.g., Grolier Online, Current Events, Current Science) are also great but require a subscription	www.scholastic.com/teachers/teaching-resources

(continued)

Continued

Resource	Description	Link
The Poetry Foundation	Resources for teaching poetry including a wide array of poems	www.poetryfoundation.org
Project Gutenberg	Over forty-two thousand free e-books that are now in the public domain; all of the e-books were previously published by bona fide publishers	www.gutenberg.org
Creative Commons Website	Access to search services that have images, music, and sites that carry the Creative Commons license	http://us.creativecommons.org
History and Social Studies		
Time for Kids	A weekly classroom news magazine and a great resource for teachers	www.timeforkids.com
National Archives Historical Documents	Documents include Declaration of Independence, Bill of Rights, Louisiana Purchase, Emancipation Proclamation, and many others	www.archives.gov/historical-docs
National Archives Online Exhibitions	Includes exhibits, on human and civil rights	www.archives.gov/exhibits www.archives.gov/exhibits/documented-rights
Science		
Exploratorium	Isn't just a museum; it's an ongoing exploration of science, art, and human perception	www.exploratorium.edu
Eco Kids	An environmental education site from Earth Day Canada	www.ecokids.ca/pub/index.cfm
Kids Do Ecology	The National Center for Ecological Analysis and Synthesis promotes education and outreach.	http://kids.nceas.ucsb.edu/index.html
Smithsonian	Asks and answers questions about science	www.si.edu/Kids
National Park Service: Learn NPS	Features educational resources for teacher lessons and student research	www.nps.gov/learn
National Park NYS Reference	Provides information about all NYS national parks and other places of historical significance	www.nps.gov/state/ny/index.htm?program=parks
Explore Nature: Science in Your National Parks	Includes programs such as Biodiversity Discovery, the Climate Change Youth Initiative, and Geoscientists-in-the-Parks	www.nature.nps.gov

Resource	Description	Link
NOAA (National Oceanic and Atmospheric Administration) Educational Resources	Invaluable resource that provides information and incredible photographs relating to climate, weather, bodies of water, and marine life	www.education.noaa.gov
NOAA Fun for Kids	Environmental science page that includes information for getting free grade-appropriate science materials from NOAA	http://oceanservice.noaa.gov/kids
Fish and Wildlife Service: Let's Go Outside	Kid friendly activities, photos, and games	www.fws.gov/letsgooutside/kids.html
Why Nature Rocks	Nature Conservancy program designed to inspire play and nature exploration; includes kid friendly activities based on time available, location, and age of child	www.naturerocks.org/why-nature-rocks.aspx
US Department of Agriculture Image Gallery	Photos of animals, crops, and scientists	www.ars.usda.gov/is/graphics/photos
US Forest Service: Forest Service Kids	Information and resources related to agriculture	www.fs.fed.us/kids
National Archives Teachers' Resources	Enables teachers to find and create interactive learning activities using primary sources, including documents and images	www.archives.gov/education
Metric Conversions	Provides conversion to and from metric for temperature, weight, length, area, and volume	www.metric-conversions.org
Science for Teachers and Kids	Government site that includes grade-appropriate material about life science, inventors, scientists, and our planet	http://kids.usa.gov/science/index.shtml
US Environmental Protection Agency	Teacher resources about the environment and conservation	www.epa.gov/students/teachers.html
National Institute of Environmental Health Sciences for Kids	Student friendly materials for all ages, including vocabulary	http://kids.niehs.nih.gov/index.htm

Photograph Resources

Thanks to Steve DelVecchio, Lauren Mayer, and Cindy Spruce for compiling this list of recommendations.

Resource	Description	Link
Library of Congress Prints and Photographs Online Collection	More than 1.2 million digitized images	www.loc.gov/pictures
America's Library See, Hear and Sing	Explores US history through animation, songs, images, and quizzes	www.americaslibrary.gov/sh/index.php
Centers for Disease Control and Prevention Image Library	Not just about diseases; links to more than a dozen different sites containing millions of images	www.cdc.gov/healthyplaces/images.htm
ThinkQuest Photo Gallery	Small collection of student-taken images; includes flora and fauna of various climates	http://library.thinkquest.org/05aug/00101/PhotoGallery.htm
The Field Museum Photo Archives Collections	More than three hundred thousand images related to anthropology, botany, geology, and zoology from the history and science museum	http://fieldmuseum.org/explore/department/library/photo-archives/collections
Smithsonian Animal Photo Galleries	Images taken at the National Zoo of animals from all over the world	http://nationalzoo.si.edu/Animals/PhotoGallery/default.cfm

(continued)

Continued

Resource	Description	Link
National Park Service Digital Image Archives	Features public domain digital images of maps, nature, and historic photos	www.nps.gov/pub_aff/imagebase.html
NOAA (National Oceanic and Atmospheric Administration) Photo Library	Invaluable resource that provides incredible photographs relating to climate, weather, bodies of water, and marine life	www.photolib.noaa.gov/index.html
US Fish and Wildlife Service National Digital Library	Images and videos of conservation, birds, aquatic species, and threatened and endangered wildlife	http://digitalmedia.fws.gov/cdm
US Department of Agriculture Image Gallery	Low-resolution (72 dpi) photos of animals, crops, and scientists	www.ars.usda.gov/is/graphics/photos
NASA Images	Archive of images of the universe, solar system, Earth, aeronautics, and astronauts	www.nasaimages.org
National Gallery of Art Images	Includes portraits of iconic Americans	https://images.nga.gov/en/page/show_home_page.html
US Environmental Protection Agency Image Gallery	Images of agriculture and the Great Lakes	www.epa.gov/newsroom/pictures.htm

Great Online Mathematics Resources

This is an incomplete, ever-expanding list from Steve Leinwand and Eric Milou.
https://sites.google.com/site/greatccssmathresources/

What Do the Standards Mean?	
Illustrative Mathematics	www.illustrativemathematics.org
Mathematics Progressions Documents	http://ime.math.arizona.edu/progressions
EDC—Implementing the Practices	http://mathpractices.edc.org/
Achieve, Inc.	www.achieve.org/achieving-common-core
Turn On Common Core Math	http://turnonccmath.net
Learn Zillion	www.learnzillion.com
Inside Mathematics	www.insidemathematics.org
NCTM Illuminations	www.illuminations.nctm.org
Mathalicious	www.mathalicious.com
Dan Meyer's 3-Act Lessons	https://docs.google.com/spreadsheet/ccc?key=0Ajl qyKM9d7ZYdEhtR3BJMmdBWnM2YWxWYVM1UW owTEE
Thinking Blocks	www.thinkingblocks.com

(continued)

Continued

Yummy Math	www.yummymath.com
Engage New York	www.engageny.org/mathematics
Mathematics Vision Project	www.mathematicsvisionproject.org
Emergent Math	http://emergentmath.com/my-problem-based-curriculum-maps
Achieve EQuIP Exemplars	www.achieve.org/EQuIP
Khan Academy	www.khanacademy.com
Robert Kaplinsky Lessons	http://robertkaplinsky.com/lessons
K–5 math teaching resources	www.k-5mathteachingresources.com

Tools

National Library of Virtual Manipulatives	http://nlvm.usu.edu/en/nav/vlibrary.html
Desmos	www.desmos.com
Geogebra	www.geogebra.org
Conceptua Math	www.conceptuamath.com
Tools for the Common Core	http://commoncoretools.me
Common Core Database	http://commoncore.pearsoned.com/index.cfm?locator=PS1cO9
Balanced Assessment	http://balancedassessment.concord.org
Mathematics Assessment Project	http://map.mathshell.org/materials/index.php
Howard County Formative Assessments (K–5)	https://grade1commoncoremath.wikispaces.hcpss.org/Grade+1+Home
PARCC sample items	http://practice.parcc.testnav.com/#
Smarter Balanced sample items	www.smarterbalanced.org/practice-test/
K–12 Assessment Center	www.k12center.org

Miscellaneous Collections of Resources

Math Munch	http://mathmunch.org/
Dana Center Math Common Core Toolkit	www.ccsstoolbox.org
Colorado Department of Education	www.cde.state.co.us/standardsandinstruction/instructionalunitsamples

Miscellaneous Collections of Resources	
Georgia Department of Education	www.georgiastandards.org/common-core/pages/math-k-5.aspx www.georgiastandards.org/common-core/pages/math-6–8.aspx www.georgiastandards.org/common-core/pages/math-9–12.aspx
Ohio Resource Center	http://ohiorc.org/standards/commoncore/mathematics
Learn NC	www.learnnc.org/lp/editions/ccss2010-mathematics
Southeastern Comprehensive Center	http://secc.sedl.org/common_core_videos/index.php
National Science Digital Library	http://nsdl.org/search/standards/D10003FB
Student Achievement Partners	http://achievethecore.org/dashboard/300/search/1/2/0/1/2/3/4/5/6/7/8/9/10/11/12
California Mathematics Project	http://caccssm.cmpso.org

Kid Curators Rubric

Rubric for Label Copy

Name _____

Trait	Excellent 5	Very Good 4	Adequate 3	Needs Improvement 2	Not Acceptable 1
CONTENT AND ORGANIZATION: The content and order of our exhibit labels help visitors understand our big idea.					
Our exhibit title communicates the big idea of our exhibit and captures visitors' attention.					
Our interpretive text panels are written in short paragraphs that address one key idea at a time and are accompanied by a visual device.					
Our captions clearly label specific objects, artifacts, images, and interactive devices.					
We include non-interpretive labels when appropriate (credit panels, orientation signs, etc.).					

(continued)

Continued

Trait	Excellent 5	Very Good 4	Adequate 3	Needs Improvement 2	Not Acceptable 1
RELEVANCE: Our writing is relevant and useful to the visitor.					
Our text is relevant to visitors because it relates to their personal experience, asks a question they might ask, poses a provocative question, or includes a quotation that draws them into the content.					
Our text is useful to visitors because it gives them something to "do" intellectually (agree or disagree with an idea, make a decision, draw a conclusion, or discover something new).					
Our text encourages conversation among visitors.					
VOICE: The tone of our writing is clear and consistent.					
Our copy is written in a consistent voice and it is clear who is "speaking" to the visitor (the school, an expert, a friend, a specific real or fictitious personality, etc.).					
The voice of the writer conveys enthusiasm for the topic.					
Our language is clear; technical terms are used when appropriate and explained to the visitor.					

Trait	Excellent 5	Very Good 4	Adequate 3	Needs Improvement 2	Not Acceptable 1
PRESENTATION: The visual quality, organization, and structure of our text make it easy to read.					
We use typographic devices to make key ideas obvious (e.g., bullet points to highlight certain ideas; italics, underlining, and boldface to make words stand out; and variations in font and size for emphasis).					
Our text is visible to the visitor; we use a 20-point font or greater for body text and 28-point to 48-point font for titles or text to be read at a distance, and we place copy within the visitors' field of vision.					
Our text panels are appropriate for a museum audience—fifty words or fewer per panel.					
Our text is legible, presented in a readable font and with high-contrast typography.					
GRAMMAR: The text in our exhibit is grammatically correct.					
Our text panels are grammatically correct, are free of spelling errors, and include proper punctuation.					
Label Copy Score					
How could you improve? List one or two goals for upcoming work.					

Initiatives That Build a Positive Classroom Culture of Differentiation

Initiatives are extended activities that can help build a classroom culture that values diversity and pushes students' thinking. Initiatives help students and teachers understand that we all have strengths and gifts, and that our success often depends on our background, experiences, and desires, rather than our innate ability or intelligence. They also reinforce the notion that struggling in something doesn't mean struggling in everything, and, conversely, being strong in something doesn't mean being strong in everything. Here are a few.

RECOGNIZING AND RESPECTING DIFFERENCES: STAND IN LINE

Ask students to line up from "novice" to "expert" using a series of academic and non-academic prompts (e.g., paddling a canoe, reading nonfiction, playing soccer, solving algebraic equations, teaching foreign language, cooking).

RESPECTFUL TASKS: MIXED RHYTHMS, ONE SOUND

Ask participants to self-assess and put themselves into one of three groups based on their comfort with making and sustaining a rhythm:

1. I'm willing to try.

2. I can do this.

3. I'm up for a challenge.

Select three rhythms, from simple to complex, that complement each other. Start by coaching the 1s through their rhythm, while the other groups talk about their favorite rhythms and things they love about music. Coach 2s, then 3s. Have 1s start with the beat, then 2s come in, then 3s. Sustain rhythm and consider inviting improvisation. Allow time for a reflective discussion that touches on the underlying meaning of the activity. What was it like to choose different groups? Should everyone have been doing the same activity (Why? Why not?) What did it sound like when the groups were each doing well?

COLLABORATION: WALK THE LINE

Tape a long line of masking tape on the floor.

Round 1: Blindfold a volunteer and tell that person she has to walk the line, staying on the tape as much as possible. The rest of the group can help the person by yelling directions, giving advice, and so on. When the person gets to the end, she takes off the blindfold and sees where she is. Debrief: How did others help or hinder the effort?

Round 2: The same person walks the line, but this time with no help from the group. Usually the person is way off in a corner by the time she gets near the end of the masking tape line. Take off the blindfold and debrief. Debrief with the following questions: "When does working together help or hinder?" "When do you just have to do it solo?" "How does a group support solo efforts?"

COLLABORATION: WORD ASSOCIATION

The goal is to keep a "chain of words" going so all participants have a chance to call out at least once. Each participant has a buddy across the circle to call on for help if stuck. An appointed person begins with a word and the person to his or her left calls out an associated word in less than 5 seconds, or points to the buddy across the circle if in need of help. Association then continues clockwise (from the buddy, if she or he called out the next word). If it comes to a participant a second time and the student still can't think of something, he may call out "Skip" to keep the association moving around the circle to those who haven't had a chance. Do this with important differentiation ideas such as "fair" and "equal."

References

Alber, R. (2013). Five powerful questions teachers can ask students. *Edutopia*. Retrieved from www.edutopia.org/blog/five-powerful-questions-teachers-ask-students-rebecca-alber

Baker, S., et al. (2007). *Effective literacy and English language instruction for English learners in the elementary grades*. Washington, DC: National Center for Education Evaluation and Regional Assistance, Institute of Education Sciences, US Department of Education. Retrieved from www.p12.nysed.gov/biling/bilinged/documents/el_practice_guide.pdf

Baker, S., et al. (2014). *Teaching academic content and literacy to English learners in elementary and middle school*. Washington, DC: National Center for Education Evaluation and Regional Assistance, Institute of Education Sciences, US Department of Education. Retrieved from http://ies.ed.gov/ncee/wwc/pdf/practice_guides/english_learners_pg_040114.pdf

Ball, D. (2003). *Mathematics in the 21st century: What mathematical knowledge is needed for teaching mathematics*. Remarks prepared for the Secretary's Summit on Mathematics, US Department of Education, February 6. Washington, DC. Retrieved from US Department of Education, n.d., http://www2.ed.gov/rschstat/research/progs/mathscience/ball.html

Beattie-Moss, M. (2015). Probing question: Is art an essential school subject? [Web log post]. *Phys.org*. May 25. Retrieved from http://phys.org/news/2015--05-probing-art-essential-school-subject.html

Bennett, S. (2007). *That workshop book: New systems and structures for classrooms that read, write, and think*. Portsmouth, NH: Heinemann.

Berger, R., Rugen, L., & Woodfin, L. (2014). *Leaders of their own learning: Transforming schools through student-engaged assessment*. San Francisco, CA: Jossey-Bass.

Berger, R., Woodfin, L., Plaut, S., & Dobbertin, C. (2014). *Transformational literacy: Making the common core shift with work that matters*. San Francisco, CA: Jossey-Bass.

Blackwell, L. S., Trzesniewski, K. H., & Dweck, C. S. (2007). Implicit theories of intelligence predict achievement across an adolescent transition: A longitudinal study and an intervention. *Child Development, 78*(1), pp. 246–263.

Carnegie Corporation of New York Institute for Advanced Study Commission on Mathematics and Science Education. Executive Summary. *The need for new science standards.* Retrieved from http:// www.nextgenscience.org/overview-0#1.%20Carnegie

Chapin, S., & Johnson, A. (2006). *Math matters: Understanding the math you teach.* Sausalito, CA: Math Solutions Publications.

City, E. A., Elmore, R. F., Fiarman, S. E., & Teitel, L. (2009). *Instructional rounds in education: A network approach to improving teaching and learning.* Cambridge, MA: Harvard Education Press.

D'Acquisto, L (2006). *Learning on display: Student-created museums that build understanding.* Alexandria, VA: Association for Supervision and Curriculum Development.

Darling-Hammond, L., & Richardson, N. (2009). Teacher learning: What matters? *Educational Leadership, 66* (5), 46–53.

Dobbertin, C. (2013). *Common Core unit by unit: Five critical moves for implementing the reading standards across the curriculum.* Portsmouth, NH: Heinemann.

Drabowska, A. (2015). Five ways doodling improves learning and creativity. *Inform Ed.* Retrieved from http://www.opencolleges.edu.au/informed/features/doodling-improves-learning

Duckworth, E. (1991, March). On thinking about teaching: A conversation with Eleanor Duckworth. *Educational Leadership,* 30–34.

Dweck, C. (2006). *Mindset: The new psychology of success.* New York, NY: Ballantine.

EL Education, Liben, D, & Liben, M. (2015). Concept paper: What literacy instruction should look like. New York, NY: Author.

Ellis, R. (2012). *Language teaching research and language pedagogy.* West Sussex, UK: Wiley-Blackwell.

Farrington, C. (2013). *Academic mindsets as a critical component of deeper learning.* University of Chicago Consortium on Chicago School Research.

Freeman, D. E., & Freeman, Y. S. (2011). *Between worlds: Access to second language acquisition* (3rd ed.). Portsmouth, NH: Heinemann.

Friedman, T. (2014). How to get a job at Google. *New York Times* opinion editorial, Feb. 21. Retrieved from http://www.nytimes.com/2014/02/23/opinion/sunday/friedman-how-to-get-a-job-at-google.html?_r = 1

Fullilove, R. E., & Treisman, P. U. (1990). Mathematics achievement among African American undergraduates at the University of California, Berkeley: An evaluation of the Mathematics Workshop Program. *Journal of Negro Education, 59*(3), 463–478.

Gardner, H. (1985). *Frames of mind: The theory of multiple intelligences.* New York, NY: Basic Books.

Genesee, F., Lindholm-Leary, K., Saunders, W., & Christian, D. (2005). English language learners in US schools: An overview of research findings. *Journal of Education for Students Placed at Risk, 10*(4), 363–385.

Goe, L, & Stickler, L. (2008). *Teacher quality and student achievement: Making the most of recent research*. National Comprehensive Center for Teacher Quality. Retrieved from http://files.eric.ed.gov/fulltext/ED520769.pdf

Good, C., Aronson, J., & Inzlicht, M. (2003). Improving adolescents' standardized test performance: An intervention to reduce the effects of stereotype threat. *Applied Developmental Psychology 24*, 645–662.

Green, E. (2014). *Building a better teacher: How teaching works (and how to teach it to everyone)*. New York, NY: Norton.

Greene, R. (2008). *Lost at school: Why our kids with behavioral challenges are falling through the cracks and how we can help them*. New York, NY: Scribner.

Hetland, L., & Winner, E. (2004). Cognitive transfer from arts education to non-arts outcomes: Research evidence and policy implications. In E. Eisner & M. Day (Eds.), *Handbook on research and policy in art education*. National Art Education Association. Retrieved from: https://www2.bc.edu/~winner/pdf/cognitive_transfer.pdf

Himmel, J. (2012). Language objectives: The key to effective content area instruction for English learners. Retrieved from http://www.colorincolorado.org/article/49646/

Hoffer, W. W. (2012). *Minds on mathematics: Using math workshop to develop deep understanding in grades 4–8*. Portsmouth, NH: Heinemann.

Hsu, E., Murphy, T. J., & Treisman, U. (n.d.). Supporting high achievement in introductory mathematics courses: What we have learned from 30 years of the emerging scholars program. Retrieved from: http://math.sfsu.edu/hsu/papers/Hsu-Murphy-Treisman-final.pdf

Hyde, A. (2006). *Comprehending Math: Adapting Reading Strategies to Teach Mathematics, K-6*. Portsmouth, NH: Heinemann.

Kang, C. (2013). Survey finds gap in Internet access between rich, poor students. *Washington Post*. Retrieved from http://www.washingtonpost.com/business/technology/survey-finds-gap-in-internet-access-between-rich-poor-students/2013/02/27/3718ca4c-8152--11e2-a350--49866afab584_story.html

Kennedy Center ArtsEdge (n.d.). Take two: Teaching revision through the arts. Retrieved from: http://artsedge.kennedy-center.org/educators/how-to/take-two

Koetsch, P., D'Acquisto, L., Kurin, A., Juffer, S., & Goldberg, L. (2002). Schools into museums. *Educational Leadership, 60*(1), 74–78.

Kohn, A. (2015). Who's Asking? *Educational Leadership, 73*(1), 16–22.

Leki, I., Cumming, A., & Silva, T. (2008). *A synthesis of research on second language writing in English*. New York, NY: Routledge.

Maxwell, L. (2014). U.S. schools gear up for surge of young immigrants. Retrieved from http://www.edweek.org/ew/articles/2014/06/27/36unaccompanied.h33.html

McDonald, J. P., Zydney, J. M., Dichter, A., & McDonald, E. C. (2012). *Going online with protocols: New tools for teaching and learning*. New York, NY: Teachers College Press.

McKibben, S. (2015, April). Music on the brain. *Education Update, 57*(4), 2–3.

Minahan, J., & Rappaport, N. (2013). *The behavior code: A practical guide to understanding and teaching the most challenging students.* Cambridge, MA: Harvard Education Press.

Mueller, P., & Oppenheimer D. (2014). The pen is mightier than the keyboard: Advantages of longhand over laptop notetaking. *Psychological Science.* Retrieved from http://pss .sagepub.com/content/early/2014/04/22/0956797614524581.abstract

National Association of State Boards of Education. (2003). *Ensuring a place for the arts and foreign languages in America's schools.* Retrieved from http://www.nysaflt.org/ advocacy/pdf/SG_Complete_Curriculum_Arts_and_FL_2003.pdf

National Center for Learning Disabilities Editorial Team. (n.d.). *What are learning disabilities?* Retrieved from http://www.ncld.org.php53-22.ord1-1.websitetestlink .com/types-learning-disabilities/what-is-ld/what-are-learning-disabilities

National Center for Teachers of English, 2008. English language learners: A policy research brief produced by the National Council of Teachers of English. National Council of Teachers of English. Retrieved from: http://www.ncte.org/library/NCTEFiles/ Resources/PolicyResearch/ELLResearchBrief.pdf

National Clearinghouse for English Language Acquisition. (2011). *The growing number of English learner students.* Retrieved from http://www.ncela.us/files/uploads/9/ growingLEP_0809.pdf

National Coalition for Core Arts Standards. (n.d.). *National core arts standards: A conceptual framework for arts learning.* Retrieved from: http://www.nationalartsstandards.org/ sites/default/files/NCCAS%20%20Conceptual%20Framework_0.pdf

National Council for the Social Studies (NCSS) 2013. *The college, career, and civic life (C3) framework for Social Studies State Standards: Guidance for enhancing the rigor of K–12 civics, economics, geography, and history* (Silver Spring, MD: NCSS).

National Governors Association Center for Best Practices, Council of Chief State School Officers. (2010). *Common core state standards.* Washington, DC: Author.

National Governors Association Center for Best Practices, Council of Chief State School Officers. (2010). *Common core state standards (Appendix A).* Washington, DC: Author.

National Math and Science Initiative (2014). STEM Crisis Page, Stats, and References. Retrieved from https://www.nms.org/Portals/0/Docs/STEM%20Crisis%20Page%20 Stats%20and%20References.pdf

Schwartz, K. (2015, Jan. 13). How integrating the arts into other subjects makes learning come alive. *Mindshift.* Retrieved from http://ww2.kqed.org/mindshift/2015/01/13/ how-integrating-arts-into-other-subjects-makes-learning-come-alive/

Schwartz, M. (2008). The importance of stupidity in scientific research. *Journal of Cell Science 121*(11), 1771.

Shanahan, T., & Shanahan, C. (2008). Teaching disciplinary literacy to adolescents: Rethinking content-area literacy. *Harvard Educational Review, 78*(1), 40–59.

Stearns, P. (1998). *Why study history?* American Historical Association. Retrieved from www. historians.org/about-aha-and-membership/aha-history-and-archives/archives/why-study-history.

Sternberg, R. J. (1984). *Beyond I.Q.: A triarchic theory of human intelligence.* New York, NY:Cambridge University Press.

Stigler, J., & Hiebert, J. (1999). *The teaching gap: Best ideas from the world's teachers for improving education in the classroom.* New York, NY: Free Press.

TESOL International Association. (2013). *Overview of the Common Core State Standards initiatives for ELLs.* Alexandria, VA: Author. Retrieved from http://www.tesol.org/docs/advocacy/overview-of-common-core-state-standards-initiatives-for-ells-a-tesol-issue-brief-march-2013.pdf?sfvrsn = 4

Tomlinson, C.A. (1997). What it means to teach gifted learners well. National Association for Gifted Children. Retrieved from: https://www.nagc.org/resources-publications/gifted-education-practices/what-it-means-teach-gifted-learners-well

Tomlinson, C. A. (1999). *The differentiated classroom: Responding to the needs of all learners.* Alexandria, VA: Association for Supervision and Curriculum Development.

Tomlinson, C. A. (2011, March). Keynote. Speech presented at Expeditionary Learning National Conference in Portland, OR.

Treisman, P. U. (1985). A study of the mathematics performance of black students at the University of California, Berkeley. Unpublished doctoral dissertation, University of California, Berkeley.

Treisman, U. (1992). Studying students studying calculus: A look at the lives of minority mathematics students in college. *College Mathematics Journal, 23*(5), 362–372.

Treisman, U., & Asera, R. (1990). Teaching mathematics to a changing population: The Professional Development Program at the University of California, Berkeley. In N. Fisher, H.Keynes, & P. Wagreich (Eds.), *Issues in mathematics education: mathematicians and education reform: Proceedings of the July 6–8, 1998 workshop* (pp. 31–62). Providence, RI: American Mathematical Society in cooperation with Mathematical Association of America.

Trefil, J., & O'Brien-Trefil, W. (2009). The science students need to know. *Educational Leadership, 67*(1), 28–33.

Tyre, P. (2012, October). The writing revolution. *Atlantic.*

Van de Walle, J. A., Lovin, L. H., Karp, K. S., & Bay-Williams, J. M. (2013a). *Teaching Student-Centered Mathematics: Developmentally Appropriate Instruction for Grades Pre K–2.* Pearson.

Van de Walle, J. A., Lovin, L. H., Karp, K. S., & Bay-Williams, J. M. (2013b). *Teaching Student-Centered Mathematics: Developmentally Appropriate Instruction for Grades 3–5* (second edition). Pearson.

Van de Walle, J. A., Lovin, L. H., Karp, K. S., & Bay-Williams, J. M. (2013c). *Teaching Student-Centered Mathematics: Developmentally Appropriate Instruction for Grades 6–8.* Pearson.

Van Oech, R. (1998). *A whack on the side of the head.* New York, NY: Warner Books.

Watson, J. D., & Crick, F.H.C. (1953). Molecular Structure of Nucleic Acids: A Structure for Deoxyribose Nucleic Acid. *Nature, 171,* 737–738.

Wieman, C. (2012). Effective teaching should create students who think like scientists. Retrieved from http://www.aaas.org//news/releases/2012/0608noyce_wieman.shtml

Wiggins, G. (2010). What is a Big Idea? *Big Ideas e-journal*, June 10, 2010. Retrieved from http://www.authenticeducation.org/ae_bigideas/article.lasso?artid = 99

Wiliam, D. (2014). The right questions, the right way. *Educational Leadership, 71*(6), 16–19.

Willis, (2012). A neurologist makes the case for teaching teachers about the brain. Edutopia. Retrieved from: http://www.edutopia.org/blog/neuroscience-higher-ed-judy-willis

Wilson, M. (2014). Asking strategic questions. *Responsive Classroom Newsletter*, Winter. Retrieved from https://www.responsiveclassroom.org/asking-strategic-questions/

How to Use the DVD

SYSTEM REQUIREMENTS

- PC with a DVD drive

- PC with a Web browser such as Chrome, Safari, Firefox, or Internet Explorer

- PC with Microsoft Windows 7 or later or Mac with Apple OS version 10.1 or later

USING THE DVD WITH WINDOWS

To view the items located on the DVD, insert the DVD into your computer's DVD drive or your DVD player. Follow these steps to access the DVD:

1. Double click the Home.html file.

2. Choose the desired option from the menu.

IN CASE OF TROUBLE

If you experience difficulty using the DVD, please follow these steps:

1. Make sure your hardware and systems configurations conform to the systems requirements noted under "System Requirements."

2. Review the installation procedure for your type of hardware and operating system. It is possible to reinstall the software if necessary.

To contact Product Technical Support and get support information through our website, visit http://wiley.custhelp.com/. To speak with someone in Product Technical Support, call 877-762-2974 or 317-572-3994.

Before calling or writing, please have the following information available:

- Title of product and if possible, the ISBN

- Type of computer and operating system

- Any error messages displayed

- Complete description of the problem

Index

Centers for Disease Control, 157

Chaffee, S., 282, 304–307

Challenge: in arts instruction, 247, 253–267; benefits of, 6; description of, 6, 9t; differentiated instruction and, 281; engagement's relationship with, 7; guiding questions for, 6; incorporation of, into high-quality lessons, 18, 24–28; in mathematics, 185

Challenging questions, 52

Change, fear of, 64–65

Changing one's mind, 103–104

Chapin, S., 219

Choice, 308–311

Christian, D., 322

City, E. A., 17

Claims, evidence-based, 107–109

Clairemont Elementary, 131, 135

Clarifying questions, 52

Classroom culture: of arts, 235–239; conversation norms and, 99; for differentiation, 282–283, 375–377; grappling in, 49–50; for mathematics learning, 176–179, 217, 219, 220; to support inquiry, 168–169

Clay, V., 74–75, 80

Close reading: for differentiation, 292–294; guide for, 351–354; in literacy instruction, 95, 96f; scaffolding for, 118–119

Codman Academy, 77–79, 305–307, 309–310

Cognitive Rigor Matrix, 25, 26–27t

Cognitive skills, 288

Collaboration: in arts curriculum, 231; for arts instruction, 271; building positive classroom culture for, 375–377; for differentiation, 283, 298–300; in discovery cycle, 36f; importance of, 7; in Japanese lesson study, 58–59; lack of, for science/history planning, 172–173; leadership's role in creating, 60, 117; for schoolwide initiatives, 57–58; of teachers, 58–59

College acceptance, 16

College readiness, 125

Common Core State Standards: as basis of learning expeditions, 34; differentiation and, 289–294; for English language learners, 319–321; learning targets and, 28; for literacy in content areas, 76; literacy learning targets to address, 84–85; for mathematics, 179, 180, 201, 208; questioning in, 51–52; in science/history assessments, 144; for science/history instruction, 129, 169, 172; workshop model for, 29; in writing, 163–164

Communication skills, 21–24

Community partners, 252–253, 270–271

Community service, 149–150

Compare-contrast structure, 110

Competence, 11

Complexity: of reading texts, 81–82; of students' writing, 111

Conceptual understanding, 19–24

Concord Review, 120

Connections, making: example of, 44–45; in mathematics, 185, 209–212

Conservatory Lab Charter School, 227–229, 236–238, 250

Content areas: arts instruction in, 238–239; challenges of, 12–13; Common Core standards in, 76; differentiating instruction in, 77; literacy instruction in, 74–79, 117, 119, 169; primary sources for, 80, 131–133; teachers of, 75–76; text selection for, 79–84; using literature in, 74–75. *See also specific content areas*

Conversations: bolstering arguments during, 102–103; changing one's mind during, 103–104; norms for, 99; online venues for, 98–99; protocols for, 99–102

Council of Chief State School Officers, 80, 172, 179

Courage, 203–206, 219

Craftmanship, 112–113

Crash Course, 313

Creative intelligence, 286t

Crick, F.H.C., 77

Drabowska, A., 257

Drawing conclusions, 36*f*

Drawing tasks, 238

Duckworth, E., 93, 99

DVD: contents of, vii–viii; use of, 385–386

Dweck, C., 177, 180

E

Economics, explaining concepts in, 22–23

Educational system: founding of, 3; goals of, 4

Ekmalian, M., 40–41, 55

EL Education, 75; achievements of, ix; approach to standards in, x–xi; arts instruction and, 13; curricular structure of, 34; differentiation and, 293; overview of, ix, xxv; popularity of curriculum, xi; principles of, xxv; science/history instruction and, 126–127; strategic questioning of, 155

El Sistema approach, 227

Electronic response systems, 54

Elementary and Secondary Act of 1965, 318

Ellis, J., 220

Ellis, R., 321

Ellison, R., 74

Elmore, R. F., 17

Emotional skills, 288

Empowerment: in arts, 251, 257–258; deep literacy instruction for, 71; description of, 7–8, 10*t*; differentiation and, 281–282; guiding questions for, 8; in high-quality lessons, 18–19, 40–44; in mathematics, 181–182

Engagement: in arts education, 245–246, 252–253; versus attention, 28; challenge's relationship with, 7; content-area texts and, 80–81; curriculum as requirement for, 29; description of, 6–7, 9*t*; differentiation and, 281, 308–311; guiding questions for, 7; in high-quality lessons, 18, 28–40; importance of, 18; in mathematics, 189–190, 195–203; planning high-quality lessons for, 28–40; in science/history instruction, 125–126; using

hooks for, 46–47; using learning targets for, 47–48

Engineering design process, 159–161

English language learners: content-area literacy of, 77; differentiation for, 318–323; expectations of, 321; honoring culture and language of, 322–323; pre-assessment of, 318–319; scaffolding for, 319–321; standards for, 319–321; teaching writing structure to, 109–110

Equalizer, 302–304

Essay templates, 306*f*

Evergreen Community Charter School, 161–162

Evidence: as basis for scientific/historical models, 161; for research papers, 147–148; to uncover big ideas in science/history, 123–124; as writing strategy, 106–109

Exhibits, 252, 269

Exit tickets: to check for understanding, 54; to close math lessons, 194, 214–215

Expectations, of students: challenges to setting, 62; differentiation and, 292; of English language learners, 321

Expeditionary Learning, 118, 120

Experiential entry points, 287

Experts: engaging, 137; students as, 170

Explaining concepts, 19–24

Expository texts, 81*t*

Extending instruction, 297

F

Failure, importance of, 94

Fair treatment, 282–283

Family involvement, 237, 269

Farrington, C., 10

Feedback: in arts, 250, 263; in mathematics, 202; technology for, 312; on writing, 112–113

Fiarman, S. E., 17

Fieldwork, 136–141, 170, 173, 240

Fine, S., x, xi, 16, 17

work in, 118, 119; professional development in, 117; reflection in, 91; scaffolding in, 86–87, 118–119; schoolwide implementation of, 116; sequencing in, 87–88; technology for, 98–99; text-dependent questions in, 85–87; using the Four Ts for, 72–92

Literary nonfiction texts, 81*t*

Literature: in arts instruction, 254–255; partnering informational texts with, 74–75

Logical-mathematical intelligence, 286*t*

Logical-quantitative entry points, 287

Loring, A., 244, 254–255

Lovin, L. H., 195, 197, 198

Low-income students: academic achievement of, 1–2; access to technology of, 313; arts instruction for, 232; mathematics and, 181

Lyons, D., 269–270

M

Mahoney, S., 16, 17, 40

Manzanita SEED Elementary School, 109–110

Maplewood Richmond Heights school district, 268–270

Marts, J., 307

Math Design Collaborative, 199

Math Matters: Understanding the Math You Teach (Chapin & Johnson), 219

Math stories, 219

Math Workshop 2.0: benefits of, 194; description of, 186–189; discussions in, 203–208; example of, 32–33; lesson closure in, 193, 213–215; mini-lessons in, 209–212; practice in, 2112–213; problem solving in, 32–33, 195–203, 212–213; structure of, 186–194

Mathematica, ix

Mathematics: African American students and, 181–182; arguments and reasoning in, 207–208; arts connection to, 265–266; assessments in, 194–195, 199, 214–215; avoiding challenge in, 185; basic skills in, 221; Bloom's taxonomy in, 199; common

challenges of, 221–222; curriculum for, 176, 178, 194–195, 221–222; differentiation in, 192–193, 213; discussions in, 190, 203–208; feedback in, 202; grappling in, 189–190, 191, 194–203, 209–212; importance of, 179–180; leadership actions related to, 217–218; learning targets in, 191, 209; lesson closure in, 193, 213–215; lesson structure for, 186–216; lesson studies in, 196; low-income students and, 181; making connections, 209–212; making connections in, 185; mindset for, 176–177, 180, 181, 203–205, 217, 219–220; mini-lessons in, 209–212; note catchers in, 207; online resources for, 367–369; problem selection in, 195–203, 222; problematic instructional practices in, 182–186; professional development in, 218; remedial instruction in, 192–193, 217; role of teachers and students in, 186–188*t*; schoolwide initiative for, 178; standardized tests in, 221; standards for, 179, 180, 201, 208; student empowerment in, 181–182; student engagement in, 189–190, 195–203; synthesis in, 193–194, 213–215; teachers' role in, 13; textbooks for, 195, 197, 221–222; transforming culture of, 176–179, 217, 219, 220; vocabulary for, 206–207

Mathematics Assessment Project, 199

Maxwell, L., 323

Mayer, L., 361, 365

McCray, S., 1, 164, 166

McKern, V., 328, 329

McKibben, S., 234

McMains, R., 47, 50–51

Meaning, levels of, 82

Meaning making, 95–104

Media, 312

Meehan, K., 293–294, 299

Mehta, J., xiii, 16, 17

Memorization, 210, 221

Menus, 310–311

Metacognition: importance of, 7–8; reflection to build, 55

Opinions, 103–104
Opinion-seeking questions, 52
Oppenheimer D., 257
Our Rivers, Our Future, Your Choice (public service announcement), 149–150

P

Palombo, M., 98–99
Pannell, S. W., 254
Patterns/trends, 156–157
PBT. *See* Problem-based tasks
Peer learning, 43–44
Performance arts, 264–265
Perkins, D., 123
Persistence, x, 263
Personal narratives, 1
Persuasive argument writing: purpose of, 104; strategies for, 106–109
Photographs, 365–366
Physical skills, 289
Pierce, L., 160
PISA test (Programme for International Student Assessment), 179
Plaut, S., 12, 51, 117
Plyer v. Doe (1982), 318
Pocatello Community Charter School, 42
Point of view, 75
Polaris Charter Academy, 134
Polaris Expeditionary Learning School, 264–265
Portfolios, 43
Power of Pictures (Olshansky), 226
Practical intelligence, 286*t*
Practice, 264, 312
Praise, Question, Polish protocol, 261, 262*f*
Pre-assessments: for differentiation, 300–301, 330; of English language learners, 318–319; in mathematics, 194–195
Presentations: in arts, 265; providing opportunities for, 113–114
Primary sources: in arts instruction, 253–254; background knowledge and, 131–132; close reading guide for, 351–354; for content-area instruction, 80, 131–133; credibility of, 134; curation of, 133–134; selection of, 133–134

Prior knowledge. *See* Background knowledge
A Private Universe (film), 20–21
Problem selection, in mathematics, 195–203, 222
Problem solving: importance of, 18; in Math Workshop 2.0, 32–33, 195–203, 212–213
Problem-Based Tasks (PBT), 220
Process standards, 150–153
Products, in science/history, 148–149, 164, 165*t*
Professional culture, 59
Professional development: in arts instruction, 271; leadership's role in, 60; in literacy instruction, 117; in mathematics instruction, 218
Proffitt, J., 211–212, 221
Programme for International Student Assessment. *See* PISA test
Project-based learning: approach to standards in, xi; shortcomings of, x
Protocols: for building background knowledge, 338–340; description of, 33, 343; for discussions, 99–102; establishing, 345; example of, 34–35; length of, 33; to provide feedback on writing, 112–113; rationale for, 33–34, 343–345; for science talks, 341–342; for Socratic Seminars, 335–337; for student engagement, 33–35. *See also specific protocols*
Purpose: of arts instruction, 229, 241; description of, 6–7; for learning, 46; of literacy, 69, 71–72, 93; of questions, 52; for reading, 83; of synthesis, 55, 213–214; for writing, 71–72, 104–114

Q

Qualitative complexity, 82
Quantitative complexity, 82
Question Formulation Technique, 52–53
Questioning techniques: to check for understanding, 53–54; Common Core

reading in, 172; leadership actions in, 169–171; learning targets in, 129–130; literacy instruction in, 75–79; models and simulations in, 161–163; need for deeper instruction in, 124–125; original research in, 157–159; practicing inquiry in, 124–127; process skills in, 150–153; protocol-based lessons in, 34–35; questions in, 153–155; real-world assignments in, 136–141; reflection in, 150; schoolwide implementation of, 168–169; standards for, 126–129, 169, 171–172; students' role in, 167–168t; teachers' role in, 167–168t; text selection for, 130–134, 169; uncovering big ideas in, 123–124, 127–135, 174

Science journals, 77–79

Science Process Standards, 150–151

Science talks, 34–35, 341–342

Scientific thinking, 150–153

Scientists, 76

Secondary research, 144–147

Section 504 of the Rehabilitation Act of 1973, 315, 316

Self-directed learners, 18

Self-efficacy, 11

Sequencing, 87–88

Shanahan, C., 76

Shanahan, T., 76

Sharing, 214, 218, 250

Shi, J., 77–79

Short tasks: for differentiation, 301; in writing, 105–106, 112

Short-term memory, 284

Sierra Expeditionary Learning School, 47

Silva, T., 323

Simmons, B., 37–38

Simpson, A., 44–45, 46, 53, 201–203

Simulations, 161–163

Skill sets, 287, 288–289

Smallwood, E., 63

Smith, J. Q., 249

Social skills, 288

Social studies. *See* History instruction

Social-emotional learning, 323–325

Social/relational groupings, 299

Socratic Seminars: Bloom's Taxonomy in, 97–98; common questions asked during, 100–101; for debriefs, 41; as literacy instruction strategy, 96–98; protocols for, 335–337; rating scales for, 101–102; reflection after, 101–102

Solar system, 19–20

Song writing, 264–265

Southwest Baltimore Charter School, 74–75

Spatial intelligence, 286t

Speaking, 321–322

Special needs, students with: in arts education, 247; content-area instruction for, 77; differentiation for, 314–323

Springfield Renaissance School, 16–17, 34–35, 40, 71, 104, 157–158

Spruce, C., 361, 365

Stainer, E., 232

Standardized tests: arts instruction and, 232; effects of deeper instruction on, 5; effects of, on student achievement, 4–5; in mathematics, 221; as obstacle to science/history instruction, 173–174

Standards: for arts, 240; differentiation and, 289–294; in EL Education approach, x–xi; for English language learners, 319–321; learning targets and, 24, 25t; for mathematics, 179, 180, 201, 208; in science/history assessments, 144, 171–172; for science/history curricula, 126–129, 169, 172

STEAM education, 234–235

Stearns, P., 125–126

STEM coursework, 159–161

STEM majors, 124–125

Stereotypes, 181

Sternberg, R. J., 285, 286t

Stickler, L., 17

Sticky notes, 171

Stigler, J., 185

Story Corps (National Public Radio), 105

Strand, M., 264–265

in, 163–164; critique lessons in, 89–90; essential questions of, 104–105; feedback on, 112–113; grappling with, 104; indicators of high-quality in, 111–116; instructional challenges of, 109; lack of student motivation for, 105; online environments for, 98–99; purpose of, 71–72, 104–114; rubrics for, 113; songs, 264–265; strategies for, 106–114; teaching of, to English language learners, 108–109; of textbook chapters, for student assessment, 142–144

"The Writing Revolution" (Tyre), 92

Y

Z